BARE HANDS AND STONE WALLS

MATER TRIUMPHALIS

Thou art the player whose organ-keys are thunders,
  And I beneath thy foot the pedal prest;
Thou art the ray whereat the rent cloud sunders,
  And I the cloudlet borne upon thy breast.

I shall burn up before thee, pass and perish,
  As mist in sunrise on the red sea-line;
But thou from dawn to sunsetting shall cherish
  The thoughts that led and souls that lighted mine. . . .

I have love at least, and have not fear, and part not
  From thine unnavigable and wingless way;
Thou tarriest, and I have not said thou art not,
  Nor all thy night long have denied thy day.

—Algernon Charles Swinburne.

WENDELL PHILLIPS

"Therefore he went
And humbly joined him to the weaker part,
Fanatic named, and fool, yet well content."
—*Lowell*

BARE HANDS
AND STONE WALLS

Some Recollections of a Side-Line
Reformer

By

CHARLES EDWARD RUSSELL

NEW YORK
CHARLES SCRIBNER'S SONS
1933

TO
JOHN RUSSELL
FELLOW TRAVELER
ALSO INGENIOUS ACCOMPLICE
IN DARK DEEDS OF REVOLT

PREFATORY NOTE

Not much of the *pars fui* excuses these pages. Sometimes from the side-lines, sometimes from the rear rank, sometimes from other view-points, certain things have been observed that are here set down in order for what they may be worth, if anything.

The struggle for the emancipation of man is long. A half-century is hardly a watch in the night. Yet there have been changes, great changes, in these fifty-two years, and any change may possibly be worth the attention of souls still loyal to the hope that has lightened so many millions across so many centuries, often seeming faintest when in reality it was strongest.

Contents

Contents

ix

Illustrations

BARE HANDS AND STONE WALLS

Chapter I

SNUB–NOSE, HIS WAYS AND WORKS

How others may have found this I have no guess, but in my own experience the crises of life have usually pivoted upon things or events that for size were like pin-heads. The first of these minutiae that fixed the way for me were a paste-brush ten inches long and a tin bucket of flour paste.

These and the ministrations of a lank, ungainly, snub-nosed and freckle-faced cicerone of fifteen years that by the back door thrust me into journalism.

My father was editor and part proprietor of a morning news-paper at Davenport, Iowa. He being hale, active and in the full bent of his career when I was passing out of adolescence, it was deemed that I could best sustain the family fortunes by learning and practising the business instead of the editorial branch of newspaper enterprise. This was a plan to which my father was the more inclined because he had always been dis-satisfied with the conduct of the business office and thought he would fare better with one there that had been trained after his own ideas. Inasmuch as up to that time the rainbow of promise had shone on me but fitfully if at all, and most when I performed as second baseman on the local nine or as an ama-teur pilot on the Mississippi river, it may be thought that des-peration had something to do with the parental decision. At the time when my impresario did his fateful work, my training for a strictly commercial efficiency had reached a stage, prosaic but needful, known as "doing up the mail." This meant that I must rise at the ghastly hour of half past three in the morning, proceed (under protest) to the press room of our establishment and there wrap and label certain copies of our influential journal as they came from the press.

The labors of the sprawly young person that had in his hands the strings of destiny were in the same fragrant precincts and might be classified under two heads. Those for hire and salary consisted of folding copies of *The Gazette* and delivering them about the business part of the town. This function he viewed with an inviolate disdain. The other, which alone had his conscientious attention, was the making of trouble. I was never able to tell surely whether his name, his imp-like face and turned-up nose, or his rare gifts and inexhaustible resources in bedeviling the walk of the sober-minded would have been the richer asset to a writer of farce comedy. Certainly the combination would seem now beyond price. I hesitate to mention the name; it will seem merely incredible and cast at once an air of improbability upon all the chronicle to follow. Yet I have the proofs; look in the records of St. Anthony's Church, doubters, and be overwhelmed. It was Willie Shine—no more, no less.

His custom, though by no means his rule, was to enter the press room about 4 A.M., after which life there took on a new and vivid interest for all concerned; so that it might indeed be said of him that when he came in at the door, peace flew out at the window. He was thin as a rake, agile as an eel, restless as a thing on springs, ingenious as the powers of darkness that he seemed to serve, and when brought to book, possessed of the trick, maddening to the uninitiated, of erasing from his countenance the last trace of human intelligence.

Back of the press room was the engine room, whence power was brought by shafting, pulleys and a belt. Suppose the attention of Frank, the imperturbable pressman, to be drawn elsewhere while the machine was running. This limb of Satan would whisk out a stick he had concealed for the purpose, throw off the belt and be diligently and earnestly at work when the machine stopped—hard at work and singing with a mournful air, "Far Away from Wife and Children," which was his favorite lyrical offering. Of a sudden he would look up in startled fashion and pipe, informatively:

"Say, Frank, the belt's off!"

All the tools in the press room had a way of disappearing mysteriously when he was present, the wrench in one direction, mallet in another, oil can somewhere else. Once after fifteen minutes of search punctuated with sweating profanity we found the planer in the pressman's overcoat pocket. Another day he tried the experiment of pouring a bottle of vinegar into the ink fountain and produced results upon the printed page that astonished all beholders. Not always were his achievements confined to our favored neighborhood. He went once to a Sunday-school Christmas festival and enlivened the proceedings for some of the children by substituting roller composition for jujube paste in the gift boxes.

We printed our herald of light and leading directly from the type on an old-fashioned flat-bedded press with a single cylinder like a huge barrel, a curious contraption then common, but now, museums excepted, quite vanished from the knowledge and affairs of men. Single sheets of paper were gripped by the revolving cylinder and pressed against the type as it slid by on the flat bed. While this was in deliberate process, it filled the air with a loud, discordant song of its own, did the old hurdy-gurdy. "Bur-r-r-r-r—clomp-clomp," it quavered, the "bur-r-r-r-r—" signifying that the bed was sliding out and then back again on the ratchets and cogs, and the "clomp-clomp" announcing to a waiting world that there had been completed and bestowed upon it another copy of the champion of civilization. The paper for the printing came in flat bundles instead of the rolls familiar to present and happier days, and these bundles, piled along the walls of the press room, provided excellently for the ease of itinerant printers, seeking repose after labor or libations.

My father held stern views as to the duty of journalism to be the guardian and nourisher of civic virtue, and about the time I began to be shaped for a commercial career he had discovered in our local government that which gave him pain and occasion for much remark. I must observe here that our town, though not exactly young, had still many marks of the region primitive. We had a volunteer fire department, for instance, and up to that time no electric fire alarm. One was now proposed and two companies were rivals for the contract. My father became convinced that at least one was tampering with the rectitude of city officers. Some of the men involved were of great respectability and power, but he did not hesitate to denounce the whole scheme. He had written two or three editorials on the subject and as these did not produce the desired reaction of public wrath, he wrote for the local page a news article describing the situation. It was a thing he did seldom, and only on some such occasion as this, when he hoped to terrify evil-doers and arouse the communal conscience, which seemed to have fallen asleep at the switch.

The Gazette consisted of four pages, each about the size of a bed quilt and observing by immemorial custom a strict division of reading matter. The first page had the telegraphic news, the second the editorial and correspondence, the third the miscellany and the fourth was sacred to the news of the city. As the quaint old rattletrap on which we printed would operate upon but two pages at a time, the second and third pages, known as the inside, went to press about 1 A.M. and the first and fourth about 4 o'clock.

On this particular morning I had cooked at the boiler a bucket of fresh paste and was laying out the printed address slips to be pasted upon the papers as they should come from the press. The composing room was on the third floor, press room on the first; the pages, called "forms," were lowered, one at a time, with windlass and chain. The first and fourth had now arrived. Pressman Frank Rohm was busily adjusting them upon the bed of the press, which he had run out for that purpose. On some bundles of print paper lay a solitary wayfarer, sleeping off a vinous exaltation. The wheezy old engine had started, the shafts and pulleys were revolving, the momentous printing operation was about to be launched. At this moment Master Shine, on whom time had hung but heavily, conceived a funny entertainment for the relief of himself and his bored confreres. With my brush and bucket of paste he would paint the shoes of the sleeping printer. With him, thought and its execution were one motion. He had adorned one of the shoes and was progressing well with the other, when the sleeper awoke with a start, perceived what manner of art work was toward, and launched a vicious kick at the artist. It missed his face but knocked from his hand the paste brush. This flew toward the ceiling, described a graceful curve and descended upon the press just as the bed with its "Bur-r-r-r" was sliding under the cylinder for the printing of the first copy. The next instant we heard a crunching sound, and the bed passed under the cylinder and came out on the other side.

Frank snorted and stopped old hurdy-gurdy before the operation could be repeated. When the type was examined, consternation seized the assembly. The brush had fallen in the middle of my father's article about the electric alarm swindle (or whatever it was) and the wire wrapping had so smashed the type that for a space of more than two inches there was just a mush of metal. Where only the wooden handle had lain, the type was injured, but hope remained because the matter there was still legible.

The next misadventure was that in trying to lift out the metal mush it fell into pi.

Here was an ugly situation. The paper could not go to press in this shape. Upstairs the regular force had long departed, the composing room was empty and dark, but the remorseful printing gentleman from the paper bundles promised to reset what had been destroyed if we could get him the manuscript or a proof. By the law of disaster that seems to rule in such cases, we could find neither, although we all but tore the office to pieces in the search. In those days each editor read the proofs of his own department as he could, and I believe it was afterward discovered that he of the city department had inadvertently carried off the manuscript in his pocket, but what had become of the proofs we never learned. An extra set, called "dupes," by which the printers measured and were paid for the type they had set was locked securely in the composing room drawer and not to be taken thence; a strike would probably have followed any burglary upon this precious hoard. The telephone had been invented but not introduced. My father lived too far away to be reached by messenger.

There can be little doubt that in those days I was "fresscher than the May with floures newe." Easily sat the emergency upon my impudent shoulders. "Leave it to me," said I with airy confidence. "I know what my father thinks about this business. Get me some paper." With that I sat and wrote, the printing gentleman, having found the spot where Slug 1 hid his composing stick, set type as I wrote, and in a few minutes the gap was filled, the type in place and hurdy-gurdy renewed her doleful song. We made the mails and in the sweet consciousness of duty done, I went home and to sleep.

Seldom, I think, has a tyro in literature made with the like small effort an equal hit. Two threats of libel suits in twenty-four hours and an irate and red-faced gentleman of the German persuasion puffing up the office stairs, a stick in hand to commit assault and battery, may be viewed as unusual fruitage of two inches of type. I had, indeed, not spared the epithets. "Thieves" and "scoundrels" rang through my stickful of type with the emphasis of an awakened righteousness. And any way, the deal stopped short.

With that my career in commerce came to an abrupt end. On impartial review, I cannot pretend that commerce was the sufferer thereby. I found myself transferred to the editorial end of the game, and the State Fair coming on soon afterward at Cedar Rapids, I was sent there to show if I could write something about it. One piece seemed to attract attention—not on its merits, certainly. The mayor of our town, the Honorable Jeremiah H. Murphy, stopped my father in the street to commend it. As the mayor was a vehement Democrat and my father a Republican of the strictest sect, the portent was viewed as too momentous to be overlooked. Hope springs eternal in the parental breast. It was now conceived that with a little more training something might be made of me; I might even some day be fitted to take my father's place at the steering of *The Gazette*. About that time the religious press, with which most households were richly supplied, had much to say about the flawless orthodoxy and superior instruction dispensed at St. Johnsbury, Vermont, Academy, and thither it was decided to ship me to be bettered by special courses in Latin, political economy, and history.

Some years later, I had the curiosity to look up in the files the early triumph of my untutored pen that had wrought these marvels. It seemed to demonstrate that the Honorable Jeremiah's taste in literature needed much amending but to be otherwise insignificant. However, to St. Johnsbury I took my way with no great heart in the business and never a suspicion of what was at hand.

Chapter II

OLD JIM DOW, NOTCHER OF BEAMS

IT was a beautiful place, notably beautiful even in a region plethoric in natural charm. The wide streets, lined with rows or double rows of great, awesome elms; the faultless precision of the trimmed and garnished lawns; the houses, often in excellent colonial, all kempt and gleaming as if new tricked in paint; the ordered avoidance of the least maculation; the air of a settled, approved and durable competence—you are to imagine what impression all this would make on one raw from the helter-skelter and catch-as-catch-can of the prairies. A trifle chill, perhaps, the totality; a trifle too rigid the rectangle of the seemly and the regulated, but all the more novel, and striking the newcomer into a gasping admiration. It is a pleasing fancy of proud American communities to try to typify themselves. The symbol for St. Johnsbury, as I knew it, would be a young and pretty New England house-wife, faultlessly attired, perfectly sure of her métier and intolerant of a speck of dust.

All about were noble hills, clothed upon with delectable greens in the summer, dazzlingly white in winter, and in autumn the dream of an incredible glory. That part of the town I was to inhabit, called St. Johnsbury Plain, stretched for half a mile along a hillside shelf or plateau that was the legacy of an old glacial river. Three hundred feet below it, the silvery, idyllic Passumpsic, last living descendant of the glacier, went among green hillocks and fertile farms. The Academy buildings and dormitory stood at the south end of the plateau. So did the Academy boarding house, where I came to rest, and where from the one window of my room I looked eastward

8

up a long winding valley exactly like that of the Lotus Eaters.

But the people that dwelt in this favored spot seemed to me for a long time merely enigmatic. The transition from the frank, outspoken, headlong, and main-strength West was too abrupt. Where I had lived nobody cared much for appearances and everybody moved more or less in the open; but here reigned the iron restraint of an invariable convention. It seemed to me at first that the Vermonters were chillier than their climate and the east wind that blew down their valleys had turned their marrow, if any, to ice. Their poise of an extreme reserve, their coldly formal greetings, their plain horror of the outre and the novel, their suspicion of strangers, in contrast with the hearty manners to which I had been accustomed, seemed unendurable. They had a fashion of speech that with its slow, deliberate drawl wearied me into an acute resentment. They said "he-ow" for "how" and "ke-ow" for "cow," and spoke of the Deity as "Ge-od." My own name they translated into "Russyell," which on the ball field was not so far out of the way, but when it came to "Love-yell" for the quiet Aldus Lovell that was my chum and confidant, I felt that even unintentional burlesque had gone too for. Despite all protests, they insisted upon calling my native state "Ee-oh-ah," and their way of looking me over with a cool and unhasting appraisal gave me the fantods. From what was said to be the common topic of their conversation, I thought they were making mental estimates of my probable worth in coinage of the realm. It was months before my dull perceptions sensed the fact that with these hill-folk the outward was only a mask. Under their frozen exterior no other people were more kindly, friendly, neighborly, and good to know, and I think I could cite no other community in this country blessed with an equal variety of the permanently sterling. In truth, the people there wore austerity as they wore their painfully formal Sunday clothes, in obedience to some tribal tradition unmeaning and inept; if they were close bargainers they were usually upright; and if day by day they seemed absorbed in trafficking they as sedulously maintained a standard of general culture, high and rare.

The Academy was in many ways an admirable institution. All the instructors were experts, and what was more worth, all were enthusiasts, each in his own line. The man of science seemed to me to know more than any one human being ought to be allowed to know; the whole vast range of scientific research was tucked within his beetling brow. With an unfaltering courage that was not less than appalling he followed the changes in each line and accepted them all, impervious to the fact that the discoveries of one day were sure to be the jest of the morrow. Similarly, he was able by mental gymnastics to reconcile perfectly the materialistic cynicism of the leading lights of his time with the ideology of what is called revealed religion, a feat that seemed more disconcerting the more it was examined. Others of the faculty were of his pattern for ability and integrity. The Latin drill was the best I have ever encountered, and for an American institution, really notable. The rhetoric man dug down to the roots of things; the political economist led with joy his panting flock over desert wastes. Everything was as good as the best and the discipline was so relentless and granitic that it would have filled Jonathan Edwards with a recondite joy, if indeed anything except the doom of the wicked could ever truly pleasure that soul of steel and ice.

There may be devices more ingeniously conceived to keep in ever watchful care the walk, morals, conversation, and religious fervor of the young than those practised in this bustling academe, but I do not know what they could be. With reason the advertisements stressed the fact of an argus-eyed supervision. The Academy dormitory, it is true, sheltered under one roof young men and young women students, but the prospectus hastened to reassure parents, alarmed, perhaps, by this architectural slip. It pointed out with emphasis that a solid wall of masonry from ground to roof effectually separated the sexes. The principal lived on one side of this wall and the assistant principal on the other, and either or both would have been sure to detect any outbreak of levity, as, for example, an attempt to tunnel the wall.

Attendance at morning prayers was sternly exacted of each and all—no excuses. Besides the reading of the scriptures, the hymns, and the prayers, the man of science, the principal or some visiting clergyman usually said a few words of reproof upon the sins of youth or of exhortation to godliness. While the prayer was on, the principal was accustomed to hold his hand over his eyes in such a way that he could see between his fingers and note an unlucky student whose attitude bespoke not the required sanctification. The mental athleticism involved in this operation always caused me much speculation and sometimes alarm. The least reflection will show that it must have comprised a duplex mechanism approaching the uncanny. While from his lips flowed smoothly and evenly the petition for heavenly grace, the other side of his mind was making (and retaining) notes about the student body before him, so that his total activities must have proceeded in about this fashion:

"We pray for [there's Blodgett looking out the window] thy guidance this [Hopkins is lolling in his seat and playing with his watch-guard] day in all we do [Hatch is writing something on a piece of paper] that we may be [Is Waterman trying to flirt with somebody?] guided aright," and so on.

At eight o'clock every evening the Academy bell rang and after that signal no student could be out of his or her room without the express permission of the principal—difficult to obtain, except on Wednesday night to attend the weekly prayer meeting at the North Congregational Church. It was customary for some member of the faculty to go about with careful scrutiny to learn of possible backsliders in this respect. As the Academy dormitory and Academy boarding house, which stood close by, could accommodate but a small part of the student body, the rest lodged variously about the town. This made a perfect supervision sometimes difficult, but the emergency was bravely met, one of the principals sometimes disguising himself with false whiskers that he might the better pursue this branch of useful knowledge.

Sabbath attendance upon church was required of all, likewise upon Sunday school, and was obtained by compelling each student to make a virtual affidavit every Monday morning that he had not been remiss in his devotions. He must return to the principal a signed affirmation reading as follows:

I, ..., do solemnly declare upon my honor that I attended the morning service at............ Church, on Sunday ...., that I was present at the beginning of the services and remained until the close. I also attended the Sunday school at the .... Church.

The whole thing reeked with piety; aggressive, militant, grim, implacable. It was like smoke from an ill-draughted stove; it oozed from every pore of the buildings and projected through the crannies of doors and windows. To show to youth the steep and thorny way to heaven was not enough; he must be driven thereon with incessant goading and the terror of imminent damnation. His soul must be saved while his mind was being informed; otherwise what was the use? And as all Right Minded Men knew perfectly well that salvation was to be had only through the Congregational Church, why allow any of the young, tender, and inexperienced beings committed to our shepherding to wander into the fields of sin disguised as other denominations? Therefore, when one matriculated, the first question, asked with a mingling, it seemed to me, of righteous asperity and a fear for the future of the interrogated, was "At what church are you accustomed to worship?" and if one were

unlucky enough to say "Methodist" or "Baptist" one met with
a merited disfavor. To be an Episcopalian was to dwell in the
tents of the wicked: I shudder to think of what would have
happened to one professing the abhorred doctrine of the Uni-
tarians or of other lost creatures that denied God had created
most of his children for an everlasting bonfire. An avowed
sceptic would have been slammed through the office windows.

The use of tobacco in any form was proscribed as the un-
pardonable offense; a single drink of any kind of liquor would
have been instantly fatal. Playing cards were strictly forbidden;
likewise all games of chance. My chum used to smoke a little
on the sly; so did I. He was discovered and compelled to make
a humiliating confession before the whole school—at prayers.
A diligent devotion was always a means of grace and sometimes atoned in a measure for slips in scholarship. One of the
students, who planned a missionary career and was duller than
ditch water, was assigned a place where he could sell tracts and
books of religion, the profits thereof being applied to his tuition fees. I regret to add that to the element given over to sin
and scorning, this youth was always an object of extreme dislike, being viewed as an obnoxious favorite of the authorities.
I name no names, but I remember that one dark night early
in the autumn two of the students, eluding him of the false
whiskers, went up the Passumpsic to Henry Ross's place and
hooked watermelons out of the back lot. As they were return-
ing they encountered this youthful missionary coming back
from prayer meeting, passing along the street quietly and nice-
ly, harming nobody, and they pelted him home with water-
melon rinds—a most disgraceful performance and the more
reprehensible because both were old enough to know better
and one was a student of political economy, the just principles
of which would have condemned the whole proceeding.

But to return to the Academy, dancing was strictly forbidden, but at intervals dismal assemblies were allowed where the

students could meet, walk around in a circle and engage in improving conversation. Unseemly mirth was sternly repressed. Robert J. Burdette, the humorist, came to town with one of his amusing lectures. A committee waited upon him with a petition that he should not be too funny. A gracious revival was going on among the Academy students; many precious souls were being saved, and it was felt that a burst of laughter might dislocate the enginery of redemption. It was, the committee well knew, Mr. Burdette's business to be funny, and far be it from them to interfere with any man's business; but would he please restrain his side-splitting jokes and be but moderately comical? He gravely assented and the revival went on triumphantly. The authorities would have been much astonished if they could have foreseen the subsequent careers of some of the converts thus snatched from the burning, as they would have been to hear the sulphurous opinions of the town that Mr. Burdette expressed.

But what I am aiming at through all this prolegomenon is a certain reaction' upon the raw Westerner, essential to the straight way of narrative. The dead weight of the intensive and, as it seemed to me, smug religious formalism drove me into violent revolt. From it was no possible escape, short of leaving the institution, which I was loath to do in view of its great excellences, but my soul yearned for a protest, and yearned not long in vain. There was at that time in Chicago a man named G. S. Baldwin to whom I turned for a certain relief. I think he was by vocation a barber or something like that, but fatefully designated to a service in literature. In those days Robert G. Ingersoll was building his great reputation as an orator and agnostic. Whenever he spoke in Chicago, one newspaper, the old *Chicago Times,* reported his lecture, virtually in full. Mr. Baldwin would send around the next day, buy the matrix of the page that had contained the report, cut it up, cast metal into it, and behold, he had at an infinitesimal expenditure the type for a pamphlet, which he accordingly issued and sold for five cents. As fast as these appeared I sent for copies. It was my custom when I came home from enforced attendance upon the dreary church service to take from their secret hiding place "Gods," "The Mistakes of Moses," and "Liberty of Man, Woman, and Child," and refresh myself with copious extracts. Before long by discreet inquiry I found a few student souls harassed as I was and willing to indulge in similar revolutionary gestures. These I was wont to gather into my room of a Sunday afteroon and read to them (with admiring exegesis) from Ingersoll.

There was in my environment still another condition to stimulate and nourish whatever spirit of insurgency might be. In plain terms, the town was a barony, and so far as autocratic rule was concerned, reproduced neatly the status of a Rhine village in the Middle Ages. The baronial family lived in the castle on the height; the townspeople kow-towed below. The place was the site of the Fairbanks scale factory; members of the Fairbanks family were the barons; in effect their word was law. Without assuming any ostensible place or reachable responsibility in the government, they ruled it absolutely. Whatever they wanted they had, and no man made question thereof. Whosoever might hold office, they ran the machine. The generation of my time comprised the sons of the two men that had invented and developed the beam scale; the huge factory they had built, and year by year had enlarged, stood at one end of the village. Six hundred men were employed in and around it and the community was believed to live and thrive upon its prosperity. Enough; the owners were the barons. Their word was law.

The whole thing struck my Western soul into dismay and then into rebellion, the more, perhaps, because the two forms of feudalism that gravelled me were really identical. It was the Fairbanks family that sustained, managed, and inspired

the Academy and was responsible for the puritanical luna-
cies practised there. It was also the Fairbanks family that ruled
St. Johnsbury with an unassailable sway. Privilege building
toward autocracy—it was the old story. The castle utterly
overawed the villagers. I had never seen the like; it
seemed as menacing as strange. In the West we knew that
some men were richer than others, but had any one of the
richer assumed dictatorial powers because of his wealth he
would have been torn out of his estate. Here the thing that
among my people would have staged a riot was accepted, tolerated, and even defended.

I made inquiries about this mystery and gained valuable enlightenment. It was the first time I had encountered in ponderable form the problem of the Power of Accumulated
Wealth, the persistence of autocracy in a professed republic,
and here are some of the lessons I gained from it. The Fairbanks barony was defended upon these grounds:

1. The great Trickle and Filter Theory of Social Existence,
then all new and strange to me. It was well that a few men
should have all the wealth in the nation because through them
the rest of us had a chance. They spent it and we got some of
the spending. It reached and enriched in this way the lower
strata that otherwise would have been but barren.

2. They were Good Men that were endowed with this abnormal sway and they used it for good ends. Of this, no doubt.
They were all good men; the eulogies upon them that used to
be poured forth in the religious weeklies were in a way merited. They represented, as we were told, the highest type of the
Christian Business Man; aptly were the Scriptures cited in their
laudation, "Not slothful in business, fervent in spirit, serving
the Lord"—and the Republican party, which in the view of
Vermont at that time was the same thing. They gave money
for good objects, they financed the Academy, built and presented to the town the really remarkable Athenæum, stocked

it with a marvellous library, added an excellent collection of
paintings. Liberally they subscribed to foreign missions; they
had built one of the most beautiful churches in all New England; they were flawless in the performance of every pious
duty. All were good men. Governor Horace was a good man
and much interested in the politer forms of horticulture. Colonel Franklin was a good man and was forming a natural-his-
tory collection to be presented to the town. Professor Henry
(he had once held a chair at Dartmouth) was a good man and
ready at any time to supervise anybody's education and conduct. The Reverend Edward was a good man, goodness beamed
in his face. But it seemed to me, on farther reflection, that Good
Man-Bad Man had not a stricken thing on earth to do with
it. These men might be so good they were blue in the face and
still the fact remained that in a so-called democracy they were
clothed with autocratic power; without mandate from the
people they were the government.

Being at the time deep in the study of the French Rev-
olutions, I knew well enough that many of the nobles of the
old regime were exceedingly good men, using their money
for good purposes and sincerely desirous of good for the
people they governed. But I saw vaguely that the system that
supported them was hopelessly bad and that the fault in
it was just this same thing of irresponsible and autocratic power. I began to grope between these two dimly sensed facts,
that somehow the existing organization tended to gather great
wealth in the hands of a few, and, second, that wealth being
always power, there existed (under other names) the germs of
the old struggle between power and the masses.

I grieve to have to remark here that in regard to the perfect
righteousness believed to permeate the scale industry, an investigation, forced some years later by impatient stockholders,
seemed to indicate more than one fly in the precious ointment.
There seemed, indeed, but too much reason to think that Satan,

ever wily and ever restless enemy of mankind, had laid his snares right there in our exemplary community and led some of our best citizens into paths no better than those trodden by the weak and unregenerate. But over this painful chapter of the history of St. Johnsbury it is better to draw the charitable veil and press on with the defense.

3. The argument weighing most with persons of a practical turn of mind was that the power wielded by our barons was properly theirs because they owned a factory and the factory gave work to many men.

This was deemed conclusive and axiomatic. After a time, for a reason I will now explain in detail, its validity seemed more and more questionable.

One of the inmates of the Academy boarding house, the modest hostelry where I had found shelter, was a man so remarkable that he remains to this day clearly silhouetted upon my memory. He was employed at the Fairbanks works in the capacity of a machinist, had been many years so employed, and was now drifting toward the western side of middle age. A well-set-up man, a well-favored man, slightly above the average in height, all the handsome Saxon in appearance, with light-brown hair and beard and clear, dauntless blue eyes; a wholesome man that had walked circumspectly and mastered himself not because of dogma and convention but because of reading and reflection.

A New Englander born and bred, his public-school education had been thorough so far as it went but he had far surpassed in his resolute self-culture anything the schools could have done for him. He was, in fact, one of the best-read men I have ever known. With as much choice as diligence, he had careered over the whole range of literature and so went about a living confirmation of Lord Bacon's apothegm. Indeed, his reading had made him much more than a full man; it had given to his manners so fine a polish and to his conversation so much of research that he was a joy to know. He had even the voice of the highly educated man, soft, melodious, restrained, and he had won to a philosophy of life that highly educated men might not always attain. I exaggerate nothing when I say I can hardly think of the earthly presence in which Jim Dow would have been embarrassed. Not because of effrontery; you could have screened his whole make-up and not caught enough of that to make a trace; but because of a fine native instinct of practical democracy, and because of conviction driven into his being. He had thought of many things, but not much of class consciousness. In his view, all men worked—kings, emperors, governors, presidents, potentates, or what not. He, too, worked. One style of work was the same as another; one worker was equal to another.

Altogether, here was a specimen of the American proletariat of whom patriotism might reasonably vaunt.

Until he knew one, it was difficult to draw him out of a habitual reserve. When he talked freely, his comments being spiced continually with the dry, pungent humor of New England, he was like found money. The man was, in fact, a walking encyclopædia. All human history he seemed to have stored in his broad, capacious head, and curiously enough he kept unflagging watch of all current events that really meant something. With other equipment, I think he knew more about European politics than any other man in that region. I will give one illustration.

The time was that of Gambetta in France. To the average educated American, Gambetta was either a name or vaguely a menace. The British press, which regularly every year for forty-four years beheld at hand the downfall of the French Republic, had heralded this man as the appointed besom of the desired destruction. Gambetta was to be the dictator. He was to repeat the exploits of Napoleon the Little and abolish the detestable Republic. Americans, if they gave any heed to the matter, accepted about this the British press as oracular.

"They are all wrong about Gambetta," said Jim Dow. "This man is not playing for himself; he is playing for France, to get it back upon its feet. If you offered him on a salver this dictatorship he would not take it."

I asked him how he could be so confident. It turned out that he had been digging into Gambetta's life and career and speeches and being accustomed to his own intellectual processes had disregarded predigested and ready-made opinion and reached an independent conclusion about this as about everything else.

It seemed most strange that a man with such qualities should be drudging over a stupid machine in a huge factory, since he seemed in every way fitted for a more spectacular career. I was once imbecile enough to ask him, after we had become friends, why he did not, in my dull phrase, branch out for himself.

"How branch out?" says he.

"Go into some kind of business."

"What kind of business?"

"I don't know."

"Neither do I. But let me tell you something. A cousin of mine had this notion of doing something, going into business, making his fortune and the rest. Well, he went into business. Do you know what he has to show for years of worry and hard work? Debts and bankruptcy. Here I am. When the whistle blows at six o'clock I drop the whole concern. Until the next morning I haven't a thing to bother about. I get my book and draw up my chair, and I don't care what goes well or what goes ill. With an absolutely free mind, I can concentrate on what I am reading. No man can do that if he has what are called business cares."

But while he went his own way and made his own opinions about other things, Jim Dow was like all the rest, a henchman to the barony. It was well known that the way to economic safety and the way to soul's salvation were in that town identical. The religious estate of their employees was not overlooked by the good men of the castle. In their view, a man that was regular in his attendance upon divine worship was a better workman than one that sat in the seats of the scornful. To mingle thus the notching of scale beams with hymnody seemed to me to carry zeal to extremities, but every Sunday morning at exactly the same hour one might see Jim Dow, faultlessly attired in his Sunday suit of black, holding in a black-gloved hand a black-bound hymn-book, wending a solemn way to the North Church. I had some reason to believe that his views upon this sacrificial ceremony differed little from my own and once was crude enough to twit him upon the fact, but this was an error I did not repeat.

It was Jim Dow that shattered for me the ill-jointed structures of accepted theories about Trickle and Filter and the beneficent giving of work to men. Nothing was given to him, certainly. All the giving was the other way. The thing that he contributed to the finished scale was indispensable. An error on his part of the half breadth of a hair would ruin 500 scales. All the worth of the contrivance depended upon his accuracy. Yet when at the end of the week he had paid the slender stipend due at the boarding house he had left for his clothing and all other expenses the sum of four dollars. There were stockholders of the company that contributed nothing to the enterprise, not even their gracious presence, and drew from it in a week more than Jim Dow received in a year. To speak of giving him work was a huge irony. He gave his skill, knowledge, careful attention, labor, but nobody gave him anything.

He was withal a lonely man, looking forth upon a bleak prospect. He had never married because he felt that with his slender wage, marriage would be unfair to the woman. To save anything substantial against the inevitable doom was all but impossible. All the instincts of a finely educated man revolted against any hint of squalor; he must keep an environment that would not rudely shout discord to his soul. To maintain his tasteful attire and have the cultural enjoyments that were his real life made sore inroads upon his meagre surplus. Grimly he faced the realities. "I suppose I shall notch beams until I am too old to run the machine," he said. "Then what? Old men's home, I suppose. A man must take what comes to him."

The political economy text-book that we chiefly used at St. Johnsbury was the work of Arthur Latham Perry of Williams College. I think there was never another man equally gifted to make an abstruse subject not only clear but attractive. Under his skilful touch what the world knows as "the dismal science" became almost fascinating, for he not only wrote with a rare lucidity but he actually fired up over the laws of exchange, monetary standards, and the like succulence; fired up himself and caused the same pleasurable interest in others. I had in those days a kiddish trick of trying to discern the man back of his written page, a process futile and not always safe. I conceived Arthur Latham Perry to be an exceedingly kind man, gentle in his ways but firm and clear and a little positive in all his convictions, with a mind incessantly active, frank, and quick. And I conceived, I do not know why, that he must have a gray beard and twinkling blue eyes. It was one of the few times in my life that guessing came out right and when a little later I met Professor Perry, I felt as if I had known him long and intimately.

I will give one illustration of his ways and character.

He was strongly opposed to the use of tobacco, which he regarded as an economic waste, since it meant no nourishment for the human frame nor addition to the human equipment. Once a week there used to come to his back door in Williamstown a vagrant creature known as Aaron Blue, a ne'er-do-well that the town rather avoided. Upon his appearance Professor Perry would always go to the back door to meet him. One

Sunday afternoon, the sage economist was in the midst of an animated discourse against the evils and wastefulness of the tobacco habit, when Aaron was announced and the Professor made his usual trip kitchenward. A friend that had often noticed this singular performance made bold on his return to ask about it.

"Why do you have this Aaron Blue coming here to your house? Why do you bother with him?"

"Well, you see," said Perry, "he hasn't any tobacco money, so every Sunday I give him enough to get his tobacco for a week."

The farther I went with him in his way through these flowerless fields, the more I thought I saw the answer to the problem of Accumulated Wealth and Accumulated Power that overhung the barony. Easily I bound cause to effect. The root of the evil was the accursed tariff. Under its operation the wealth that should be for all was seized by the favored few. Give us but a chance to buy wherever we could buy the cheapest and all these troubles would pass like the mist. The next grand struggle of the race was to free commerce from tariffs as labor had been freed from the other blight of slavery.

Under the spell of this illumination, it seemed to me that I had a call if not to the housetops at least to some place where I could ease my burdened chest with winged words conveying to my fellow men the glad tidings of emancipation. Accordingly, on February 3, 1881, at the town of Peacham (auspicious name!), Vermont, while I was still an Academy student, I made my first appearance on the lecture platform, discoursing on "Free Trade *vs*. Protection." Luckily, history has preserved no record of this unepochal effort, but my private conviction is that it was fairly bad. However, I had a good house. Lecture engagements were few in Peacham. In the audience, about three rows from the front, I noticed a tall, weedy youth whose arms and legs seemed to have sprouted suddenly from his clothing and whose round eyes were fixed without wavering upon mine. He seemed so strange a being that I asked about him and learned that his name was George Harvey, native of the village. Forty years later he was the American Ambassador to Great Britain. In 1887 when he and I had adjacent desks in the office of the old *New York World,* he told me without blinking that the stuff he heard that night made him a Free Trader. George was always a merry soul and would have his little joke.

Anyway, I was launched into the fight, although in the rear rank where no one but myself knew I was fighting. To my fevered vision, the redemption of the West was clearer than crystal, and simple the remedy for all our ills. Abolish the tariff and the thing was done. Inclined toward this satisfactory creed, I came a little later upon a copy of *Progress and Poverty,* and that settled my case. Infallibly I conceded the voice of ultimate wisdom, and saw in Henry George the apostle of a new gospel. Poverty was not normal but abnormal; poverty came because some men had too much and others therefore too little. Why too much? Assuredly, the tariff.

About this time also I became lucidly aware of a spirit much greater. With other substantial advantages, the Academy was blessed with an instructor in elocution of singular and pre-eminent ability, the only exponent of his art I have known that based it all upon reason, good sense, and the scientific principles of sound and music. His name was Wendell Phillips Stafford; long afterward he came to be an honored judge of the Supreme Court of the District of Columbia and a noted orator. Though not related to the great agitator, he had naturally keen interest in the man and his works and he early drew my attention to some of Phillips's matchless orations as models of style and construction. From this beginning, Phillips grew to be the god of my idolatry. I got the published volume of his speeches. I pored over them, not alone as achievements in a most difficult art but as revelations of the man behind them. I read with what

serene courage he faced the mob in Faneuil Hall, how he had
dared to stand out against the return of fugitive slaves, how
boldly in the market place he had arisen to cry aloud against
the illimitable crime of slavery, how he defied the Southern
slave oligarchy before which most men of his time cowered
and quivered. Pages I memorized from his *Simms Anniversary,*
Idols, his *Harper's Ferry,* and that still unequalled classic
among all elegies, his speech at the grave of John Brown. The
Doric simplicity of his style, its exquisite music, the structural
strength of his reasoning, his perfect command over all the
resources of speech, filled me with an inexpressible admiration.
Once I had heard him on the lecture platform. It seemed to
me now as I bent over his pages that I could hear again his
silvery voice with its great range of feeling and expression and
see again his impressive figure. While I was still in pupilage he
delivered his great Phi Beta Kappa oration, "The Scholar in a
Republic." It seemed to me to contain the whole duty of man.

I thought then that he was the greatest of Americans; I
think so still. By so much as service for an ideal is above service
for a man's own fortune or glory he towers above all others we
have elected to call great. I was never crazy enough to imagine
that I could emulate his deeds any more than I could imitate
his style, but the mere existence of such a man was strength
and light to the rank and file. The theme that rang through
his Phi Beta Kappa address, the theory that a man's gifts, whatever they may be, are not bestowed upon him as possessions but
lent for use toward the common good, struck me as better than
anything in any scheme of instruction I had ever heard of. I
wondered that the reverend dodo that harangued us with a
stodgy baccalaureate had not mentioned something of this
kind instead of lunging at us with the sun-dried remnants of
an outworn theology.

Chapter III

THE CITADEL OF PRIVILEGE

O<small>H</small>, well," said Ted Eagles, who kept the Locust Street grocery in my native town, "farmers are always grumbling."

True was the word; we all said so. Everybody knew that farmers were the world's worst fault-finders; knew it and glibly we repeated it on the least occasion, or none. In an Iowa town chiefly for its life dependent upon agriculture, this notion was a perdurable part of the amused contempt with which we were pleased to regard the yokels of the granges. But what must seem puzzling to the historian, for a long time nobody took the least pains to learn what on earth the farmers were grumbling about. Between the plow-tail and a petulant spirit is no apparent connection; men have tilled the soil since before Noah was a sailor and have not developed a notable specialty in girding.

Least of all, one might think, had they of Iowa, on the face of things, good reason to curse their lot and give over. They possessed some of the most fertile soil the sun ever shone upon; they were engaged in producing things all men must have to live. We used to boast that in the whole State was only one-half acre of land that could not be cultivated. The vaunt once reached the ears of Lincoln and he made a jest about it, but it was substantially based, nevertheless. For ages the prairies had lain fallow, burned over every autumn or so by the fires that loaded the soil with the salts of fertility. When it was touched with a plow-point, behold, it leaped into an unprecedented harvest. And yet farmers grumbled.

The real burden of their jeremiads was not the hard work they must do nor the chances of the weather, although we always said so. These were only handy themes for surface relief; the cause of trouble went much deeper. It lay in the fact that for all their toil, skill, care, fortitude, and privations they had nothing to show except the bare fact of an existence kept by a hand-to-hand fight against adversity. Except in rare and favored instances, no one could win to even a moderate fortune at farming. The average Iowa farm in those days was a quarter section, or 160 acres, of phenomenally rich earth, and the net result of a year's grinding labor upon it was relatively less than a French peasant reaped from a patch perhaps a twentieth of that area. Year after year the Iowa farmer turned the black loam, sowed the seed, watched his crop to an abundant harvesting, took it with expectancy to the market and came away with enough to pay the interest upon his mortgage and little besides.

To win to even this barren fruitage he must not only work like a horse in a treadmill but endure a horrible isolation. In town, the children of even the poorest had some chance of culture, some measure of human society, some change from the grim and the gruelling. The farmer's child in those days must fight to win even the rudiments of an education and dwell meanwhile in an immitigable loneliness. Industry, sobriety, integrity, frugality, all the virtues bepraised in song and story might work gloriously elsewhere but they broke down at the farm gate. Blight overhung the entire business. A man might work his hands to the bone and deny himself all ease, and the result would be an identical defeat. The farmer fed all other men and lived himself upon scraps.

Especially in the fall of the year we would see them coming in processions to the town, jolting along in their rough, springless wagons. Sometimes their wives sat with them, two care-worn faces instead of one. Their gaunt frames and labor-loosened joints had become the standard jest. The jolly husbandman was a myth; I think I seldom saw a farmer in those days that did not look worsted in the battle of life. Not because they were ill-spirited they lost in that battle, but because they were gripped helplessly by a huge and lop-sided system that denied them a chance to win.

Almost any other industry could claim some fostering care or substantial help of government. Farming, the industry upon which all the rest depended, could go hang. Manufacturers of articles in iron, steel, wood, textiles, ceramics, were enriched by a tariff that shielded them from competition. The farmer not only had no such shield but in a way vital to his interests he must face in a foreign market the fierce rivalries of the world. The cost of everything he must buy was artificially enhanced for him by the tariff that swelled the profits of the manufacturers; the price of his staple products was fixed for him by an uncontrolled competition. Deeply and in a thousand ways the thing cut into him. His chances for successful contention in that foreign market to which he was assigned were dependent upon transportation to the seaboard. Yet here again the cost of all such transportation was wantonly increased by the tariff upon all things that entered into the building and upkeep of railroads. In the last analysis, the essence of the protective tariff was a tax levied upon the consumer for the benefit of the producer, since the price of the domestic article was the price of the foreign article plus the amount of the tariff duty. No tax was levied for the benefit of the farmer; daily he paid taxes for the benefit of other men.

Fresh from contact with the discerning mind of Arthur Latham Perry, it seemed to me as clear as day that the only chance the Iowa farmer had of winning out of his slough of despond was by emancipation from the crushing burden of the tariff. While still in the Academy I had written for my father's newspaper a series of articles on this entrancing subject—perfectly sophomorical, I have no doubt, foolish and ineffectual, but at least stumbling toward this point. When I came home I found the fight far advanced and in abler hands. One other journal in our State, *The Leader,* published at Des Moines, the capital, was whanging manfully at the fortalice of iniquity and had been for some months. Its assaults were so clear, forceful, varied, and based on research that I was moved to ask about the author. I found his name was Henry J. Philpott, he was editor of *The Leader,* and within a space remarkably short he had won for his newspaper a position of power and influence.

The more I read after him the more I wished to know him. After a short correspondence I went to Des Moines for that purpose, and there in December, 1881, we founded the Iowa State Free Trade League, the first of its kind in the country.

Free Trade was the traditional policy of the Democratic party; Protection was supposed to be the sacred white cow of the Republicans. *The Gazette,* my father's journal, was an old-line Republican organ and the course we were pursuing brought out a plenteous crop of protests, including one from Major William McKinley. Yet there were many other seceders in the West that shared our views. The president of the State League, Orrin W. Mosher, a banker from an interior city, was a Republican; so at that time was the vice-president. Philpott was secretary; Lowry W. Goode, publisher of *The Leader,* was treasurer. We four virtually constituted the League. A few others came in spasmodically or nominally, but we four did all the work, and with the aid of an imposing letter-head, a colossal assurance, and some well-chosen literature, got away with it.

Early in the fight the cause had sudden help from an unexpected and perhaps equivocal champion. I am to suppose that the name of W. H. H. Murray hardly lingers now upon the human memory, but in the seventies it was to the religious world second to none except that of Beecher himself. No stranger figure has appeared among us. He was an ordained minister in some orthodox sect, Congregational, I think, and a pulpit orator of a genuine eloquence. In the Civil War he served with some distinction and wrote about it with extraordinary power. He was about half-mad over out-door life, and may be said to have discovered the Adirondacks, writing about his fishing and tramping adventures there with so much of charm and enthusiasm that he was known as "Adirondack Murray." Almost equal with fishing in his devotion were trotting matches, the driving of fast horses and horse lore. About these matters he wrote articles and stories that became classics. At the top of his prestige, he established in Boston a religious weekly called *The Golden Rule,* in which he made an equal division of interest between evangelism and horse flesh, and I do not see how any one could say fairer than that. At that time one famous driver of racing horses surpassed all others in glory, and scoffers used to say that a reader of *The Golden Rule* could never tell St. Paul from Budd Doble. Whether by reason of these features, somewhat unusual in religious journalism, or for some other cause, *The Golden Rule* attained for a time to great circulation and popularity; after the mid-day Sunday dinner in a well-ordered household, if one took up *The Golden Rule* and allowed one's eyes to stray from the Sunday-school lesson to an account of Budd Doble's latest triumph, why, no harm done and no reputation injured.

The Reverend Murray was temperamental and impulsive; also vagarious. For a time he was pastor of the Park Street Church in Boston; then he went to independent sermonizing in a public hall. *The Golden Rule* waned and went out. Suddenly, Mr. Murray startled his followers, who were still many, by swift and highly mysterious exit to Europe. He was gone some months and people had begun to forget him when one day he reappeared in Boston (without an explication), hired the

Boston Music Hall, packed it, and then came forth and delivered one of the ablest arguments for Free Trade I have ever encountered. Out in Iowa we fell upon it with shouts of joy. It was a marvellous piece of reasoning, bristling with facts and buttressed with a knowledge of economics that few of his admirers had ever suspected him to possess. By all accounts it thrilled and deeply impressed his hearers and won respectful attention even from the most rabid of the Protectionist organs.

Then he lapsed back into obscurity, dwelling in a little house in a remote part of Burlington, Vermont. If any one can tell what moved him to this single spectacular display of a really remarkable equipment, such a one is wiser than I.

Considering its numbers and means, I cannot but think now that the Iowa State Free Trade League of four persons did a fairly good job. It issued a flood of pamphlets and leaflets, it held public meetings, it came down with thumping letters of protest upon Iowa newspapers that dared to commend Protection to the Iowa farmer, it kept up an incessant fire in the friendly journals, it roared, shouted, and bellowed and for a time drove the forces of evil back to their trenches. It certainly did. In the election of 1882 it carried on the tariff issue five of the Congressional districts in the state, a thing without precedent and enough to start the echoes in the reverberate hills. And it did this in the face of constant assurances that its members were depraved and desperate characters, Anarchists in disguise, public enemies, seeking to overthrow the foundations of our holy and perfect system and deep in the pay of the Cobden Club of England. All of us were wallowing in British gold; some of our opponents even knew and did not hesitate to reveal the exact amounts each received.

The League did more than to send five good Free Traders to Congress. The uproar it made in the Woolly West resounded across the continent in a way out of all proportion to effort or deserving. Old-line Free Traders in the East perked up and became active as soon as they grasped what was going on in the hinterland. A group of first-rank economists united to further the work. The New York Free Trade Club was revived, followed by the American Free Trade League. Professor Perry, Professor Sumner of Yale, David A. Wells, Horace White, Thomas G. Shearman, R. R. Bowker came forth with articles, books, and pamphlets. Some of the work done by these men naturally eclipsed for solidity and worth the best we had ever accomplished in the West. I remember a book written by Mr. Bowker, an *Economic Hand Book*, that built up with statistics, facts, and logic a case against Protection no one was ever able to gainsay. About that time, *Progress and Poverty* was making its sure way from coast to coast and wherever it went it made proselytes. Altogether, we might well think we had the enemy on the run.

For all the share in this that the Iowa League had, the credit belonged to one man, Henry J. Philpott.

Here was one of those strong but uncelebrated figures that exist behind every movement if at all it revolves, men that do the work or inspire it or lead it, and of themselves leave no other memorial. He was about twenty-six when I first knew him, rather tall, almost gaunt, with a student's stoop, a pallid complexion, burning blue eyes, and a short brown tangled beard. He had been born and bred upon a farm but had managed to obtain a classical education, and showed a combination, most unusual, of the fiery zeal of an agitator and the cultural taste of a recluse. He loved equally to fight and to sit alone and devour poetry, and I may remark that the first time I heard Poe's "Annabel Lee," read as it should be read, read with understanding and sympathetic interpretation, it fell from the lips of Henry Philpott. He was almost passionate about art and would give up anything (except a tariff fight) to see a good picture.

One night we were in Chicago walking down to the old

Michigan Central station at the foot of Lake Street to take a train for the East. Of a sudden he darted from my side and went scurrying rapidly from shop window to window, peering in and loping on, I pursuing under the impression that he had gone mad. At the end of two blocks I caught up with him.

"For the Lord's sake, what ails you?" I panted.

"It's a picture of Christ that used to be in one of these windows and I wanted you to see it."

Taking him by and large, I think he was the ablest polemical writer I have known. No one engaged in a dispute with him on any phase of the tariff question that did not emerge in defeat. For every statement, great or small, he had the authority ready, book, chapter, and verse. Despite his guileless and unsophisticated appearance, he could never be trapped into an erroneous statement. In controversy, of which he had always two or three examples going on at the same time, he struck out right and left and spared not, so that many persons knowing him only from his writings visualized him as a fearsome creature going about seeking whom he might devour. As a matter of fact, about anything but the tariff he was the gentlest and kindest of men. His voice was not good for public speaking, a fact he never regretted, for all his preference was for battle in the press; he never did himself justice before a larger audience than four. All the bitterness he had absorbed flowed upon his pen; when he laid that down he was just an old softy. If in his articles he attacked the tariff barons as plunderers and bandits, he was without personal ill-will toward them or anybody else. He lived simply, studied conscientiously, fought honestly, and had as little of fame as of fortune.

The intensity of his feelings about the tariff led back to his youth. Every phase of the farmer's hard lot he had known and had tasted the last drop of its bitterness. He had seen his father and mother in his own phrase "battling up stream and carried down." The grinding toil, the fruitless sacrifices, the deadening weight of the vast loneliness, the incessant struggle against the forces of nature that were hard and the greed of men that was harder, the early risings, the late laborings, the piled-up crops that melted away like snow and left as little trace—the whole wretched and murderous business was burned into his soul. A sensitive man, he thought back upon his mother wasting her life in such an environment and the thought was like burning thorns in his flesh. He knew there were in the State at that moment thousands and thousands of such women caught in the same hideous machine and he conceived of himself as chartered and destined to release them.

He had gone into the tariff question far more deeply than I had ever dreamed of going. To his mind the Protective system was more than the source of the Western farmer's poverty, the piler of senseless fortunes, the machine that impoverished the many to enrich the few. Against the theory of Protection he charged a national decline and moral degeneration. He saw in it the origin and nourisher of the notion that the government existed for no purpose but to make its citizens rich. He traced back to Protection's evil influence and example the corruption of politics, the black scandals of the fraudulent pensions, the disguised raids on the treasury, the river and harbor swindles, the breaking down of every ideal of service and public virtue. If one set of men could invoke the aid of the government to provide them with profits by taxing their fellow citizens, another could reasonably demand appropriations that were merely a magnified grand larceny. If one man could be helped by the government to build his private fortune out of a nail factory, another might as reasonably use the same means to win illegal grants of the public domain. The idea of using the government for personal ends, originating in the Protective theory, had spread through the nation and in his judgment was turning it into a society chiefly composed of plunderers and the plundered.

"THE COMMERCIAL CLUB OF WASHINGTON"

Puck's cartoon on the United States Senate and the Interests

Nothing really mattered except to combat this huge evil and to try to rescue what was left of the democratic ideal. For himself, he would, I think, have lived as contentedly upon six dollars a week as upon the twenty dollars that constituted his salary. He cared nothing for money, something for kudos, nothing for personal appearance, and, as you are to learn in the sequel, as little for health.

The memories of his boyhood on a farm were strong upon him, but most his recollections of his mother. He recalled her as the patient, uncomplaining, sad-eyed drudge and slave in a company chained to the chariot wheels of a kind of Moloch of profits. She arose early, she toiled late, she had no joy more ennobling than the cleanliness of her kitchen and the excellence of her pies at harvest time. No existence could seem more barren, and with research and energy he cursed the system that seemed to crush from even the most aspiring spirits the last chance to know the good of life.

Once a blizzard descended upon them when their fuel supply was all but exhausted. Eight persons, I think he said, were huddled in the kitchen. At some distance from the house was a pile of cord wood, their only hope. From time to time a hardy soul would dash from the house to that pile and bring in maybe two sticks or three. So dense was the driving snow, so dark the air and so cold, that this pioneer must go with a rope tied around his waist, the other end attached to the house, lest he be lost, for the snow obliterated everything. In the house was only an old hand-saw. With this they sawed from the log laid across a chair enough wood to keep the fire going and themselves from freezing.

Nature seemed at times to conspire with human greed to add to their afflictions. In August, 1876, when there had been every promise of improving conditions and the yield looked most fair, of a sudden came a visitation of grasshoppers and he saw every green thing destroyed while he gazed. All the corn was eaten to the bare stalks, the little patch of potatoes and cabbage, that his thrifty mother had planted in the door yard stripped to the ground, the trees left bare as in December, grass cut to the roots. An illimitable army of destruction oppeared from the southwest and vanished, leaving only ruin behind.

"You may not believe it," he said, "but it is a fact that they were so thick they delayed trains on the railroads. The locomotive drive wheels slipped on the tracks made greasy with their ground-up bodies."

From time to time the newspapers in our part of the world would burst into cackle about the marvellous prospects for abundant tilth, chortling over what they called "a bumper crop." This never failed to arouse his savage irony.

"Crop of what?" he would say. "Crop of callouses and old clothes to turn. Who'll get the good of the big crop? The money sharks and the Iron and Steel Association. Big crops only mean more work for smaller returns."

The net result of his father's effort had been like the net result in so many other cases. A lifetime of toil had won a roof over the family's head and a semi-annual interest charge in lieu of rent.

The hopes of the Free Traders were centred upon the Democratic party, but they leaned there upon a flimsy reed. From time immemorial the Democratic party had stood for "a tariff for revenue only" and down with Protection. Of later years it had continued in its platforms the same old declaration, but as the power of the Protected manufacturers increased one could see that the Democratic tongue was being thrust the farther into the Democratic cheek. The Democrats won in the Congressional election of 1882 complete control of the House. It was necessary to make some gesture about the tariff. They brought in the Mills bill, which provided for a reduction of about ten per cent in the prevailing duties and some additions to the free list, and with this we were forced to be content, but with expectant eyes turned upon 1884, when there would be a President to elect and we might expect plain speaking and resolute acting.

This reminds me of a historical incident that may well be recorded here. Among the eminent recruits to the Free Trade cause that appeared in the East was Henry Ward Beecher, still holding forth weekly at old Plymouth Church in Brooklyn. His most intimate friend was Thomas G. Shearman, who was superintendent of his Sunday school and had been of his counsel in the famous Beecher-Tilton trial. "Tearful Tommy" and "Shammy Tearman" a cynical press had dubbed Shearman then because of the emotion he showed. Before the jury he had thrown his arms around Beecher and shed tears down the back of the Beecher neck; yet ordinarily was he cold as a fish. Shearman, putting himself unreservedly into the Free Trade fight, had won his pastor to the same faith, although the pastor had always been a strong Republican. In the Spring of 1882 Mr. Shearman came to Iowa and consulted with the Free Traders there, followed a year later by Beecher himself, who was then on a lecture tour. At these conferences it was agreed that if the Democrats should take any definite stand in Congress about the tariff issue, and should nominate in 1884 a respectable candidate, the Western Republican Free Traders would support the Democratic ticket in the national election. The provision about the candidate was put in because there was much talk at the time about Sam Randall as the Democratic nominee and the Westerners regarded him as Satan's own. Mr. Beecher was included in this agreement.

The next year, the Democrats nominated Grover Cleveland and the Republican Free Traders generally kept to their word and supported him, among them Mr. Beecher. Attempts have since been made to show that Beecher's support was given out of sympathy for Cleveland in the Maria Halpin scandal. "Beecher had been in a woman scrape himself and had a fellow feeling for another in the same predicament," says one of these detractors. The fact is, Beecher's support was assured months before he or any one else knew of the Maria Halpin business and was based entirely upon the tariff issue.

In June, 1883, we had progressed with the agitation to a point where we might venture to call the first national Free Trade convention. It was held in Detroit and drew an unexpectedly large attendance. The Detroit Opera House was crowded to its capacity. Everybody rejoiced; we had driven the Monster Protection to its lair and were now about to exterminate it. The speeches were eloquent and able and all that, Professor Perry delivering one of the best. The Mayor of the city, although a leading Republican, went so far as to urge an American zollverein to take in all South America and have absolute free trade with all American countries. The resolutions were grand and full of pith and moment. The American Free Trade League, headed by George Foster Peabody, occupied the centre of the hall; the vice-president of the Iowa League was the convention's secretary. There was even on exhibition a victim of the cause. He was the former editor and proprietor of a newspaper in some highly Protected region where he had talked Free Trade and been thrown to the wolves by way of example salutary. I looked upon him with mild curiosity never the least surmising that the same thing could happen to me.

But it did, and that right early. In a way to be related hereafter my father's long fight against corporation monopoly ended in his ruin. *The Gazette,* which had always been regarded as a family heir-loom, was suddenly wrenched from his grasp and the whole Russell tribe found itself slung upon the sidewalk. Confronted with the grim necessity of daily bread-getting, I must for a time give over the hunting of the tariff jobberwock.

The next disappointment fell in quickly and was more grievous. By a change in ownership, we lost *The Des Moines Leader*. Henry Philpott, being likewise out of a job, started a little Free Trade weekly called *The Million*. It was of few days and full of trouble. We that knew, admired, and loved him had long been uneasy about his health. His emaciated frame, evident lack of vitality, burning eyes, and constant cough were danger signals of the worst kind, and particularly to me that had seen others go that way. A short time after he had begun *The Million* he was stricken down. Galloping tuberculosis it was, and almost before we were aware, he was gone. If he had been shot down on a battlefield he could not have been more truly a sacrifice to a cause.

The movement in Iowa never recovered from the blow of his passing. Other reverses came to shatter the rosy dreams that had entranced us. The Democratic platform of 1884, which we had hoped and expected would be a ringing clarion call and that kind of thing, emitted no more than a squawk. The Presidential campaign, which we had hoped would be fought on the tariff issue, came to turn on some miserable degrading stuff about two children born out of wedlock, and when the Democrats had finally won, Free Trade had won nothing with them because the Protectionists, whether Republican or Democrat, and that made no difference, were in a position to block everything—and did so.

Things drifted thus, with the Free Trade hope slowly dimming as the power of the Protected manufacturers grew, until Cleveland's historic and reviving message of December, 1887. In the existing conditions, it was the boldest step any President had ever taken; so far as it goes, he is entitled to all the credit that can be given to him for so outstanding a course. Putting aside every other topic, on the eve of a Presidential election in which he knew he was to be a candidate, he sent to Congress a message that forced the whole tariff issue upon the nation. In plain terms he said the time had come when the Protective theory must be curtailed and the nation turn about face toward the policy of treating all of its citizens alike.

Thus challenged outright to combat, the Protected manufacturers made a mighty response, put forth all their strength, and won. With the aid of John Y. McKane, boss of Coney Island and afterward a convict in Sing Sing, they scraped through in New York State and got the Presidency.

But Cleveland's message had made the tariff issue national and inevitable. For the next four years it went on before an electorate always growing more hostile to the tariff barons. It was evident that the next election, that of 1892, would be fought on this question and that if Cleveland were again nominated he would win. The Protected manufacturers tried valorously to prevent his nomination. They manipulated things so as to steal the New York delegation to the national convention, they tried to snitch delegations in other States. Then appeared upon the scene a man of singular and commanding genius, a big, masterful, intrepid, resolute man, that brought all the machinations to naught. Political conventions have known nothing more abnormal. William C. Whitney was not a politician; he was a lawyer, business man, speculator, financier, society leader, aristocrat, but he outwitted, outmanœuvred, and outfought the shrewdest political leaders of the East. It was he that kept the Cleveland forces together; it was he that frustrated every assault and won daily upon the enemy. Tammany was all against Cleveland; the ferocious tiger of the New York jungles was only a poor old alley cat when W. C. Whitney started in to shoot.

And now a strange thing happened. Cleveland was at his summer home in Marion, Massachusetts. He had a private wire between his house and the Cleveland headquarters in Chicago, where the convention was held. Later it was transferred to the convention hall itself. Over this wire, Grover Cleveland, foremost champion of tariff reduction, bold assailant of Protected monopoly, sent message after message urging that the utterance on the tariff be conservative, and trying to restrain those that wished it to be explicit and brave. Explain this in any way you please, it is the fact. All of his thick-and-thin adherents were ready enough to follow his ideas. The Western Democrats, led by Tom Patterson of Colorado, fiercely resented it. They declared that if the platform shilly-shallied on the tariff, they would walk in a body out of the convention, and as their purpose was manifest and the party on the brink of a fatal split, they had their way, wrote the tariff plank as they desired, and Cleveland was obliged to accept it.

He won on it, the Democrats swept the country and for the first time since before the Civil War, were in complete control of the government. The nation had responded on the tariff issue, not consciously accepting our doctrine of absolute Free Trade, but determined that the most vicious features of the Protective tariff should be abolished as the beginning of a better system. With joy, young and susceptible spirits in the movement looked forward to the Happy Day.

It never came. For then was revealed the fatal weakness in the Free Trade cause. The Democratic platform had in plainest terms committed the party to drastic tariff reductions. When the attempt was made to carry out this pledge, sincere Democrats like Representative Wilson of West Virginia ran plump against the stone wall of the individual interest. The moment reduction was suggested in the duties on lumber, up sprang the whole lumber trade with a passionate scream of protest—the Democratic members of Congress from the lumber districts screaming as loudly as anybody. If the attack approached woolens, a fierce cry went up from the woolen interests and members from the woolen districts led it. If one spoke of cottons, New England roared aloud; if of iron and steel all Pennsylvania revolted. Except acorns, there was no one item in the list that could be touched without bellowing rage and threats of widespread ruin. Always Democratic Congressmen were as eager to help the bellowing as any Republicans, and for the same reason. Both had from the moment of election centred their thoughts, souls, minds, and aims upon re-election, and neither would take the risk of offending wealthy manufacturers, particularly when the manufacturers could marshal behind them their employees, panicky with the created fear of loss of employment.

Under these conditions the sessions of the Ways and Means Committee, of which Wilson was chairman, might as well have been held in the Place of Wailing. Little was heard except complaint and protest. Each interest was quite willing that the tariff should be reduced on some other commodity than its own product but pictured limitless woe if on its own the duties should be lowered in the estimation of a hair. As each had its own member of the House or the Senate committed, for purely selfish reasons, to its defense, when the bill was driven through both houses its own father would never have known it, and the total reduction it effected in the wretched tariff was hardly discernible.

It seemed to us of the radical Free Trade wing that the ultimate blame for this rested upon Cleveland. He that had made the tariff fight virtually abandoned it now. With his great prestige and influence he might have forced the recalcitrant Democrats into line and compelled them to keep their promises. So far as we could see, he made no such effort, and allowed the bill to become a law without his signature, thereby signalling to the country the hopeless impotency of the Democratic party and paving the way for its overwhelming defeat. The change that seemed to have come over him is a historical mystery. All the fortitude he had displayed in December, 1887, seemed to have oozed away and left him flabby. Bold declarations he had made against the interference of the money power with the functions of government. Before he had long been President it was evident that this same money power had won to a complete mastery upon him. When he passed over to a gang of respectable racketeers in Wall Street the power to enrich themselves at public expense by controlling the national bond issues, the element that had been most earnestly devoted to him turned away with a bitter disillusion. Their idol had but feet of clay, and mushy at that.

Mr. Cleveland has been widely praised for his reputed courage. The courage displayed in these transactions, including his private wire messages from Marion, was certainly nothing to stir pulses to a gallop.

There is one other phase of his conversion to the money power's side that I mention here because of its philosophical interest. In June, 1894, the poorly paid and badly treated employees of the Pullman Company at Pullman, Illinois, went on strike and their strike, spreading to the railroads, became a momentous struggle between capital and labor. It might have been avoided with a little of decent regard for justice on the part of the companies, but it was not; I think the companies rather wished it. To support their side in the controversy, Cleveland ordered out the federal troops. Now, the Constitution says that this shall be done in cases of domestic disturbances only upon the request of the Governor of an affected state and his certification that the state authorities cannot deal with the situation. The Governor of Illinois made no request for troops in this instance; on the contrary, he protested against their intrusion, declaring that the state authorities were fully able to control the disturbance. Cleveland persisted in violating the nation's organic law in this respect and was strongly upheld in his course by Richard Olney, then his Attorney-General.

In 1874, President Grant, at the request of the Governor of Louisiana and upon the required certification, had sent troops into that state to quell disorder that amounted to a rebellion. At a public meeting in Faneuil Hall, Boston, on January 15,

1875, this same Richard Olney had vehemently denounced this course of President Grant as an intolerable violation of a state's sacred rights.

But to return to our Free Trade muttons, the movement was dead. It had gone against the stone wall of profits and been smashed there. A cynical indifference settled upon its one-time advocates. The nation was shackled by the chains of selfish interest to the tariff chariot; the procession would have to take its course.

Autopsy. The Free Trade movement died of a profound constitutional malady. Like so many other well-meant reform-ing inspirations, it had attacked symptoms but stopped short of causations. All that the Free Trade champions said against Protection and its evils was true; it was indeed an overflowing fountain-head of trouble. But it was only the outgrowth of an underlying condition. So long as the profit system was to be retained, Protection or Free Trade could make little difference to the lives of the masses, and even Henry George purposed to leave the profit system virtually intact. The real source of the world's distress was production for profit and nothing could remedy or seriously affect the disorders arising from that source except the substitution of production for use.

I cannot but think, also, that we of the Free Trade move-ment were singularly dumb about another matter. We might have seen that as the world was organized, Free Trade for any one country would be in the long run impossible. In the frantic international competitions for markets to which civilization has been reduced, any country without tariff barriers would be overwhelmed by its neighbors. In those days we made much of the example of England, which kept up a tariff for revenue only and apparently thrived under it. But we failed to observe that England was in effect protected by the low wage scales and low living standards of its workers and that this protection would collapse as soon as another nation developed its manufacturing facilities to a point where it could undersell the English producer. Exactly that condition we have since seen arriving and Free Trade seems now as dead in England as it is in the United States. It is in fact dead everywhere, however excellent its theory, and will be until we learn from panic, depressions, and disasters to abandon an insane for a sane method of providing mankind with its needs.

Chapter IV

THE RED GAME COCK

BUT Free Trade was not carried from the stage without a singular episode well worth recalling and remembering.

While we had been urging the main battle charge against Protection as a governmental policy, Henry George had been stating a far higher view of the same subject. *Progress and Poverty,* that epochal work, had gone of its own momentum from one thinking mind to another. Its reasonable proposal to abolish not only the Protective tariff but other forms of our crazy, lop-sided, unjust, and absurd taxation methods and adopt a plan at once scientific and beneficial, made a deep impression upon all that took it into serious thought. We had proposed to end Protection; he hoped to end also poverty, the slums, the huge degradation of the masses, the acute inequalities of condition that curse and threaten all modern social structures.

Almost without his effort or knowledge followers began to gather around him. In 1886 he was nominated by an independent labor movement to be mayor of New York.

The campaign that followed was a liberal education to any one not well versed in the varied resources and powers of Accumulated Wealth. I happened to see it all—from a seat on the grand-stand. Frst the terrified huddling together of the wealthy at the growing menace of a reform that would curtail their rentals; then the sudden dropping of all other interests and antagonisms to meet this peril to purses; then the means by which unified wealth did battle with an aroused proletariat. Henry George was the greatest and most practical of all Free

46

'Traders. I saw men that had loudly endorsed the Free Trade
faith as a theory, men of wealth and property, scuttle out of all
their professions to join hands with extreme Protectionists
against the menace of Georgeism. The New York Free Trade
Club, with which I was then connected, lifted not a hand to
help him. Most of its members openly or secretly yearned for
his defeat. They were men of wealth and property; he threatened rents. I do not know how one could more plainly state the
underlying impulses of the privileged. Something else, it is
true, had power upon them. Caste was no fantasy in those
precincts; it was an existent fact. Most of the members were
college bred. Henry George's followers were working men. As
much as we please we may seek to evade the class distinctions
wrought by our mad system of educating 7 per cent of the
population, but it persists nevertheless. The thought that the
government of the city was to be delivered over to mere workers was to many of my associates intolerable.

But the extreme fright among the propertied was shown still
more comically in the situation that developed in the Democratic party of the city. It was then split in two factions, Tammany Hall and the County Democracy. Tammany Hall represented the vulgarians, County Democracy what was called
the respectable element, men of means and standing, business
and professional men. Up to that time, the two factions had
glared at each other across the polling place with far more
bitterness than either felt toward the Republicans. It was the
announced conviction of County Democrats that all Tammany
was corrupt, vile, composed of low persons, ignorant foreigners, denizens of the slums, and no one of the least respectability could ever be found in such company. All this antagonism vanished magically at the mere mention of Henry
George's name. The spectacle of a high-hatted and silk-stock-
inged aristocrat of Fifth Avenue (as it was then) getting into
bed with an unshaven and beer-fragrant dive-keeper of the

Bowery was not exhilarating but lost much of its shock by becoming familiar. Tammany Hall and County Democracy buried every difference, met in sweetest amity, and nominated a coalition candidate in the person of Abram Stevens Hewitt, Peter Cooper's son-in-law and a melancholy dyspeptic with a disordered liver and millions of dollars.

Also, he was a member in good and regular standing of the New York Free Trade Club and had been a Free Trade member of Congress.

But the George movement swept on without experienced direction, impelled irresistibly by the revolt of the workers and the propertyless. Skilled observers saw it heading for an assured triumph. Such election laws as we had in those days were loose and gave every loop-hole for manipulation. The Australian ballot had not been introduced; anything was a ballot that was found in the carelessly guarded boxes. Registration was haphazard; repeaters were always handy when needed. All of these resources of evil were cheerfully employed by aroused righteousness combating the red menace of the abolition of poverty, and all were insufficient. When the last vote had been deposited that day, Henry George was elected mayor of New York. In the next three hours he was deprived of his victory by the simple process of manipulating the returns. Twelve years later Richard Croker, speaking to an intimate friend, admitted the manipulation. His version of it was simple but sufficient.

"Of course," said he, "they could not allow a man like Henry George to be mayor of New York. It would upset all their arrangements."

The precious arrangements were salvaged, landlords' profits were rescued from the wicked beings that would destroy them, society was saved, and Henry George was left beating in vain upon the stone wall.

The precincts of conservatism had not heard the last of him. Backed by an enthusiastic following, he continued his agitation.

"THE MEPHISTOPHELES OF TODAY—HONEST LABOR'S TEMPTATION"

Puck on the menace of the Single Tax, October 20, 1886

Early in the fight he had been joined by Father McGlynn, a priest of the Catholic Church and one of the most eloquent men I have ever heard. Archbishop Corrigan made every effort to silence him; he defied his archbishop, held to his course, and so was unfrocked. Ominously the movement spread. The great Anti-Poverty Society was formed; George and Father McGlynn addressed Sunday after Sunday its immense crowds. The idea of eliminating the slums, of emancipating the dwellers therein, of obtaining for every human being a chance to live and to have in his life something of sufficiency and comfort, laid tremendous hold upon the imaginations of the sympathetic. Now and then a man from the propertied class came and joined hands with the workers to win to these ends. Among them, Bolton Hall, a rising young lawyer, the son of the Reverend Doctor John Hall, pastor of the Fifth Avenue Presbyterian Church and one of America's most notable divines. The son split with the father on this issue and went his own way as an able and learned Single Taxer.

But in all these movings of the waters a distinction is to be made and is not made easily. It is between those that enlist because of profound conviction and those that merely hop along, keeping a cheerful step for a time to drop out at the next corner. In 1887, Mr. George, encouraged by his notably big vote in New York City, held a state convention and put into the field a full ticket with himself at the head as candidate for Secretary of State. The hopes of the convinced Single Taxers went high, but the ticket won in the state no more than 80,000 votes. By one of those curious vacillations familiar to all observers of American politics, the tide was far on the ebb, but the Single Taxers did not know it. The next month came out Cleveland's tariff message, Henry George announced that because of the issue thus raised he should support Cleveland in the coming election, and the movement he had inaugurated dwindled toward its end.

Many of his followers insisted upon struggling forward and in 1888 nominated a candidate for President with the backing of what was called the United Labor Party. The votes it won were inconsiderable. *The Standard,* a Single Tax magazine George had founded, continued for a time to preach his gospel. Then it too drifted its way to the Saragossa of forgotten things.

Mr. George was slightly undersized, bald on the top of his head above a fringe of reddish-brown hair and an adornment of reddish-brown beard. We reporters used to call him "The Little Red Rooster" or "The Little Game Cock," thereby signifying his temperament as much as his appearance. He was for a fight. Among those he fought were many of his own adherents if they ventured to disagree with him. He was of a masterful will, more than a little vain, more than a little domineering and arrogant. It is not now with such qualities that successful leaders of men are equipped. Besides, so far as I could ever discover, he lacked a sense of humor—fatal want. He took himself with a seriousness that amounted to the solemnity of a religion. This again does not help leadership. Even Father McGlynn quietly sheered off after a few months.

As is to be set forth later, we had by this time acquired in New York a Tenement House Commission. One day Mr. George appeared before it with the information that all its deliberations, proceedings, and even its existence were foolish and vain. Tenement houses were unnecessary. Why have a commission to consider of them? Adopt the Single Tax and they would melt away. He might have said something with this significance in a way that would offend nobody. He did not say it in that way; he said it with a red face, a vehemence of shouting, and an angry air that aroused anger in return. At that hearing was another man of the quietly forceful type like Henry Philpott, although of a totally different physique. He was an earnest, zealous, sincere little labor man named Edward King. No trump of fame has ever sounded his glory, but he spent a lifetime in behalf of the workers and had no other reward than the consciousness that he had done what he could. He took it upon himself to rebuke Henry George, the celebrated author and publicist, and did the task with a calm dignity and power of reasoning that left Mr. George rather pathetically silent.

George was of humble origin and not college bred. In his early life he had been a compositor on a newspaper in California and afterward a reporter. His newspaper training seemed not to have developed in him anything of that half-cynical tolerance that is so often met in most old-timers of this craft, and no less it failed to give him any sympathy for his fellow-craftsmen. He was not an easy man to approach. Yet we of the reporter guild never doubted his sincerity or the nobility of the vision that led him on. With unflawed honesty he planned a world without slums and without poverty, and those of us that had done police work could not but warm to a man that came with such a message.

The strength of his hope was that if all taxes could be abolished except only this one tax laid upon the actual value of the land-site without considering any improvements thereon, the resulting stimulus to building, business, and industry would transform all the existing conditions of life. There would not longer be any reason to crowd and herd people into filthy tenements, but capital would be eager to provide ample housing for all; the great revival of industry would furnish ample employment, diversify it, improve it. The better distribution of wealth and products thus obtained would lift the masses to a standard of living never before known. The abolition of tariff Protection would take with it trusts, monopolies, and the piling of great fortunes. The sure economies resulting from a simplified tax system would free the hands of government as the resulting reduction in tax burdens would free those of industry. For the first time, then, life would be normal, released from the fear of poverty that has always brutalized it, and the world would be remade.

To inspire so much and so great faith in a plan so largely theoretical is plainly a work of genius. Looking back over the movement George founded, it is clear that he was a most extraordinary man and the mark he left upon the world and its thought will never be erased.

With pen and the spoken word he labored for his ideal, not at all overlooking the limelight, which he was human enough to enjoy to the full. He had a good, round penetrating voice with a medium register and was an effective public speaker, though somewhat prone to over-gesticulation and emphasis. Doubtless, his natural gift was larger in writing than in oratory; when he spoke it was his doctrine rather than his eloquence that convinced. But otherwise was the fact with Father McGlynn. He had been a parish priest in the great teeming unhappy East Side; he had known only too well the dun miseries of that submerged population; and when he spoke of poverty it was with a heart full of sorrowful sympathy gained by his own experiences. One that knew what he knew could never wonder that he swayed vast audiences to an unwonted tenderness when he dealt with this subject. I have seldom known a more admirable figure; it was of a quality of both physical and moral sturdiness. His very poise was magnetic and impressive, his perfect mastery of himself, his magnificent honesty, the power of his sentences. He seemed an intellectual and moral giant. There was something poignantly pathetic about his defeat; he had done so much and endured so much!

At one time the Anti-Poverty Society promised to become a towering force. It never realized its prospectus, but I am convinced Father McGlynn was a power of permanent good. Through him, thousands of persons that had never given a thought to the terrible evils of the tenement house were led to confront themselves with the fact that in modern society a man must be his brother's keeper and there is no escape from the communal responsibility. Tuberculosis and crime are stern avengers else.

In 1882 Mr. George and his family went abroad, visiting Ireland first and then England. In London they were the guests for a month of H. M. Hyndman, the great Socialist leader. Hyndman seems to have had a somewhat troublous time with the restless prophet of a slumless world, and afterward spoke disparagingly of his guest's intellect. "It is far from a first-class mind," he said. But for this low estimate two allowances are to be made. Hyndman, though in other respects broad-minded and liberal, had some slant of the anti-American prejudices of his countrymen. Besides, George had wounded his British sensibilities in their tenderest spot. How? Why, in a London street one day he stopped and ate whelks from a push-cart[1] at the curb. That, of course could never be forgiven.

Among the followers with whom George openly quarrelled was J. W. Sullivan, a man worth more than a passing note. He had been a journeyman printer through the West, but having a bent for writing cultivated it assiduously and became the master of an incisive, vigorous style. He was for a time editorial writer on *The Standard;* then he fell out with his peppery chief, and became an irreconcilable and tireless enemy. He used to charge that George took his entire theory ready-made from an obscure Irish writer named Dove, who lived in the early part of the nineteenth century. If this was true, I have no doubt that by a process of the human mind not at all unfamiliar, Mr. George came to believe implicitly that the thing was all his own.

Father McGlynn stayed outside of the church as long as he could. After the collapse of the Anti-Poverty societies and the visible ebbing of the Single Tax tide he made his peace and was restored. But not to a parish in New York City. In a re-

---

[1] The English, in their barbarous dialect, call it a "barrow," but of course they mean a push-cart. One must make allowances for a backward race.

mote village on the Hudson he disappeared from public sight. Years after his name had ceased to be mentioned in the public press he was performing there the humble duties of a rural priest.

In 1897, to run far ahead of our story, a peculiar condition existing in the political situation when the first election was to be held in the Greater New York gave an opportunity for an independent candidate and Mr. George was again nominated for mayor. He was proceeding vigorously with his campaign when he was stricken suddenly with heart failure and died two weeks before election.

Among those that received into their souls the Single Tax gospel were men that clung to it ever after as the sign of human salvation. Men's minds run to types, like plants or birds. The men I mean were of the highest character, intensely sympathetic, weighed upon by the sorrows of mankind, eager to help, full of kindness and mercy, but still unwilling to think that the only hope for the common weal was a complete reorganization of society; men like Mr. Hall, Mr. Louis Post, Mr. Frederic Howe. Years after the Single Tax doctrine in America had ceased to lift a head, and the thing it represented had been forgotten, when the whole movement seemed to have dried up and blown away, these men held unshaken to the faith, conscientiously sure that in the fullness of time the splendid dream that had inspired them would be realized.

Now and then came from the far-away world a sound or an echo to give them cheer. New Zealand adopted the principle of a tax upon actual land value. It was hailed as a triumph for the George philosophy, but no momentous results followed; the social status in New Zealand was unchanged. For this apparent failure was reason sufficient. The tax on land values was there but other kinds of taxation persisted as before. In 1907, that greatest of all slack-wire artists, Mr. Lloyd George, being then chancellor of the British exchequer or something of the kind, announced his government's conversion to the same principle and introduced a land tax that was prophesied to herald the downfall of the land monopoly in Great Britain and the coming of the glad, glad new day so long expected. It was but another gesture of futility. The government imposed a tax upon land values, but the land monopoly did not crumble, the rosy-fingered dawn appeared not, and any one that cares to see how trifling a figure the land tax cuts has but to look at its returns in the British budget.

Autopsy. The disease that chiefly laid low the Single Tax movement in America was the same malady that proved fatal to the Free Trade movement. It has no scientific name as yet, so far as I know, but it consists of medication for symptoms instead of for causes. Any attempt to retain the capitalistic organization of society and still be rid of its inevitable sequellæ is like dosing the symptoms of malaria without removing the origin thereof. Mr. George always intended to preserve production for profit. So long as we have that poisonous fountain-head we shall have its evil overflowings no matter what kind of taxation we may introduce. If we are to have taxes at all, there can be no doubt that the Single Tax is the most scientific, just, and reasonable that has ever been devised. But the question is whether in any enlightened state of civilization we are to have taxes, and anyway a great constitutional ailment is not to be remedied by giving it a new kind of plaster.

To the death certificate above offered, one addition may be made. Besides its inherent weakness, the Single Tax movement suffered because of a peculiar bent in the American psychology. If Henry George had been allowed, in 1886, to take the office to which he was elected, his subsequent story might have been different. In this country, an immediate and unequivocal success is demanded of everything we undertake. If a movement can show nothing in this line, we cannot stop to bother with it. The Hindus have a million gods; we have but this one. Sceptics, may be, agnostics, infidels about all else, to this one cult of Success we adhere with faultless fidelity. To plod along after an ideal, year by year, accepting defeat and still unwavering—that is not for us. Show us results or hence upon your way and take your creed with you, O good Reformer.

"How many tall ships, think ye now, have I seen laid aboard and how many brisk lads drying in the sun and all along of this same hurry and hurry!"

Chapter V

"GREENBACK THE WEAVER"

To the power exercised in this country by the railroad corporations throughout the last three decades of the last century there is surely no parallel in the history of democratized nations. Absolute, irresponsible, arbitrary, often tyrannical, to find its like we must go back to the grim annals of an acknowledged feudalism. I despair of causing one of this generation to grasp the conditions of the preceding. Occasionally, some guileless youth arises to declare now that the railroads ought not to be regulated. If he knew American railroad history he would never play poll parrot to that propaganda. So long as railroad companies were at liberty to charge what rates they pleased, to ruin an opponent and reward a knee-crooker, to corrupt government, to silence and control the press with passes, to gag criticism with rebates and privileges, they, having the arteries of economic life, created in the heart of the Republic an absolute monarchy. It is not enough to say that throughout the West they controlled the government. The truth is, to all intents and purposes they were the government.

Political parties and political conventions lay in the hollow of their hands; nominations and platforms were at their nod and beck, they filled the legislatures with puppets of their own choosing, they hand-picked Senators and Representatives, they dominated the ruling of every city, town, and village through which their lines passed, they wrote laws to suit themselves, their marionette governors signed on the dotted line. Finally, for any matter in which they had the least concern, they held over courts a power that made justice look like a satirical comedy.

When I was a boy in Iowa it was notorious that an average citizen could win no verdict against a railroad company. Law, equity, justice had nothing to do with the issue. Let him have the best cause in the world and if the railroad thought best to fight it he could get nowhere with it. Governor Larrabee once cited a case in which a farmer in Northern Iowa had an unassailable claim for damages against a railroad. He lived at a distance from the county seat. When the case was tried there, he lost it. Coming home he travelled for a distance in the same railroad car with the judge, several of the jurors, the attorney for the railroad and his own counsel. He seemed to be the only man in the car that paid fare. Judge, jury, attorneys for plaintiff and defendant—everybody else travelled on passes.

So did everybody in a prominent or controlling position in town, county or state government. Sheriffs that drew jury panels, clerks of court, mayors, aldermen, all party bosses *in esse* or *in posse,* police magistrates, well-known attorneys, could get passes whenever they asked for them, and often were supplied without request. No newspaper man ever paid his fare anywhere. One might be puzzled at times to think where the revenues of the company came from. Merchants that in politics or otherwise did any valeting for the company had their freight bills halved. The rate sheet was as flexible as a rubber band. Only the unknown and the powerless were guided by it.

Against the oppressions of this autocracy there was no protection. My father was one of the first to perceive the new tyranny and to rebel against it. The railroad shut off his coal supply. He had to take wagons, diggers, and shovels to a spot in our county where a thin vein of nearly worthless coal came near the surface and there dig up the fuel to keep his presses going. He conceived that relief from the transportation monopoly might be had by extending the water ways and so became the father of the Hennepin Canal project to unite the Upper Mississippi with the Great Lakes and afford water transportation to the sea. It proved his doom. While he was in Washington urging his plan, the railroad and Protected Interests, through the minority-stockholder dodge, threw the concern into the hands of a receiver and my father into the street, as previously recorded.

Of the historic agrarian insurrection of 1872–73, the uprising in the West that shook so many portly fortunes with novel alarms, we are to speak hereafter. It was the product not only of a long series of unquestionable wrongs heaped upon the poor farmer, but also of the agitation of the railroad-monopoly issue by a few outspoken and liberally hated spirits that saw in the revolt only another form of the old struggle between man and irresponsible power.

Among the men of this order in Iowa was one so fearless and inappeasable that he came to embody in himself the idea of resistance to the growing absolutism of Accumulated Wealth. His name was James Baird Weaver and he hailed at that time from Bloomfield, Davis County, which was south of the centre of the state. He was a lawyer of distinction in his own region, having served with notable success as district attorney and in several celebrated cases. But what at first marked him above others was his record as a soldier, wherein he had performed in a way to surpass romance.

He was born in Dayton, Ohio, in 1833, and was ten years old when his father pioneered from Cass County, Michigan, to Iowa, where he was among the first settlers to get land after the legalized spoliation of the Sacs and Foxes. The boy was reared on a farm in the hardest of conditions, wrested what education he could from primitive facilities, at twenty drove an ox team through the barrages of hostile Indians to California, came back by Panama, made his way through a law school and began to practise. He threw himself into the fight against the slave-owning oligarchy, helped to form the Republican party when he was barely of age, and was already noted as a brilliant campaigner when the Rebellion of the slave-owners broke. Bloomfield was a small town in a sparsely settled region. President Lincoln's call for 75,000 men brought out in fifteen minutes 105 volunteers in little Bloomfield. James Baird Weaver was the third man to reach the recruiting place. He enlisted as a private and fell into Company G, of the Second Iowa Infantry, a regiment that afterward won a notable fame. He had hoped to get into the First, but it was already full.

Virtually undrilled and rawer than a March day the regiment was ordered into active service in Northern Missouri. From that time on Weaver saw almost incessant fighting and marching. It appears that from the first his courage made men talk and wonder. I think there never was a braver man. He rose to be second lieutenant, first lieutenant, captain, major, colonel, and brigadier general, and each promotion was won by daring or skill, or both, on the battlefield.

We must believe from the record and from abundant testimony that this iron fortitude was not at all of the order that is called animal. He was one of those strange birds, a Christian soldier; Havelock, O. O. Howard, and all that. His men worshipped him. He had the quiet, restrained poise of a man perfectly sure of himself, never shouted, never blustered, never play-acted, but when he gave an order gave it in such a way that men leaped to carry it out. A laconic man, not much of a conversationist, even in the pinches noted for courtesy. This is high praise, but in truth it falls short of the testimony afterward multiplied by the men he had commanded.

Three incidents. At the battle of Resaca, it was Weaver that discovered the rebel position, laid a pontoon bridge under fire, led a part of his command across and charged upon the enemy's rifle pits, driving him in a rout.

At the battle of Shiloh the Second Iowa was caught in the

"Hornets' Nest," and was in a way to be annihilated. It was Weaver that led them out of their mess and against the enemy. As he was charging at the head of his troops, Colonel Samuel A. Moore fell, struck with three wounds. Weaver stopped, turned, came back, picked up Moore at the imminent risk of his own life, carried him to safety and went on with the fight.

When he became a commanding officer he was entitled to a horse. On a long march he would spy some private soldier that was limping or worn out; then Weaver would drop from his horse, give it to the disabled private and plug along afoot.

Such a man in such times as followed the end of the Civil War would be an inevitable power. When he took up the fight against the railroad monopoly he led it in a drive like that at Resaca. The companies saw in him a foe most dangerous and marked him for their peculiar attentions. In 1874 he was the popular candidate for nomination to Congress from the Sixth Iowa district. The railroads swarmed in against him and beat him—by one vote. His friends declared that even that narrow victory was won by a trick. The next year, he was the idol of all outside the Amalgamated Brotherhood of Political Valets for the Republican nomination for Governor. The opening was alluring. From Governor he would go on to be United States Senator and so have probably a lifetime eminence, for that was the way in Iowa. His popularity was immense; if there had been a primary he would have swept the state three to one. There was no primary, the nomination lay in the hands of the state convention, to which Weaver delegates were being chosen every day.

The railroad Interests, thoroughly alarmed, worked overtime to stem this tide. For once, they found that the free-pass system and their carefully built political machinery were not working with the usual faultless rhythm. Weaver was going to a certain nomination and an overwhelming election—Weaver, avowed anti-railroad man. They had clever managers in those days, the embattled railroads. One of their men, John H. Gear, who was backed by the Burlington, became a candidate, with others, in a desperate attempt to block Weaver by a division of strength that would prevent a nomination on the first ballot—the good old "favorite son" racket that has been played upon so many conventions. The railroad strength was back of Gear and brought him many delegates. Then came the jiu-jitsu. At the right moment Gear suddenly withdrew and whisked to the front old Samuel J. Kirkwood, who had been the adored War Governor.

To affront this revered figure was more than many delegates could endure. It smacked of treason to the eternal principles of the Union. Kirkwood had been an efficient Governor and his name was linked with what Iowa regarded as a holy cause. A stampede took place. Two hundred men stuck by Weaver; others ran like sheep to herd with the railroad delegates and gave Kirkwood 268 and the nomination.

The saloon men had helped the railroads. Weaver was an ardent prohibitionist. The respectable and solid business Interests helped the saloon men. Weaver was a demagogue, a pestilent agitator, a reckless person plotting against the best business interests of the country, and once more the Respectable Element snuggled up to Low Brow, Hickory Shirt, and Beery Breath.

The disappointment was heavy, but Weaver did not sulk. He accepted Kirkwood and the ticket and was allowed to be nominated for the State Senate.

Then the railroads came in and beat him again.

Often some knocks like this are required that a man may learn how lumpish is all this loyalty to party in the face of real issues. When this man got a lesson he got the whole of it and needed not to have it twice. He perceived now that the grip of the railroad Interests upon the two old parties was too firm to be shaken and if he was to continue the fight against railroad and other monopoly he must climb out of the familiar reservation. There had been formed in Ohio and other states to the East of him the nucleus or skeleton of a new party called the National or Greenback party. In 1877 James Baird Weaver shocked Iowa and amazed and disconcerted a large part of his following by announcing that he had allied himself with this despised and rejected company from the caves of Adullam.

Instantly he was accused on all sides of acting upon a personal spite, of seeking to revenge himself upon the party that had disappointed him, of sacrificing principles to his personal vexation. Many times in after years he assured me most positively that he had not been influenced by such considerations but by something different. As he was so singularly frank and so careful about all his statements, and as he had no reason in the world to deceive me, I believe he was in this regard also honest.

He said that there seemed to him two issues that overshadowed all else in America. One was the threat to our institutions and liberty that lay in the swift advance of corporation power—this railroad monopoly, for instance. The other was the menace, quite as great, that lay in the control of the world's finances by a group of bankers and large bondholders. By another road he had come to the position that Thaddeus Stevens held, the doctrine that brought down upon Stevens's head the wrath and misrepresentation still potent at the mention of his name. Weaver held that all banks and other private interests should be dispossessed of the power to issue or control the nation's money; the national government should furnish all the currency. By unmistakable motions the country was then approaching a single monetary standard of gold, the reserves of gold to be manipulated at a profit by a group of English and American bankers. He thought this was equivalent to giving government into the bankers' hands. As he came before long to be called the dangerous lunatic who believed a circulating medium should be provided by printing an unlimited supply of paper dollars, it may be well to observe that he never believed anything of the kind nor advocated it. But he did believe that the national currency issued by the government in the Civil War should be retained and that all future money issues should be from the same source, and he did believe that the process of contraction, then going on as the date neared upon which specie payments were to be resumed, meant a certain danger.

Right or wrong about this, there broke upon his head such a sirocco of condemnation as few Americans have known. The propertied foamed at the mouth at the mention of his name; millions of the unpropertied, believing with the national fatuity whatever they might read in newspapers, concluded that he was a public enemy and often clamored to have him suppressed or locked up. He, and pestilent demagogues like him, were disturbing the national tranquillity and preventing the national return to prosperity. In the campaign of 1875 one of the railroad organs had applied to him a term that had for a later generation a meaning of greater interest. According to this authority, he was a Communist. Hundreds of other publications that knew as much about Communism as of Cherokee folklore took up the word with glee. Weaver was a Communist, rang the chorus. Sometimes he was also a Nihilist, occasionally an Anarchist. At all times, by whatsoever name one might prefer to call him, he was an unmitigated rascal and national menace. Many an editorial writer of that day would have been greatly astonished if he could have looked forward fifty years and seen the greater part of the world forced to accept the basic principle that Weaver advocated, and nation upon nation doing business on a circulating medium unsecured except by public faith. Weaver himself recognized Great Britain as the main source of the stalwart support in this country of the gold standard. He, in his own turn, would have been no less astonished if he could have foreseen the chief champion of gold becoming the first to abandon it under the first great strain it encountered.

The next year, 1878, after his desertion of the party he had helped to form, he was nominated for Congress by the Greenback and Democratic parties in the district where four years before he had been defrauded of the prize. The rest of the state jeered and jested until the morning after election. Then it discovered to its amazement and the terror of the Interests that his old neighbors had given him a memorable vindication. They had elected him over the man that had nosed him out of the honor four years before.

It was a time of uproar in Washington. President Hayes had been at work forcing his Southern policy upon reluctant or hostile Republicans and in the hullabaloo the expiring Congress had failed to pass the necessary appropriation bills. The new Congress must be called in special session and Weaver found himself in his seat early in March. Almost at once he soared into a distinction few newcomers there had ever had. They knew him well, the Interests, and the first evidence of their tender regard came in the distribution of committee places, which was then in the sole hands of the Speaker. Samuel J. Randall of Pennsylvania, alleged Democrat, held that powerful office, and he expressed the dislike in which all good mossbacks and true held Weaver by giving him places on the Committees on Waste Baskets and Liver Pads. The imperturbable Weaver did not care; he knew his game. He had two resolutions, one declaring that all currency should be issued and controlled by the Federal government, the other that the government's bonds should not be refunded but paid off as they should mature. Randall refused to recognize him for the presenting of these resolutions. Monday was private calendar day when by unanimous consent the rules were suspended and measures could be introduced and passed, pension bills and the like. Every Monday Weaver blocked this business by uttering one little phrase that threw the machine off the track.

"Mr. Speaker, I object."

Under the rules of the House that upset the calculations. As fast as a new attempt was made to proceed, Weaver placidly interjected:

"Mr. Speaker, I object."

That was enough, but Weaver added upon other days a varied repertory of annoyances. A master parliamentarian, one of the best debaters the House ever saw, clever, witty, always on watch, he made life a burden for the magnificent Speaker.[1] For weeks the battle went on. Members fumed and fretted, appealed, threatened and swore, partisan politicians screamed, partisan newspapers thundered against the wild-eyed Greenbacker from Iowa. Little cared the wild-eyed. He had throughout his life an extraordinary poise of courtesy. To all denunciations as to all appeals he made the same extremely polite response, but altered not his procedure. Day after day the same:

"Mr. Speaker, I object."

Samuel J. Randall was accustomed to have his own way. In those times the Speaker of the House of Representatives was a Czar. Proud man and Czar and all, he must yield at last to the quietly persisting man from Iowa, the hated Greenbacker, demagogue and enemy of society. James Baird Weaver, the patient, had his full reward. The time came when he achieved his point, the Speaker surrendered, and the wild-eyed got his resolutions in and won to a vote on them, which was all he wanted.

Wall Street loathed him, and all really respectable persons turned upon him the stern brow of a virtuous reproof. Nast relieved many a struggling but inarticulate soul when he made cartoons for *Harper's Weekly* representing Weaver as Nick Bottom with his ass's head. "Greenback the Weaver," he called it, adding apt quotation. Everybody said it was a prime hit and cut the cartoon out and pinned it to the wall.

In 1880 he was nominated for President on the National or Greenback ticket, and received 308,678 votes, to the grief and consternation of many observers.

For to the conservative majority of the nation, to be a Greenbacker in those days was to be beyond the pale of humanity. It

[1] Congressional Record, Forty-sixth Congress, Second and Third Sessions.

"GREENBACK THE WEAVER"

Nast's celebrated cartoon on James Baird Weaver, printed in *Harper's Weekly*, March 6, 1880, with this quotation from *Midsummernight's Dream:* "I see their knavery; this is to make an ass of me; to fright me if they could. But I will not stir from this place, do what they can; I will walk up and down here, and I will sing, that they shall hear I am not afraid"

is odd to reflect that the Greenbacker of 1880 stood in exactly the same pilloried position as the Socialist of 1910 and the Communist of 1932, representing the sum of human iniquity. All three were bad, wicked men engaged in nefarious plottings to overthrow the holy structure of a perfect social order. The editorials appearing in the American newspapers against the Greenbackers in 1880 might have been reprinted in 1912 against the Socialists and in 1932 against the Communists, with but the change of half a dozen words. Look back upon the newspaper files and see.

In 1880 the chief weapon with which detestable agitators sought to assail the sway of the Right Minded was a horrible thing called Fiat Money. This meant, according to the sage and judicious editorial writers of that day, that the government was to print immense quantities of paper dollars with which everybody was to be endowed and so become rich. Careful searching of the platform adopted by the Greenback convention in 1880 fails to discover anything of the kind, but does reveal this paragraph, which to the initiated will sufficiently explain the detestation with which the whole movement was regarded:

The civil government should guarantee the divine right of every laborer to the results of his toil, thus enabling the producers of wealth to provide themselves with the means for physical comfort and facilities for mental, social, and moral culture; and we condemn, as unworthy of our civilization, the barbarism that imposes upon wealth-producers a state of drudgery as the price of a mere animal existence. Notwithstanding the enormous increase of productive power by the universal introduction of labor-saving machinery and the discovery of new agents for the increase of wealth, the task of the laborer is scarcely lightened, the hours of toil are but little shortened, and few producers are lifted from poverty into comfort and pecuniary independence.

The rest of the platform demanded that the national government should alone have the right to issue and to control the nation's circulating medium, that the government bonds should be paid off and not refunded, and paid in legal-tender currency instead of bank notes; that the system of national banks should be abolished; that there should be free coinage of silver as well as of gold; that there should be an eight-hour working day, the inspection of factories and workshops, the abolition of convict-labor competition, a bureau of labor statistics, an end to child labor, and that wages should be paid in cash. Chinese labor immigration should be prohibited, forfeited land grants should be reclaimed, interstate commerce should be regulated by the national government, monopolies should be discouraged, bondholders should not have special privileges, there should be a graduated income tax, the right of suffrage should not be restricted, there should be no large standing army, the rules of Congress should be democratized.

That was all, except a final thundering denunciation of the existing governing class. "We are not content to endure farther discipline from our present actual rulers, who, having dominion over money, over transportation, over land and labor, over the press and the machinery of government, wield unwarranted power over our institutions and over life and property."

Here you are, then, O Philosopher, interested in the Human Comedy. Take good note of this episode. At the end of May, 1933, the Congress of the United States formally adopted as the national policy the demand of the Greenback convention of 1880 in regard to the payment of the national bonds in currency. It had previously adopted in essence the demand of that Greenback convention in regard to the free coinage of silver and taken the first steps toward the national control of the circulating medium. This left nothing unfulfilled of the Greenback program except the abolition of the national banks, and three bills were pending to achieve that result. Every other plank in the Greenback platform of 1880 had either been adopted by the government or had come to be regarded as a manifest truism. Like it or dislike it, this was the situation in 1933, was it not? Then please note next that in 1880, the party that held these doctrines was composed, according to contemporaneous comment, of rogues, cranks, lunatics, knaves, and traitors and all the ends they aimed at plain treason and sub-version. Is not that worth thinking about? The land resounded with indignant denunciations of these perilous revolutionists. It was worse than any ordinary public condemnation; to admit sympathy with the detestable Greenbackers was to be ostracized socially, commercially, and culturally. Respectable men refused to speak on the street to Greenbacker acquaintances, brothers and sisters withdrew the right hand of fellowship at the prayer meeting, and it was seriously debated whether a Greenbacker ought not to be expelled from the church. A man might better have the smallpox than an attack of Greenbackism. And yet in the light of the foregoing record, it seems that to be a dema-gogue, a pestilent disturber of the public tranquillity, a noisy agitator and an advocate of financial vagaries is only to be fifty-three years ahead of one's times.

Weaver inspired the parts of the platform that he did not actually write. It embodied his own conviction. Good man—bad man—what is it all but a date?

He did not run for Congress that year but at the next election, 1882, and the next, 1884, he was triumphantly returned from the Sixth Iowa district. This was personal popularity, for the Green-back party was waning. Ben Butler of Massachusetts, with all the prestige of his bold career as Governor, could poll in the Presidential election of 1884 but 175,370 votes.

In the early part of 1883 I was with Weaver in a little town in Southern Iowa. We sat in the poor little office of the poor little hotel and compared notes. On the wall opposite us hung a map of the United States. Weaver said:

"Do you know the costliest swindle ever perpetrated on the American public?"

I said I didn't but supposed it was the annual river-and-harbor steal. He said:

"No; it's right on that map in front of you. Here is the Union Pacific [indicating with a pencil], 990 miles, and here is the

Central Pacific, 785 miles [or whatever it was; he knew and I did not], and every mile of each was marked with a fraud for which the people have been paying ever since and will continue to pay as long as the railroad exists as a private corporation. Do you know how much they have paid so far?"

I didn't, but he knew to a dollar and promptly informed me; so many million dollars a year that must be extorted from the public in freight and passenger rates to pay the interest and dividends upon a fictitious capitalization created by one huge fraud after another. His next question was if I knew who were the strongest men in history. Once more I confessed my ignorance. He said they were the four projectors of the Central Pacific, Huntington, Hopkins, Stanford, and Crocker, for they had moved the entire Sierra Nevada range of mountains thirty miles nearer the sea. The government had allowed them a double rate of plunder for work done in mountainous country and they had claimed and been paid at the mountain rate for work done upon the plains.

He next spoke of the railroad land grants, about which he had at his tongue's end an array of figures that dazed me. He knew all the grants to all the companies and how each was a bigger swindle than the other and could recite them in order like the multiplication table. I picked up enough energy to say I thought the main issue before the American people at that time was the tariff. He said the tariff was something but the real issue went far deeper; it was the control of the government by the money power. If that were not destroyed or checked it would produce an iron-heeled autocracy.

From this one might suppose that he was inclined to be aggressive, voluble, or self-assertive. On the contrary there was never a milder-mannered man. For one that had been pictured as the arch devil of the times and the most dangerous factor in American life he seemed so quiet, reserved, and always so scrupulously courteous that I wondered at him.

He was about the average height, notably erect and soldierly in his bearing, spare as an Indian, one of those wiry, tireless, alert, but notably self-controlled men that seem to carry about them a certain unescapable aura of power and distinction. He never walked down the street or entered a public assembly anywhere without instantly drawing all eyes to himself. His aquiline, high-bred features, commanding gray eyes, curling gray hair, closely trimmed military mustache were parts of the total impression of him but there was something else. I think everybody that looked at him attentively had a feeling, however vague, of involuntary respect, and I think that what really caused the respect was an actuality of character.

He had an excellent voice, mellow and yet of great carrying power. When he was speaking in public, one liked to listen to him no matter how much one might disagree with him. His oratory was a little too much of the Webster Websterian, a hangover from the country school and the debating society, but he had good funds of sarcasm and invective and being always in control of himself was a powerful champion.

He had his share of human inconsistencies. It was odd to see one so invariably gentle, deferential, quiet, and modest off the platform became so hard, so implacably militant, when he stepped before the footlights. On the stump, the relentless crusader, grim, bitter, sarcastic, cutting straight ahead like a meat axe; off the stump, the example of a kind of old-school and courtly politeness—it was strange enough. But more of the incongruous is to follow, for he that was of so marked a courtesy in his private walk was also of an equally marked sententiousness of speech, and how these two qualities can be reconciled in one man is too puzzling. And again, here was a man essentially a Puritan, rigid as iron in his faith, with his hands set to a task likely to daunt the hardiest evangel, and yet having an exquisite sense of humor. Laughing little himself, he could make all others roar. About the Money Power and the exploiters he seemed harder than nails and fierce enough to command at a street barricade, and when he walked forth he would give his last cent to a beggar and go home a-foot, having no carfare. You would yourself be harder than he seemed if you loved not such a man.

He wrote a book, *A Call to Action,* in which he set forth in plain terms the perils he saw gathering for democracy in America, the virtual impossibility of adjusting Accumulated Wealth to popular government; a perfectly bold, outspoken book, that was received with the groans and execrations of the good and has since been so far verified that its boldness seems now composed of commonplaces.

As to the manners of man, he saw no reason why courtesy should be entangled with circumlocution and embroider its pith with the ruffles of verbiage. Once he received from a convention the offer of a nomination that he thought he should not accept. A committee was appointed to confer and sent him a long telegram setting forth the general desire with reasons and advantages and ending with a question if he would accept. He wired back this and no more:

> "To the Committee etc.,
> No.
> J. B. WEAVER."

After he had demonstrated his peculiar hold upon the people of the Sixth District, Greenbackism being now deemed to have died the death, many Republicans in the state were thinking what a grand thing it would be if he could be wangled back into the party. One of the United States senatorships was becoming vacant and it was felt by the management that it offered a perfect bait to lure Weaver inside the reservation gates. On a certain night he was to travel from Burlington to Omaha to fill a lecture engagement. Some exceedingly able gentlemen were detailed to ride with him and show him the Promised Land. They took a drawing-room in a Pullman and sat up all night to do the showing. One of them afterward furnished me with a vivid account of the proceedings. The best of the talkers opened the meeting with an exordium on the respect that people had learned to have for the former Greenback pariah, how the Greenback issue was dead and its party deader, how the fundamental principles of the grand old Republican party must be ever dear to the Weaver heart, how the chance had providentially come by which he could once more align himself with those that had always loved him, and so on, world without end.

Weaver sat bolt upright, listening but uttering not a word. When the orator paused and looked at him for an answer, he gently murmured:

"No."

So they began again and this time showed him the kingdoms of the earth, how election as Senator on the Republican ticket would open the way to greater honors, to which none could dare to put limit—great, great as any in the world. How at the time there was a dearth of leadership, how Divine Providence had gifted the Weaver mind with this priceless talent and so on, and paused again. Weaver sat bolt upright and gently murmured:

"No."

So others took up the burden of the song with variations. They reminded the General that he had been one of the founders of the Republican party, that he had fought for the Union, that the cause he had upheld on the battle-field was now again imperilled by insidious foes, how his duty was to come to the rescue, and so on, and paused. So Weaver sat bolt upright and gently murmured:

"No."

Daylight was beginning to shine through the windows when, having exhausted all their resources in argument and entreaty, one of the missionaries said:

"Well, General, will you not tell us exactly why you refuse this offer?" So Weaver said:

"Yes, I will tell you. I am standing for a principle, not for Jim Weaver."

So he walked his wild road whither that led.

He was a shrewd observer and knew the political game as well as any man that played it, but he played in it with clean hands. There was no more trickery in him than there is in a gridiron. Once he and I were attending a Democratic national convention, and walking about the lobby he said to me:

"The Solid South is no asset to the Democrats. It is a terrific liability to party and nation. There is no political vision in the South, no political enlightenment and no political principles. They come up to national conventions one year and vote for free silver and the next vote for single gold and neither know nor care a hoot which they vote for. There is but one issue in the South. That is competition to see who can most hate the Negro. The man that wins gets the nomination. The whole thing is a dead drag upon the country. When the Democrats get into power they have to struggle under the burden and handicap of it. When they are out it keeps them from getting in. Slavery must be the greatest of crimes. Here we are, all these years after it has been abolished and we are still paying the penalty for it."

Once at a Republican state convention he told me that there were eighty-four Methodist clergymen among the delegates.

"Suppose there were eighty-four Catholic priests at a Democratic convention," said he. "The country would rock and you would not hear the end of it for a generation."

A wave of Republican sentiment in the Presidential year of 1888 defeated him for Congress, but not long afterward he began to be interested in a new revolt of the unfortunate farmers that developing rapidly threatened to be a powerful factor in the next election.

This was the Farmers' Alliance, originating in the South with a purpose to take up some of the activities dropped when the Grange withdrew. After a time, its political destiny becoming probable, it was organized as a party called the People's.

Its foundation was an expression of the old indignation of the farmers because they worked hard and got nothing but a bare living and sometimes not much of that. For years they had been discontented with a condition that gave to them the bitter toil, and reserved for what they viewed as parasites all the joys of living. A member of the Chicago Board of Trade or Minneapolis Chamber of Commerce might make $100,000 in a year by the juggling of farmers' products and the farmers get from the same products the crusts of existence. The Alliance people thought this condition could be remedied by abolishing monopolies, regulating the railroads and coining silver freely, with a few other things. They were dead set against the controlling money power and as this was Weaver's favorite theme and had been for many years, he naturally went along. In many respects, the Populist party was a revival or reincarnation of the Greenback party and speedily succeeded to the Greenback party's place as the National Bugaboo. For apparently, unless we can believe that some band of miscreants is plotting our imminent ruin, life has no zip for us and no real happiness.

Month after month grew the People's party steadily and grew likewise the anxiety of the Wardens of the Flesh Pots. In the West and South particularly it gave to old-party managers many a weary hour. Western farmers actually seemed about to break from the Republican faith that had been with them sacerdotal; Southern farmers threatened the everlasting phalanx of the Solid South. Those that had seen the rise, supremacy, and toppling of the Granger movement, being for a time sceptical, came in the end to surrender. For behold here, the real thing; this had a definite program and this time the farmers were really mad.

The party held at Omaha, July 2, its national convention for the Presidential campaign of 1892 and turned out a notable show. Ignatius Donnelly was chairman and wrote much of the platform, which was a humdinger. Not often has a political party come forth with so much plain speaking and so little bally-hoo. One curious thing to be noted now in it was the prediction that the narrowing control of finance and the segregation of wealth would result in terrible social convulsions, the overthrow of civilization or an absolute despotism. The demands were for the government ownership of railroads ("the time has come when either the railroad corporation will own the people or the people must own the railroads"), of telegraphs, telephones, and the express business; the free coinage of silver at sixteen to one; the Farmers' Alliance sub-treasury plan to keep money in circulation; a graduated income tax; a postal savings bank; the Australian ballot; restriction of immigration; the eight-hour work day; abolition of privately hired armed forces to overawe working men on strike; the initiative and referendum; the election of Senators by direct vote of the people.

The wording of the platform crackled with earnestness, and made the sloppy verbiage of the other parties sound like the perfunctory routine blather of a pop-corn vendor. On this platform Weaver was nominated for President. He went forth, made a whirlwind campaign through the West and ran up the amazing total of 1,065,191 votes, carrying six states and winning twenty-two votes in the electoral college, an achievement, all things considered, the most remarkable of its kind in our political history.

The vote in the South especially. In Alabama it went above 100,000, although fraudulent counting cut it down in the returns to 85,181; in Kansas, 163,000; Nebraska, 83,000.

Three states had Populist Governors, the next Congress contained three Populist Senators and seventeen Representatives rated as Populists. With pain, the Old Guard admitted that the outlook was bad.

In the next two or three years, the new party added to its

strength. It won more Senators and more Representatives, it cast bigger votes in the West and South, it gave every promise of being an important factor in the election of 1896.

And then Privilege brought out its heavy artillery and began to shoot to death the red menace from the West. To shoot it with what? With ridicule. Nothing else is so effective in American politics. The kept press ran over with daily jibes and uncontrollable laughter about the uncouth barbarians that had come out of the West to glimpse civilization. One of the Populist Senators, Peffer of Kansas, wore a long beard. It was worth a million dollars to the jesters of the Eastern press. Congressman Simpson of Kansas was supposed to be too poor or too savage to wear half-hose. "Sockless Jerry" was worth easily another million to the pen and crayon artists. The party name itself, shortened to "Pop," was a ponderable asset of price to these blithe souls. When merriment failed, there was always denunciation handy. The proposal to coin silver for instance—invaluable to editorial writers! It gave a perfect chance to stand erect in the forum and with voice of thunder demand "Honest money," righteousness, and full interest rates.

The Populists themselves added much to the stores of ammunition discharged so liberally upon them. They fell to quarrelling within the ranks about the same old issue that has split almost every reform movement that ever existed. "Who shall be greatest"—it gets them all, soon or late. Also, orthodoxy. This fellow does not really believe the whole creed to the last syllable, as we do. Out with him! Here's a brother rather weak about free coinage. To the outer darkness with him! After a time, rifts appeared and factions and internal fighting, whereupon the end came into sight. When in 1896 the party voted to endorse William J. Bryan for President and then quarrelled as to its own candidate for vice-president, hari-kari was seen to be in the offing.

Slowly Populism dwindled and went out. In 1904 there was

enough left to hold a convention and nominate Tom Watson for President, and that signalled the end.

I came into it too late to be of the least use, even if I had known how. But I followed the corpse to the burying-ground.

Autopsy. The People's party died of a jab in the jugular vein by a cartoonist's pencil; also of symptomititis and atrophy of the cerebellum. That is to say, from a fine running start it went more or less dotty, anyway; but the chief trouble with it was the complaint that took off Single Tax. It was aimed against symptoms and overlooked causes.

But may I please recur for a moment to its platform of 1892? Poor old ridiculed thing as it was, it demanded that year more reforms that have since been incorporated into our system than both the other parties together proposed that year and four other Presidential years combined. It is said of the People's party that it was a failure. Yes? There are a dozen traces of it in the national polity today but not one mark of the successful parties that rolled the car of triumph over Populism's forgotten grave.

What is success? And what is failure?

Chapter VI

THESE FROM THE TENEMENTS

THE classics are well, books are well, the institutions that at different times tried to pour, as from vials, knowledge into my empty head were well; but the only education I ever had that amounted to anything was when I was a police reporter on the East Side of New York.

Take that swarming region that stretched from Mulberry Street to and across the Bowery and so to East River, and from Brooklyn Bridge northward to Harlem, one might say—one could learn there more about life as it really was than in any formal school of cloisters and dons that ever existed. One item alone in the scope of its curriculum was worth more than the sum of all professional tuition. It was the fact, driven relentlessly home upon any observer, that the great majority of mankind lived in poverty, want, privation, and squalor; that what we called prosperity, and so worshipped and so sought sedulously, was a savage jest, since at its height it meant only the welfare of a certain comparatively small class. To the generality of mankind it signified nothing. Good times, bad times—what difference to the Lung Block?

This and the cognate facts of the dreariness of the life of the poor, and still more, its illimitable waste. Come now, see the great Theory of Filter and Trickle as it actually works. Of all the gleaming wealth poured into the laps of the Wardens of the Flesh Pots, what could be discerned flowing along these stinking kennels? To be born in a hideous and mephitic tenement, to grow up in hideous surroundings, to labor without hope and so exist without joy, to sink back to earth at last like worn-out ox or abandoned ass, this was the manifest lot of the population cooped in these repulsive purlieus.

Let a man be bred in fullest faith that his country was indeed the land of opportunity where all were the free architects of their own fortunes, he would not go far into this hard school without taking on a loathing for all such plenary platitudes. The glorious opportunity that glittered before these dwellers in the abyss was that somehow they might be buried otherwise than at public expense.

Of the contrasts forced upon a reporter's attention, since he was one hour interviewing a murderer in the Tombs and the next a merchant in a sumptuous home or a lawyer at a club, one need not speak; they are obvious. But the best of what he saw, for instruction and things to think about, was not Fifth Avenue but Mulberry Bend.

The tenement-house region in 1886—nobody knows what it was like that did not work in it. Shall we hark back and have a look at it? Suppose we start at James and circle around to Essex and Hester. The streets are uncleaned, the pavements hidden beneath matted filth. Look up, look down, turn this way, turn that—here is no prospect but the unkempt and the disorderly, the slovenly and the grim; filth everywhere, trampled on the sidewalks, lying in windrows, collected in the eddies of door-steps—horse-droppings, desiccated rubbish. Here is a line of ash cans set out on the sidewalk and uncollected; the wind, scant and heavy laden as it is, blows from each a drift of ash-powder that trails across the sidewalk and adds itself to the accumulation there, to the flight of dirty papers and the slush of frag-mented garbage. The buildings are all ugly; the freedom of a free country includes also this that any man shall be at liberty to deface the scene with any horrible structure he may be willing to inflict upon the world, and the result is a conglomerate of ugliness and jagged discord likely to wrench the nerves of any uncalloused beholder. Miles of such atrocities and nothing else. Dismal little triangles like Rutgers Square and the thing called in derision Paradise Park mock at the primal necessity of some place where man can breathe uncontaminated air and see grass and blue sky.

The tenements are generally above poor little shops. The door is at the side. Go in and fill your lungs with the odor of a million poor meals and of a score of leaking sanitaries. How do you like it? Hundreds of thousands of human beings breathe that atmosphere and know little of any other. The lower hall seems never to have known a broom. There is a staircase with dirt on the steps and may be the visible evidences of bronchitis. The railing is greasy from a million unwashed hands. Come upstairs. Here is a room without a window or visible means of ventilation. People sleep in it. The housewife makes some effort to battle against the flood of dirt that is engulfing her. It is like combating a sand storm in the desert. Notice the squalid and frowsy furnishings. How can people live in this way? Take a look out of the windows. Here is the gray, forlorn, and dirty street, there a dreary court. That is all. It is what they see year in, year out. Millions of people. It is what they breathe, this foul air. Then they get tuberculosis. The white plague wings its way out of this place and threatens us that do not have to breathe this air, do not have to live in these conditions. Then medical science ransacks materia medica to find a remedy. Remedy! While we keep on manufacturing disease at one end of society and drugging it at the other!

I tell you again that no man knows about these things that has not seen them. No man knows what an almost palpable pall of gloom hung over the whole region.

In it was said on eminent authority to be bred vice and crime. Vice and crime were my business. I should know about them if anybody knows. Well, then, how about it? Why, I say to you that after a time was left in me no more of gaping wonder at so much of vice and crime. What puzzled me was that there was so little. Take the boys, for instance. They grew up in something akin to Mr. Fagin's academy. From their earliest consciousness they were aware of criminal ways and deeds. Men and boys that made easy livings and did no work furnished examples; environment, conversation, suggestion, need, supplied the impetus. They knew all about the gangs whose bold deeds were recounted daily in their hearing and whose members were pointed out with a certain distinction of heroism. Yet not all the boys turned criminal, only a small percentage of them.

Or the girls. What a place in which to rear the future mothers of a race! Street walkers plied their trade in every thoroughfare. Streets perfectly well known to all the inhabitants of the region were given up to houses of prostitution. We reporters knew well about the gang of white-slave catchers that for a price went about to lure girls into these places, picturing the life of ease there with the hard drudgery that was the lot of the honest. Yet not all the girls turned prostitutes, only an infinitesimal percentage of them. Vice and crime brought grist to our mill, but I know that more than one of us thought far more wonderful than any story of robbery, suicide, or murder (and far more worth writing about), the marvellous persistence of the essential goodness of the human heart in the midst of every influence that could trample it into the mire.

Some of the girls went wild—oh yes! I will tell you about one of them; you can judge of the rest. Elizabeth Garrity was her name. She lived with her mother in two wretched rooms at 153 Leonard Street. Mother, most respectable, hard working, honest, made a scanty living for herself and her one child, this Elizabeth, by sewing and by doing the work of a cleaner. Elizabeth was born in a tenement, and bred there. By all accounts she was from the beginning unusually good-looking, the pet baby of the block.

EAST SIDE STREET SCENE IN OLD NEW YORK

Harper's Weekly, April 9, 1881

She had dark, curling hair, dark liquid eyes, an olive complexion, oval face. The neighbors agreed about this and said, too, that she was notably active and vivacious. She wished to play. Where was a playground? In the street; nowhere else. She wanted playmates. What playmates? Older children already indurated by an incessant passing show of debauchery and license. Four saloons on the next corner, with ruffians or criminals going in and out, and she playing around their swinging doors. Prostitutes going by or soliciting in the streets. And the air—you know now what the air was in those regions; that, and the patch of occasional sky!

Her mother tried hard to keep her straight, sending her to school and to church. She ran away from school to play in the streets. Before she was fully grown she was dissolute. At seventeen she left home and went upon the street. Then she fell in with Danny Driscoll and went to live with him in Pell Street— terrible Pell Street.

Just another choice flowering of the slums, Danny Driscoll; he might have been Bezie Garrity's brother, for he too had been born in Leonard Street and had known nothing else but the sidewalks for a playground, criminals for his familiars. Literally true it was in his case; his mother was "Apple Mary," who sold fruit around the Tombs police court and could identify on sight most of the noted law breakers that entered and left it. When Danny was fourteen he was sent to the penitentiary for six months for picking pockets. Some time after his release he illustrated the deterrent of punishment under our wonderful code by robbing a man of a watch in the old *Herald* Building, having meantime committed innumerable petty thefts for which he had escaped detection. This time he was caught and sentenced to eighteen months.

All the time he was noted throughout the old Sixth Assembly District as a fighter and a daring criminal, for he was already named as the captain and leader of the celebrated Whyos.

We were prone to think in the year 1933 that gangs and gangsters were the development of our own epoch. As a matter of fact, they are almost as old as the Bowery. There was no time in my experience as a reporter when they were not at work in the tenement-house regions. Not so bold as they became after Prohibition, not operating on so grandiose a stage; but in other respects akin. Of them all, most we heard of the Whyos, a name coined from the clan call of the members; but often came also news of the gangs of Corcoran's Roost and Hell's Kitchen, close rivals for bad eminence. And of the Whyos, Danny Driscoll at twenty was captain with his old-time chum and fellow-graduate of the tenements, Danny Lyons, for first lieutenant and confidant. And then with Bezie Garrity for his girl.

More than his girl. She was clever, restless, ingenious, smart as a whip, nimble of wit, two per cent educated, absolutely fearless, and retaining her good looks, for she was trim as a swallow and went fairly well dressed. She planned the best robberies of the gang and got the robbers away.

At 162 Hester Street, John McCarthy kept a rooming house, none too savory in repute. Driscoll gathered a grudge against him, for one night when the Whyo was drunk and uproarious, McCarthy, who must keep the police warily in mind, put him into the street. So Driscoll swore to be even.

On the night of Friday, June 24, 1886, he and Bezie began to make the rounds of the saloons open after hours and to tank up. At four in the morning, both being drunk, they went to McCarthy's place and rang the bell. McCarthy came and recognized Bezie, for she had often been there in the pursuit of her profession. He opened the door for her. Then quickly seeing who was with her, he tried to shut it, after she was inside. Driscoll thrust a foot forward and blocked the door. The men struggled. Bezie threw her arms around McCarthy to help Driscoll. McCarthy took fright, broke away and ran into a back room, Bezie following him. Driscoll stood in the hall, revolver in hand. Bezie opened a rear door to let him reach McCarthy. In the dim light of the June morning he thought she was his enemy, fired, and she fell with a mortal wound.

Policemen heard the shot and ran in, catching a fleeting vision of the Whyo in retreat. There followed some hours of pursuit over roofs and down scuttles, through cellars and dark passageways, but he was caught at last—in "Apple Mary's" grim quarters. Bezie died that night in St. Vincent's Hospital, her lips clenched hard and saying no word about her slayer.

So we tried Danny Driscoll in the Court of General Sessions, tried him quickly and easily, found him guilty, and on September 30, 1886, sentenced him to be hanged by the neck until dead and gave thanks we were about to be rid of a knave. We did not hang Ed. Stokes, millionaire, for shooting Jim Fisk, nor many another well-dressed murderer, but we made short work of Danny Driscoll, thug. He had not intended to shoot Bezie Garrity nor harm her but that made no difference. Hang him anyway.

His lawyer took advantage of the liberal chances for delay the law allows for the poor as for the rich and by appeals and more appeals stood off the fulfilling of that sentence. But on the night of January 23, 1888, old Joe Atkins (which was not his name) came into the yard of the Tombs prison and erected there the ingenious framework for killing people that had made him in a curious way, famous, and in the gray winter dawn they wakened Driscoll from his cell and marched him to the foot of that frame and put on the black cap and Atkins adjusted his cunningly devised knot under the left ear and cut the cord that held the weight and the body shot into the air and came down to tug at the end of the rope and we were shut of Danny Driscoll, criminal, and dangerous leader of the Whyos.

We had made him what he was. So we took our finished product and choked the life out of it and believed we had done a good job—some of us. Scarcely anybody thought of the perfect machinery we had set up to manufacture his sort, nor of the colossal irony of hanging the victims of that machinery instead of abolishing the machine. A few had some such revolutionary notions as they went out of the prison yard or as they read next day of what we had done there. Among them two or three reporters that had seen Driscoll in his prison cell and talked with him and been impressed with a feeling that under all the madness and stupid violence there had been in him a certain capacity for use if society had but the wit to find it out.

Why do I go back now to all this sordid story of a drab and a murderer? Well, for two reasons: First here was the huge East Side teeming with human beings, the East Side with a birth rate much larger than that of the pretty districts. Future men and women of the Republic were being bred in that hive. What chance had they to become creditable citizens? This was the answer.

Also for another reason. Why do we retain in an age of enlightenment the capital punishment that is so strange a relic of darkness?

That it may deter others from committing murder, says Reversion. Yes? Deter whom?

Danny Lyons was Danny Driscoll's first lieutenant, co-mate and confidant. While Driscoll was a prisoner in the Tombs, the two managed to keep in communication. Driscoll was under sentence of death for murder. While he lay there Lyons acquired a grudge against an athlete named Joseph Quinn, shot him down in the street, and on September 30, 1887, exactly one year after the sentencing of Driscoll, and in the same court, Danny Lyons was convicted of murder and sentenced to be hanged. And a few months after we had broken the neck of the leader of the Whyos, on the same gallows in the same place, we broke the neck of that leader's first lieutenant and pupil. Again, who is deterred?

Wise society, ours! Not for a moment will we disturb the causes of wrong-doing but with stern and implacable justice we will punish the wrong-doer—when he comes from the tenements that we tolerate.

Is this enough, or shall I take one more instance out of the sample case of my recollections?

The ancient town of White Plains in 1887 was far different from the White Plains of later days. It was remote, old-fashioned, quiet and sedate. With other customs inherited from the past, the stores kept open after 6 o'clock. About half-past 9 on the evening of Thursday, January 20, 1887, Mead's bakery was still open, but young William Mead, who was in charge in his father's absence, thought the time had come to close it. He was in the back room reading; his younger brother was in the shop. A customer entered, bought something, went away, and the boy was moving to lock the door when two men came in, having their hats pulled down upon their eyes and their overcoat collars turned up about their chins, and ordered him to hold up his hands.

He ran in terror to the back room. William came out and thought some one was playing a joke. One of the visitors drew a revolver and shot at him. The bullet went through his heart.

There were neighbors all about and hearing the shot they came running and wondering. The two men ran into the street and down it toward the railroad tracks. The crowd, as soon as it could understand what had happened, began to follow. The night was dark but the snow everywhere made the movements of the men dimly visible. An always increasing multitude was upon their heels. They halted and fired at the crowd and checked its advance. Then they seemed to disappear.

Every person in and around White Plains that had any form of firearm added himself to the pursuit, weapon in hand. The chief of police commandeered a sleigh and went tearing up one road and down another, looking for the fugitives. Outside of the town behind a stone wall that fenced a field, he thought he saw a darker clump than the bushes. He halted and shouted at it. The two fugitives stood up and began to fire with revolvers.

The crowd, keeping under cover, was now hemming them in. There was an incessant fusilade. One of the posse took the heavy pistols of the chief of police, worked his way behind fences and walls to within a short distance of the trapped desperadoes, and fired at them. Both were seen to fall. Then, in the dim light, he saw one of the figures raise himself upon one arm, put a revolver to his own head, and discharge it.

After that first shot he was still in the same position. Then, to the amazement of the beholder, the same figure again raised his revolver to his head and fired a second shot, after which he too fell down.

There ensued a long pause in which no one dared to advance upon the faintly descried heap upon the snow. At last the man that was nearest crept up and found two bodies, one dead, the other dying, literally shattered with bullets.

The chief and his aides carried the bodies into a store and looked at them—and they were two boys.

Each had two revolvers and in every pocket a supply of ammunition; each had a dagger carried in a belt. They were poorly dressed, they wore no underwear, they had between them only a few cents in money. Nobody in White Plains had ever seen them before.

They lay that night in the police station. The next day, two young men arrived from New York and identified them.

James J. Tristram had come to America many years ago from Dublin with his young wife to make a good start in the land of golden opportunity. He was a tinsmith, a decent, sober man and a hard worker when he could get work to do, for his was largely a seasonal trade. In Monroe Street, they occupied a tenement in a typical tenement-house region. Five boys were born to them. Father and mother tried as well as they could to educate their children in the public school in Vandewater Street.

There was no playground at the school and none elsewhere in that region—except in the streets.

The eldest son, James J., Jr., came through well and developed a little business in the making of some form of wire goods, into which he took Richard, the brother next to him. Thomas and John, the next in point of age, were taken from school to work for their brothers. None of the family was known to the police in any way; none had attracted the least unfavorable attention from the neighbors. The Tristram family stood well.

The third boy, Thomas, was now nineteen, the fourth, John, was seventeen. On Thursday, January 20, Thomas and John said they did not wish to work that day but were going to take a vacation trip. With the youngest brother, William, they went to the Grand Central Station, boarded a train for a station above White Plains and walked back to the town. Then at nightfall they gave William enough money to take him to New York and sent him home. They seemed to have hung around the shadows of the town until 9.30 when they entered Mead's bakery. An hour later they were dead, shattered with bullets.

James J. Tristram, Jr., intelligent and respectable, and Richard, his brother, could offer no explanation of this episode. Thomas and John had always been good boys. They had never mixed with the gangs of the neighborhood, had never stayed out at night or shown any inclination to be wild. I went up to the Tristram flat on the third floor and tried as considerately as I could to draw information from the father and mother, beaten to the floor by this disaster. The father, more composed, corroborated the account of James junior. The mother could only wring her hands and say over and over, "They were such good boys! Such good boys!" There were two windows in the front of the flat and two in the rear, which was the kitchen. The boys' room had a window on a tiny dark court that was no better than an air shaft. Well—that was the story. They had, year in and year out, looked forth from the front windows upon roaring, dull, and dirty streets; from the rear upon black roofs, smirched walls and chimneys. The whole prospect was contained in things drab, forlorn, down at the heels, hopeless. At the next corner was a newsstand. It sold weekly papers, then popular, containing stories of wild adventure. For ten cents one could get a paper-bound novel purporting to be about detectives and criminals. The boys loaded themselves with this literary slop. We found some of it in their room. No doubt they lay awake at night and read it as the only possible relief from the deadly dreariness around them. It offered a new world and glimpses of a life that had interest. They slipped away that day and made this sudden blind, stupid, foolish lunge at their vision of an existence that might be not all monotony.

It was Thomas the elder that, already badly wounded and seeing himself surrounded, had shot himself. Often I wished I knew what thoughts and sensations were in his poor little stunted boy's mind as he did that.

All the ordinary decencies and kindnesses of human life were threatened in the jungle; it seemed wonderful and glorious that any good survived. Not all the children reared in that hothouse of evil went to the bad; only a few. Of better stuff than I, the majority of these self-salvaged ones. Well enough I knew and at times admitted that if I had been born and reared in such conditions I should have been a drunkard or a criminal or both, and at such times of wholesome reflection the sense of superiority that naturally goes with a state in which one does not have to live in a tenement house sagged fairly low.

The reaction, of course, differed with different victims of such environments. A house-painter with his wife and two small children, a boy and a girl, lived in a tenement in Third Avenue. For some weeks he had been out of work. The neighbors said that every morning he went out and walked from one place to another looking for employment and came back at night not having found it. Always the same report—no work. One night the children were in bed and asleep. The house-painter took a revolver and shot his wife dead, then he shot the two children in their sleep, then he killed himself.

The next morning the neighbors hearing no sound from that flat and remembering the shots of the night before, notified the police. We found the four bodies stark and cold. On a bureau was a letter the wife had addressed to her husband's mother, who lived in another tenement half a mile away. We went there. The house-painter's brother, an East Side youth of eighteen, met us at the door. No one there had heard of the tragedy. It was our painful business to break the news. When he comprehended what had happened, the only comment of the loving brother was this:

"Holy Jesus Christ, did he kill them all? Well, I always thought that fellow was nutty."

We were an evening paper; at 9 A.M. I must begin my ministrations at police headquarters. It happened that a few mornings after this episode, the city editor called me on the telephone and said that the Tantivy Coach, or some such name, a famous society stunt, was to start that morning from the old Brunswick Hotel, the man that should have covered the auspicious event was sick or drunk or something, and could I find time to dash up from Mulberry Street and write a story about it, for it was very important, indeed. So I made a hurried arrangement about the police news and dashed up accordingly. It was a clear, high-stringing morning in March, spring just beginning and everything tonic and lovely. Brave men and beautiful women and all that. Eminent lights in the social world. A four-horse coach of the strictly classical model, to be "tooled"—that was the word; you must be careful to use it—"tooled" by Mr. Frederick Somebody (most eminent of all the eminent social lights). The coach was glittering, the costumes were gay, the horses spirited. Back of the eminent one that

was to do the "tooling" sat a lackey, or something, resplendent
in livery, high boots, and things, and holding a long straight
coach horn. Another, similarly attired, held the horses' heads.
When all the Eminent Ones had climbed to their places, Mr.
Frederick Somebody took the reins, one liveried creature raised
his horn and blew a mellow blast, the other released the horses'
heads, and away went the machine, headed for Pelham Manor
or somewhere, just as you read in Dickens, you know. It was
perfectly lovely. I was told that on a modest calculation, more
than a hundred million dollars were represented on that coach
roof. And what were the Eminent Ones doing there? Oh, they
were playing at coaching, just as Marie Antoinette played at
dairying—for lack of something to do.

The Old Brunswick, Fifth Avenue, Twenty-sixth to Twenty-
seventh—resort of fashion. All Fifth Avenue then was residential and the home of the élite. The flat where the house-painter
slew his family was not half a mile away as the crow flies. In
the psychology of the coach-load that went to Pelham Manor
that day it was farther away than Mars.

It seems incredible now, but most of the streets of the East
Side were then ignored by street cleaners. Fifth Avenue was
cleaned, so was Madison. Hester Street reeked in its native dirt.
Now and then some strange person piped up about the dangers
to public health in the neglected streets. Then we sent (sometimes) a reporter to see the street cleaning commissioner and
he showed that with the appropriation at his command he
could do no better. Whereupon the subject lapsed to its former
state. When snow fell, it was removed from Broadway and
the up and down thoroughfares. Hester Street waited until nature removed what nature had showered there.

Cranks, Socialists, reformers, and other pestilent persons continued from time to time to protest about our tenement houses.
They reminded us that tuberculosis, for instance, was no re-
specter of persons, and that from the tuberculosis factory we

were thoughtfully maintaining on the East Side the germs spread and invaded far holier precincts, with direful results. Same way about other diseases. They pointed out that the most productive of all these disease factories were the tenements that had neither sunlight nor ventilation and that of these were thousands in New York. By dint of continual protests, supported by doctors and health authorities, they succeeded finally in securing the appointment of a Tenement House Commission, which had hearings and took testimony and made investigations and reported the momentous discovery that unwholesome surroundings made unhealthy people.

Reports of this priceless character dragged their slow length along until by some means legislative attention was fixed upon the matter and we harvested a crop of salutary tenement-house laws—salutary so far as they went, I mean. Effectually they prevented the building of any more of these human slaughterhouses but they did nothing to demolish those that were then at work. No, not even those owned by Trinity Church and devoted to the service of God, which were among the worst in the city. That section of urban hell in the Fourth Assembly District that I have mentioned as the Lung Block got its name because of its conspicuous fertility in tuberculosis. It was denounced by the Tenement House Commission. Twenty years later it was still standing and still making business for undertakers and grave-diggers.

It and its compeers bred disease much more than they bred crime. This continued to puzzle me. Sometimes I was tempted to think that the huge pressure of the Egyptian darkness that brooded over the region was squeezing from the human make-up all impulse to revolt and leaving only a dull, stoical, mechanical submission, particularly in the young.

Not always. There was a woman of great wealth and high social standing that had a palatial residence somewhere on Long Island, I have forgotten where. It was her custom to be driven to the city for afternoon functions, and then to be driven home again by way of the East Thirty-fourth Street ferry. One day her secretary or major domo or butler or somebody, came to headquarters bursting with indignation to make complaint of intolerable wrong. For several nights now, my lady's carriage, driving through East Thirty-third Street, had been stoned by young ruffians. At first, little attention had been paid to this outbreak of the riotous spirit of the hoi polloi, but last night the coachman had been struck on his cheek with a flying missile and cut so that the blood flowed. And another rock had smashed the rear window and narrowly missed my lady. And it was manifest that such rowdying must be suppressed.

Chief Inspector Byrnes, to whom the complaint was made, inquired how my lady happened to be driving through Thirty-third Street on her way to the ferry which was at the foot of Thirty-fourth. It appeared that this route was chosen because there was less traffic in Thirty-third and the carriage could move at a swifter pace, which, of course, was highly desirable. My lady, having nothing to do, was always in much haste to do it.

Ours was a journal wholly devoted to law, order, and the better classes. I was delegated to make further inquiry into the circumstance of the ruffian children, and discovered that about a week before, a carriage like my lady's, driving at top speed through Thirty-third Street had swept into a knot of children, playing in the street. Where else should or could they play? A thoughtful government that had spent millions on Riverside Drive had never deemed the tenement-house dwellers to merit any consideration, and the children in that section of the tenement-house hell might play on the pavement or not at all. So the carriage swept into these from the tenement kitchen of miseries, ran over one and hurt it so it died. Whereupon the children that had escaped its flying wheels took careful note of it, gathered missiles, and lay in wait. When next they saw an elegantly upholstered coachman sitting upon the box they let go with the debris.

There was a certain mixture of the same impulse or something like it in the vague, muddled, lumping mentalities of the youthful criminals of Hell's Kitchen and Corcoran's Roost; I mean a dimly perceived sense of injustice in the fate that had caught and held them. I am aware that this statement does not in any way click with the pet belief of the well-to-do that the criminal is a creature specially designed and furnished with a separate psychology, if any, but my conclusion is based upon intimate observation of crime and criminals and I am going to let it stand. There is such a thing as a criminal mind, but in every instance it can be traced back to environment and living conditions. If society insists upon maintaining such environments and such living conditions, it ought not to grumble about the crime bill it must pay—or the gangsters, hold-ups, and lawlessness that beset us.

As to all of which it is sufficient to go back to the thesis with which I started. The obvious fact that overturned my previous notions about all these things was that not all the girls became prostitutes—only a marvellously small number. Not all the boys became gangsters or thieves; only a comparatively small number. Most of those that slipped, slipped because they could not stand the pressure of the horrors around them. But the tremendous converse of the tenement-house situation that erased pessimism and refreshed faith was the suggestion of what men and women would be if they had a chance. In the midst of this grim perdition, surrounded with every influence that could debase and ruin, the essential goodness of mankind was not utterly obliterated. The terrific and bestial struggle for daily bread, the degradations of dirt and uncomeliness, the pangs and shames of poverty could pervert some of it and obscure much more but could not utterly destroy it. If man under such conditions did not become wholly devil he must have in him in the mass the unconquerable angel, he must have ineffaceably in some mysterious way the image and likeness with which he started.

Therefore, all he needed was a chance to let this indestructible good grow and the alien evil fall from him. And if something could take from him the fear of want and the necessity to snatch bread from his fellow's lips that he might have it for his own, it seemed as if life in the world might cease to be horrible and become something to have delight in and joy.

Chapter VII

FOR THE FAIR NAME OF OUR CITY

FIRST Sunday of August, 1884. Mr. Frank Keenan, a lal-lah-paloosa reporter of the good old school, is passing through City Hall Park in New York. He notices with some surprise a small group of aldermen going into the municipal building. At the entrance to the Park he sees two other aldermen, talking earnestly as they steer up for the same harborage. The circumstance strikes him as so strange for a Sunday afternoon that after a time he turns back and betakes himself curiously to the same building.

Up he goes to the chamber of the Board of Aldermen. The doors are fast locked but he hears voices within, voices plainly raised in debate. He worms himself into the cloak room whence he can make out two things. The board, in extraordinary and secret session, is debating something about money, and over its deliberations sits Mr. Henry W. Jaehne, vice-president, and eminent political leader. Of this no mistaking. Jaehne, known by his bland, mellifluous voice. Once heard it can never be forgotten, that voice.

A man of note is Mr. Jaehne, distinguished in many ways. Some persons insist that he is the best-dressed man in New York; by all he is admitted to be faultlessly heedful of his attiring. That silk hat he always wears is polished like a mirror; his four-button cut-away coat, perfectly molded to his svelte form, his trousers of an unimpeachable stripe, his gloves, his buttonhole bouquet, his well-trimmed brown mustache, are subjects of admiring remark. Also noted he is for urbanity and surpassing grace of manner that few can resist. Vice-president of the Board of Aldermen, third place in the city government. Also, a chieftain in the County Democracy, that great organization of our best citizens and highest of brow, existing, as we have seen, to uphold the purest standards of politics and ever to flout the despicable Tammany, composed of rag-tag and bob-tail and of other persons, low indeed of brow. The high brows of County Democracy beam upon Mr. Jaehne. They hold him to be an excellent counsellor and one that knows how to win in politics.

What is Mr. Jaehne's business? He is a real-estate operator and capitalist. In these callings he must be successful; he has much money, and do but look at his clothes!

Mr. Keenan continues to ponder about that strange secret Sunday session of the Board of Aldermen. Presently, he and others of the tribe of the sophisticated begin to see a light.

The city is chiefly dependent for its intra-mural transit upon street cars drawn with horses. Broadway is the grand artery and thoroughfare of traffic, but Broadway below Fourteenth Street has never had a street-car line. All the wise men are agreed that such a thing would be impossible there. The jam of other vehicles is too great. All day long their slowly moving procession fills the pavement from curb to curb, pounding heavily over the Belgian blocks and producing a Niagara of tumultuous uproar the equal of which is not to be found in any other street on earth. A composer translates it into musical notes, all played on the lowest strings of the double basses with an obligato of trumpets in discord and a thundering racket of kettle drums. From time immemorial, transportation of passengers in Broadway has been achieved with what are called stages—old-fashioned omnibuses, lumbering, horse-drawn, not pretty to look at, but able to steer from side to side as occasion may demand. Which is virtually all the time. As a street car is confined to its two tracks, the answer is plain. Street cars are impossible.

Yet the traffic and the tolls would be goodly if street cars could be made to run, and at this time two companies are trying to get the right to make the experiment.

Of a sudden, the Board of Aldermen passes an ordinance granting to one of these companies a franchise in Broadway for the term of 999 years and without compensation to the city.

The burghers gasp and the mayor immediately vetoes the ordinance. The Board on the same day passes it over his veto, twenty-two of the twenty-four voting for it.

So this is the circumstance that the wise Mr. Keenan connects with the secret Sunday session and surmises that the money topic under discussion that day is something to make the burghers more than gasp if they knew the whole of it. Without knowing the whole of it, the burghers surmise without difficulty the probable links. All are convinced there has been crooked work, the more because of the peculiar performance of Mr. Jacob Sharp, president of the respectable company upon which this vast benefaction has been bestowed. He takes no chances on injunctions, Mr. Sharp. The day the ordinance is passed he gathers his workmen and materials. When night falls and no courts are open and no judges easily to be found, he turns loose his workers, opens the pavement, lays down his rails and in the morning by the bright light, behold, the Broadway surface railroad completed and in operation. It is swift and clever—but too suggestive. All men know that something is wrong. All demand punishment for the wrong-doers.

But common knowledge is not evidence upon which grafting aldermen can be sent to Sing Sing. The months go by and fructify in nothing upon which warrants can be issued. The district attorney turns loose all the resources of his office and gets nothing. A committee of indignant citizens conducts an investigation and gets nothing. The press fumes and frets and gets nothing. Cynics urge that the figure of justice on our city hall be taken down since the old lady has so evidently gone out of business—in our community.

All this time Vice-President Jaehne holds unswerving the tenor of his agreeable way, bland, courtly, gentle of speech, correct of deportment. Interrogated about the Broadway franchise, with brow serene he assures one and all that the measure was passed solely in the public interest that citizens might have a chance to ride instead of walking, always walking. He even praises the aldermen for civic virtue. More than ever he is known and admired.

Known by many, known and not admired by a stoutly built man of strange ways that sits all day in a big, bare office in Mulberry Street. He knows many things, Inspector Byrnes of the detective bureau, among them when to speak and when to be silent. He is accustomed to keep one eye warily fixed upon certain men of wealth and power in Wall Street. These have interested themselves in the Broadway scandal and some of them urge Inspector Byrnes to give them the help of his knowledge and experience in running down the bribery that all men are sure must lurk somewhere in the smelly precincts of the old city hall. Mr. Byrnes is pleased to say he will do his best.

It is March, 1886; nearly two years have passed since the scandal broke and nothing has been done. Mr. Byrnes invites Vice-President Jaehne to come up to his house and pass a social evening. The vice-president comes, urbane, faultlessly dressed, buttonhole bouquet of the best. He has reasons of his own to be on good terms with his host of that night. Mr. Byrnes's front room upstairs has two closets and some doors. The house has guests this night the vice-president knows not of. They are five detective sergeants from the Byrnes staff who adjust themselves in the closets and behind the doors.

Mr. Byrnes is himself no punk performer in the urbane line and greets the vice-president with distinguished affability.

They sit and talk about indifferent things, Shakespeare and the musical glasses, may be, until Mr. Byrnes suddenly loses his amiable bearing and produces from his pocket certain pieces of paper that have a marvellous effect upon the vice-president. He looks at them and turns pale and shakes, and Mr. Byrnes, holding them before his terrified eyes, proceeds to extract from him a full and detailed confession of how the Broadway franchise was obtained, how the company headed by Mr. Sharp and composed of most respectable citizens had found itself in competition with the other company and had bought the twenty-two aldermen for $20,000 each. Also, that the special secret session that puzzled Mr. Keenan was held to discuss which of two bribes was the better. For the rival company had offered temptingly a handful of cash and a block of stock and as any one could see this created a situation perplexing to statesmanship. But at last the aldermen had agreed with eminent authority and decided to take the cash and let the credit go.

And the five detective sergeants in the closets and at the doors hear this confession and take it down in note books. And when the vice-president goes home that night, he knows that the game is up for him, anyway. Because the pieces of paper he was invited to examine in Mr. Byrnes's hospitable home are the evidence that he is not a real-estate operator nor a capitalist but the proprietor of the most successful "fence" in New York and the money he has dispensed so liberally was drawn from thieves and burglars.

The next day Mr. Byrnes takes the notes of his sergeants to an astonished and grateful district attorney and the warrant is issued for the vice-president's arrest on the charge of accepting a bribe.

At the news consternation falls upon the twenty-two, hitherto boldly confident and defiant. One of them is Mr. Charles B. Waite, manager of the fashionable Hotel Brunswick. He loses not a moment's time. So fast he runs to the district attorney to turn state's evidence that as Mr. Keenan sagely observes you could throw dice on his coat tails.

Many of the others beat the warrant servers to the Grand Central where without baggage they catch the night train for Montreal. The extradition treaty does not cover aldermanic grafting.

Two others make confessions, Aldermen Michael J. Duffy and L. A. Fullgraff—Fullgraff, at whose name the Tuneful Nine must shout with glee.

The whole city rises with joy and inexpressible relief—for a time. The confessions are full, explicit, indubitable. Justice can now resume her sway. Dishonest public servants are about to be punished as they deserve, the city's name is about to be purged. Ring out, joy bells, for now all is to be set right.

Six or seven aldermen that have not confessed and have missed the night train to Canada's inviting shores, are under arrest and out on bail. To trial then, with them, beginning with Jaehne, the dapper, the urbane, the glass of fashion and mold of form, now fallen. Easily he is convicted, May 15, 1886, sentenced to imprisonment for nine years and six months and on May 22 is whisked to Sing Sing.

"One!" cries Justice, imitating Edmond Dantes. "Next!"

This is Arthur J. McQuade, a ruddy-faced, jovial politician, man about town, good fellow, and all that. He puts up a vigorous fight, but on December 14, he likewise is convicted and sentenced to seven years and six months.

It is January 18 before his various motions for delay collapse upon him and he must take the cold plunge after Jaehne. I go up to the prison with him. All the way he sits in the smoking car chained to a plain-clothes man, and laughs and chats and smokes with perfect unconcern, so far as we can see—except that under the constant laughter is a certain nervous titter, now and then.

As the train pulls into the Sing Sing station, he springs to

"FROM CITY HALL TO SING SING"

Puck's cartoon on the Jaehne case. April 21, 1886

his feet in advance of the detective, cracks another joke, trots unconcernedly to the waiting hack. At the prison gate he jokes again, this time with us because our hack has beaten his. Merrily he goes through the questioning, merrily he turns toward the great iron door. And then as he is stood up to be measured for his prison suit, the whole thing seems to fall upon him at once and most strangely. All the unspeakable horror of the ruin of his life seems to reach out and beat him to earth as with huge clubs. Whether he has so far put it resolutely out of his mind, whether in an instant all his power of bluffing drops from him and leaves him infantile, I know not. In a flash, all his face goes ghastly white, his knees give way under him, he falls shaking against the wall and must be seized and supported.

Two! Next!

The next is old John O'Neill, the grandfather of his district, always known there as "Honest Old John." Everybody knows and likes him. He keeps a little shoe shop in Centre Street, but his real business seems to have been as a patriarch among his people and to keep the young men going straight. When his case is called he comes into court without a lawyer and asks if the trial cannot be postponed for a time. The shoe business is good just now in Centre Street but it will be slack a few months later. Almost no defense he makes. Quickly he is convicted. Three years and six months in Sing Sing. No appeal in his case, no attempt to postpone. Off with him to Sing Sing and I am assigned to accompany him.

It is a miserable cold, gray morning. They start him early, waking him in his cell before it is daylight. He does not jest nor smoke but lies huddled in the corner of the car seat, a bundle of human rags, shaken together. Not a word he says all the way. The detective to whom he is manacled, out of the pity of his heart, tries once or twice to say something. He never responds. At the Sing Sing station he totters and nearly falls.

The detective must lift him to his feet and all but carry him to the hack. Scarcely has he voice to answer the questioning at the prison office and scarcely, I think, knows when the great iron door closes on him also.

Three! Next! The interests of virtue are thriving in New York. The stain upon the city's name is being erased. Next!

But now the car of justice begins a little to bump and go awkwardly. The next case is that of Thomas J. Cleary, janitor of the Equitable building, alderman from the First District. He has strong friends, he puts up a vicious defense, strangely powerful interests are enlisted in his behalf. All the state's evidence men testify against him, the confessions are there, the evidence is the same as in the other cases, even stronger, for this man is proved to have money resources most unusual for a janitor. But the case goes not the smooth road to conviction. Cleary hires from Philadelphia Daniel Dougherty, the most famous living forensic orator and one of the highest-priced lawyers in America. He has Cleary's weeping family exhibited in the court room, he makes a thunderingly long and doubtless eloquent plea based on the theory that this poor, honest man is the victim of a horrible conspiracy,—and the jury disagrees! On the same evidence deemed conclusive in three cases, the jury disagrees. And about this time, McQuade's attorneys succeed in obtaining from the Court of Appeals a reversal of his conviction and he goes free.

And with these defeats, virtue apparently ceases to rear her angered front and the pursuit of the wicked to slacken in our neighborhood. For we are now reaching that second stage in all warfare against revealed graft that has so puzzled and disconcerted reformers. The public, habituated to find in its newspaper every morning a fresh dish of tabasco, has extracted from the graft story all its thrills and demands something new. If reminded of the morals of the case, the man in the street that at first has burned with indignation against these corruptionists now begins to laugh at the performance as rather clever. The bribe-takers snitched the money and are safe. Well, money is money. The virtuous and public-spirited among the rich recall to themselves that after all they have other things to do than to vindicate official honesty. The juries pluck up enough courage to follow their natural instincts against informers, and the whole campaign comes to an inglorious end. Gradually the fugitives return from Montreal to which it appears they need not have journeyed, and former Aldermen Waite, Duffy, and Fullgraff are left to meditate upon the foolishness of panic.

There remains still the bribe-giver to be dealt with. Our newspaper, always stalwart for the Right, clamors that Sharp must be tried. He is, and convicted, whereupon Civic Virtue takes heart a little. Not for long. The Court of Appeals reverses his conviction, also, and his death forestalls a second trial, if any were intended. Thus the whole Broadway scandal that has once shaken New York to its foundation stones, slips smoothly away to oblivion, where it has no end of company.

But the franchise the aldermen sold for their own profit is nailed upon the city of New York for 999 years and fifteen years later becomes, by its mere existence, the pivot of a gigantic swindle for which New York pays heavily and is still paying. No doubt it was clever, that franchise theft. But it was costly.

The last stage of the fight to save Cleary was still on when I was hurtled out to Chicago for *The New York World,* and found another city going through an almost identical experience, with one contingent of its aldermen slipping nimbly to Toronto two leaps ahead of a warrant server and others brazening out indictments and trials that never achieved anything. Afterward, indignant Chicagoans did indeed on one occasion frustrate the franchise-grabbers by thronging to the council chamber and hanging rope nooses over the edge of the balcony in full view of aldermen that had intended to vote away the public's streets, but this effective revolt had too few imitations. As a rule the corporation got what it wanted. Accumulated Wealth marched easily to more privilege that it might have more wealth and so more power to win more wealth; and citizens that still believed in public virtue were left sucking their thumbs.

City after city and state after state went through experiences identical with those of Chicago and New York. Public utility companies were the common offenders; public utility companies composed of good men that wished illegal privileges and cared not a rap who was corrupted so long as they got their chance at profits. Railroad companies rotted state legislatures and county supervisories; street railroad companies and gas companies bought the city councils. As a reporter, I covered at different times graft stories in seven states and nearly twice as many cities. Rich men that wanted to buy Senatorships supplied an incessant sewer-tide of scandal but the corporations were far worse.

Strange and disheartening incidents came always upon one that investigated these conditions. I have seen a man revealed as the high legislative corruption agent of a great corporation endorsed nevertheless by the chief civic body of his city, endorsed as pure and honest. I have seen a legislator that resigned rather than face charges of corruption, scandalous throughout the state, received in his home town with a brass band, a street parade and a eulogistic banquet. I have seen state legislators tagged all over with the labels of graft and triumphantly re-elected by their fellow citizens. I have seen notorious grafters re-elected to the chief offices in the cities they had betrayed, and re-elected with full and perfect knowledge of their crimes.

Everywhere, men of virtue cried out against this foul tide and apparent degeneration. Courageous public prosecutors like the late Joseph W. Folk of St. Louis labored still with sincerity to bring punishment upon the guilty. Everywhere they duplicated the story of the great Broadway scandal in New York.

The most poignant, the most dramatic, the most memorable of all these conflicts took place in San Francisco, and since the Civil War we have scarcely had in this country another development so subtly and profoundly indicative. We should deal with it now, although it will for the time steer us away from chronology. In the San Francisco struggle before it was done, men threw off all disguise, all pretense of decency, and reverting to the naked candors of the Stone Age battled with pristine ferocities and hesitated not at murder in the cause of profits.

The city, haunted still by some occult but compelling memories of the mining camp, had always been free, easy and unconventional, and I think had always been corrupt. The Southern Pacific Railroad of that day usually ruled there, and of course ruled rottenly. Protected vice and the public utilities supplied the rest of a total tribute that must have been enormous.

Respectable business, honest business, admired business, going hob-nob with the lowest orders, an ulcerous strumpet on one arm, a lumping beer slinger on the other; the same old spectacle familiar then in almost every American city.

Out of the welter of these conditions in San Francisco arose two men of master minds upon whom was presently fixed the attention of the community.

One was Patrick Calhoun, president of the street railroad company; the other Abraham Ruef, Republican boss.

The next compelling figure in the story is that of a newspaper man of indomitable courage and Roman fortitude that, becoming aware of the rampant corruption around him, highly resolved to end it. He was Fremont Older, at that time managing editor of *The San Francisco Bulletin*.

Day after day passed before him in his professional ministrations the evidences of a vast social decay that filled him increasingly with disgust and alarm. Such of his fellow citizens as knew of the advancing putrefaction seemed indifferent or indurated. What was needed was a bold, strong move that would arouse them to action. He was moved to undertake such a demonstration if only he could find a fearless prosecutor and come by the necessary financial backing.

Francis J. Heney was then bringing to a close his efficient prosecution of the timber thieves of Oregon, in which he had made and deserved a national reputation. Mr. Older sought Mr. Heney, laid before him the terrific facts he had accumulated and asked for help. Mr. Heney had been born in San Francisco. He deemed it his home. When he had comprehended the full extent of the villainy then going forward in it, he said that he would enlist to combat it. When asked what his fee would be, he replied that it would be nothing; he would do the work as a public service to his native city, and in all the furious conflict that ensued he received not a cent and paid his own expenses, the one fact that lightens the gloom of the rest of the narrative. It shows that after all the sense of the citizen's public obligation, often supposed to be extinct, still survived.

To carry on the investigation, employ detectives, make researches, it was estimated that a fund of $100,000 would be needed. Mr. Older laïd the matter before James D. Phelan and Rudolph Spreckels, public-spirited and clean-handed citizens of San Francisco. Mr. Phelan was then in private life but in three terms of office he had demonstrated that he was the best mayor San Francisco ever had. Mr. Spreckels was a banker and the only one of the kind of whom we have record. He ran his bank on his own independently conceived lines and seemed more eager to have it an institution of public benefit than a mill to grind profits.

With these two remarkable men pledged to finance and stand by an effort to shake their city free from the greasy folds of the graft constrictor that was strangling it, and they kept their word. Through all the storm that followed, often raging with thunder crashes about their ears, they never flinched.

Mr. Older started the campaign in *The Bulletin* and made the most extraordinary fight so far known in American journalism. Daily he volleyed with whole pages of revelations. At first they had to do with vice protection; in a short time they began to lay bare the crooked operations of the public utility companies, and chiefly those of Patrick Calhoun.

Mr. Calhoun's street railroad company had sought a franchise that would allow it to disfigure the streets of San Francisco with overhead wires and trolley poles. The citizens were against the proposal, demanding the underground electric conduit system in use in New York and Washington. The decision lay with a public body called the Board of Supervisors, answerable to a city council elsewhere. Mr. Calhoun took $200,000, gave it to his attorney, who gave it to Mr. Ruef. Eighteen supervisors, through the incessant labors of Mr. Older and his clever manœuvres, were forced to confess that they had shared in this bribe fund and because of it had voted the objectionable franchise.

An emissary of Calhoun's now sought Mr. Older and asked at what price he would abandon the fight against the street railroad company. Mr. Older replied that there was not money enough in San Francisco to induce him to desist, as he purposed to have Mr. Calhoun in the penitentiary.

Soon afterward a desperado from Mexico was discovered to have been brought to the city to kill Mr. Older. It was after the earthquake and a new building was in process of erection across the street from *The Bulletin* office. The plan was to have the bandit shoot from the second story of this construction with the idea that the noise of the electric riveters would drown the sound of the rifle. The gunman sought out the chosen place but did not like it, believing, as he himself said, it afforded too little chance of escape. He then arranged to do the killing elsewhere but did not know Mr. Older on sight and was waiting until he should receive the right signal from another man better informed.

This plot having been discovered and frustrated, the next great idea was to blow up with dynamite the cottage Mr. Older occupied at the beach, for it was his custom to swim every evening in the ocean. This also was discovered and foiled by the two plain-clothes men that had now been assigned to guard Mr. Older. A few days later he was walking in mid-afternoon along a street some distance from the business centre of town, a street to which he had been called by telephone. An automobile filled with armed men drove up to the curb, four leaped out, seized Mr. Older, thrust him into the machine, and drove him away. Several stations down the railroad line, they boarded the night train for Los Angeles on which Pullman reservations had been made for the whole party. Every time Mr. Older thought to escape a revolver was thrust into his side and he was told that at the first motion he would be shot. The intention, as one of the plotters afterward acknowledged, was to take him from the train into a lonely place and kill him. All this was to be done under the cover of what purported to be a warrant of arrest for criminal libel. The story was to be given out that Older, while in the hands of officers, had attempted to escape and had been shot in consequence.

This plot was foiled, largely by accident. A young lawyer, a passenger on the train, that did not know Mr. Older, observed the party and suspected or inferred that something was wrong. He made inquiries, learned who the prisoner was, hopped from the train, telephoned San Francisco, and Rudolph Spreckels and Mr. Heney did the rest. Older was rescued from his captors at Santa Barbara and enabled to return to San Francisco, where with undiminished energy he resumed the leadership of the fight.

The men that effected the kidnapping were directed by well-known agents of the street-railroad company. All were indicted. Then witnesses against them were spirited away and none could be convicted.

The reign of terror went on. Almost daily a new attempt was made to ruin Older, to inveigle him into something that would result in a criminal charge, to discredit or intimidate him. The house of the chief witness in the street-railroad case was dynamited, other witnesses were induced to leave the state or were frightened into silence.

Schmitz, who had been elected mayor on a labor ticket, was indicted, convicted, and sentenced to five years' imprisonment but escaped on a technicality. Ford, Calhoun's attorney, was tried and acquitted. Abe Ruef was tried, the jury disagreed, and he was being tried the second time, Mr. Heney conducting the case with skill and energy. One day, as court was re-assembling after the noon recess, a former convict crept up behind Mr. Heney and shot him down. He was taken to a hospital and believed to be dying. The criminal was seized and locked in a jail cell. A few mornings later he was found dead with a revolver lying beside him.

By a miracle the bullet intended to end Mr. Heney's life went through the fleshy part of his neck and he escaped with the permanent loss of hearing in one ear. In a few weeks he was able to return to the prosecution. While he was incapacitated, Hiram W. Johnson, afterward Governor of California and still later United States Senator, sprang into the breach, took up the trial, and most ably pressed it. Ruef was convicted and sentenced to fourteen years' imprisonment, the limit of the law.

Calhoun was tried and the jury disagreed. He was to be tried again. With the overwhelming evidence against him, his outlook was dark. But he knew well his San Francisco. At the crux of the struggle he precipitated a strike on his street railroad. Then he brought in thug strike-breakers. Rioting ensued in the streets. He took an open automobile and rode up and down Market Street, defying the strikers and commanding the strike-breakers. As the strike was bitterly opposed by all the business elements of the city, the spectacle of Calhoun daringly exposing himself to the vengeance of any violent-minded men won him an immense popularity. When with his thugs and imported strike-breakers he had won and ended the play-acting and the strike, everything else was forgotten and he was hailed as the savior of the city. He might be a corruptionist but he had beaten organized labor.

While the case against Calhoun was still to be tried, an election came on. Mr. Heney was nominated for district attorney, and of course his nomination involved the whole issue of the prosecution of the grafters, which in turn was the issue of the public utilities against public honor, the power of profits against the law.

But meanwhile the same change that had been noticeable in the public sentiment of New York and of Chicago under the like conditions was now still more visible in San Francisco. The business element that at first had endorsed the prosecution now declared that it had gone far enough, that it was hurting the city, finally that it was bad for business.

It is a cry that has seldom been raised in vain anywhere in America.

The election drew near and thrust before the people an issue as plain as daylight, straight as a die. If the prosecution of these men, guilty of the most perilous of all possible betrayals of a public trust, was to continue, Mr. Heney must be elected. His defeat would mean a mandate to protect vice and perpetuate it. Which did the people of San Francisco wish, crime or probity?

The centre of the battle swirled around Calhoun. The strange disagreeing of the jury on his first trial had aroused in thoughtful minds the gravest suspicions. Every citizen might easily reflect that the influences that bribed county supervisors would not hesitate to bribe jurors, and that with the bribing of jurors would disappear every vestige of safety for every average citizen's life and property. This man, singularly adroit and supple, was to be tried again if Mr. Heney should be elected, but would probably go free if Mr. Heney should be defeated. Again, which did the voters wish?

The campaign that ensued was something that should never be forgotten in this country. All the open resources of Accumulated Wealth and Big Business, and still more those resources that are always covert, were brought to bear against Mr. Heney. The assertion that the graft prosecution was injuring business was diligently repeated with impressive warrantry. Financial interests pulled the department stores, the department stores pulled the newspapers. The banks (not the bank owned by Mr. Spreckels) used the subtle and almost irresistible influence that they wield over their depositors and creditors. Citizens' associations and women's clubs were brought into line. There was even a resort to the whispering campaign, that last weapon of the political scoundrel, and stories were invented reflecting upon Mr. Heney's private life.

I arrived in San Francisco in the midst of this campaign and it was plain even to the stranger, if he happened to be an old political reporter, that Mr. Heney was to be defeated. The stedfastly honest element in the city would not believe such a thing possible. How could any community turn against a man that had given to it his best and ablest services and so doing for the purest and highest of motives, had been shot down and permanently crippled? The thing was not in nature. No community would do it.

Yet that is exactly what San Francisco did. When the votes were counted that night Mr. Heney was found to have been beaten by 10,000.

Then the man that had defeated him went into court and

obtained the dismissal of the indictments against the street rail-road head and the whole graft prosecution came to an end with but this barren result obtained.[1]

One man in prison.

Autopsy. The graft prosecutions and civic virtue movements to demand and support such prosecutions perished of garrotting by the public utility and other Powerful Interests.

But something else was involved. San Francisco offered only a typical case. So often had the like failure followed the like attempt to convict of such crimes that the attention of experts was now fixed upon this curious problem in American life. Why should the bribery of public officers, the deadliest of crimes against the security of the state, be here a crime immune against punishment?

As to this, may I, with due humility, beg leave to offer the suggestion of a reporter of many of these incidents?

Mr. Older was profoundly discouraged when the prosecution of these public enemies collapsed. He need not have been. Only one man went to prison. But San Francisco will never again be as bad as it was under Calhoun and his like. Never by any possibility. It may not be what its high-minded citizens would like to have it, but it will never again sink to the old levels.

Only two men served prison terms in New York for the Broadway franchise bribery, but New York was never again as bad in that way as it had been in 1884. Nobody went to prison in Philadelphia's festering scandal, but even Philadelphia began to reform.

That is one undeniable fact and disposes of the theory that men are monkeys and hopelessly bad. They are not hopelessly

---

[1] For the details of this great drama of municipal misrule, see Mr. Older's wonderful book, *My Own Story*. Nothing more significant has appeared among us. It is the surpassing indictment of the capitalist system.

bad, they are magnificently good whenever they have a chance to be good. But suppose we go a little farther.

Everywhere, in San Francisco as in New York, the prosecution of the grafters came to an identical end. Well, why?

Because in each case the public lost interest in the matter and no longer cared. In each case if that interest had survived the prosecutions would have gone through to the end. It was not alone the evil influence of the public utility companies that perverted the public will about these matters. And it was not that the people in America were by nature more knavish and less moral than people elsewhere. Great efforts have been made to cause this to be believed, but it is baseless, nevertheless. Beneath the seeming apathy, beneath the wide-spread appearance of a slovenly and neglectful attitude toward public probity, was a vague, unformulated, unexpressed but persisting intuition of a pivotal fact.

Not the bribe-giver nor the bribe-taker was the real offender. It was useless to imprison men for doing under one guise what we are all engaged in doing under some other.

For in the existing system of society, what are we but all little crooks together? How is it possible for man to be honest so long as for his daily bread he must strive to outwit or overreach his fellow?

Honest business? There is no such thing.

What? Shall we marvel that under a system of vast, complicated, intricate but inevitable corruption men are in some ways corrupt? Nay, again, in a different way, the true marvel is that in the midst of the most debasing environments there are still gropings after integrity. Not even a social system, insane, lop-sided, essentially dishonest, and essentially brutal, can crush from the human heart all its longings for things good and clean.

Chapter VIII

DOWN WITH THE BOSSES!

MOST things in this world that go well are fortuitous. The curious delusion we pursue under the name of success is chiefly chanceful; the Brisbane notion that men carve their careers by sheer will and brain-power is a fantasy. In our times there has been not one man that rode in the whirlwind and directed the storm. I doubt if there ever was such a man, outside the realms of febrile imagery. Here are two wheels revolving close together. Each has on its rim a single projection. One is an individual, the other occasion. They turn at different rates of speed. Some time the two projections may click and the electric contact be completed. Then a man comes forth with a cheap automobile or a new kind of chewing gum or a patent nursing bottle, and makes the success reef. The rest of the time the two wheels can revolve and revolve until perdition freezes over and there will be nothing doing along the Brisbane avenue to glory.

These reflections, as you are now to see, are illustrated by an incident, which must first of all have a background.

Columbia Heights in the city of Brooklyn, year 1893, presented to the world the picture of a senile decline achieved with dignity and an invincible respect for the opinion of mankind. Once it had been the fashionable region of a city of pride and distinction. When it had been left far behind in the march of development, it clung tenaciously to the traditions of vanished grandeur as to those of civic virtue. Erstwhile mansions of the great might become boarding houses and their stables be turned into carpenter shops; nothing could obliterate the facts of history. The houses that once sheltered merchant princes and eminent statesmen still strove against too much decay and the boarders boasted at Macy's and elsewhere of the view from their back windows over two rivers, the Upper Bay and the Orange mountains.

Not without reason was all this pride of place. The old Pierrepont mansion stood at one end of the street, that of Moses Taylor, once the first name in the shipping trade, at the other. The great house of the Claflins rose not far away, and beyond it had lived that weird and incomprehensible genius, Ferdinand Ward, while he carried on the moling operations that wrecked Grant & Ward, laid low a national hero and precipitated a national panic. The old Beecher home was at Hicks Street, a short distance away and over all the region was flung the odor of an incomparable sanctity, for close by was Plymouth Church, renowned in history. But for newspaper men, all these had not so much interest as the rather ornate dwelling at the corner of Pierrepont Street, built by A. A. Low when lord of the China trade, and occupied by Seth Low when as reform mayor of Brooklyn he had driven the bosses, parasites, and plunderers right and left.

On my way to my work one morning, I was passing along this respectable if somewhat grass-grown thoroughfare, bound to Manhattan by way of Wall Street ferry. In front of the Low house I ran plump into old Bob Kelly.

Never tell me that in this life all men find the places for which they are best fitted and rise or fall according to their modicum of brains; come not at me with old flaccid soothsaying about the just rewards of industry and purpose. Here was a man that by natural gifts was fitted for high positions in the state and his job was to keep a smug boarding house in an obscure street. Dress him up a little and you could pass him off anywhere as a member of the nation's cabinet, at least. He had the head of a philosopher, the mind of a historian, the voice of an orator, the most astonishing flow of pithy expressions ever heard on human lips, and he lived in a poke and died uncelebrated. "Full many a gem of purest ray serene," and that sort of thing. It was no figure of speech in his case. He knew more about the inside of politics in Brooklyn than most of the insiders themselves; knew and could tell you the result of any election six weeks before it happened; knew all about all the public men of his day and could estimate them to a hair. No, kind but suspicious friend, contrary to your half-formed thought, he was not a victim of bad habits. He did not drink, used tobacco but sparingly, and was not half as lazy as I was.

He used to come into my office when I was in charge of the Brooklyn edition of *The New York Herald* and tell me things about the actual government of the city to make one gasp and wonder; things that on investigation invariably turned out to be true. And with other matters, he initiated me into the arcana of the Kingdom of Brooklyn, as instituted and conducted by Hugh McLaughlin.

We had had a succession of excellent, amiable gentlemen of the greatest respectability that occupied or rattled in the high position of mayor—Mr. Whitney, Mr. Alfred Chapin, and others. There was not one of them that was, other than in name and title, any more a mayor of Brooklyn than a rubber stamp. The real government of the city was not at all in the city hall. It was situated in a corner of an old building in Willoughby Street, at one time a church and now Kerrigan's auction room. There unheralded, undesignated, uncrowned, and unsung, sat a large, rather lumbering man, with a heavy and ruddy face, shaggy eyebrows, side-burns, shaggy brown hair turning gray under a silk hat worn summer and winter; a man with sharp wary eyes and mysterious, silent ways, that was the real mayor, and aught else besides. He was Boss McLaughlin, head of what was known as the McLaughlin political machine and holding in his hands the strings at the pulling of which mayors and all others danced and spun.

The performances of this group were not exactly ethical but for a long time had been above questioning. The eminent gentlemen that had been one after another elevated to lofty positions knew perfectly well to whom they owed both election and obeisance, and proceeded accordingly. They must also have known, and equally well, the rotten conditions that prevailed in the city that by a handy fiction they were supposed to govern. Never a word said they in protest, but only applied themselves diligently to the more docile obedience and an attempt, through the favor of him of the auction room, to pluck down a nomination for Governor.

Old Bob Kelly's revelations were always of the intimate workings of the controlling machine. I think that since Tweed's day there had not been an equal of the combined power and arrogance of the group that managed Brooklyn. To their success the peculiar status of the city lent much. It was the world's hugest lodging house. Most of its population worked or did business in New York and until it should be pinched unendurably had no great interest in the place where it slept.

So we met that morning in 1893 directly in front of the Low house and Kelly proceeded upon his favorite theme, which was the shame of Brooklyn and the lost hope of its redemption.

"There was one man they couldn't ride," he said, and jerked his thumb over his shoulder to the bright red-brick house where Seth Low had lived.

I went my way to the office and when W. C. Reick, who was chief commander of *The Herald* forces, came in, I said:

"I believe it is about time for an open revolt against the Brooklyn ring. There hasn't been one for some years and it must be about due. I think we could make a hit if we started on it."

Reick lived out at Jerome Park and knew about Brooklyn as

he knew about Hackensack. He asked if I thought we could win. I said we might, if things went all right, for we certainly had case enough, but other rebellions had failed, and I told him the outline of the story. He fired up, said it was a good chance and we'd take it.

He of the auction-room corner had not been able to walk his way without criticism, though of that not a word appeared in the daily press. Edward M. Shepard, a man of wealth and high character, with an old Brooklyn tradition back of him, had been one crying in the wilderness against all this carnival of pillage. Not long before he had written a magazine article, to which no attention was paid, on the subject of municipal mis-government and had spoken in the plainest terms about the style of misgovernment we had in Brooklyn. Another sturdy and unafraid opponent of the ring was William J. Gaynor, an able, prominent, and mildly eccentric lawyer. We consulted with these and also with the representative in Brooklyn of *The New York Times,* who had made what headway he could against the tide of currupt politics and was most sympathetic with our purpose, thrusting away the least restraint of that newspaper rivalry that has spoiled so many good enterprises.

The first attack came in one of our Sunday issues and gave a general and somewhat startling view of the gang-ridden city. A cartoon by a famous cartoonist was better than the article and started things off with a zip. The tradition of morality that was Brooklyn's more or less proud possession was felt to be outraged by these iniquities and righteousness arose (more or less) to the work of purification. Conferences were held, the familiar cry was voiced that now was the time for all good men to get together, and a non-partisan movement was started to oust the ring at the coming election.

When it became evident that the motion was genuine and formidable, some squabbling began as to nominations. Mr. Gaynor had his heart fixed upon heading the ticket as the can-

"THE MAKING OF A SENATOR"

Puck's cartoon on the old style of politics

didate for mayor, but was obliged to be content with the chance to be a justice of the Supreme Court. After long debate, the reformers picked a business man, which was then a popular fetich. He was Charles A. Schieren, a reputable leather dealer with a store in The Swamp region of New York. The other places on the ticket were filled without difficulty and likewise without anxious scrutiny.

So the issue was joined and for some time afforded much innocent merriment to the gentlemen that were accustomed to gather around the auction room. The hunting of the political snark was an old-time and familiar diversion, much approved in our best circles when they happened to think of it, but never bagging any game. The sophisticated had long given up any notion that reform was anything but a handy word with which to win the mild applause and comfortable checks of the silk-stocking brigade. Only school boys and the half-witted believed that politics could ever be purified. After a time the prospect did not seem so full of first-class amusement and about three weeks before election we settled down to a hard gripping contest, with him of the shaggy brows putting forth all his strength. Nominally, he was a Democrat. The opposition was non-partisan. After a time, a new source of joy was injected into the fight by the discovery that fervent Republicans whose personal fortunes were not wholly dissociated from the existing condition, were giving active support to the Democratic ticket. Party lines were much more strictly drawn then than they have been since and the people in general were not so ready to understand that graft and privilege have no party.

One day I had another access of amusement that could not be shared. It occurred to me of a sudden that the situation created by the Bad Men of Brooklyn was not essentially different from that created by the Good Men of St. Johnsbury. The humor of it was the thought of the horrible shock that would go over the Good Men at such a suggestion. Yet the fact was beyond denying. Methods were different; results were identical. In each case the government was conducted by persons that had no relation to the will of the electorate. Nobody chose Hugh McLaughlin to govern Brooklyn; nobody chose the Fairbanks family to govern St. Johnsbury. In each case the form of totally unauthorized and illegal government was complete, perfect, absolute, and autocratic.

It was a bitter fight, and toward the end, as usually happens in such cases, the fury of combat carried each side fairly far. One thing is to be said in behalf of the machine. In one respect it had kept Brooklyn in a state of moral cleanliness, being the only great city in America, or perhaps in the world, of which the same boast could be made. This advantage we owed to Hugh McLaughlin's personal character, for his private walk through life was irreproachable. Under his rule the social evil, which raged in its most repulsive forms on the other side of the river, never dared to cross the Bridge. We understood that dive-keepers and the like had made the most tempting offers and had been sternly repulsed. The machine had a close working alliance with all the intra-mural public utility companies, and these with the universal support of the saloons and the banks constituted the bulk of the machine strength. Nay—I forget! The truest element of its strength was the chronic indifference of the average citizen. There and everywhere else. The one conspicuous point wherein the American school system has failed is in the education of the citizen to a sense of his grave and incessant civic responsibilities. We have made, doubtless, good workmen, good bond salesmen, good lawyers, good electric technicians. Not equally have we made good citizens.

It was the certain alliance of the bosses with the corporations and the saloons that made the success of reform doubtful. The corporations had shown that they could exert a tremendous pull; the power of the saloon everybody knew. I think that, to the last, most of the reformers felt we were leading a forlorn

hope. But behold, on election day, the boarding-house population that ordinarily had been inarticulate or somnolent,
awoke, went to the polls, and delivered itself of one resounding
protest against the whole machine idea. By 9 o'clock it was
evident that the ring had been overwhelmingly beaten and the
entire reform ticket had gone in with a bang.

Then in a speech to an immense and cheering crowd, Mr.
Gaynor, judge-elect and afterward mayor of the Greater New
York, paid a graceful tribute to the part *The New York Herald*
had taken in the fight.

The reign of King Hugh was broken that night and never
restored. The organization continued to hold together for a
time but it ceased to be any real power in Brooklyn affairs. I
think McLaughlin's spirit failed after that wallop. He had regarded with pride the fact that he had kept Brooklyn free from
the one form of moral taint that he regarded as most important
and he was hurt to find the excesses of his followers out-
weighing what he regarded as a notable achievement.

Reform's victory in Brooklyn had certain repercussions not
long after in New York. That winter down came the Lexow
committee, famous in history, to see if Doctor Parkhurst's excursions into the city's moral sewers might yield something for
partisan advantage. We had been so long accustomed to conditions of police graft and commercialized vice that no one in
the newspaper offices had the least hope of any other result but
the usual gestures. A committee headed by Theodore Roosevelt
when he was an assemblyman had beaten in vain on that stone
wall and retired to nurse its bleeding fingers. A committee
headed by Sloat Fassett had been no more successful. It was the
same old story; why repeat it?

But this time it proved different. The appalling revelations
came day after day, each worse than the foregoing, until the
truth was laid bare that vice had formed a partnership with the
paid defenders of law and order, and too often with respect-

ability itself, to manufacture prostitutes and share in their earnings. Police captains in precincts where the traffic went on had collectors called wardmen that gathered the tribute from the disorderly houses. On the basis of a recognized percentage, the wardman got his share, the captain took out his portion and sent the rest along up the line until the final residue rested in some pockets of most eminent gravity.

There was a Tammany mayor. Not a thing was brought out against him nor, indeed, against his administration except that he had made no attempt to root out an admitted evil. That was enough. A great wave of revolt against the whole existing municipal system had started. Reform became suddenly the universal topic. Often came to mind then that familiar sentence of Macaulay's about the comic aspect of the British public in one of its periodic spasms of virtue. Good Government Clubs were formed and swept into their membership an army of most excellent gentlemen that had never before taken the least interest in the management of any public affairs—college graduates, rich men, even society leaders, and the wealthy curled darlings of our nation. Good Government Club A, Good Government Club B, and so on until the city was covered with these pious and alphabetical sodalities and many an elegant social favorite found himself near to touch elbows with persons he would not otherwise have recognized. It was a lovely and inspiring sight; more civic righteousness was preached in New York from May to November, 1894, than had been uttered there before or has been since, I trow. Herman Ridder brought into line the citizens of German descent with his German-American Reform Union. Some one immediately imitated it with a Latin-American Reform Union to take in the Italians. The Citizens Union was co-ordinate and led all these efforts for betterment. The occasion was too obvious to escape the attention of the comic poets, and rhymes about the Goo-goos, Garoos, Laroos, and See Yous came in floods, and for the most part, it is creditable to record, were thrust into the waste-basket.

There was one phase of the reform movement that might well be saved for future instructors in the troubles of democracy under our competitive social system. Many a time and then again, year in and year out, the charges had been made, and believed, that the defect in our politics was that our best people would take no interest in it but left it to low persons, who, coming from foreign lands, were of course without our own high ethical standards. But now our best people, having rallied thus nobly to the standard raised by these Good Government clubs, pressed eagerly along unwonted paths to Zion. More young men of elements theretofore indifferent to civic duty came forth with enthusiasm, and to show how much their class had been slandered, and that their interest in the country was as great as that of any low-brow going, attended the club meetings and expressed the noblest sentiments in favor of reform and the uplift.

The slogan commonest then upon the lips of every reformer was that there had been revealed an unholy compact between vice and government and all reformers understood this to mean that government must be rescued by putting Tammany out and putting nice and good men in. The Good Government clubs said this at every meeting. They invited the public to come in and hear the truth forcibly expounded and in a short time the hideous monster Vice was being hunted all the way from Houston Street to the Harlem river—with words. It was felt that a new era had come upon us, since citizens that had always been careless of the public welfare had now taken hold of it and would make it hum. Some of the clubs rented elegant quarters and prepared to become a permanent feature of city life. Their members felt that upon them rested the responsibility of freeing the nation's metropolis from the blot of the unholy alliance before referred to, and felt this for as much as six months—in some instances. After which the fervor chilled, the enthusiasm declined, the noble crusade came to an end, and Goo Goo was erased from the metropolitan memory.

In the midst of this lifting of hearts and freeing of souls it was felt that there must be in New York, as there had been in Brooklyn, a movement in which all partisan feeling should be subordinated to the common good. The regeneration across the river, which after all had been more or less accidental, became an inspiration and a model. Brooklyn had cleaned its house: New York must do likewise. The coalition was formed; it nominated William L. Strong for mayor and a full ticket, not always too carefully selected. In the election Tammany, although led by Hugh Grant, went down to a signal defeat.

Alas, for the bright hopes of the forces of the uplift! Wolves had slipped into the fold—also asses. The excellent but inexperienced leaders of the revolt had been so intent upon the heads of the tickets, in New York as in Brooklyn, they had paid small heed to the rest. In both cities some queer birds had been nominated in the sacred name of purification and rectitude. Before long certain gentlemen that reform had elevated to office in Brooklyn were under indictment on charges highly unbecoming the heralds of the better day. In New York a series of unhappy events and complications slubbered the shield with unseemly marks. That formidable person, the man in the street, began to feel that we had exchanged a gang of crooks for a band of chumps, a state of mind all to the good for the grafting business, which had only retired to cover and was waiting.

A conscientious police captain named Chapman was assigned to the Tenderloin district, where at that time most of the vice had its lair. He took his task seriously and began to eliminate some of the worst offenses and restrict the rest. Times were hard; the depression started by the panic of 1893 was still heavy upon the land. Business was slow. The notion was adroitly started and assiduously fostered that for the sluggish state of business reform was responsible; what New York needed was a wide-open town to make business good. Buyers from the bushes, we were told, no longer came to New York because the ban had been put upon the rich raciness formerly pervading the Tenderloin. For all this was not a particle of basis in fact. Business was bad in New York because it was bad everywhere else and must continue to be bad until consumption should catch up with and pass production. But a great number of shop-keepers, hotel men, and the like were tricked into accepting the superstition about the wide-open town, and Upper Broadway repeated with cheers and jeers the famous battle cry of Asa Bird Gardiner, "To hell with reform."

The police department had been reorganized with much fanfare from Albany. Four good men and true had been chosen to direct it as commissioners, Theodore Roosevelt being the head. None of the new commissioners had any practical knowledge of the great and complex business of policing a large city. They forced out of office the only man that could have saved the situation for them—Thomas Byrnes, I mean, the old superintendent—and gave over the chieftaincy to one incompetent after another, while the commissioners chiefly quarrelled.

The squabbles in the police board, which became a public scandal and helped to disfigure the rather homely features of reform, had some interesting sequelæ. The reform law made the board to consist of four members, two Republicans and two Democrats. The Republicans were Theodore Roosevelt and Colonel Frederick Grant; the Democrats, Avery D. Andrews and Andrew D. Parker. Differences arose almost at once between Roosevelt and Parker. Roosevelt was always impatient of opposition. He lost a temper over which he had at all times incomplete control and so made a bad situation worse. Parker was a lawyer, cool-headed, quick-witted, and usually the victor in the disputes. The board split in unexpected fashion. Colonel Grant came to believe that Parker represented the better policy and the better method; Andrews, the Democrat, sided with Roosevelt, Republican. The board was therefore tied and to a certain extent impotent.

Roosevelt never forgave Colonel Grant for what he deemed a desertion. Years afterward when Grant had returned to the army and Roosevelt was President, he blocked Grant's advancement. But he showed his appreciation of unwavering support by making Andrews special investigator of the State Trust scandal, with the result that when Andrews found little to condemn in the actions of the Trust Company's officers, he and Roosevelt came in for criticism, the more acrid that men involved in the scandal were personal or political friends of Roosevelt.

But about the Holy War on Bosses: The quarrels of the police commissioners, which made up a great part of all their meetings, added to the general disgust, and when the next election, that of 1897, came around, Tammany rode back to power wearing bells.

It is interesting to the philosopher to recall the next chapter. Under Mayor Strong and the reform administration there had been a serious attempt to enforce the laws, to stop graft and to curb vice. These strivings after the more excellent way having been ridiculed, fiercely denounced, and then repudiated at the polls, the Tammany government seemed to accept at face value the notion that the way to restore prosperity led through a wide-open town and so threw the throttle all the way. The good old times came back with a rush—and more. Graft boomed on all sides. A police captain having died suddenly, his desk was opened and found to be literally crammed and bursting with money. Lexow, Parkhurst, the Uplift all forgotten or derided; Good Government Club A, B, C, D, and the rest, Garoo, Laroo, See You—so many badges of foolishness. The disorderly house graft alone was estimated at more than $7,000,000 a year. The net result of reform seemed to be that every bad thing was worse than it had ever been before. Whole streets were filled with brothels that flaunted their trade with breath-taking audacity, until a private citizen was moved to organize a volunteer force and attack with axes the dens of iniquity.

Girls were seized in the street and dragged off to these sinks from which no power seemed able to rescue them. The daughter of a Jewish rabbi was one of the victims. She was located and an appeal made to *The New York World*. To the astonishment of its editors, they found that even the potency of the press was nothing in such a case.

The inevitable result was another popular revolt and this time the spirit of it closely resembled that of the vigilance committee in a western mining camp. It picked Seth Low to lead the assault. The manifestations were of a new order for the metropolis; little noise, much grim determination. They threw into Tammany a shiver of fear. To save a desperate situation, it nominated for mayor the Edward M. Shepard that had been the courageous assailant of corruption in old Brooklyn. Mr. Shepard was weak enough to accept the nomination, and so blasted an otherwise admirable career. It was the same trick that had been tried in 1894 with Hugh Grant and again it failed. Mr. Shepard had been universally respected as a good citizen and sincere reformer. His alliance with the forces of evil turned against him. Among the things that the American electorate will not endure is the notion of compromising with principle for the sake of a personal ambition, and Mr. Shepard led the way to a memorable overthrow.

Then New York cleaned house again and did this time a thorough job. Tammany returned to power at the end of the Low administration, but the wide-open-town conditions never came with it. No one that vividly remembers the old days will question the immense and genuine improvement. Under the existing system of society, the government of all large cities is more or less crooked and must be. This is true whatever pharisaical pretenses may be made to the contrary. But take at their worst and all together the complaints since made against government in New York. They represent, bad as they may look, an enormous advance. After all the vicissitudes and shifting aspects, New York is a far better city than it was in 1894. Men are but men; there is no place on this earth, so far as my observation has gone, where they dwell in a state of grace and perfection. There is graft in New York, and vice and gangsters and immorality and works of the devil. But slowly conditions better, evil loses, good wins, and faith is justified. Any one that knows what New York was when Lexow boomed down upon it and what it was in 1932 will not be moved by the comparison to exultant and immoderate hosannas, but if he is honest he will admit the sure signs of advance and once more give thanks for that same ineradicable sense in all mankind that leads it with many slips and turnings in a hunt for something better.

Autopsy. Movements to turn out the bad men and turn in the good perished of infantile paralysis or pernicious anæmia.

"The purification of politics is an iridescent dream," said John J. Ingalls, Senate jester, and everybody laughed. Similarly everybody laughed when he said, "Please pass the mustard." He did not add that the dream consisted only in thinking the source of corruption to be the badness of the bad. As a matter of fact, it is the social system and so long as we retain that cause we shall have corruption, for corruption it breeds as it breeds hatreds, strikes, war, and poverty.

Chapter IX

MUCK-RAKING AND MUCK-RAKERS

ANY qualified chemist can take a pint of common sea water and by the application of his curious and recondite craft tell you how much of chloride of sodium it contains, how much of magnesium, calcium, iodine, or what else, down to the thousandth part of the division of a scruple or a trace. But no character analyst could by any skill or wisdom determine how much of Thomas W. Lawson was business acumen, how much megalomania, how much love of the spotlight, how much resentment against his business associates, and how much a sincere desire to expose and correct great evils. All these he had, which perhaps was a blessing. The mixture enabled one to choose the element best suited to one's reaction and so fortify praise or vehement wrath as the case might be.

Up to July, 1904, the world knew him, if at all, only as a daring and eccentric operator in the stock market that had grasped at the ever elusive light of celebrity by building a yacht to try for the America's Cup defense and then by having a pink named for him. But in the July issue of *Everybody's Magazine* he appeared as the author of a bomb-shell article that startled the nation and left Wall Street breathless.

It was the foreword to a series that the magazine announced from the same pen devoted to a revelation of business as actually practised in this happy land, ranging from the picking of pockets to the buying of judges, and including arson and murder. That was all.

I think nothing stranger has happened in our national life.

Mr. Lawson proceeded to make good all the promises of his foreword, and a little more. He told a story that for lurid details exceeded the imaginations of the wildest of shocker writers and in its disclosures of reckless viciousness seemed to show new capacities in the human spirit for the cruel and the avaricious. It was a nightmare of savagery, man returned to the jungle, still fashionably clad and boasting the ordinations and amulets of civilization—a staggering showing. Every paragraph contained material for a libel suit. What still puzzles one is that the men thus revealed in a delirium of lust and bestial conflict made no motion to protect themselves from the onslaught, made even no denial. The country gasped and wondered and gasped again. For a time it talked of nothing else. Then it seemed tacitly to agree that the whole thing was part of the helter-skelter and insanity of modern life and turned to something else.

Lawson was a good-looking man, past forty when I knew him, rather stocky in build, so strongly featured that anywhere he would command instant attention for his appearance. He had dark-chestnut hair, thick and curling; excellent blue eyes, steady and cool, rather heavy jaws, a well-trimmed brown mustache, and a dimpled chin. One thing that struck me as peculiar was his neck, which was short and pugnacious, shaped at the back like John L. Sullivan's, thick and bulky. He dressed with exceeding care and was well aware of his pulchritude.

He had one fad that seemed to most men inexplicable. His office in Boston contained more carved images of elephants than I have ever seen in any other one place, even in a shop devoted to such things. In the centre was a huge flat-topped writing table that had become so covered with these figures that it had been abandoned to them and another desk brought in. Every style and variety of elephant was there, carved in teak, mahogany, ebony, ivory, and all else, elephants with trunks curled up, elephants with trunks bent down, elephants with long tusks, elephants with short tusks. Alfred Henry Lewis cherished a pet theory that every man resembled some animal and, as a jungle inheritance or something, had a predilection for the thing he resembled. It is a far-fetched notion that Lawson was a reincarnated elephant, but the back of his neck did somewhat support the fantasy.

In the hey-day of his tourneying he was the centre of national attention, being hailed by many as a social savior and even as a candidate for the Presidency. To that dream he made speedy end, first by coming out in an article in which he denounced the public as made up of shrimps, and then by still more effectual means.

For he began at once to use his prestige and power to help him in his operations in the stock market. He would telegraph great advertisements, half a page at a time, to leading newspapers, advising the purchase of one stock and the selling of another. The public was not shrimp enough to fail to perceive what this meant. In fact, the public is not shrimp at all—this public. It seldom fails to detect the clinking of false metal. For a short time, Lawson was the most influential figure in the country; with almost the same swiftness he declined into obscurity. Some years later he suddenly reappeared with sensational charges that the Secretary of State and other men in the government were conniving at the rigging of the market with inside information. There was an investigation before a committee of the House of Representatives. Mr. Lawson was summoned as a witness. He made a rambling statement, unsupported by evidence. When some of the accused men went upon the stand and shattered his charges he became so excited that he had to be put into his seat by the sergeant-at-arms and finally led from the room. After this he was not again in the public eye. He died penniless—after all his daring and sometimes bewildering exploits in the market.

He was the most conspicuous of the school that afterward

came to be known as muck-rakers, but not the pioneer of the guild. An accurate history of this singular phase of American letters must acknowledge that in point of time the first of this particular group was Henry George, Jr., who appeared in *The National Magazine* with a critical exposition of the United States Steel Corporation and how it was put together. Miss Ida Tarbell's masterly survey of the Standard Oil Company eclipsed this effort and came to be a classic of its kind. All of these articles served to direct the country's attention to one invaluable and unescapable fact. It was that the passion for great and sudden wealth had bewitched men's minds to such an extent that what was called Big Business became not otherwise than a colossal and ably managed piracy, above and beyond all law, all restraint, and all moderation.

Of course muck-raking was no new thing, although it seemed to many persons only a strange outburst of a solely modern spirit. Even in this country there had been much of it years before Miss Tarbell and Thomas W. Lawson arrived upon the field. As far back as 1881 Henry Demarest Lloyd in the staid old *Atlantic* had laid bare some of the black secrets of the oil monopoly, subsequently expanded in his *Wealth Against Commonwealth*. In London, in 1885, William T. Stead had gone to jail for exposing the traffic of certain aristocrats in little girls. Newspapers had carried on many campaigns of the exposé nature. *The Herald* had exposed the operations of Ludlow Street jail and of the New York coroner's office. If we wish to go farther back, Charles Dickens did a great job in muck-raking the boys' schools of England and Charles Reade still greater when he relentlessly exposed the prison system, the private insane asylum and the old labor union of the Broadhead type. Assuredly, we lacked not precedent nor good company. Once I had the curiosity to look back at contemporaneous comment on the excursions of Dickens and Reade into these realms and found that they had been liars, rascals, and low, dangerous persons like those that now were defaming the best business men of their own time and land.

With us the impetus to these revelations was helped along by an investigation through a legislative committee of the state of New York, into the scandalous operations of the great insurance companies. Mr. Charles Evans Hughes appeared as counsel for the committee and conducted the examination of witnesses, thereby laying the foundation for his political career. Mr. Hughes bore himself with extraordinary skill. He pressed his inquisition far enough to show that the methods of the insurance companies were exceedingly bad and needed reforming but not far enough to imperil them or the men that misdirected them. It was enough to make him a popular hero and not enough to cause any financier to think him a dangerous man, and beyond this in discretion and wisdom it hardly seems possible to go.

But months before this development, all the great corporations had come to be more or less under searching scrutiny and suspicion, signalling a curious revolution in the national thought. All America had been accustomed to laud and bepraise the makers of great fortunes, inquiring not at all as to means so long as the fortune-maker kept out of the penitentiary. Money had become the touchstone and perfect measure of worth. The process of reasoning was naïve, but satisfactory. To become rich required intellect; the greater the riches the greater the intellect. Besides, these men that began with nothing, may be, and sat presently upon heaped-up sacks of wealth had a certain patriotic symbolism. They illustrated with a peculiar glory the land of opportunity. Where else were such achievements possible? Sound the loud timbrel: here was hope and blessed inspiration for us all! What these men had done, of course, others could do (with sufficient intellect), for here stood all doors open to him that had genius and industry—and that kind of thing.

Now, of a sudden, men began to discover that these great and adored fortunes had been gathered in ways that not only grazed the prison gate but imposed burdens and disadvantages upon the rest of the community; that vast hoards for one man meant so much less for others. In the shock of this discovery, a literature of exposition arose and daily the magazine editors looked for new dark, malodorous corners of money-grabbing upon which the spotlight could be turned.

Pure accident cast me, without the least desire, into the pursuit of this fashion. I had finally withdrawn from the newspaper business, and having enough money to live modestly I was bent upon carrying out a purpose long cherished in quite a different line. From my fifteenth year I had been a humble follower and disciple of Theodore Thomas. Much more than a great musical genius and the father of the American orchestra, he was of learning and research, and a thinker on many subjects. Some casual remarks of his led me to the conclusion that what we call the separate arts of music and poetry are really but one, and I now conceived that with a piano, my Swinburne, and some sheets of music paper I could demonstrate this priceless fact to a palpitating world. Upon this task I was intent when the whole business was upset with a single telegram.

One day, Mr. J. W. Midgley, who was a famous expert on railroad rates and conditions, was testifying before the Interstate Commerce Commission and let loose a flood of startling facts about the impositions practised by the owners and operators of refrigerator cars. My friend, Mr. Erman J. Ridgway, was then editor of *Everybody's Magazine*. He read of Mr. Midgley's testimony and instantly saw the chance of an exposé. Mr. Midgley lived in Chicago. So did I, at that time. Mr. Ridgway wired asking me to see Mr. Midgley and get him to write for *Everybody's* an article along the lines of his testimony. I conferred accordingly and Mr. Midgley positively refused all offers to become an exposé writer. I reported this to Ridgway and retired to the piano and the sheets of paper, blissfully unprepared for the next turn out of the box. It was a wire asking me to furnish the article *Everybody's* wanted.

I had not the least disposition to do so, except only that Ridgway was my friend and I wanted to oblige him. I thought I could get together enough material to meet the requirements of the case and return to my real employment. The next thing I knew a muck-rake was put into my hand and I was plunged into the midst of the game.

One reason why I was reluctant was reminiscent, whereby hangs a story. When we started *The American,* Mr. Hearst's journal in Chicago, there was a shortage of water supply in the city. Householders were begged and implored to conserve what we had and waste none of it, and for one summer the watering of lawns was prohibited. This in a city bordering upon Lake Michigan seemed lunatic. We had on *The American* a bright and able young reporter named James O'Shaughnessy. He acquired a notion that the reason the water supply was short was because somebody was snitching it. Encouraged by the management, he obtained a permit to dig up the streets at certain intersections near the packing houses. Then with workmen he went at night, made the excavation and discovered that the city mains had been surreptitiously tapped and certain packing houses were drawing off millions of gallons for which they paid nothing.

The revelation, not too modestly proclaimed in our columns, naturally caused a sensation, but so great was the power of the packing firms that no penalties followed, though the stealing was stopped. From my experience with this expedition I was aware of the virtually absolute power of these companies and knew that any one attacking them would have an unpleasant time. Now packing-house firms or companies were the owners of the bandit refrigerator cars. It was impossible to expose the refrigerator-car impositions without exposing also the methods of the Beef Trust, and frankly I had no taste for trouble, much preferring the amphibrac foot upon which I was then engaged. Besides, other experiences had caused me to believe that for all such things there was no real cure so long as we maintained the existing system of society.

But like it or not, I was in for it. I wrote two or three articles on the refrigerator-car scandal and then went on to write a series on the methods of the Beef Trust and was not in the least astonished to find that I was become an unmitigated scoundrel, a hired assassin of character, a libeller of good men, an enemy of society and of the government, and probably an Anarchist in disguise.

Theodore Roosevelt was then President. The packers' good friend and sturdy champion in Congress and out of it was William R. Lorimer, who for years had represented the packing-house district. Mr. Lorimer was an able politician and known as the Republican boss of Chicago. The packing houses were liberal contributors to the Republican campaign fund. One of them in the campaign of 1896 gave $200,000. Colonel Roosevelt was himself no slouch of a politician and in his own words, "a practical man"; in politics, none was more practical, or could be. When the attacks began on the Beef Trust, Mr. Lorimer assured him that the Trust was a myth and the packing houses were harmless and respectable business enterprises, operated for the public good and innocently. Roosevelt was (at that time) on most intimate terms with Lorimer and accepted this vindication at its face value. But the attacks continuing and being reinforced by vehement complaints from the cattle raisers, he instructed his Commissioner of Corporations, Mr. James R. Garfield, to make an investigation. Mr. Garfield returned a report that Mr. Lorimer himself might have written. It found that there was no trust among the packers and that the business in general was impeccable.

This finding caused the greatest satisfaction to our best business circles, to the President, and, I think, to all Right Minded Persons. A large part of the press chuckled with glee and the gentleman that was then President Roosevelt's Director of the Mint went about a million miles out of his way to write and publish articles along the same lines. The packers had a bank in Chicago and were unwilling that a good deed like this should be forgot. They made this gentleman president of their bank, which was a nice position, indeed.

But the agitation against the Beef Trust only increased. The cattle raisers of the country had long writhed under a system by which they were deprived of a normal market and forced to accept whatever prices the packing-house combination might offer. The produce commission men had been in a state bordering on revolt because of the lawless exactions practised upon them by the bandit refrigerator-car companies, which were only disguises for packing-house firms. The fruit and vegetable raisers joined in the outcry. Roosevelt saw that the tide was running all the other way. He presently decided to go along with it and became the country's embodiment of the idea of opposition to the trusts, though nobody could ever mention anything he ever did to oppose them beyond burning words uttered between large white teeth, firmly clenched.

To the Beef Trust warfare Upton Sinclair's powerful novel, *The Jungle,* was the most efficient aid; people would at any time rather take their exposé stuff in fiction.

Even before the magazine series on this subject had been completed, the writer of it was engaged upon another. Indeed, we were all up and away, full of the pleasures of the chase, I suppose, or something of the kind, and all that business about poetry and the music sheets forgotten. It was exhilarating sport, hunting the money octopus. *Puck* printed a cartoon in which we all appeared, lance in rest, furiously charging. Everything that had a crooked look was certain to be upturned to the public gaze. Lawson continued his breath-taking disclosures, Samuel Hopkins Adams pilloried the men that were imposing upon the nation with patent-medicine nostrums. Wherever an exploiter showed his head we were ready with a brick to heave at it. John L. Mathews wrote the first exposures of the Water-Power Trust and predicted its rise to perilous and overshadowing might. Ray Stannard Baker attacked the injustice with which colored people were treated in the South, and shed additional light upon the railroad evils. "Every man that has a million dollars must show how he got them, for he is under suspicion," said Charles Michelson. The histories of various utility enterprises were recalled to show that virtually all had been attended with fraud and swindling on a gigantic scale. Fortunes that had been admired as evidence of the glorious opportunity existing in our happy land, turned into exceedingly shabby exploits in thimble-rigging. Gustavus Myers came out with his *History of the Great American Fortunes,* in which he shattered any fiction that any of these had been made honestly. *Everybody's Magazine* took up the terrible conditions in the Southern prison camps and forced at least a temporary improvement.

The crusade swept into politics and headed for a wholesale redemption. In the election of November, 1905, Mr. Hearst was a candidate for mayor of New York on a platform of public ownership, no bosses, and a general cleaning up, thereby threatening privilege on its two most stupendous angles, exploitation and Tammany. On the face of the returns he came exceedingly near to election. So many scandalous irregularities were employed to beat him, there was so much repeating and fraudulent registration, that many persons believed he had been honestly elected but had been counted out as Henry George had been counted out in 1886. Subsequent investigation showed that the fraud had not been committed in the counting of votes but in registration and illegal voting. About a year later *The*

"THE CRUSADERS"

Puck's visualization of muck-raking

Cosmopolitan Magazine printed a series of articles on election frauds, how they were committed, and why. A member of the New York Assembly conferred with the writer of the articles and introduced the present election law, which makes fraudulent voting all but impossible and gave to New York the first honest elections it had known in its history.

Early in the game, *McClure's Magazine,* in which Miss Tarbell's work had appeared, broadened the inquiry to take in again the good old subject of graft in city governments, and on this quest Lincoln Steffens had started his extraordinary series called *The Shame of the Cities.* One of the cities in which shame was then at its worst was Minneapolis and in sifting out the truth concerning Minneapolis Steffens achieved what must always remain among the great historic feats of reporting. He managed to obtain the ledger in which the graft collectors entered the sums they collected and the persons to whom the money was paid—obtained it and photographed its pages. Against such evidence as this the usual cries of "liar!" and "scoundrel!" fell flat and Minneapolis had no escape from the duty of cleansing herself.

One rather curious element that entered into the enormous success of Steffens' articles may afford to the philosophical a glimpse of humor in the midst of a fairly grimy chapter. It was a roundabout touch upon that racial prejudice from which the Nordic seems powerless to free himself. Frequently the bribe-taking aldermen in our great cities, and still more frequently the political bosses that managed the huge system of graft, were of foreign birth. This mightily relieved the mind of the native patriot. Always he had felt that these low foreigners would bring the nation to ruin and if with shame he must contemplate the total iniquity he had at least the consolation of the prophet approved. It was to be noted that this soothing emollient was best when the name of the offending alderman or political boss began with an O or a Mac. Long had the patriot felt that these Irishmen in politics boded trouble. Look at Tammany Hall!

Then Mr. Steffens reached Philadelphia, the most American city in America, and showed that the corruption elsewhere looked almost like purity compared with the Philadelphia brand. But was the complacency of the native patriot disturbed? Not in the least. He had a congealed belief that all the trouble was of foreign origin and nothing could melt it out of him. It was vain even to show him the roster roll of the grafters in Philadelphia and invite him to pick a name not conspicuously native. As vain as to call his attention to the fact that Philadelphia was the only city on the continent where a band of corrupt aldermen having for graft given away a public franchise closed the doors and sang in derision:

> Hail, hail, the gang's all here,
> What the hell do we care, what the hell do we care?

That Nordic belief in the futility of all effort that does not reap a swift and tangible result—how many an illustration we had, before we were through, of the trouble that fantasy can make! Yet it is but another evidence of uncompleted thought, again a Nordic inheritance. In truth any effort for any good cause is worth while although it may seem at the time as vain as thorns crackling. As to which kindly note the next incident.

One day early in 1905, I was sitting in the press gallery of the United States Senate observing the proceedings which were, as usual, but languid. Directly in front of me on the floor below was a row of well-fed and portly gentlemen, every one of whom, we knew perfectly well, was there to represent some private (and predatory) Interest. Each was supposed to represent the people; each was in fact representing some division of the people's enemy. Looking over the rest of the Senate, I was struck with the patent fact that almost nobody in that chamber had any other reason to be there than his skill in valeting for

some powerful Interest, and I thought a series of articles might
well be written on the fact that strictly speaking we had no
Senate; we had only a chamber of butlers for industrialists and
financiers.

When I returned to New York I outlined my idea to Mr.
Hearst, who had lately bought *The Cosmopolitan.* He liked it
and I had begun to accumulate facts when I received an assignment from *Everybody's Magazine* to go around the world and
write of popular movements in different countries. My task
for Mr. Hearst was passed along to David Graham Phillips,
in whose hands it finally took shape in his notable series called
The Treason of the Senate.

Phillips wielded a scathing pen and when aroused on a
question of right and wrong spared nobody. His vitriolic attacks on the Senatorial Brotherhood of Bankers' Footmen
aroused furious indignation. In about the fourth installment
he scored unmercifully certain friends and political cronies
of President Roosevelt. This moved Roosevelt to his celebrated "muck-raker" outburst in which he denounced us all as
defamers of the good and the true, but shot chiefly at Phillips.
In its real source his phrase, which was from John Bunyan's
allegory, was not happily chosen. As a matter of fact, the
creature that Bunyan pilloried was the creature that we were
pursuing, the man that wastes his life in raking in the muck
for money. But Roosevelt managed to fasten the name upon us
and thus to check crusading. Phillips remained philosophical
under this thrust and continued his series, but the next turn
found him far less stoical. When the series ended, there appeared in *Collier's* a savage attack upon it and its author and I
had an anxious time with him that Sunday, walking him
around the streets while I tried to comfort and console him
under the blow. He was terribly cut up, but need not have
been. If he had once considered the philosophy of reform he
would have laughed the whole thing off and thought no more

of it. For of course, every muck-raker is a liar, a slanderer, a calumniator, and a low, dangerous person, and cannot possibly be otherwise. Every man that objects to any existing condition and tries to change it is a bad man and always has been. All reformers are rascals. Good men are always perfectly content with things as they are and recognize clearly in them the divine command, to oppose which is impiety toward God and treason against the state. Whenever a depraved reformer suggests any change in this holy and perfectly authenticated order, there is first laughter, then contempt, then alarm, then a rapid banding together of the forces of righteousness, then a struggle with the subversive red element trying to overturn the Constitution, then a glorious victory for the right and the total defeat of the forces of unrest.

Then the good men, having vindicated their superior virtue and the perfect state of everything in general, presently proceed in a quiet way to remedy the evil complained of and to that extent straighten their walk.

It was so in this instance. *Collier's* was by no means the only organ of the Right Minded that pronounced a sentence of scorn and damnation upon poor David Graham. The reactionary press rang with his name as chief among sinners, while the President was everywhere praised for rebuking the slanderers of the upright and the good. And when all the excitement had subsided, virtue had been vindicated, and all that, the men Phillips had named were one by one retired from the Senate until scarcely one was left. More than that, the *Treason of the Senate* had a powerful effect in furthering the great reform that took from the legislatures the power to elect Senators and put it into the hands of the people, where it belonged.

But Phillips could never see the good he had wrought and to the end regarded his series as the one failure of his career. Failure! Few exploits in muck-raking have achieved a more certain success. In his time the Senate was probably the most reactionary legislative body on the face of the earth, being popularly known as "the Rich Men's Club." From that condition it changed in a few years and became the truly popular branch of the national assembly and led whatever progress was achieved by legislation.

But muck-rakers we were thereafter. Wonderful is the power of an epithet. That one word so applied did more to discredit reform and assist financial buccaneering than the whole mass of newspaper and other literature published in defense of the buccaneers. They were supposed to hate Roosevelt. He himself diligently fostered that notion. "Wall Street expects every lion to do his duty," he said to his newspaper friends as he was sailing for his African hunting. As a matter of fact, he was Wall Street's white-haired boy and the real extent of his antipathy to its operations was finally disclosed when Mr. Hearst made public the secret correspondence of the boldest of the financial crew. Probably no other man in history has ever made so great a reputation on so slight a basis.

Many of the magazine editors took fright at the Presidential command and abandoned exposé stuff. Others continued it, more or less timidly. There were other forces than any emanating from the White House, and more ruthless, to check the tide. Speaking at a chamber of commerce banquet in a Western town, the president of a New York City bank made the emphatic declaration that there would be no more muck-raking in this country. In plain terms he declared that business had suffered all the attacks it intended to endure and that the slanderers of the leaders of the nation's commerce would be silenced.

He was right. Silenced they were and without delay. And the manner in which the silencing was done, of which you are soon to hear, may seem of considerable philosophic interest.

The public did not wish to have it stopped, if circulation figures mean anything. In 1907 there was a feeble magazine in New York called *The Broadway,* mostly devoted to stories a little off color and to pictures of undraped ladies. It had a total circulation of about 12,000, none of which it deserved. One of the most successful advertising agents of that day was Benjamin B. Hampton, a man of unusual parts and capacity. He bought the tottering *Broadway* and in three years built its circulation to 480,000 chiefly by intelligent muck-raking. One of his earlier feats was a series of articles on the rotten tenement houses owned by Trinity Church, among the worst and most dangerous in all the tenement-house cursed city. The series, with its photographs of conditions and its array of indubitable facts, started a cyclone of resentment, particularly in our highest social circles. A talented playwright made a drama of the series and Olga Nethersole acted it with great success, despite a furious denunciation from all the best elements. The whole front of righteousness and Things as They Are was livid with rage. George Harvey, with the aid of constant subventions from the rich, was then conducting *Harper's Weekly* as an organ of respectability. He dutifully burst into screams of indignation. Muck-raking had now attacked not only the financial stability of the nation but our citadel of faith and religion. Many articles appeared in many quarters condemning the author of the Trinity series as even more depraved than the rest of his hellish crew. To the writers of some of these outbursts he put one question.

"You say these tenement houses are not really bad. Would you like to live in one of them? Take the best of them all. Would you like to live in it?"

And the answer was always the same.

"No, but it is good enough for the people that dwell in it."

"How do you know it is good enough?"

"Well, that's all they are fitted for."

I submit these questions and answers as a pleasing illustration of the mind of superior virtue—at that time.

The Reverend Morgan Dix, chief pastor of Trinity, died in

the midst of the engagement and it was poignantly suggested that grief and chagrin over the attacks upon his corporation had caused his death. Muck-raking had become murder.

The smoke of battle finally cleared away. Trinity had the usual vindication, the wickedness of the muck-raker was satisfactorily demonstrated and all was once more peace. Then Trinity began quietly to pull down its objectionable tenements. According to a worker in the Tenement House Bureau, in the next three years some scores of these filthy old barracks disappeared from the face of the earth.

Chapter X

NORDIC BLESSINGS IN INDIA

A BDUL KHAN—Mohammedan of the Mohammedans, tall, spare, as dark in hue as the average American Negro, finely featured, thin delicate nostrils, keen black eyes, black crisping hair, black curling beard, clothed from neck to heel in spotless white that made contrast with his bright red turban and black beard—he was a sight not to be forgotten. The more notable because of his bearing, which was of an incomparable stateliness; for he went plumb-line straight, carried his head with a bit of quiet defiance, and had about his blazing black eyes something almost daunting and undeniably wary, appraising, and suspicious.

By profession he was what is called in India a "bearer." Why, I do not know; I never saw him bear anything. In reality he functioned as guide, courier, interpreter, and instructor of the swallow-flight tourists. All of that order migratory in India must have such service. For most of the unloved guild the duties also include valeting. The rest is necessary; the valeting is pure snobbery.

It was Mr. Khan's fixed habit to keep his English-speaking employers under a careful observation quite devoid of trust. "Yes, sir," "No, sir," "This way, sir," "That is the Jain temple, sir," was about all the conversational pleasure he allowed himself, and but for an accident we might have gone through India and known no more of him as he really was than was to be gleaned from these and the like desiccated comments. The

148

accident revealed to him that whatever other errors we might entertain, we were under no illusion as to the real nature of the British occupation of India. When at last he had mastered this phenomenon, when he had enwrapped it in the tentacles of his mind and absorbed it as verity, he registered joy in a way unconventional and highly embarrassing. Of a sudden, he flopped to the floor and tried to embrace my knees. Being raised from this position, he declared with some mystic insignia beyond my ken that Abdul Khan was my friend for life, which, incidentally, he proved to be. We had previously been able to cure him of the habit of addressing his tourist as "master," which is the badge of the bearer tribe most disconcerting to the stranger in search of tolerable comfort in Indian travel.

It appeared that when this wary and resolute son of Mahomet gave at last his reluctant confidence he gave it without reservations. In many ways the change made for the betterment of impartial inquiry in his unhappy land, for it furthered the clearing of mysteries. For example, why the attitude of the generality of British was toward the generality of the dusky people Britain had assumed to govern an attitude of gratuitous arrogance and overlordship.

Let us have a few illustrations from scenes of life in India as I knew it:

What is called there a European, which means merely a white man, was coming down the broad, handsome stairway of the Taj Mahal hotel. Midway of the long flight a native was at work chasing the last elusive speck of dust. Intent upon this precious task he did not notice the approach of the representative of the superior race. Of a sudden he looked up, terror swept his countenance, and swiftly he fled like one detected in a crime. At the bottom he turned, flattened himself against the wall, and so stood quaking until the stranger had passed.

It was against the unwritten but still invincible code of India for an Indian to meet a European on a staircase.

The visitor went out and rode about the city in a carriage. Everywhere the native policemen saluted him as he passed. He was of no more rank or station than the town pump, but the policemen invariably saluted. He was white. By the unwritten but iron code they must salute all white men in carriages that all natives might be reminded of the white man's superiority and their own lowliness.

In a by-street a native walked on a sidewalk, carrying upon his head an inverted basket with a heavy wooden rim. The basket limited his vision. A European met him on one side and struck the basket a savage blow, adding a curse. The rim rang sharply upon the native's head and he uttered a gasp of pain. The next instant another European struck the basket upon the other side and again drove the rim against the native's head. He uttered another gasp of pain. The second European cursed like the first. The native had no right to carry a basket on the sidewalk. The place for him was the pavement with the other beasts.

In the rooms of a hotel at Rangoon was posted a notice that read thus:

Guests are respectfully requested not to beat or strike the native servants. Please report all causes for complaint to the manager, who will do what is necessary in the premises.

Once we saw what was deemed necessary and how it was administered. By the manager. With a long blacksnake whip.

At the Residency grounds at Lucknow an intelligent native showed us about, explaining the different points of historic interest connected with the siege. When we approached the ruins of the Residency building he asked to be excused and said we must make our way without him. It was fifty years since the siege and yet no native was allowed to enter that building. Natives must still be reminded of their futile revolt and of the dreadful things at the Alumbaugh.

At all times we were under watchful though not unkindly

scrutiny to see that we failed not to coincide with the general scheme of race superiority. At Bombay we had developed a strong liking for Abdul Khan and talked with him as we should with any other fellow creature. An English subaltern observing this came close and said:

"Excuse me, you know, but really I must caution you against treating your boy there [meaning Abdul] in this way. You will ruin him for service. Really, you know, one mustn't be polite to these people. It puts false notions into their heads. It is necessary to be strict with them."

I made inquiry as to why this was necessary. He said:

"Well, you see, there are 300,000,000 of them and only 140,-000 of us and we've got to keep them in their place."

Often the place-keeping operation seemed to be going on with awkward joltings. Ostensibly the natives submitted to it with a stoical patience, but he must have been an unskilled observer that could not see the signs of resentment. In cities like Calcutta, Bombay, Delhi, and Agra, where the Sikh policemen were at every corner and detachments of soldiers marched to and fro, it was one thing. But when one visited Jaipur, for example, where a native prince and native government still ruled and the total European population was a score or so, the situation was different and distinctly uncomfortable. Novel experience for the superior race to be in a position where its superiority was so openly challenged and hardly demonstrable! For Jaipur could get along perfectly well without the white man and frankly desired to do so. And to ride through its streets and encounter only ugly looks and muttered curses and clenched fists in that vast disparity of numbers was nothing to pleasure the nervous.

But what the natives felt and showed at Jaipur they felt and concealed (more or less) in other places. The notion that such frightful license of revenge as attended the failure of the Revolution of 1857 could be erased from a people's mind, or could fail of results troublous to the rulers, was merely mad. The British thought they understood the Hindu. They never understood him. They do not understand him now. Every cannon shot at the Alumbaugh that scattered a native in hideous fragments over the plain was registered in the Indian mind and assured there of red fruitage.

"I hate the English," said Abdul Khan, when he became communicative. "Every Indian hates the English. He may not show it; it is there in his heart all the time. All castes [meaning religions] just the same—Mohammedan, Hindu, Jain, all the same. My father, he fought in the war in 1857. When I was a little boy he used to take me on his knee often and tell me about that war. All about it. He told me what the English did. He told me, 'This is what the English have done. Never forget it. Keep it in your mind as long as you live and hate the English. Teach your sons to hate them. Some day there will be a chance to drive them out of India. In your time, may be, in your sons' time. Whenever it comes, be ready for it.'"

He said his father had been at the defense of Delhi where he had captained a gun, and he showed us from the city wall the spot where the gun had been placed.

I said that all the histories of those days that I had been able to find referred to the disturbance as a mutiny—the Sepoy Mutiny was its fixed name in history. He said it was no mutiny; it was a revolution, the great majority of the people sympathized with it, and it had for its object the ending of British rule in India. Also, that it would have succeeded but for the native princes. They helped the British.

"Mutiny!" he said. "The Rani of Jhansi—would she have fought in a mutiny?"

We talked much about the uprising, with the history of which he seemed rather astonishingly familiar. The whole story is a memorable illumination of the fatuity of human judgment, the folly of reprisals and the perils of that view of mankind that accepts surface demarcations as evidences of profound inward differences. So nearly as one can make out now, the British of that day took no more pains to learn the psychology of the people they assumed to rule than they expended upon horses, donkeys, and dogs. The British theory of superiority was to the British mind so manifestly just and right that it was open to no question. According to subsequent testimony there had been for months or years abundant evidences of restlessness among the governed people. Plain warnings were disregarded. The patient and inviting stoicism of the natives was taken at its face value. Always they had submitted to the superior race, therefore always they would submit. Abdul assured me the matter of the greased cartridges was but an incident—the striking of the match when the train had been well laid. The British thought it was the beginning and the end. Their indifference to the mentality around them was fatal. They remedied the complaint about the cartridges and believed all was again settled forever. The next moment the storm burst and caught them unaware, first that May day at Meerut, 1857, and then everywhere.

Then they thought with a showing of frightfulness to stay the flood. It seems to have gone only the faster. Little has been said about this phase of the red story, but it appears that the British initiated the policy of ruthless cruelty and when Nana Sahib ordered the appalling slaughter at Cawnpore he was but following and exceeding a lesson already abundantly set for him. The tale of villages destroyed, of ferocious floggings, of innocent persons wholly unconnected with the revolt that were sent with the rebels to instant death, is not a chapter likely to add anything to Nordic glory. When at last after stern and often doubtful battlings, the better guns, better training, better discipline, aided by the native princes, had subdued the revolution, the British thought (not unnaturally, perhaps, in view of their equivocal position in the country) that there should be exacted so terrible a punishment as should vindicate race superiority and discourage forever any impulse to the like disobedience. They carried out that purpose with a relentless fury that surfeited revenge and at home appalled even some of their own countrymen.

One of the punishments devised by victorious Superiority and inflicted upon captured insurgents was to tie them over the mouths of heavily shotted cannon and then discharge the cannon. If any one entertains now a doubt that this was done at the Alumbaugh and elsewhere, one has but to refer to the records. In Ball's two-volume *History of the Indian Mutiny,* Volume I, opposite page 410, one will find a picture of this operation, showing a gun exploding and fragments of an Indian hurtling through the air. It appears that some of the bystanders were struck by the flying pieces, heads or legs or arms, and complained that the guns were too heavily loaded. That seems to have been the only complaint in the ranks of the Superior.

The operation may have made revolt impossible for the rest of that generation, but it had etched in fire an ineradicable hatred upon the Indian mind and after seventy-five years the results were apparent in the most difficult and dangerous problem the British Empire had ever encountered.

For India is the keystone of the imperial arch. If that goes, all goes, and the most resolutely optimistic of Britons cannot fail to see the keystone slipping. It is saved one year by one desperate and devious expedient and next year by another, but it slips, nevertheless. The choice that really presents itself to the imperialist is between more Amritsars and infinitely greater, more turning of machine guns upon defenseless peoples, more slaughters, more tigerish conflicts, more hatred and more seed sowing for future revenge, or the invention of constantly new tricks to win for another brief span another delaying of the inevitable clash. And when it comes the discerning will hear in it the echoing guns of the Alumbaugh.

For they will not learn, these rulers, they will not learn; therefore they are unfit to rule even if their motives were pure as the driven snow, still unfit to rule. The horrors of the revenge of Superiority after the revolt of 1857 are indelible in the Indian mind, yet must they be burned deeper by other acts of wanton and savage cruelty reminiscent of the Apaches. As note:

January 14, 1872, fifteen years after the Alumbaugh, a band of mad fanatics, about one hundred all told, made an attack upon a town of the Punjab and were easily beaten off and captured. Religious fanatics they were, Sikhs and so on, not political plotters. So what was done with the madmen? Forty-nine of them were tied over the mouths of cannon and shot to pieces, fashion of the Alumbaugh. No trial, no inquiry, no delay; bind the captives, tie them thus, now the match and so an end, with natives to gather up the pieces and clean away the blood. Good work for the natives; teaches them to respect Superiority.

Yes, but there is more still. It is April, 1919, sixty-four years after the suppression of the Rebellion; there is unrest among the Inferiors, agitation, aspirations for freedom, arguings against an alien domination. Meetings of the dissatisfied are held, there is what is called disloyal talk, though how an Indian that talks for India can be disloyal is a puzzle. Criminals take advantage of the prevailing unrest to come into the open and practise their iniquities. Some commit murders, some robberies, some arson. The British commandant in his own words thinks it necessary to teach the mob a lesson and to strike terror into the native hearts everywhere. A peaceful meeting of unarmed folk is held in a public square. The British commander turns his machine guns upon it and kills then and there about 1200 men, women, and children, wounding more than 3000.

I think I will let one of the victims speak of it. She is a native woman and she is testifying under oath in a court. She is asked:

Q. When did you come to know of your husband's having been killed in the square?
A. Soon after the firing I heard in my street that thousands had been killed. I got very anxious and I thought of going to the square at once. Two female neighbors went with me. I saw the whole place full of dead bodies. I went around and looked for my husband among the dead bodies. I had to pull my husband's body from under a heap of dead bodies. There were pools of blood all over the place.

The witness then described her failure to get help to carry her husband's body home and went on:

I turned back and came to the side of my husband's dead body. I remained watching there the whole night. I had to watch the dead body with a stick in hand because there were dogs about. About 2 A.M. I heard the groans of a wounded Sikh. I went to his help and put his wounded leg in position. There was a wounded boy of about twelve years of age that kept crying the whole night. He was entreating me the whole time not to leave the place, as he was very much terrified. There was another man crying for water in a most piteous manner. No water was to be had there and I felt helpless. Except the cries of the wounded, the only thing I heard was the barking of dogs and the braying of donkeys. At 6 A.M. Sundar Das came with a cot. We then brought the dead body of my husband home and later took it to the cremation ground.[1]

Year 1919, at the hands of Christian Superiors. Trying to shoot the gospel of Jesus into subject races. Is it any wonder the Indians hate the British name?

But we are not yet done with this story. To demonstrate to the world beyond question the extent of the superiority of the Superiors they opened a public subscription for a testimonial to the general that ordered the butchery.

In this way was obtained a purse of $150,000, which was presented as the gift of a grateful people. Few men of our time have had more substantial tokens of public approval. No touch of the Dark Ages seemed lacking except a Te Deum in St.

[1] Quoted by Edwin Thompson, *The Other Side of the Medal*, pages 115–16.

Paul's. But that April day is fixed in the Indian calendar and every year it is observed with mourning—and menaces.[1]

It is urged as some excuse for the gift that the heroic recipient, having been dismissed from the army, had lost his pension. Surely, if one can find in this the least palliation for a backward lapse so significant, one should make the most of it.

There are two hoary old fables about India that are overdue to be eliminated from the judicious mind. The first is that England is in India for India's good. As a matter of fact, she is there for her own profit and for nothing else under the sun. The pretense of altruism is no more than a peculiarly flagrant flaunting of the racial hypocrisy. Casting up all to account, debit and credit, the net result is that England in India has been more of an injury than a benefit. Oh, yes! Full weight is given here to the achievements about Suttee and Thuggism. It was well to break up the band of Thugs, although their numbers and menace were alike small in comparison with the total population. The practice of Suttee, revolting to the Occidental mind, was not revolting to the Oriental. The superstition was that by ending her life in this terrible way the widow attained to supreme bliss in heaven. It was racial. Well may we remember, before we condemn, that all races have their superstitions, including our own. The superstition of the widow's attainment of bliss by horrible self-slaughter was more directly and obviously fatal than the superstition that life consists of snatching bread from one another's lips, but may be doubted to have done more harm in the world. The mere fact that we commonly, nay, almost invariably, refuse to recognize any psychological process different from our own might in itself be counted as a superstition if it were only intelligent enough to attain to that distinction.

[1] In an American magazine some time after, a titled Englishman appeared with an article defending the general for the ordering of the massacre at Amritsar on the ground that it was necessary and declaring that the United States had done the same thing under similar circumstances, but omitting a citation. *Tu quoque*—if that is a defense.

Against the suppression of Thuggee and Suttee is to be placed the black fact that in 150 years of rule, England had established no national system of education, that the percentage of illiteracy was greater than it had been when England took charge, that, so far as the records indicate, the people of India were happier, richer, and more prosperous under their native rulers and native system than they have been under the English.

In 1750, almost every Indian village had its school and probably 60 per cent of the population was literate. The schools have perished under British rule; today, 90 per cent of the population is illiterate. Nay, I understate the indictment. Total population, 320,000,000; total of literates in any language, 22,-600,000.[1] After 150 years. Are these people fit to govern?

In these 150 years, England had done nothing to relieve the poverty of the teeming Indian masses but had only exploited them.

You do not know what the word poverty means until you have looked at typical Indian villages and assimilated the fact that as these wretched beings before you breathe, spawn and fester in their human rabbit-warrens, so breathe, spawn and fester millions upon millions of other fellow creatures of yours in a land that is potentially the richest on earth.

Well, how do they live?

In inconceivable mud huts, perhaps twelve feet by fourteen, often smaller, with a thatched roof, no window, a doorway with a strip of calico or bamboo for a door, one such hovel to a family —so live millions upon millions of them and never know anything else. Pigs are not usually housed so anywhere in America. So their fathers lived, so their children will live, and the government over them has cared not a rap.

For this the excuse is urged that it is impossible to induce these people to live otherwise because the East is the East and the West is the West and nothing else is so comical as the

[1] *Statesmen's Year Book.*

American or European that thinks any improvement can be introduced in India.

So sang Kipling, Poet Laureate of All Reaction; so echo all the wise men of the West that come East to pick up good profits.

Yes. But the same things used to be said about Turkey, exactly the same. The Sick Man of Europe was beyond all help or hope. Never would a new idea be tolerated on that soil; all must go on forever traversing the same monotonous everlasting invariable routine, around and around. And then came Kemal Pasha and with a turn of the hand, Turkey underwent the greatest and swiftest transformation ever recorded among men. Let no man sing again that the East is the East and the West is the West, but let him remember that the Caliph was flung forth without ceremony and that on the prayer rugs of the Mosque of Omar operates today a vacuum cleaner.

But the point of the indictment against British rule is not so much that it has done nothing to abolish the mud hut; it has not tried to do so and has not seemed to care.

No doubt there are and have been innumerable kindly souls among the exploiting people that have looked with commiseration upon these miserable millions. I am not speaking of them. I am speaking of the ideas that have ruled the ruling class and the government, and as nearly as I could ever make out these ideas may be summed thus:

We are the Superior Race and were so created. They are the Inferior Race and were so created. It is the divine will. Let it go at that.

Now it is quite useless for any one to urge upon me that there are child marriages in India, that the people have ways that are strange to us, that they are superstitious and believe in a million gods. I know nothing in these conditions that justifies the government over them in allowing them to live like moles and die like flies. Elsewhere in modern times government exists to further the welfare of the people governed. In India it exists to enable Manchester cotton-mill owners to become rich or richer and other aliens to have great salaries and pensions.

It is India that has made England wealthy, and making it wealthy has made it powerful.

But come back once more to poverty in this land once the richest in the world. I say to you that the spectacle of a typical native village in India, or still more, of the flimsy mud huts that cluster under the walls of an Indian city, is enough to shake one's belief in triumphant humanity.

The furnishing of these wretched lairs is below the barest needs of human existence—a pot or two, a few rags, sometimes a make-shift bedstead. Floors of mud, walls of mud; not an object however poor or sorry to suggest beauty or relief from the drudgery of daily grubbing. If there is handy the wall of a compound it will be plastered with the manure picked up by little children as it falls in the road and exposed to be sun-dried for fuel. The thatched roof is scarcely high enough to enable an average man to stand upright. In the monsoon season come the heavy rains when work outside is impossible. Then the whole family sits upon its heels in these dark and dismal dens, inert, damp, unspeakably miserable, without even the animal sufficiency of hibernating bears. For of the whole 150,-000,000 or so of ryots in India the mass goes underfed from birth to the grave. "There are 350,000,000 of human beings in what you call Christendom," protested Wendell Phillips, "and 200,000,000 of them do not have enough to eat." What he would have said if he could have seen India, I know not, but here on the richest soil under the sun, the majority of the population goes half starved; yes, even in the best of times, half starved. And then come famines, unnecessary famines, huge ironic famines, that make civilization and Christianity and progress look contemptible, and sweep off millions.

Millions, said I. And you thought it an exaggeration or a

figure of speech. Yes? Since the beginning of the present happy century of Christian peace and good will to men, more persons have perished of famine in India than were slain in the World War. Humanity cried out against the horrors of the battlefield. They were like tender mercy compared with the unspeakable horrors of the famine areas. And observe that these visitations, instead of diminishing under the rule of Great Britain have increased in number and in fatalities.[1] Look at the figures. Divide into quarters the nineteenth century. Here are the reported deaths from famine in each.

PERIOD	NUMBER OF FAMINES	DEATHS IN EACH
1800–1825	5	1,000,000
1825–1850	2	400,000
1850–1875	6	5,000,000
1875–1900	18	15,000,000 to 25,000,000

In the great famine of 1900–1902, more than 10,000,000 persons perished and since then even these appalling figures have been exceeded. If you have ever examined the photographs taken in the Indian famine of 1900 you must be haunted still by their fearful revelations.

And no less by their unanswerable indictment of the governing nation that would allow such conditions and thereby prove itself unfit to govern anything. If there were nothing else to destroy in the eyes of the world the last claim of Great Britain to remain another day in India it is the record of the Indian famines.

But come back to these mud huts. Take a look at the beings that dwell therein. Note their bony frames and gaunt faces; these would be enough, but stay long enough to notice their expressions of fixed melancholy. They seem incapable of

---

[1] If minded to pursue farther this subject, look into an illuminating book, *India in Bondage,* written by a returned missionary, the Reverend Doctor J. T. Sunderland. After that the cry of the "White Man's Burden" will be fairly fulsome in your ears.

laughter. I think a happy child would be so rare among them he would be viewed as a portent. Grave-faced and sombre little men and women, these children. Who ever saw Indian children playing, or romping, or running with laughter after a kite or a ball? Kipling says they are a sad-faced lot. They are, but Kipling does not inquire why they are sad. Neither does any other Englishman. Nor care. It is so because it is so. Let us drive on to the gymkhana.

And if the children are sad that should be merry, having tasted so little as yet of the bitterness of life, what shall be said of these mournful women, young or old? For years seem to have nothing to do with it. There is not upon this earth, I am convinced, another company like theirs, with so profound a melancholy looking from their eyes and so brooding a shadow of fate that is much more than the unescapable curse of drudgery and pain. The typical Indian woman is a figure of her nation, born into bondage and doomed to drag out an existence without hope. It is the sad-visaged, silent children and the sorrowful, wistful faces of the women that most of all make this land the symbol of despair. Truly, life without hope—it is the living death.

There are these frightful huts and frightful people and frightful conditions around each great bustling thriving city. Delhi, for example. Masses of miserable people dwell thus, fed upon a handful of rice a day, sleeping on rags, living worse than horses live. Yes. And when I was in Delhi the memory was still strong of the last Durbar—a marvellous spectacle, millions upon millions of pounds spent in a senseless and barbaric display over the crowning of another king on the other side of the globe. Just that. Millions of pounds spent upon a pageantry to celebrate this dreary event, the native princes coming covered with spangles and gee-gaws, all tricked out in the gorgeous native costumes, seed pearls and diamonds, rubies and emeralds, estimated soberly in bushels, trains of kow-towing servants, music brought from far off, special lighting, colorful picturings, every conceivable flash or glitter of glory, and outside the wretched masses, cowering in the mud huts.

All about these huts and their inhabitants are the potentialities of wealth and comfort for every one. As you ride through India you will notice great areas of land that produce nothing. It is unfertile then? you ask. Oh, no; it is exceedingly fertile, but it is owned in some great estate and the rajah or princeling or sensualist or fattened parasite that owns it does not care to have it cultivated. He is in London being entertained, or in Calcutta being flattered, or he is amusing himself with his women, or gone hunting, or something. He does not care, his lackeys do not care, nobody cares.

In the last analysis this delectable state of sans souci seems to include the government. Its business is not to bother about the hut dwellers, but to maintain the British supremacy that profits may be good and the golden tide halt not. Such are the fruits of imperialism.

I have said that famines in India were unnecessary. Let us look into that. Indian famines result from drought and failure of the water supply. But how a failure of water supply? The rainfall in some parts of India is the heaviest in the world. In the dry season the Jumna River is a trickling stream stealing timidly between baking banks. In the wet season it is a torrent a mile wide rushing to the sea. If the water supply were properly conserved there would never be a shortage, there would never be a famine in India. In 1900 the British had been for 140 years in possession of the country and had provided no adequate system of water conservation. Then another famine came and these millions died of it in agonies that sicken you now to read of.

Then a water conservation system is begun but still inadequately and the scant supply of water is sold at a price no poor ryot can afford.

The fruits of imperialism, the deadening blight upon oppressor and oppressed, exploiter and exploited. Here you can see it all.

An American friend of mine reported a conversation he heard among highly superior individuals at a time when bubonic plague was raging and other millions were being snatched by it from the mud-hut existence.

"Isn't the plague very bad there in Cawnpore?" says one, toying with his gold cigarette case.

"Oh, yes," says the other, "but it is confined entirely to the natives, you know, so we are not alarmed."

At last what is called by a pleasant convention medical science gets up a serum that when injected into the veins of these low, obstinate creatures, always so stupidly prone to fall sick with the plague, may heal them. Or else it will keep them from having it, I forget which. Twenty dutiful Inferiors are stood in a line and the bug extract shot into their arms, and eighteen of the twenty drop dead at once. These natives are so unreasonable.

It is not in nature that these conditions should last without murmuring and insubordination; would not be in nature if there were no poignant memories of cannon slaughtering and the like to goad to unrest. But the Superiors have thought of this contingency; thought of it deeply and well, thought of it much more than about famines and water supply. No native is allowed to have a weapon; no firearms, no gun, pistol, no knife with a blade longer than so many inches. No visitor is allowed to carry in any kind of firearm. If he has a revolver it is taken from him to be restored when he leaves the country. Periodical searches are made of hut thatches and the like lest by chance the law should be disobeyed and some Inferior have secreted a fowling piece or pistol or knife with a blade an inch too long. Wise and careful government, it overlooks nothing —along these lines. Profits must be safeguarded. Yes. And yet even I was made aware that all the time arms were being passed over the border from Afghanistan and secreted in nooks and corners the Superior mind had not discovered.

Because, under the Inferior's attitude of stoical resignation dwelt unextinguished, unsubdued, the passion for freedom and the passion for revenge, and it was no difficult trick for the obsequious babu in the sahib's prosperous store to say "Yes, sir," "No, sir," "As you wish, sir," and have all the time in his heart a thought of murder.

They dwelt upon the crust of a volcano, the happy, well-fed Superiors, with their five meals a day, their elegant amusements, their exclusive society. They counted on the lesson of the cannon practise at the Alumbaugh. They forgot that the heart of the Inferior is exactly like the heart of every other human being. And they forgot the Rani of Jhansi.

This young and beautiful woman, deserving of an imperishable place among the heroines of history, was the queen of Jhansi, one of the territories fraudulently annexed by the British. At the outbreak of the Revolution she threw herself into it with an amazing energy, donned the uniform of a soldier, marched, fought and bivouacked with her troops, was at the front in many battles, led charge after charge, and when killed at last was found still grasping her sword, facing the foe and with all her wounds in front.

The British counted upon the Alumbaugh as a great deterrent, and I think most of them counted securely upon the devil's own institution of caste.

Not all of them. I know there were kind-hearted and wide-visioned among the Superiors that felt the evils of this system and some even that tried to discourage and combat it. Many of the sincere missionaries did this. They could hardly do otherwise and preach with any aplomb the fatherhood of God. But I am equally sure that the governing class and its fringing congeries looked upon caste as an asset and sedulously upheld it. So long as caste prevailed there could be small chance of union among the Inferiors. You cannot unite men that are superstitiously bound not to hold the least communion, one with another. Everywhere, union is strength for the oppressed, division is the asset of the oppressor. Caste was the most powerful of all dividing influences.

The number of castes varied with the part of India one might be in. About 55 were most commonly recognized; in some regions the number might run to 200. The principle was the rigid and impassable segregation of the population into layers or strata, one below the other. Religion (at that time) enforced the segregation, snobbery enjoyed it. As in England today, some esoteric satisfaction seemed to pertain to the reflection that somebody else was down stairs. The perils that attached to it may have added some zest for the adventurous. If, for example, a high-caste man allowed so much as the edge of his robe to touch the robe of a lower-caste man, the high-caste man was defiled and must to the temple to be purified, a work of difficulty and cost. You can see at once the economics of the system; the priests got the price for the invisible laundering. Similar degradation and need of rigid purification attended such a calamity as sitting upon the same bench with a low-caste man, or touching anything he had touched, or entering under the same roof with him. The ways in which one could be defiled were so many that the visitor must wonder how any one managed to keep clean.

It was the common remark among the Superiors that caste was impregnably entrenched in the Indian mind, Indian tradition, Indian usage, and could never be eradicated. A great part of the common belief that nothing could be done with India except to exploit it centred around this pleasing doctrine. And yet there before the faces of persons that averred this and probably believed it, caste was steadily breaking down. Any visitor that used his eyes knew perfectly well that it was breaking down, that it was already doomed. Not because of any influence put forth by the Superiors nor even because of well-meaning missionaries, but for another and more powerful reason.

Before the march of modern inventions and machines, caste melts like snow upon the desert's dusty face.

Here is something for philosophers to ponder. The introduction of the street railroad in Bombay did more in one day to break down caste than a million preachments could have done in many years.

The inevitable promiscuity of a railroad passenger car—whoever thought of that as a moral agency? Here were under the same roof and sitting upon the same benches, high caste, low caste, and all the castes between, touching robes, even touching hands. It was necessary to invent a rule that the deadly contamination belonging elsewhere to roofs and benches did not work in a railroad car. In Bombay one was transported in a tiku gary at a cost of thirty-two cents, or one rode in a street car for two. In the face of that difference, caste proved not to be worth thirty cents. It was necessary to make a rule that contamination did not work in a street car. The sending of a telegram frequently involved the same defeat. One must use the pencil that a low-caste man had used, one must stand to write at the same desk.

And again, in these times it is not possible to keep any people wholly in a state of ignorance concerning the marching of the rest of mankind. The Indians began to be aware that the world outside moved toward equality and liberty. To the restlessness resulting from the memory of the reprisals of 1857–8 was added the goading knowledge that other peoples had won or were winning free, and when the Young India movement came upon the field it found the ground ready plowed for new ideas. Under that harvesting, caste began to vanish forever on a brightening horizon.

There remains still the problem of the pariahs, the Sudras,

the last dregs of this ill-formed society, the melancholy creatures that burrowed in caves and cleaned the streets and fed upon garbage. The accumulation of centuries of prejudice must be cleared away before these dreadful beings could be admitted within the pale of humanity, but in view of what has already been accomplished, no one can really assert that the task, difficult as it is, will not be accomplished.

But the freedom of India, complete, absolute, untrammelled, is indispensable to this as to the other phases of her restoration to a place among the nations.

I wrote on a foregoing page of this chapter that there were two great fables about English rule in India, one being a benevolent purpose. The second is the theory that the English keep the peace between the Mohammedans and Hindu religionists and but for the presence of English troops these factions would be forever at battle, murder, and sudden death. This seemed on examination highly improbable for the reason that in many places where no English troops were visible nor any evidences of English restraining influence, Mohammedans and Hindus dwelt together in amity. It was a fact so striking that we were moved to take photographs of men of the two sects that we found, for example, walking with their arms around each other. Abdul Khan's dearest friend, whom he brought to call upon us, was a Hindu. In the Revolution of 1857 members of the two religions fought and worked side by side. "Half of the men that worked the gun my father commanded," said Abdul, "were Mohammedans, half were Hindus. There was no trouble between them."

He said that when a disturbance broke out in these elements it was always the work of the English. Agents provocateurs were sent for the express purpose of fomenting trouble and he told how they did it, reciting incidents he himself had seen. He had history on his side, for in the reign of Akbar the Great, when India reached its highest point of prosperity and safety,

there was perfect religious toleration and Hindu and Mohammedan kept the peace.

Altercations between the sects were certainly assistant to the
English rule, no matter how they came about. They gave an
excuse for the military demonstrations that were relied upon in
the great place-keeping manœuvres and another excuse for the
occupation of the country.

When it is urged that in return for these uncounted millions
of pounds sterling that have been minted from the sweat and
misery of India, England has blessed the land with the Christian religion and the exhilarating spectacle of a more exalted
code of morals, excuse me if I smile. The blessed privilege of
accepting Christianity (Anglican version) has not mitigated
the mud huts nor lightened the dark frown of melancholy that
broods over the whole peninsula. And even if the Christian
religion were indeed all that my lord bishops say of it, after
150 years of effort the dent it has made upon the mass of India
is virtually indiscernible. They may still (in the hymn) call
us to deliver their land from error's chain, but the deliverance
so far won is nothing to write home about.

All this was before the rise of Gandhi, that I knew India, but
even then there were those that believed England would in the
end voluntarily consent to restore to the Indian people the
country that had been reft from them. The theory was pleasing, but chimerical. So long as the purpose of organized society
is profits and India remains profitable to possess, England will
not give up so great a source of profits. Passive resistance is a
noble idea, but under the existing system inherently unworkable. At the end of 1932 the Gandhi movement had virtually
dissolved, and India was left facing the choice between sullen
submission and armed revolt. The concessions England was
willing to grant were but salves and nostrums. So long as the
government of India remained in alien hands the causes of unrest would never be mitigated. Nothing could obliterate the

actuality of the alien over-lord; nothing could erase from the Indian mind the bald fact that the country was not allowed to determine its own destiny; nothing remove thence the memories of 150 years of degradation and exploitation.

The world is to hear more of India.

Britons and the apologists of imperialism have been pleased to speak contemptuously of the Indian mind, of which they know nothing. It would be dull indeed, and inept, that mind, if it did not clearly perceive where the case for Britain breaks down. In all respects and at all points the British performance in India is historically, humanly, fundamentally, inadjustable to the march of mankind. Even if, as is falsely pretended, the British were in India for India's good, that would help nothing. Because good is not to be done in that way. The whole attempt to hand down benefits to an alien people and coerce them into an alien standard of conduct or even of comfort is indefensible. Peoples sometimes perish under such dispensation; they never really advance. The first law of the forward march is that it shall be with volition, not coercion; that it shall come from within and not from without. Civilization is to be achieved; it is not to be cast down in packets from a height like bonbons from a Christmas tree. Imperialism scoffs at the notion that every people has its right to determine its own destiny but the right remains still persisting and still with a spear point at imperialism's heart. Below its shifting and evanescent troubles, the world has no greater question than the fate of India; and if it could be determined in any other way than by complete independence and national freedom, mankind would double upon its own line of advance.

Chapter XI

AN ADVENTURE IN ARBITRATION

SURELY, some allowance is to be made, even in this harsh world, for men that stumbling about in the dark take a bush fire to be sunrise and a corn-bin the walls of the New Jerusalem.

New Zealand, for instance—New Zealand, once in its history the World's Sign of Blessed Hope. How it came to be so is a fair story—let us have it next.

"We are what suns and winds and waters make us," sang Landor, to an unheeding world. He should have seen New Zealand first. Then he could have added another stanza and more convincing. Possibly one making for more tolerance and less of the delusion of race.

For if there are on earth any people supposed to be of a settled order, of sure addiction to tradition and background, it is the worthy excellent people of Scotland. But neither the inheritance of rugged conservatism nor any other mental armor plate could stand long against the idyllic beauty and soft climate of the newest of the new worlds. When the Scotch emigrants that settled that lovely land sailed out of the Clyde they might be as dour as ever a covenanting forefather of theirs. A few years on the Wanganui and they were of all men the most sceptical of the sacred past and most avid for a better way to do everything. They were even developing at the end of the earth a new habit of thought, a new language, and a new pronunciation. Contacts with new interests, new scenes, new problems, contact with the natives, with wholly new conditions of life, were making a new nation, and one looking at them was led to ponder the folly of trying to hold together an empire scattered over all the face of the map. The demands in the struggle for existence are too rigorous for sentiment, and modern life is too practical. New Zealanders might speak with a pathetic fatuity of England as "home," and might be willing in battle to attest what they deemed a devotion to the mother country; the granitic facts of geography were all against a tie that led so tortuously around and around the inhabited globe to end at last in another island, no bigger, no better, and pointing far away toward the opposite pole.

You can carry to a new clime the names of an old; you cannot carry there its society, mentality, or customs. All life in the old country was laid out in the iron-bound strata of caste. In New Zealand, caste was virtually unknown. Not long before my arrival a man that had been a great and controlling power upon the country, had held its highest office and planned its progress, ended a picturesque and masterful career and nobody had thought it strange that before he had been prime minister he had been a working coal miner or something of the kind. Richard Seddon was his name, too little celebrated in the world's annals, for he was one of its constructive and inspired geniuses. Besides a large and notable gift of governing, he had other traits. He was honest, unselfish, understanding, and strange to say, at the height of his glory, never lost his sympathy with the men that toiled. He knew better than schools or books could have taught him that the welfare of the state rests upon the welfare of the producers therein, and he had a purpose to make of New Zealand a workers' paradise.

It was his belief that even under the existing system of society this was possible without shaking off the parasites and without largely disturbing them in the enjoyment of their accumulations.

It was time something of the kind should be attempted in New Zealand because not long before the state of the workers had been anything but paradisiacal. There had been a great strike, a strike of the maritime workers, and transportation had come to an end. Consider what this meant to an island country. All of its paths, channels and chances were upon the sea. Of a sudden these were cut off. Paralysis fell upon the nation.

The rest of the community coalesced to meet this emergency by defeating the strikers. The choice seemed small; beat the strike or starve, was the way the people translated it. All kinds of men volunteered to do transport work, and of course the strikers were routed. Not easily, but surely; no strike can succeed in the face of strong public opinion.

As soon as this one had been properly crushed and the emergency was over, a thing happened that always seems surprising and yet is always most natural. Many men that had been insistent upon overwhelming the insurgents began to ask what the row was about, and perceiving that after all it had a reasonable origin, they became interested to see that it did not happen again, for it was too costly. And considering why it happened led them to see that the worker had some rights. They welded a coalition between the old Liberal and Labor parties, went to bat at the next election, made a working man prime minister and began to grope after ways to avoid strikes until they hit upon one that seemed perfect, potent, and everlasting. Seddon was the second prime minister of the New Jerusalem and for the rest of his life sailed the ship through blissful seas on a chart that seemed flawless and wonderful.

The substance of it was so to improve the state of the worker that he would have no reason to strike. Provide and insist upon sanitary working conditions, short working hours, enlarged opportunities for recreation and improvement, free and ample help to obtain work, encouragement and legal recognition of his unions, better housing, help to enable him to own his home, cheap and convenient transportation, ample protection in his rights.

Capital, which had regarded the rest of the program with no

great enthusiasm, now took heart of grace. No more strikes—
it was a noble aim, and before long the rest of the world began
to notice and applaud. The strike had come to be the sign of
dread among the nations. Strikes seemed to come more often
and be worse. What to do about them boggled all statesman-
ship. Sometimes governments tried the gendarmerie, sometimes others less advanced resorted to Pinkertons and armed
thugs. Laws were passed designed to make striking illegal. On
the street railroads of New York alleged postal cars were run
up and down (at intervals) so that a strike might be declared
an interference with the United States mails and the federal
troops brought out. But thuggery was more generally favored,
and indeed it looked good; have ready enough men with rifles
to shoot economic subjection into violent persons that are regardless of their duty toward their kind, indulgent employers,
and so restore peace. But the trouble seemed to be that the
more strikes were broken by this method, the more they seemed
to recur, and as workingmen generally did not really like the
notion that their fellows were to be shot down for resisting a
cut in pay, for instance, in most of these industrial countries
what was plainly threatened was a rift between employer and
employed akin to civil war and sometimes, as at Homestead
and Cœur d'Alene, actually attaining to it.

But here was a country wiser than the rest that had found
a plan to meet this alarming difficulty. It had abolished strikes
and still left the workingman contentedly on good terms with
the kind, indulgent, and the rest. How did this miracle come
upon us?

Not entirely by man's devising. More it seemed of the order
of the providential. It had been believed that strikes could be
avoided if there were some genial smiling body whose function
should be, when a strike was threatened, to step in and with
kind words restore the status. To this end was set up a Board of
Conciliation whose function was to take softly by the hand the

parties in an industrial dispute and lead them back to the blissful seats of brotherly love. It appears that some one foresaw the
possible failure of this glorified olive branch and there was
added an Arbitration Court to hear both sides and determine
which was right.

But suppose one side or the other should be obstinate and refuse to accept the decision of the arbitrators?

That we will prevent with penalties. So crushing fines were
provided for any possible recalcitrant. Take what the court
awards you or be mulcted to the limit. We must have peace.

This worked beautifully. No more strikes, no more lockouts,
no more riots, no more interruptions to business, no more stone
throwing in the streets. Everything as harmonious as wedding
bells.

The operation of the labor laws was under the direction of
Mr. Edward Tregear, one of the unsung benefactors of the human race that prove the existence of heaven since they get no
reward here. He was, moreover, in other ways well worth attention. The coffee-colored natives that the white men found
in New Zealand were part of the great Polynesian peoples, the
world's ethnological mystery, that sweep from New Zealand
through the Island world to Hawaii. They are among the most
interesting of earth's children, among the most attractive and
in some ways among the worthiest. In New Zealand, of course,
the superior whites at first made war upon them with the pleasant purpose to kill them off and so be rid—in the name of
Christ and so forth, as usual. But the Maoris suddenly manifested a considerable interest in this operation and a strange re-
luctance to be sacrificed upon the altar of Superiority. Being
among the best fighters in the world they managed to halt the
process of extermination (with guns, at least) and became an
integral part of the new colony, inhabiting almost exclusively
the centres of the two islands.

Mr. Tregear was a student, a lover of learning and a philosopher. The Maoris seemed to him to have immense possibilities of interest. He gave up his home and business in Wellington, went into the forest and lived for sixteen years among the native tribes. When he was done he knew more about them than any other white man had ever known and had acquired for them a profound sympathy and understanding. He proceeded to write the standard book on the subject, *The Maori Race,* filled with stores of rare knowledge, and to compile the Polynesian-English dictionary that has been in use ever since.

Side by side with his understanding of and sympathy for the native went his understanding of and sympathy for the wage worker. Prime Minister Seddon had that feeling because he himself had been of the guild. Mr. Tregear had it on another impulse. He had never been a wage worker, but he looked upon all the submerged element of mankind in all lands with the same eye of compassion, and strong upon him lay the fact that as the earth produces abundantly for all her children the lack that afflicts the great majority is absurd and inexcusable.

It was after his return from Maoriland that he became the head of the government's labor department where he remained, whatever shifts the rest of the administration might undergo, until he retired for age. I think there would have been more than a strike if he had been displaced. The reason was that he administered the none-too-easy task laid upon him with a singular combination of enthusiasm, tact, prescience, self-abnegation, patience, and firmness. In the course of a long experience with public men in many lands, I have not found in another a larger allotment of these qualities. No doubt they were a native gift, bettered by observation and reflection. I had ample opportunity to note him well and found no variation in his method. He could shut the bores off without causing them to feel that the tap was being turned on their eloquence; he could show the gratuitous complainant the flaw in his tale of wrong; he could assure the timid business man that ruin was not at

hand because wages were going up; he could do all without allowing his urbanity to slip or his versatility of tact to moult a feather.

One of the functions of his department that he superintended, and I think invented, was a complicated but efficient national system of labor exchanges that made unemployment virtually impossible. Suppose a farmer to need a hand, a factory to need a worker, a housewife to need a maid. The need was reported to the nearest government office, which immediately notified all other government offices. Lists of the unemployed were scrutinized and available workers informed. If one had no means to pay one's fare to destination, the government (owning the railroads) advanced the amount of the fare and was repaid from the wages of the worker. No charge was made to employer or worker for labor bureau service. It was the government's business to find work for the workless and usually such work was found in a few hours.

New Zealand forged ahead. Not swiftly, because of its remote situation and the world's general ignorance of its advantages, for this was its heavy handicap. Six weeks by steamer from Gravesend overwhelmed the imagination of the English emigrant. It seemed like a leap out of the world. The soil, being largely volcanic, was fertile, the variety of products hardly limited, the yield large, the climate (except in the extreme southern part of the south island) mild, genial, and still invigorating. If there is an ideal climate in the world, I should deem it to be the climate of Auckland. With ease and government assistance land could be had. The public school system was among the best, the social life in the towns as advanced as any in civilization, the beauty of the country almost incredible; and still the settlers halted because of the distance and the feeling that New Zealand was out of the world.

Nevertheless, for capital as for labor New Zealand offered the undisputed advantages of industrial peace.

Henry Demarest Lloyd went there and was fascinated with the prospect. In his judgment, New Zealand had found the long-sought philosopher's stone in industrial matters. It predestined the end of labor troubles everywhere. We had only to do what New Zealand had done, and watch the glorious results. He wrote a book, *A Country Without Strikes,* in which he set forth the triumph of New Zealand's wit and skill. Frank Parsons went there and praised the socialization experiments, the government ownership and efficient operation of the railroads, the telegraphs, the telephones, the express service. In their wake came I trundling and it seemed to me no less that in the settlement by peaceful arbitration of all industrial disputes New Zealand had blazed the world's way. We had only to follow. No more strikes! I recalled scenes on the East Side of New York, a line of policemen led by the gigantic Alexander Williams, advancing down the street with their long night sticks beating men's heads as one might chop wood; a street railroad strike in Chicago, mounted police guarding a car operated by strike-breakers and workmen from the new buildings throwing brick and tiles on the car and upon the police. I thought of the grave significance and terrible scenes of Homestead. No more strikes! What a country! Joy be its portion and happy man be his dole that thought of arbitration boards to supplant brick-bats and night sticks!

How easy after all was the solution of the problems that had seemed so disruptive! How sure in economics as well as in ethics! We begin by treating the workers kindly. We foster their unions instead of trying to break them up or make them illegal or shoot them full of holes. We give to the toilers good wages. Liberally they expend with grocer and dry-goods merchant the liberal wages we give them. The grocer and the dry-goods merchant buy liberally of the wholesaler. The wholesaler orders largely from the manufacturer. The manufacturer pays off his note at the bank and makes a new one and larger. Result, everybody prosperous, everybody happy, everybody peaceful, and a new golf course planned by our club. Why bother about these foreign theories of a re-fashioned society? Let such notions be for dreamers. For us, being practical men, here is the obvious way to all the regeneration society needs, and forget the abstruse Marx, whom we don't understand anyway.

Well—we cannot all be cold-blooded and slow-pulsed judges sitting forever distrustful upon the tripod. I thought it was all right, so thought Lloyd, so thought Parsons, so thought many another. When I came home I told Brisbane about it and he made it the text for editorials. It illustrated his favorite thesis (at that time) of Good Wages Mean Good Dividends, or something to that effect.

Yet we were wrong, the whole gang of us, and wrong for a reason that will seem now so obvious that you will wonder none of us thought of it, for it stuck out like Cape St. Vincent of a clear morning. None of us did think of it, not even Edward Tregear, the wise, the experienced, the perceptive, gone wrong like the rest.

How wrong? In this way:

The Arbitration Court was made up of three persons, one nominated by the labor unions, one by the employers, the third a member chosen from the national supreme court. This, of course, was arbitration by one person, not by three. Everything depended upon the decision of the supreme court justice.

For a long time his decisions were either in favor of the workers or so unimportant, if the other way, that the surface of the industrial pool was unruffled, and work proceeded to the dulcet strains of a lovely harmony, labor and capital apparently hand in hand, the lion and the lamb in one bed. But there came a time when the manufacturers declared that they could stand no more increases of wages. On this subject they made a move that could not be disregarded. They showed by apparently unassailable figures that any farther increase in the cost of production would ruin them and compel them to close their factories.

The next decision was in their favor and against the workers.

The workers refused to accept the decision.

"As you will," said government. "We will now proceed to apply the law to you as we have in other cases to the manufacturers," and the court levied the prescribed fines.

The workers refused to pay the fines.

"Ho, there, bailiffs, distrain me the goods of these recalcitrants!"

But, behold, it was totally different now! With ease a court could levy a fine upon a manufacturer who had machinery, buildings, a house, things to be levied upon. What shall you do, O Daniels come to judgment, with a stubborn person that has nothing but his packing-house knife and at home the family wash boiler and soup kettle?

With this problem the government wrestled long and painfully. The first conflict was in some way compromised. The next was a coal miners' strike in the South Island. The government sought to levy upon the wash boiler and soup kettle. The bailiffs removed the forfeited goods and offered them for sale to satisfy the judgments unpaid. Offered them for sale and sold them. Sold them to other miners that bought in the whole lot for twenty-five cents and immediately carried them back to the places from which they had been taken, leaving the government biting its fingers and helpless.

Strikes multiplied. The Arbitration Court decreed and decreed. The workers paid no attention, and Auckland, metropolis of "The Country Without Strikes," saw a cruiser made fast at the foot of its principal street with guns pointed to sweep the thoroughfare of rioting strikers. The whole admired structure of Industrial Arbitration as the panacea for industrial disorders collapsed, and one more beautiful dream crashed upon a hard reality.

For any errors made by Lloyd and Parsons in estimating this venture in altruism existed all the excuse suggested at the opening of this narrative, and more. They were students, they longed ardently for some way out of the industrial swamp and leaped upon anything that promised a good path of exit. For my own gross blundering there was no palliation. I had seen strike after strike; if anybody on earth should know the genesis of labor troubles and be able to detect a fallacious remedy for them, assuredly I should. "Ignorance, ma'am, sheer ignorance," said Doctor Johnson, being reproached for an error in his immortal dictionary. Even this frail shelter is not allowable to me.

For the essence of the case was as simple as pot hooks and hangers. If you undertake to compel men to work under conditions they are unwilling to accept you are merely trying to reintroduce slavery. The thing is impossible. So long as workers will assent to the award of industrial arbitrators, well and good. When they will not assent to it there is no means now to compel their assent.

The wise government saw this in the course of time, gave up the attempt, and came to rely chiefly upon conciliation as a remedy for industrial disturbance. New Zealand is still a lovely country and still offers every inducement to the settler, every attraction to the tourist. But it did not discover the panacea for industrial troubles because under the existing system of society there is no such panacea and no chance of one.

In our own country about the same time eminent gentlemen alarmed about labor disputes organized a social group to bring together in one sweet bond of unity the leaders of the unions and the captains of industry. The failure of this attempt was not so tragic and spectacular as the New Zealand collapse but it was as complete.

It is worth remembering that the late Samuel Gompers, the president of the American Federation of Labor, pointed out from the first and with sardonic amusement the fallacy of the New Zealand plan and yet went sober faced to the meetings of the Civic Federation. But what he thought as he sat there one can easily imagine.

Autopsy. Compulsory arbitration in New Zealand died of falling down a well and breaking its neck. As it never had any right to exist, flowers were omitted at its funeral.

Chapter XII

THE DEAD CARD APPEARS

"THE Madness of Much Wealth!" cried David Graham Phillips, in a magazine article of the trust-busting period, meaning the chief phase of the existing status. Few gave heed to the article, but it contained the heart and gist of the whole business. What on earth did a man want of a hundred million dollars any more than of a hundred million vest buttons that he should cheat and duck and lie and manœuvre incessantly to wrest dollars from the grasp of need? Yet it was not really the dollar that made men mad; it was the trancing vision of the power that went with the dollar, and men were not really so money crazed as they were touched with the old obsession of dominion—and kudos. What the Orient was to Tamburlaine, Wall Street was to Thomas Fortune Ryan.

Under this illusion and the spur of the public's admiring applause, they did, as we have seen (and do), fairly dizzy things, these captains of industry and leaders of finance. About once in so often an outburst of muck-raking, a Senate committee, or some other agency of searchlight reveals to a gasping country the real nature of these operations; the rest of the time they go on unobserved and unrebuked, differing in style and method to suit the shifting demands of the intermittent fever of public morality, but always in essence the same lawless exercise of the power of Accumulated Wealth to get more wealth that it may have more power to get more wealth.

One of the worst of these operations in my time was the shameless looting of the street-railroad system of New York, by which with an initial investment of a trifling sum the public was made to furnish the purchasing price for one enterprise after another until all were in one control, a process that left behind a staggering total of bonded indebtedness for the public to bear, after the same public had been preyed upon to build immense private fortunes. The round-the-world assignment, to learn what other nations were doing with the universal Problem of Accumulated Wealth and Accumulated Power having been fulfilled, a muck-raking series was projected to relate the triumph of high finance that wrecked New York's transportation system, including incidentally some passages from the career of Mr. Ryan, then the greatest financial power in New York.

A chief source of information about this dazzling episode in our business life was Colonel William N. Amory, who had been treasurer of the old Third Avenue Street Railroad and knew exactly how the pillaging had been done. He had not accepted it in silence but had printed at his own expense a remarkable pamphlet in which he gave the facts and figures. He was now the means of introducing us to a phase of Accumulated Wealth all new and full of interest to any inquiring mind.

It seemed to be a fact that Big Business walked to its triumphs arm in arm with a detective. David Ferguson once wrote an article on this subject that deserved more attention than it ever received, for it showed a condition the average man would have said to be impossible. All big business enterprises employed what were called "shadows," but were in fact only hired detectives: employed them to spy on their competitors, on possible rivals, on suspected employees, on labor unions, on all persons that were antagonistic to them. Colonel Amory had not proceeded far with his protests against the street-railroad looting when he was aware that he had the full attention of these furtive pursuers. Day and night they watched him. Even so far they went as to extract his mailed letters from a letter box, another thing one would have said offhand to be impossible, but it was actually performed.

One morning Colonel Amory and I were sitting at breakfast in the dining room of the Hotel Broztell, where I was living. A man that was evidently following Amory came in, keeping close upon his heels. To give some color to his presence he had a newspaper that he made a show of reading while he stood near our table to catch our conversation. The trick was so obvious that we could but laugh and openly guy the man.

"Look at this sleuth standing here," said Amory, "pretending to read while he tries to listen to our talk. Isn't he the great boob? Where do they find that kind? I suppose he calls himself a detective," and so on in a loud tone that the man could not but hear. He still stood wholly unabashed, and when Amory left was tagging along in his wake.

For many weeks I never left the hotel without being followed. At that time on the opposite side of the street stood a row of stables belonging to the once fashionable residences in Twenty-sixth Street. There was one man that every evening snuggled himself into the disused entrance to one of these stables and watched for me. As soon as I came out I could see him over my shoulder stealthily moving in the wake. In those days the old Hoffman House was still standing. It had two entrances, one in Broadway and one in the side street. I would enter briskly at the Broadway side, come out on the side street and then again into Broadway where I would suddenly confront the sleuth to his manifest amazement and dismay. It is not altogether the happiest sensation in the world to feel that one is always under a slinking and malignant scrutiny, but in this case the annoyance was erased in amusement. The whole performance struck one as infinitely childish, preposterous, and laying bare the stupidity of what was called "business acumen." Nothing I had been able to say against entrenched respectability warranted that I should be dogged day and night.

A close friend in those days and an accomplice in assaults upon righteousness was Alfred Henry Lewis. To him I referred the mystery and drew the short straight answer, for to him the thing was plain as sunlight.

"What they expect," says he, "is to get you into a woman scrape. Watch your step, my son."

This seemed still improbable, but was possibly illustrated a few years later when offended Interests arranged upon a Lieutenant-Governor of Illinois a woman trap by which they hoped to ruin him.

Another manifestation that puzzled me greatly was the swarm of agile-tongued prospectors loosed upon me. Not a day passed without a visit from some gentleman that had discovered the infallible way to make money, much money, make it easily and safely. I grew to expect that one of this tribe should wait for me every morning when I came down to breakfast. If a small percentage of the wonderful schemes they outlined before my vision had proved true to specifications and I had embarked in them I should now be a millionaire. I thought it impossible any one should suppose I had any money to invest, but that seemed to be the flattering belief in certain financial circles.

Again to the source of Wisdom, who regarded me with contempt and said:

"Plain as day. They want to get you involved in some shady scheme and then show that you are writing these things for an ulterior purpose."

How that may have been, again I do not know, but I recall a persistent visitor from East Orange who showed me how I could make $50,000 in a day by printing one statement in my next article and then buying or selling some stock.

The ministry of the sleuths was long continued. Some months later I lumbered through the state on a speaking tour. For a time I was followed by one male detective and two lady stenographers who did me the honor to take down everything I said. The exact source of this attention was soon ascertained. I had been writing about the railroads and one railroad company had sent the stenographers to see if I said anything that could be made the basis for a libel suit. It was a clever device. A man speaking at Painted Post is not likely to be so circumspect as when he is deliberately writing something to be printed.

But I started to set down the verification of his prophetic soul that announced to the Western chamber of commerce the end of muck-raking. Pressure upon editors, or publishers, or both, closed one magazine after another to the men with the rake. At last but two were left. One of these was strangled. For the other, I myself precipitated the ruin.

Mr. Samuel Merwin, whose character was so lovable and whose aims were so high, was editor of one of these surviving periodicals of protest called *Success,* a name that came in the end to be excellently designed for the jests of columnists. He felt, as many others felt, that fundamental conditions were intolerable; that there was steadily arising in the country a power of Accumulated Wealth with which democracy could not co-exist, and with high courage he printed articles in his magazine that sought to arouse the public to this fact. Every magazine at certain seasons of the year must have financing. When next *Success* reached this situation it found that no financing could be had and *Success* failed.

Hampton's was still left, and going strong. Mr. Hampton had an unusual editorial sense; he knew how to make his magazine interesting while he made it also an instrument of progress. It was the foremost muck-raking periodical of the world, but it contained more than exposé stuff, so that its circulation rose and its entrenchments seemed assured.

I was writing for it a series of articles on the more conspicuous railroad scandals of America, the historic swindles by which one great fortune after another had been created at an enduring public expense. In the course of time I reached the New Haven, which was then, under its old management, at the summit of its apparent prosperity, power, and arrogance. I went to Boston and elsewhere, got my facts, wrote the story, and turned it in.

Somewhere in the office of the magazine the Interests had planted a spy. We knew that well enough but could never detect him. One reason we knew it was because some one in the office had obtained a list of the stockholders, who were being bombarded with anonymous circulars attacking the credit of the enterprise and advising immediate sale of the stock. We were now to hear more of this person's mysterious art.

My story had just been put into type and the proofs had arrived, when a well-dressed and important-looking man came in and said he represented the New Haven Railroad and desired a confidential talk with Mr. Hampton. This being easily arranged he disclosed his business.

He said it was well enough known to the management of the New Haven that an article had been written for the magazine attacking the railroad; that this article was a tissue of lies, was libelous and malicious and he had come to demand that it be suppressed.

Mr. Hampton mildly inquired how his visitor knew the article was untrue. He said that it had been seen and read by persons connected with the railroad's management.

"Well," said Mr. Hampton, "we will not print in this magazine anything we know to be untrue. Here are the proofs of the article. Suppose we go over it and you point out the things that are untrue and if you can show that they are so we will omit them."

"It is all untrue," said the young man. "It is just one string of lies from beginning to end."

Hampton picked up the proofs and read the first sentence.

"BILL SIKES"

Puck on the coal situation, March 7, 1906

"Is that true or untrue?" says he.

"Oh, well, of course, I don't mean that," said the visitor. "I mean when you get down into the heart of the thing."

"You said it was all untrue," said Hampton. "We must read it all and see if you are right." He read the next sentence.

"Is that true or untrue?"

"Wait till you get past the introduction."

They went on, Hampton pausing at the end of every sentence and the young man impatiently waving him to proceed until they came to a sentence that declared that in ten years the capital stock of the railroad had been increased 1501 per cent.

"There," shouted the young man, "that statement is a damn lie."

"Is it?" said Hampton, and reached into a drawer of his desk from which he fished a copy of *The Congressional Record* containing explicit testimony to the assertion the article made.

So they proceeded to the end, Hampton referring to *The Record* or an investigating committee's report whenever a statement was challenged.

"Where's the lie?" said Hampton.

"Well, you may have documents and things enough to make out a case, but the article is injurious to the railroad and we demand that it be suppressed."

"It will be printed," said Hampton.

"Then I must tell you that if you print that article your magazine will be put out of business. That's all." And he went out.

The article was printed.

I have mentioned the fact that a magazine in the dull season must have advances from the bank to keep going. So far Hampton had never experienced the least difficulty in obtaining these advances. His was well known to be a popular and expanding enterprise. When summer came he made the usual application for a ninety-day accommodation and was astonished to be refused at the bank where for years he had been a favorite customer. The cashier was a friend of his. He asked for the reason of the refusal and was told confidentially that orders had come not to let *Hampton's* have any money.

Hampton was of extraordinary spirit and persistence. He got together a mass of unexceptionable securities and applied at another bank. Same result. First and last he offered that collateral to twenty-four banks and trust companies in New York and was refused by all. The order had come from the Supreme Satrapy, sitting at the G. H. Q. of Accumulated Wealth—and it must be obeyed by one and all.

Meanwhile the attacks on the credit of the magazine redoubled, creditors with claims became insistent, all efforts to obtain help failed, a mysterious purchaser appeared with an offer and *Hampton's* faded from the scene. The visitor had spoken sooth. The magazine was suppressed.

Colonel Arthur Little was then chief owner of a magazine called *Pearson's*. After the demise of *Hampton's* he kindly took us in from the doorstep on which we were shivering, and *Pearson's* became the last vehicle in which Big Business could be exposed. By dint of Colonel Little's indomitable will it lasted three years. Then exactly the same tactics that had been applied to *Success* and to *Hampton's* were turned upon him and he too went down, though with flags flying. And the era of muck-raking had come to an end.

Autopsy. Muck-raking in America came to its death by strangulation at the hands of persons and Interests perfectly well known.

Doubtless Respectable Business was glad. Whether the country had reason to rejoice is another question. Where there is no criticism there is no health—in a democracy, at least. After the last muck-raking magazine had gone down there was no chance, except through an occasional investigation by Congress, to check the operations of high finance or make known to the public the real nature of the conduct of its business. The whole thing went on therefore into a carnival of plundering, extortion and huge swindles until collapse came in November, 1929, and thereafter the public could learn too late the reality about investments that had been palmed off upon it. The two billion dollars drawn from the American public for worthless foreign bonds seemed a sufficient commentary on a state of business that goes without criticism and therefore without restraint.

The truth about muck-raking is that it is a wholesome and necessary influence and no republic can afford to be without it. But while it can and often does effect minor reforms, it is, like all other temporizing remedial devices, nothing against the fundamental system that is the source of our troubles. It is just one more experiment in symptom dosing. The source of the malady remains to insure a fresh outbreak in another form.

Yet no one looking impartially over this curious and interesting period of American reform can justly avoid the conclusion that great good came of it. Mention has been made of the effect of Phillips' articles about the Senate and of other muck-raking exploits. To these are to be added that the onslaughts of Mr. Adams upon the patent-medicine fakers brought about an immense improvement in that situation and drove from the field many of the worst of the impostors. Mr. Adams also contributed invaluable help to the passage of the pure-food law. The United States government took the articles of one muck-raker as its basis and chief information in suits it prosecuted against two of the most conspicuous of the trusts. As noted in another connection, the assaults of the magazines wrought a much greater restraint in the methods employed to effect the advance of business combinations. A series of articles on the reasons for the many railroad accidents in America brought about the beneficent "safety first" campaign that greatly reduced the per-

ils of railroad travel. Mr. Mathews laid the foundations for the
long-drawn-out struggle against the Power Trust. A series on
the Southern Pacific in politics, with a tremendous campaign
led by Hiram Johnson, ended a condition in California that had
virtually abolished all other government but that of the railroad. And not to string out these citations, the essence of the
whole operation is to be seen in the results, before noted, of
Lincoln Steffens' articles on municipal graft.

Steffens himself would never acknowledge this, but seemed
to hold stedfastly to a notion that all efforts to better conditions had been essentially fruitless. Some years after muck-
raking had been abolished, I was with him one day in Paris
and asked him if he had ever been back to Minneapolis to look
at the results of his work.

He said indifferently that he had not and had no desire to
go. I said:

"Well, I have been there often and watched things as well as
I could and there has been a wonderful change. Minneapolis
shook itself free from the old conditions and cleaned up in a
way to delight your heart."

"There hasn't been a particle of change," he said. "If I were
to go back now, I should find everything exactly the same."

Nothing's so dainty sweet as lovely melancholy.

As a matter of cold fact, the choice is between a slow improvement, wrought through exposures of evil, through appeals
to the ineradicable good in mankind, between that and a fundamental but not necessarily a violent change in the economics
of society.

One day in 1907, Judge Gaynor, Lewis and a few other
friends were sitting around a table in the art-embellished bar-
room of the old Hoffman House. The judge was in a sorrowful mood that day, and lamented everything in sight.

"The heart of man is so corrupt"—he began.

"The heart of man isn't corrupt," some one broke in. "The

heart of man is sound and good. See how it shows up whenever it has a chance! We make a wolf-den of the world and then wail and wring our hands because men in it have to act like wolves or die. Nearly anybody will be decent if you give him half a chance."

It was noteworthy that Judge Gaynor, who had been forty years in practise and sat upon the bench, admitted that this was so.

It is the summary of the whole business.

But about waiting on slow time, some years before the last turn of the garrotte had silenced the last muck-raker, it seemed to me that the only logical place for any one dissatisfied with reciprocal rapine was the Socialist party, which did not purpose to wait for an indefinite sunrise but to remake fundamentals. It was true that I had never read *Das Kapital* and could not have told Karl Marx from Frederick Engels if I had met them walking arm in arm up the street. Few persons can be conceived to have known less about Scientific Socialism, but the party represented a protest and the biggest protest then in sight. I had also observed two things about it. Big Business and Accumulated Wealth viewed it with shuddering horror, and having been thrown much into contact with its members I had found them to be the best people I had ever seen, and I thought I should be in luck to be allowed to go along.

It is pleasant to record that to this act of folly I went not without the grace of friendly hands outstretched to save. Jack London appealed with kindly remonstrance, David Graham Phillips with long and almost tearful pleadings, and Alfred Henry Lewis with violent denunciation. London urged I should ruin what he was pleased to call my "literary career," Phillips that I should destroy what he was pleased to call my "influence," and Lewis that I should be just a damn fool playing on a dead card. When he learned that about that time there had been a third refusal of a proffered nomination to

Congress, Lewis threw over what little restraint he had and broke into most rude and unseemly speech. If there had been any point to these arguings, doubtless I should have heeded them, since no one alive could have less taste for any form of the martyr business. But looking at it soberly, a literary career, supposing I could have had one, always seemed to me the perfect ideal of nothing on earth to have; so far as I have been able to learn, I never have had the least influence upon any human being; and as for Congress, any old Washington correspondent knew well enough that the life of a Congressman was about two degrees worse than the life of a mule on a cotton plantation. Nothing was easier therefore than to pursue the downward path, which I did to my inexpressible satisfaction.

Lewis had a circle of friends and cronies that used to meet frequently in the back room of Considine's saloon in Broadway near Forty-second Street. There they sat at a huge round table, but however arranged, Lewis was always the head and presiding genius. His position and attitude reminded one of Doctor Johnson at the Club; everybody else deferred to him. The other membership was diverse, and I venture to think unique. There were Charley White, the prize-fight referee, Inspector McLaughlin of the police, Bat Masterson, the celebrated sheriff at Dodge City in the "bad-man" period, Kid McCoy, the prize fighter, Eddie Foy, the actor, Val O'Farrell, at that time one of the cleverest of the detective sergeants at police headquarters. Also a gentleman that had led an active and I think lucrative career as a yeggman but had fallen into the mere humdrum of common honesty, and a few other kindred spirits. To this genial company having been presented by Lewis as the nation's champion lunatic, a distinction hardly to be coveted even in the back room of Considine's, I was hospitably welcomed and became part of the entourage.

As a rule, the sessions might have been directed to show the comical futility of fiction, since what is the use of belaboring one's imagination when the realities of life are so much more engrossing than anything that can be devised? Most of the narrative art represented around that table was of the highest quality because it was all unstudied, spontaneous, and genuine. Masterson, when he could be started upon one of his yarns of Doc Halliday and Wild Bill, was a fascinating narrator. I cannot recall many better stories, in or out of print, than his account of The Fight at the Adobe Houses, or his Trek of the Northern Cheyennes, which latter was an epic. Charley White had been born and bred on old Cherry Hill and his stories of life there were afterward woven together by Lewis and printed. O'Farrell had an inexhaustible fund of legends about adventures in the underworld; McCoy, who was nobody's fool, had picked up good store of legends, and occasionally the yeggman would come in with piquant illustrations of his peculiar industry. Lewis himself was a master talker. One thing to be noted about the stories was that they were clean. They might be adorned with expressions one would not hear in a Sunday school and they might be told in a manner free and easy, but they were strictly clean. I think every person in that circle had an instinctive repugnance to smut. So much can hardly be said for certain other gatherings much more distinguished.

Lewis sat there night after night and drank nothing but bottled water. He had been cowboy, practising attorney, politician, reporter, and he drank nothing but water. It was the favorite beverage in Considine's back room—including the yeggman.

Chapter XIII

COMRADES ALL!

ONE joins the Republican party by voting the Republican ticket. One joins the Democratic party by voting the Democratic ticket. In 1908 one does not join the Socialist party by voting the Socialist ticket. One can vote the Socialist ticket until the mountains melt down to the sea without ever being a member of the Socialist party. To join the Socialist party in 1908 is a motion of solemnity and port. One must fill out this application blank, must have members to vouch for him, must answer questions as to his fitness, must run the gauntlet of possible objectors, and must be balloted over by a grave and careful committee. It is nothing to be undertaken lightly; it is like joining a church. One must have had experience in grace, one must show that one has come out from the tents of the wicked and capitalism.

Even when one has given satisfactory evidence that one is worthy to be counted among the elect, there remains sometimes a kind of initiation, not always of a joyous character, as is now to be set forth.

Robert Hunter, author of the remarkable book called *Poverty* and of other powerful works, had been nominated by the Socialists for the State Assembly from the old Eighth District, which was the part of the East Side that had been most familiar to me as a reporter. I greatly admired Hunter's work, and had tried to help him in the vigorous campaign he was conducting. If De Ate could be once redeemed by the election of a man of Hunter's character and ability, it might be the beginning of a movement that would free us from the wretched political oligarchy that then dominated the East Side. I therefore wrote a letter to *The New York World* asking all possible support for Hunter as a candidate of hope and reform.

When I had been admitted to the Socialist party, I was assigned to the branch or chapter that met nearest to the hotel at which I lived. To the first meeting of this local I went with the satisfaction of an acolyte performing his first ceremonies. I had noticed that many good movements came to naught because the rank and file would not attend the meetings nor perform the routine duties inseparable from such organizations, and my pious resolve was firm that to this laxity I would be an exception by attending every meeting of my branch. So I went in and took an unobtrusive seat near the door as one that recognized his true position in the rear rank. I had not been there ten minutes when all attention was centred upon my unlucky presence. A lady member of the branch gifted with a prehensile tongue and a flow of oratory seldom surpassed even among her charming sex, arose and began to pour out upon my head the vials of an apparently inappeasable wrath. It was some time before I could discover wherein I had offended, so great was the emotion with which her fluent words were charged, but it was presently certain that my letter to *The World* had been my undoing. I had written in behalf of one Socialist candidate. But there were Socialist candidates in all the Assembly districts. By singling out one and not mentioning the others I had violated some fundamental law of the Socialist state forever essential to its well being, and apparently was deemed to have incurred eternal damnation or die the death or something. It was farther intimated that in thus transgressing the organic law I had shown that I was no better than a vile capitalist and probably a wolf in sheep's clothing and other low things. To this I made no defense, my guilt being apparent, but some one having pointed out that as the transgression had been committed before I came under the regenerating influence of the Socialist organization, there might still be hope for the erring one. Besides which, it was doubtful if the branch had jurisdiction over crimes committed by non-members, which seemed to offer a compromise whereby I might be saved, and the meeting took up something else.

There was a central committee, to which all the branches sent delegates, that sat every Saturday night in a room in the Labor Temple. After a time I was chosen to be one of the delegates from Branch One and journeyed every Saturday night to East Eighty-fourth Street, where we sat always until 2 A.M. and sometimes later, ardently discussing the points of pins and the like vital matters. The party was managed on the broadest lines of democracy and there was no limit to debate, but the meetings, though animated and prolix, were always orderly and although there were factions and often acrimonious squabbling over things of no moment, there was something else I am presently to describe that when I came to understand it, more than atoned for the wrangling and the apparent waste of time. Superficial observers used to jeer at these debates and argue from them that the Co-operative Commonwealth was impossible, since so much time would be spent in discussion that there would be none for action. This was a pointless comment, since whenever an emergency or a matter of importance arose it was in the end handled adequately; and besides, there being nothing between democracy and autocracy, democracy is inseparable from free discussion. Many of the delegates to the central committee were persons of foreign birth to whom a share in the transaction of any deliberative body was a novelty. They were only practising or indulging in a novel and luxurious experience and he would be intolerant that would grudge to these the relish they evidently took in the performance.

But the great compensating fact about the whole business was the unmistakable spirit of devotion to a cause in which all believed implicitly. That alone made everything worth while. About the Socialist creed clung a certain splendid significance of the universal man and the general fraternity that was different and obliterated the recollection of human weaknesses, whatever they might be. Personal ambitions there were, plenty of them; men that mixed much desire for lime-light with a purpose to emancipate the working class; wire-pulling campaigns to get party offices and all that, just as among other human beings. But what I mean is that above all this was a tremendous impetus to endure and to struggle that came from a faith in an actual and reachable new day for everybody. The bulk of the Socialists I knew believed in it, absolutely, unquestioningly, but not emotionally, which is the chief point here. They founded their faith upon a cold rea-soning that they were ever ready to propound, defend, and fight for. Their paradise to come they built foursquare upon incontrovertible logic and they served it with a magnificent de-votion and often at great personal cost.

Upon admission to the party, one became "Comrade," a cus-tom imported from Germany. Even in private conversation as invariably in meetings, one must address one's fellow as "Comrade Smith" or "Comrade Johnson." The presiding offi-cer of every meeting was "Comrade Chairman," the scribe was "Comrade Secretary." The title stammered a little in unfa-miliar mouths when it came to addressing the women as "Com-rade Miss Mergenthaler" or "Comrade Mrs. Heidenheimer," but the etiquette was rigidly enforced. It represented a beauti-ful ideal, doubtless, but was unsuited to America. That all members of a political party should call one another by a term of endearment awoke measureless laughter among persons ac-customed to the frank crudities of Tammany, for instance, or the big fist of Barney O'Rourke. It is quite true that at central committee meetings and elsewhere Comrade Niersteiner might express opinions of Comrade Markobrunner that were anything

but comradely, but underneath whatever squalling might break
out and whatever conflicts of personal aims, among the rank
and file was for a time a genuine and persistent feeling of
kindly co-operation. And to that I add a prevalent and sted-
fast willingness toward self-sacrifice that often left me astonished and exhilarated.

For all that, we used to do some things that were weird and
some that were weirder. The substance of the party's strength
was among Germans and Jews. It left the great American
Voter absolutely cold. Yet it was evident to the least reflection
that the American Voter was exactly the person to whom we
must appeal if we were ever to be more than a lost wail in a
wilderness. Despite all arguments and reasons, he continued to
view Socialism as an uncouth plant of foreign growth unsuited
to this soil and condition. At that time a certain part of the
great East Side was a kind of receiving tank for newly arrived
immigrants from Russia and Poland. These being still un-
naturalized were without votes. Whenever we had a Socialist
procession through those streets the enthusiasm manifested was
tremendous and spontaneous. The sidewalks were jammed
with shouting people, the windows were full of smiling faces,
old men and women wept and cried aloud, "Endlich! Endlich!" ("At last! At last!"). One would think we were about
to carry everything before us, but when election day came
around we did nothing of the kind. We had the cheering and
the old parties had the votes.

Sometimes we had promises as well as cheering. Morris
Hillquit, whose clear genius and powerful mind won for him
international leadership, made in 1906 a memorable campaign
for Congress. He told me afterward that if everybody that before election promised to vote for him had done so he would
have won hands down. And if all the persons that after the
election assured him they had voted for him had really done
so, he would still have been elected.

The one way by which Socialism proposed to bring about the Co-operative Commonwealth was through the ballot box and the convinced support of majorities. If every foreign-born voter in the United States should vote for us until Doomsday that would avail nothing without the support of the native Americans. This was obvious, but somehow we could never induce our German and some of our Jewish members to see it. The exile is seldom the impartial judge of his alien environment. To the average German Socialist in America, the strength of Socialism in his native land and its weakness here were but other proofs of the superiority of the German mind and the dummheit of the Americans. If they would not see what was so certain and plain, the fault be upon their own stupid heads; we from the Vaterland know what is what. Projects to Americanize the movement and give it a start toward its necessary goal, if it was to be anything but a back-room debate, were many and almost invariably negatived. They were not regular, they had not the sanction of the fathers in the Reichstag, it was not so done along the banks of the Spree. James Mackaye and Edmond Kelly wrote books to introduce Socialism to Americans, good books, readable books, but no effort was made to push them into a general circulation. Much of the literature that we did disseminate was unintelligible to average Americans. Some comrades argued that the theory and principle of Socialism were so simple it would make its own way. The ponderous volumes of Karl Marx contained the gospel. They had been translated and were accessible. Let the uninformed American turn to them and acquaint himself with the knowledge possessed by every educated European.

This pique was not wholly unreasonable. It must be confessed that from Ellis Island on we do nothing for the newcomer to our shores to arouse in him any feeling toward us but one of resentment and hatred. We set ourselves above him as a damn' Dago or damn' Dutchman and he responds by vaunting within his wounded and hostile soul the things he knows that we do not.

But the small band of Americans in the ranks continued to urge that to play the political game a party must play it, and some of these appeals led to rather unusual results.

One year it was resolved to open our campaign among Americans and in an American district that we might start off by attracting favorably the American thought. So a hall was chosen on the upper West Side in a good residential region and on a Sunday afternoon we let go with the oratorical artillery, extraordinary efforts having been made to bring in the unconverted. The opening speech was made by a gentleman with a name no average American could pronounce and who spoke the vernacular but indifferently and with a strong foreign accent. He began with a bitterly sarcastic exordium on the Statue of Liberty, which he denounced as a sham and a fraud. It was the first thing a visitor saw upon entering the port and it was a lie. It symbolized liberty in a country where liberty was not and never had been. Having made this running start, he went on to denounce the country and its institutions and people. He was a voluble person with much lung power. Before he had proceeded far the element on which we had proselyting designs had fled for the door and we could comfortably resume the good old task of converting the converted.

The resentment Americans showed to this method of luring them into the fold was regarded in some quarters as another evidence of the national inferiority. Germany was continually held up to us as the model, but no one seemed to reflect upon what would probably happen to an American if at a public meeting in Germany he should denounce the Kaiser. But the case of the gentleman that was enraged about the Statue of Liberty was the more interesting, since he was of Russian birth, had fled from his native land to escape military service, and if he had stayed, for two per centum of such criticism as he uttered in New York that day would have been whisked to Siberia. All of which will amuse but not much astonish those that have impartially considered the human possibilities in self-deception.

The steering of *The Call,* a daily journal that we issued for some years beginning in 1908, was another illustration of zeal overriding reason. If a newspaper is to live it must have readers; to have readers it must publish reading matter that many persons like to read. Not many persons but only a few like to read the incessant thunderings of a determined propaganda, no matter how good may be the cause; not many persons like to pay money to read every day what they already know. *The Call* came out at a time when the masses of New York people were ready for a new kind of a newspaper; they were not at all ready for a daily bulletin of Scientific Socialism.

Before long, *The Call* was headed for a lee shore and dangerously close thereto. All the elect felt that to let it go smash would be an intolerable disaster and defeat, so here began a long series of death-rattle appeals to keep the crippled thing going and a series of great and tireless sacrifices to that end. Men and women gave money to *The Call* they could not afford to give, denied themselves of every luxury, denied themselves of necessaries, sold small possessions, worked overtime that the publication might go on. Old smokers gave up their daily tobacco and put the money it would have cost into a box to keep alive something without warrant of existence.

Mr. Abraham Cahan, who had been a reporter on an American daily and one of the ablest and most brilliant that ever wore a fire-line badge, had started and conducted to a memorable success a daily newspaper in the Yiddish language called *The Forward*. It was not published solely for profits but made them nevertheless. In the most generous way it gave of its profits to the struggling *Call* and kept it alive. Even with this help the poor old lumping thing was chronically in extremis.

Three times in my own recollection it was breathing its last gasp because a wretched capitalistic company turned off the gas supply to the linotypes, the bills therefor not having been paid, and three times it was rescued by a personal contribution.

We gave a fair in its behalf at Grand Central Palace. Sympathetic painters donated paintings, authors gave books, women sent in specimens of their handicraft, musicians and actors contributed entertainment, there was a notable outpouring of help and good will and another notable demonstration of the spirit of self-sacrifice that possessed the rank and file of the party. Scores of members, headed by Graham Phelps Stokes, worked day and night to make the thing go. With a week of prodigious toil we made a net profit of $1500 and *The Call* absorbed that in two days.

Every one wished to help the paper. Robert Hunter wrote for it stirring editorials, Socialist artists sent in excellent cartoons, trained newspaper reporters covered assignments gratuitously. Lincoln Steffens took an interest in it and made suggestions from his own experience. The fact was that so long as it had the propaganda tag nobody would have the gift of it.

Which is exactly in line with all my experience and observation concerning all other propaganda publications. Nothing else in this world is so futile.

I do not know why we were all so eager to keep *The Call* alive but we were. One fact about it will be enough for any newspaper man. Any one that bought it must buy another journal to find out what was going on. That being the case, it had no right to live. The money it cost, if applied to other activities, would have produced results. There were never any results visible for *The Call* except anxiety, labor, and the bump from one risk to another.

We went on nominating candidates for every office in every election and collecting a meagre handful of votes; in the city, about 30,000. It was not wildly exciting but we kept on. In the

presidential election of 1904, Eugene Debs, Socialist candidate
for President, had polled 402,321 votes; four years later he had
only 420,993. At this rate of progress Socialism would come
about the time the devil turned religious.

The most encouraging sign was the large number of fine
young spirits that were attracted to the party. In Branch One
alone was a group of writers and intellectuals of the rarest
promise—Ernest Poole, the novelist, and his wife, Margaret;
Leroy and Miriam Scott, Robert Bruere, Howard Brubaker,
Charlotte Teller, Madeline Doty. To be remarked always in
this convocation of worth and talent was William J. Ghent, author of *Mass and Class* and *Our Benevolent Feudalism* and afterward of *The Road to Oregon,* one of the most successful books
of its time. He was an indefatigable worker; with Rufus W.
Weeks, he organized what he called the Collectivist Society,
which gave monthly dinners at large downtown restaurants
and attracted great gatherings to hear unusual speakers. Charlotte Perkins Gilman was one of the most effective of these.

Three men in this company stand out as unforgettable types.

The first in my recollections is Edmond Kelly. He had been
for many years the most conspicuous and successful of American lawyers in Paris. It was he that had been Anna Gould's
counsel when she divorced Boni de Castellane and he had appeared in many other important cases. After so many years of
brilliant career abroad he had returned to America to live in
retirement. The condition of the poor and of the wage-worker
had long been in his mind. He had become convinced chiefly
by reading and study that for the ills of mankind was no feasi-
ble remedy but the creating of a Socialist state, and after reaching America he avowed his faith and applied for admission to
the party.

He was an interesting and effective speaker, a powerful writer, and driven on by something few of us understood then to
throw himself into good causes and labor for them with a

singular and feverish intensity. He had saved rather slender means from his professional success, but enough to live on, and he gave liberally of the rest so far as he could. He always went immaculately dressed, looked like a prosperous statesman and when he attended the meeting of a Socialist branch in the back room of Karl Bodenbach's beer saloon, Edmond Kelly with his scholarly bearing, delicate features, carefully trimmed gray hair, and modish attire was something to be remembered.

He was not content to be engaged only in Socialist activities, he must have other outlets for his beneficent zeal. He founded the Liberal Club to bring together men and women not quite satisfied that civilization had reached its perfected state, and he made public addresses in behalf of various movements for social betterment. He was modest, kindly, tolerant, manifestly sincere, manifestly weighed upon by a persisting melancholy and as certainly making efforts to conceal the oppression. Something about him strangely wistful and gently sad impressed us all, but we could never tell what it was. He seemed to look out upon life with the eyes of one that tired of it all but was driven by some irresistible force to play out a part. At least, this was the explanation that was easiest of his mysterious bearing, and it was wrong. Once he was confined to his apartment with sickness and asked some of us to come to see him. We could not tell what was the matter with him; he chatted and smiled as usual but seemed like a man trying to escape some unpleasant thought and craving companionship and sympathy for something that he did not express. I think we were rather callous about it, but we did not know; as usual, we did not know: we never do know until it is too late.

His health was often bad, but he bore his part in all the activities of the party. He would not take any office or place of prominence, insisting always that he was only a private in the ranks, but he served there with a readiness to take on the humblest tasks that seemed strange to those that knew the stage he had played on in Paris. In the summer of 1909, his health growing worse, he went with his wife to the country and died there.

Then we understood what a tragedy had been enacted before our eyes. More than two years before he had been condemned to death by the doctors on the charge that he had what is called pernicious anemia. Having implicit faith in the mumbo-jumbo that is known as medical science he determined to do all the good he could in the brief span of life that should be left to him. He believed that the surest way to do good was to promote Socialism and to this he devoted his failing energy—under a death sentence.

Another figure of those days and ways without whom the Socialist story would be incomplete is that of the Rufus W. Weeks I have before mentioned, the vice-president of the New York Life Insurance Company.

Even so; the New York Life Insurance Company. The last place on earth from which you would expect a Socialist to emerge. The company was one of those that had been most severely scorched before the side-stepping Armstrong Committee; its president had died suddenly in a way that strongly indicated suicide; and the whole thing was pilloried as one of the gigantic brooms that operated to sweep up ready money from all about the country and dump it into the laps of the Central Financial Group—who used it after their own pleasure. Yet here was the vice-president of this most typical capitalist corporation not only an ardent Socialist but testifying to his faith with ponderable works. Year in and year out, his was the largest individual gift of money to the Socialist party. Never was altruism of a purer strain; he had from it nothing but the acrid criticism of his fellows, social ostracism, and at first a plenteous suspicion among those to whom he had joined himself. That an officer of a great capitalistic corporation should march with revolting wage-workers was not in nature. It must conceal some evil design—or else espionage! Mr. Weeks endured all this as calmly as the taunts and spurns of his own class, and gradually he won to the unbounded respect and confidence of the despised agitators to whom he had joined himself.

Like Edmond Kelly, he would never be edged into any prominence or recognition but went conscientiously about his tasks in the ranks. He could be counted upon to be at every meeting of his branch, sitting in a back seat, saying nothing but beaming behind his spectacles a kind of benison upon the whole performance. With his gray beard and thoughtful expression he seemed more like a college professor than a business man; yet business man he was and keen and able, being probably the first of living insurance actuaries. It must have been an unusual endowment to keep him in his place against the storm of criticism his course provoked. He had been made a Socialist by study and reflection; once converted he held with the tenacity of an evangelist to the faith he had discovered for himself.

The third figure among many that I recall with respect and gratitude was of a totally different type, the workingman coming by study and diligence to a commanding position, the true proletarian emerging from the shop to lead and speak, the apostle-propagandist. His name was William Mailly and he had made his way out of the ruck of wage-workers by native ability and application. Beginning life as a coal miner, he had won in his union to some office of distinction. At the time I first met him he was one of the editors of *The Call,* but his specialty was soap-boxing, at which he surpassed, in a way, almost anybody I have heard. He was the Socialist candidate for Assemblyman in the Sixth District, which comprised a tenement-house population some degrees lower in economic status than that of the Eighth. There he made a fight like that of a bulldog, and mostly unhelped. Every night he would start out, take position at some street corner and in a few minutes have about him a crowd that hung intently upon every word he uttered. Without the least grace or training as an orator, he had a natural gift of speech most remarkable and an intuitive understanding of the psychology of his audience. Off the soap-box he often seemed to me glum, morose, and taciturn; when he mounted his portable rostrum the words flowed from him like water from an opened hydrant. The most singular thing that I noticed was that he had no gift of humor and traversed completely the doctrines of the spellbinders, for he seldom told a story. His was a higher gift than that, an infallible knowledge of the best way to snatch and grip the tenement dweller's attention. Yet he was never vulgar, never played the least buffoonery, was always serious, had no tricks. He merely stood there and talked—but he made everybody listen.

He spoke a variable language, for, speaking every night, he did not repeat himself but came with new forged weapons. As to this, he told me once that he never wrote out a speech in advance and, more than that, never allowed himself to think of what he should say before he mounted the platform. "If I think out anything first," he said, "then I am trying to remember instead of giving all attention to a point I want to make. Wait for the inspiration of the moment—that's the best way."

He had to the full the proletarian suspicion of all persons that had any other background but the workshop. It seemed difficult for him to believe that a soul could feel revolt against the existing system unless revolt had been ground into it by poverty, distress, and grim struggling. Against capitalism and all its ways and works, all its beneficiaries, apologists, defenders, and pie-eaters he had imbibed a bitterness that did not stop to discriminate. He had battered on the stone wall until his hands were torn and bleeding, but the soul within him never stopped even to take breath. The greater part of his life had been spent in insurrection without tangible result; the hatred that rang in his speech had soaked into him from experience. I think that in one corner of his mind was a picture that, no matter what he might be doing or where he might be, was always more or less in his consciousness. It was a tenement house teeming with wretched people whose lives were just so many sacrifices to Moloch, so that it would have been better if they had not lived, or living it would be better if they were forever drunk that they might be insensible of the horror that crushed them down. I think he multiplied one tenement house into twenty thousand and that into the incalculable total of wasted lives upon a world that should be and was not, happy, and daily he contemplated the suffocating total. And I think that this goad that drove him along from corner to corner and sacrifice to sacrifice ended his life.

He was slightly above medium height, clear complexioned, ruddy faced, well and powerfully built, strong and hearty in voice, but his health was already undermined. No doubt it was his illness that made him at times irritable, quarrelsome, and unsocial. Yet he was also at times a genial, considerate, though never voluble companion, and he had a hidden substratum of kindness that not disease nor bitter reflections could spoil.

With the simple and abstemious life he led he should have endured for years. In the spring of 1910 it was evident that he was beginning to fail. Indeed, the strain he had put upon his physical constitution had been too much. The doctors ordered him upon a strict diet, but he refused to take the least care of himself. It was another Philpott going deliberately to death rather than relax. He continued to work as long as he had any strength and died in the summer of 1911.

So then here were two men, of totally diverse types, in the same situation, both condemned to death, facing the dread summons each in his own manner, one with sorrowful resignation, looking regretfully back upon a life he had enjoyed, one with bitter resentment against the injustice of the sentence, yet both finding consolation and sustaining power in an identical anodyne, which was devotion to a cause. And does not that fact, if we will but think of it, cast light enough upon the whole dark mystery?

A considerable part of the press was habituated to view such men as dangerous plotters against the safety of society, as personally wicked or evil-minded, demagogues and all that. It never seemed to occur to these writers to ask what induced such men to condemn themselves to privation and go to death along such ways. Demagogues do not usually offer their lives in defense of a cause; conspirators do not usually conspire for no advantage to themselves. Mailly was endowed to win in the material world a brilliant success; so were hundreds of men and women in this movement of whom the public never heard a word. They gave up the chance of their own glory for the sake of an ideal that they believed would cure the world's woes, and I could never understand why this obvious fact should not have been admitted by their opponents. If any of their opponents cared to be fair.

And about those rows, dissensions, personal clashings, cliques, jealousies, ambitions, that shook us, something remains to be said. When one went into Socialism one did not lay off like a vesture one's mortal frailties. Outsiders seemed to think one ought to do this, but in my experience I never knew it to happen. Morris Hillquit and Henry Slobodin, two of our ablest leaders, had a feud. I was idiot enough to think I could reconcile them, and gave a dinner at a Hungarian restaurant. The viands were delicious, the wine of the best, the speeches felicitous, everybody was happy, and Hillquit and Slobodin stalked home on opposite sides of the street. The Scientific Socialists continually derided the other kind and got hot sarcasms in return. Meetings about the desperate state of *The Call* sometimes lasted all night and were enlivened with bitter personalities. But despite all the squabblings, and strange as it may seem to one that never tried it, there was an immense satisfaction in belonging to the organization. Alexander Irvine wrote a brochure on *The Spiritual Content of Socialism,* and it was an excellent title, either way you read it. Assuredly, the spirit of man got more from this endeavor than from any other I have known. Whatever might be the personal frictions, we went home remembering that anyway this was a movement to establish a world without war, without poverty, without slums, without the spoliation of the worker, with an opportunity for all to live and know what life really means, and that was consolation enough. Actually and practically enough.

And this brings me to a point about this movement that I have never seen remarked but is worth noting among the curiosities of human conduct. In the other reforming crusades that I had observed, the crusaders had the incentive of a definite material advantage, the easing of debt burdens, the revival of business, the lessening of taxation, the cheapening of rents. The men and women that toiled for Socialism had for the most part not a chance of the least material advantage for themselves. Personally, Ernest Poole would be no better off under Socialism than under the existing system; Socialism would mean no personal advantage to Rufus Weeks or Kelly or Bruere or Algernon Lee or any one else that was most interested in it. The simple fact is that those that would reap most from it never gave a dang for it, and I think that is something to remember and ponder. For continually we are told that men will do nothing except for self-interest and material gain, but the truth is that men will do far more for an ideal of common benefit; and I point to the gratuitous labors of the Socialists as I knew them. The dream that led them on might have been impossible but at least it was a noble and beautiful dream. A world without war, without poverty, without the darkness of ignorance, without the brutalizing fear of penury, without debasing drudgeries, with light and opportunity for all—you would think that persons that could visualize such a world and the way to it would have some claim to be heard. Not Socialists. The mere name

"THE SOCIALIST TOWER OF BABEL"

Puck's notion of the Socialist party, April 4, 1906

seemed to shut up minds like a trap and start all the narrowest prejudices into action.

Not always. Some of the fortunate were inclined to give a hearing. The Reverend Percy Stickney Grant, rector of the fashionable Church of the Ascension, Fifth Avenue and Tenth Street, for instance. To the horror and sputtering indignation of some of his parishioners he gives his church every Sunday night to a Socialist clergyman who preaches a sermon of peace on earth, good will to men, only the protesting parshioners will not hear it. For the first time in its history the church is crowded night after night. Even the gallery is filled to capacity. More than half of the people that come are Jews. They make a most unusual congregation for a Christian church. When the plate is passed they contribute to it. The total revenues of the church are swelled. But the horrified ones are not the less horrified. Alexander Irvine usually fills the pulpit. He is an ordained minister of the Presbyterian Church. A dissenting clergyman in an Episcopalian pulpit—it is felt to be a slam against propriety.

After the services we adjourn to the chapel next door where there is a forum, conducted with signal ability by Darwin J. Meserole, son of a great house of Brooklyn. There are speakers on current topics and discussion in which the audience takes part.

One night an attorney for the privileged class comes and ridicules the notion that any change is needed in the social system, for it is perfect and lovely. He denounces Socialism because (so he says) it would tend to degrade the noble soul of man. Men are divine and should be left alone to work out their own salvation.

Voice in the Audience—Is there anything divine about the bread line?
Attorney for the Privileged—Yes sir; the men in it.
Mrs. Meserole, from the gallery—Mr. Chairman, if the bread line is divine, does it grow more divine as it grows longer?

It is a time of depression and general distress. A parade of the unemployed is planned to induce municipal relief. It is to converge upon Union Square. As it comes there, a mysterious bomb is exploded and a marcher or spectator is killed. Panic seizes the well-to-do. Here are Anarchists, here are revolutionists, here are reds and subversive elements broken loose. To this violence has come the unrestricted freedom of speech that has been so unwisely allowed to these persistent Socialists. General Bingham, the somewhat jumpy head of the police force, has the tantrums, and threatens everybody. William Travers Jerome, district attorney, sends his plain-clothes men to the Church of the Ascension Sunday night to listen to these dangerous persons, take down their speeches and arrest them if they talk incendiarism, murder, bombs, civil war or treason felony, for such proceedings are they charged withal. Finally he comes himself and listens to every word. No arson, murder, or treason felony appearing in the utterances there, he goes away, shaking his head. They must be deep people, these Socialists. They talk about the Prince of Peace and all that, but what they really mean, of course, is arson, murder, and treason felony.

Doctor Grant is not frightened by these mutterings but keeps his church open to the wicked plotters and subversive persons like the Meseroles. He likes the Socialists and trusts his life among them. One night he invites their leaders to come in a group to his house—about twenty of them. He wishes to be hospitable and feels sure that they would appreciate a friendly drink and glasses round. So he lays in a stock of good old Scotch whiskey and other restoratives. At a signal, the servant brings in trays and glasses. To his astonishment, nobody drinks. Queer conspirators, those Socialists.

The philosophy they offer is fundamentally that the earth produces enough for the abundant support of all her children. If there is want, scarcity, destitution on one hand and stupid superfluity on the other the trouble is the unequal distribution of products. The beginning of that wrong distribution is with the results of labor. Labor produces all the wealth of the world. It should have the wealth it produces. It does not have the wealth it produces because the tools of production and the channels of distribution are privately owned and operated for private profit. The tools of production and channels of distribution should be owned by the public and operated not for profit but for use. Dangerous men that preach this. Reds and malefactors.

One thing we try to make clear is that the existing system of production for profit has in it the seeds of its own destruction and the world's great disaster. Production being for profit, the cheaper the production the greater the profit; hence the incessant striving to supplant men with machines. This will burn the world's candle at both ends, since it multiplies the product while it diminishes employment and therefore the purchasing power that might consume the product. And we point to the steady increase of labor-saving machinery and the steady increase of relative production over consumption.

It is to be supposed that we tell this story badly, and I worst of all. We make no visible impression with it. In 1910 the Socialist party, in a fit of temporary derangement, nominates me for Governor of New York. For nine weeks I tear about the state and in 1912 for eleven, trying to put over the fact of an approaching Unconsumed Surplus. I think that outside the Socialist party not a man, woman, or child ever gives the slightest attention. It is not effective effort but amusing. To the sophisticated mind, few things in nature can be more comical than the spectacle of an elderly person scrambling madly from town to town and city to city, trying to tell people something they do not wish to hear. One night in White Plains, New York, I addressed an audience of eleven persons and recall with pride that only two went out before I was through. At Rome,

New York, I spoke in the open space near the railroad yards and some one thoughtfully sent down a switch engine to open its exhaust there. At that I fared better than some of my comrades upon these forlorn hopes. While I was speaking at Oneida Castle one night, Jack Garrity was speaking at Ilion, a short distance away, and was slung into the old Erie Canal for talking about the Unconsumed Surplus.

Sample passages from Life on a Soap Box:

Wellsville, New York.—Julian Keating of the *Hampton's* staff arrives with a bundle of my proofs and remains over night. The meeting is held in the fire-engine house. Seats have been provided. Nobody will occupy them. The crowd stands at the rear, back to the wall, in sullen silence. Fervent appeals from the chairman, from myself, fail to move one of the silent mass. I talk over rows of empty seats to this dark line away at the rear, standing without interest, without applause. Hence, I go back to the hotel profoundly discouraged.

A few days after election, Keating asks:

"How many votes did you get in Wellsville?"

"Seventy-eight."

"Good God! Did they vote the fire apparatus?"

Bolivar, New York.—I arrive on the Celery Express, an unluxurious means of transport that on down grades makes twenty miles an hour. It is due at 8 P.M., just in time for my meeting. It arrives at midnight. Station deserted; no autos, no hacks. I struggle up to the hotel. It is closed and dark. Knock on the door. Knock on other doors. Presently a dark shadow emerges from the other side of the street and advances.

"Hey, mister? Want a room?"

I do.

"All right, come with me. I'm the town policeman." Not under arrest, any way. He leads me around the corner to the back door of the hotel, takes a key from his hip pocket, unlocks the door, and says:

"Now climb up one flight, turn to your left and tumble into the first vacant room you can find. Got any matches?"

I lumber up the stairs, valise in one hand, burning match in the other, find a room with the door open and lunge in. No lock on the door. Five minutes later something is moving in the hall. Door opens, a dog as big as a horse comes in, surveys me with intense scrutiny and goes out. Night clerk at the Hotel Bolivar, no doubt.

Rattlersville, New York.—Hotel so bad I drag the bed to the window and sleep in my clothes with my head on the window sill. All the odors in hotels are not of Araby the Blest— nor even of the kitchen.

Brownsville, back part of Brooklyn.—"You take the Fulton Street L and go until you know you are lost. Then get out and it's six blocks to the right."

Woodhaven, Queens County.—"How do I get there?" "Oh, Lord! Well, you'd better go to the Atlantic Avenue station of the Long Island, get a train for Hackmetack or some such place and ask for Gus Schnitzler's beer saloon. He'll tell you the rest."

Nine weeks, night and day. When I am through I return from the wilderness and drop in upon the charmed circle at Considine's. Impresario Lewis is there. He has learned that Socialist campaigners travel at their own expense, and effectively he amends his former disparaging introduction. I am not a lunatic, as he had thoughtlessly said. To be crazy requires some sub-stratum of intelligence. I am not crazy, but only the nation's incomparable dumb-bell.

The Unconsumed Surplus remained unconsumed whether as the tangible products of toil or as the oratorical offerings from the soap-box. Nobody would give a living hoot for it. That was 1910–1912. Twenty years later I heard in barber shops, smoking cars and hotel rooms, and read in the most reactionary capitalist newspapers the exact statement that no one would listen to in 1910–1912, the exact statement for which Jack Garrity was thrown into the Erie Canal.

What? Had the world come around with contrition to hear the utterances of its soap-boxer? Not at all. He was as forgotten as the wind that blew through Pharoah's whiskers. But Evolution, which is to soap-boxing as Ossa to a wart, had come, and to its tuition men pay heed, willy-nilly.

But the soap-boxers keep right on, 1910–1912, and all other years, doggedly at their task if unheeded. A world without war, without poverty, without slums, without the spoliation of the worker, with an opportunity for all to live and know what life really means—it is enough.

Chapter XIV

THE PHILOSOPHY OF PIGMENT

O N a Saturday in May, 1908, the Republican Club, in West Fortieth Street, New York, was holding a luncheon forum. A topic of vital communal interest was to be discussed. First came a clergyman, well known to all the city, able, elocutionary, wise; then two distinguished lawyers, long practised in polemics; then a learned judge, then a man of public office. After these, one other that eclipsed all the rest. In the logical and coherent arrangement of his matter, in apt illustration, in research and knowledge, in the polished and carefully chosen cameos of his language, in the faultless fluency of his utterance —unequalled. Here was a man of manifestly unusual mind and equipment; he astonished and charmed all that heard him. Who was he? A graduate of two great universities in America and of Heidelberg in Germany, a noted scholar, a winner of honors abroad; one that had travelled and taken good note of men and manners. If you spoke with him he responded with that quiet courtesy that is the stamp of the cloister. A man to mark and to be glad to know.

Yes. And yet in no part of the country in which he was born would he, this man, be secure against daily and gratuitous insult and indignity; in no part would his great and unusual attainments have either the recognition to which they were entitled or the opportunity for exercise from which society might profit. In no part of the United States would his status among his fellowmen be essentially above that of the criminal, the gangster, or the moral leper. In no part of the United States could he pass freely without the unprovoked hostility, without the scornful or hateful gaze of most of the persons he might encounter.

If he should seek to earn his living in a profession that he was fitted to adorn, he would find every door slammed in his face and bolted fast. Were he to seek employment in some business concern or enterprise, he would find it impossible to obtain any situation adapted to his learning, worth, and native ability. Ten thousand men with much less endowment than his and with a fraction of his capacity for valuable service would be employed where he would not be allowed a toe-hold. He might, indeed, get work in sweeping the floor, or carrying out the ashes, or cleansing the spittoons; but in all the length and breadth of his country he could find not one place that his training and mentality adapted him to fill for his own benefit and the avail of the community.

If, giving up the attempt to make use of his gained knowledge, he should don the garb and take upon himself the tasks of a mechanic, he could find no factory or work-shop where he would be allowed suitable employment. He might have acquired the greatest dexterity, skill, facility ever known and he could make no use of it. He could not even join a labor union.

Men and women would go out of their way to affront him, to make him unhappy, to taunt him with his helpless state as society's captive and victim bound at the stake of its inveterate hatred.

He could belong to no clubs, and if he attempted to enter many a church dedicated to the lowly Nazarene he would be shown to the door or herded into a gallery or made to feel that he was an undesirable outcast to whom the salvation taught by Christ was denied by men.

If he were to visit the capital of his proud native land, the city supposed to give tone and example to the rest, he would have great difficulty to discover a hotel that would allow him to lodge under its roof, a restaurant where he could be fed, or if he should fall ill, a hospital where he would be treated. If he should search out such a hospital, he would find himself an object of no courtesy and scant attention, and when spoken to always by his first name, not with the use of the title ordinary among civilized people. If he should attempt to get books from a public library he would be snubbed and scurvily handled. If he should visit a public park he would find himself shunted into an area separate from other visitors. Riding in a street car, he would probably be met with resentful looks on the faces of passengers he had never offended, many of whom would pointedly refuse to occupy the same seat with him.

If through another or a ruse he should obtain a ticket to a theatre, or a concert, the ticket would be taken from him at the door, but he would not be allowed to enter. If in some manner he worked his way past the doorkeeper, he would be torn from his seat and thrown out as if he were some form of wild beast.

So it would be everywhere in Washington; but if he should venture into the Southern part of the country in which he was born, far worse would be his lot. On a railroad train he would be forced to travel in an old, ill-equipped, unsafe car, segregated from other passengers, marked with the branding of a contemned inferiority. He would not be allowed to eat with other passengers in the dining car; if he waited for a train he would be thrust into an inferior waiting room; lest he should defile with even his presence the members of the superior caste, a separate entrance or exit would often be designated for him. If he should seek to enter a hotel he would be stopped at the door; if he should urge his right as a traveller he would be expelled with clamor and violence and be fortunate if he escaped alive. If he should attempt to visit for any purpose whatsoever the office of a professional or business man in an office building he must walk up the stairs, no matter how many flights, for he would not be allowed to enter an elevator. Freely and without question a low-browed ruffian could use that elevator; a criminal, an illiterate, a thug. This man could not pass its gate.

If he should be accused of the violation of any law, he could not have the least assurance of justice, no matter how innocent; he might not be able even to obtain counsel. A vile murderer, a depraved thief, a slimy rogue would be provided with able attorneys that would battle arduously to save him from punishment. This man might not be able to assert even his barest human rights.

He might be counted as a citizen of a Southern state and yet, by a flaunted lawlessness, have nothing but the name of citizenship. Although a resident he would not be allowed to vote. The organic law of the nation would be trampled upon to deprive him of the rights that law guaranteed to him. If he were to utter a word of protest or seek to uphold the dignity and worth of that Constitution of his native land he might be lynched. If he were lynched, no effort would be made to punish his murderers. At every turn an ingenious aggression would remind him of his lowly state, a cold malignity press into him the fetters of an essential bondage. His soul would be wrung with deliberate brutalities at the hands of persons without a tithe of his learning, accomplishments or character. The helot of the ages, the door-mat of what we are pleased to call, with unconscious irony, a Christian civilization, the pariah and Untouchable of our bulwarked caste.

Well, why? Ostensibly, because of his complexion. He is about three shades darker than I am. Hated for a trifle of coloring matter beyond his control. Hated and spat upon. Even in the North, plenteously hated. If he goes to a Northern hotel, told that there are no rooms, even if half the place is empty. If he tries to buy a ticket to a theatre, told there are no seats left, with half of the tickets still in the rack. If by industry, thrift, the practise of the white man's boasted virtues, he accumulates money and tries to buy property in certain regions of the city, his house will be dynamited and his life imperilled until he moves out. Everywhere a foot upraised to spurn him, everywhere a barrier across his path to keep him back. Hated for a trifle of coloring matter.

Yet how can that be? Here is another man, still darker in complexion, and he travels about freely, occupies rooms at the best hotels, is received in the best drawing rooms, is treated with invariable respect.

He is a Hindu rajah; Doctor W. E. B. Du Bois, graduate of Heidelberg, is an American Negro.

What difference does that make? In a country called a democracy, a country that professes the doctrine of equality, boasts of its liberality, calls itself the land of opportunity, vaunts itself over the inferior European countries, feels itself too good to associate with the depraved French and the damn' Dago, here is a most extraordinary situation. How does it come about?

It comes about for two reasons. First, the Negro was once a slave; he still typifies, therefore, to the immature mind, labor in its lowest form. The Anglo-Saxon cannot rid his blood of that old taint of snobbery. The Negro being connected by tradition with this lowest form of labor, he constitutes in our society the lowest caste.

With this and still going far beyond it, infinitely far, is another reason.

The Negro in America is the victim of the sentiment of a Lost Cause, and the other sentiment of sectional pride. It was for him that the Rebellion failed and in spirit the typical Southerner has never accepted that failure.

This is plain speech. It seems to me that nothing else is appropriate. Sectional pride, sore memories of an old defeat, and Anglo-Saxon snobbery have made this country a sign of shame and sullied in the world's eyes all its best achievements.

And thus we come to the phase of the matter that requires a place in these citations.

There had been a race riot and a Negro lynching in Springfield, Illinois. In Lincoln's town, almost under the shadow of the monument raised to him men call The Liberator, a member of the race he is said to have liberated was put to death by a mob.

There was a white man in America that had long thought about this unspeakable national disgrace and its causes. If inherited tendencies are anything, his sympathies should not have been keen, at least, on the side of the oppressed dark-skinned men, for his antecedents were Southern and his grandfather had been known as a Copperhead in the Civil War. But he happened to have an exquisite sense of justice, a broad democratic faith and an inquiring mind. He had long before, in searching out the springs of the national sinning, come to the conclusion that the tattered excuse offered for the most horrible of these reversions to savagery had no application to the majority of cases; that most of the lynchings in the South had nothing to do with crimes against women but were provoked by the implacable hatred of the Southern white men. He saw also that throughout the South merely for that reason and no other, Negroes were without rights or opportunity, that basic justice and the common instincts of humanity were alike perverted that they might remain without hope while revenge should be satiated. It seemed to him that these were conditions intolerable and perilous and some protest should be framed against them.

In this spirit, William English Walling went to Springfield immediately after the lynching and investigated the crime. Coming away, he had a thought of a great national organization of fair-minded whites and intelligent blacks that should throw some form of shield between the Negro and his oppressor. He came on straight to New York and to persons that he thought might be sympathetic offered the outline of his conception. He was a Socialist. Being also an old friend, he naturally talked of it to me.

He had a small flat in West Thirty-ninth Street. There he asked us to come one afternoon in March, 1909. Five of us responded, all told. We talked informally about the possibilities of creating some society or organization that might contend against the racial madness that possessed the North only a little less than the South. The whole thing seemed comically futile. This stone wall was of the granite of prejudice, clamped with steel bars of an accepted tradition. Four or five men and women—what could their bare hands achieve except bruises and derision? Preposterous to think of it. The undismayed Walling could see nothing absurd in the proposal. Patiently he sketched his plan, sketched it many times, that day and other days. We continued to meet at his flat, sometimes five, sometimes six, once as many as eight; Mary White Ovington, Henry Moskowitz, Doctor Stephen Wise, Leonora O'Reilly, Oswald Garrison Villard, and others. Between times, Mr. Walling went about the city, talking of his dream, indefatigable, restless, pouring forth a tide of nervous energy that put all the rest of us to shame.

At last we felt in a position to issue a call for a national conference. It was held (with many misgivings) in the hall of the United Charities Association and brought out a response that astonished and rather startled us. Professor Burt G. Wilder of Cornell was there and dissected eighteen brains of white and of colored persons to show that there was not a particle of difference. We heard from unexpected lips burning protests against the national iniquity and out of that conference emerged the National Association for the Advancement of Colored People, the most efficient instrument for racial justice ever devised, attaining to more than 100,000 members, organized in every state in the Union, and having a notable record in serving the ends of justice. Scores of innocent men it has saved from hanging, other scores it has released from prison; it has carried to the Supreme Court of the nation and won there its steady protests against the insane persecution of men whose offense was complexion; it has battled everywhere for tolerance, opportunity, and equality. It has blocked repeated and lawless attempts to segregate Negroes, it has defeated for office men that stood for race persecution, it has been of inestimable value to the whole colored citizenry. For all this the basic credit is due to Mr. Walling, who conceived and founded the Association.

In the first twenty-three years of its existence it has not done all that we hoped it might do, for the stone wall of this prejudice was too strong, the jungle instinct of race hatred too deeply rooted. But it has made a notable beginning. Slowly the race conditions in America, bad as they are, tend to better. Slowly is growing among enlightened Southerners a perception of the high cost of hatred, and the obligations of the common humanity; and looking upon the progress already made, one can take heart and believe that some day Americans will cleanse their flag from the dark blotch that race persecution has flung upon it.

One reason for such faith is that on this matter all science points one way. It has already demonstrated that there is no such thing among the children of earth as a real division into races. The old-time fantasies about Semitic, Hamitic, and Indo-Aryan were shattered long ago. The Black Race, Red Race, the Brown Race, the Yellow Race are but terms of convenience, not of scientific fact. For reasons still to be perfectly ascertained, peoples dwelling in certain regions or under certain conditions of sunlight, air, and soil, tend to develop certain physical characteristics or tints, but this has nothing to do with their essential traits or capabilities. Taking them by and large, men are the same regardless of complexion or shape of nose or curl of hair.

The only real differences among them are differences of opportunity.

Theories of the superior and the inferior race are mere fictions, convenient for the purposes of imperialistic exploitation or to excuse savagery, but otherwise footless. Variations there are, of course, among nations and tribes in history, institutions, ideals, experiences, and lines of development, but these differences are so trivial that in the mass they are not worth bothering about.

It is odd that the people that have made in the world the loudest boast of their devotion to liberty and humanity are the people that have made the worst showing of race prejudice and race injustice. The condition of the Negroes in the Southern part of the United States is not much worse than the condition of the Negroes in British South Africa. The American colonists were not more savage to the natives than were the English colonists in Australia and Tasmania. Wherever the Anglo-Saxon has gone he has walked with head high and insolent mien while his iron-shod boots have ground Black, Red, Yellow, and Brown men into the dust. Let India answer as to this, and Georgia and Mississippi.

Avid pursuit of the imperialistic phantom is superficially responsible for much of the wrong, but still farther back is that same Anglo-Saxon inheritance of caste and snobbishness. It seems impossible for the Anglo-Saxon to be quite at ease unless he can feel that he is above somebody else. "The French," said Edmond Kelly in one of his fascinating lectures, "have a passion for equality." The passion of the Anglo-Saxons is all the other way. To horn in and to shoulder out with something my neighbor has not seems to be first concept of Anglo-Saxon life.

I have spoken of the persisting evil of the Civil War's aftermath as a factor in these abominations. Without the least prejudice one way or the other and looking upon the matter as if it were a judicial inquiry, come, let us see how this enters the problem. The simple fact is that for seventy years the average resident of the Southern states has felt impelled to expend upon helpless Negroes the resentment and disappointments of that conflict. Two generations have not sufficed to erase this profound feeling. Southern children are taught at their mothers' knees and in a thousand ways to keep alive the passions of the dead-and-gone struggle. The psychology is not too difficult; we must remember that the South fully and without misgiving expected to win that war. Slavery being the quintessence of the caste system, caste had reacted upon the Southerner to produce a conviction of superiority. For a full generation it had been the boast of the Southern leaders that in their own phrase, "one Southerner could whip five Yankees." These leaders believed they had made arrangements to ensure success; to almost the end they deemed eventual victory certain. No people ever suffered a greater chagrin and disappointment in defeat. The war was fought about the Negro, to determine whether his flesh should continue or cease to be subject to ownership like that of a horse or mule. Profoundly the moral defect in the Southern cause augmented the Southern resentment. It must prove to the world that the Confederacy was right, that the Negro was an inferior creature, that he had in fact neither a soul nor rights that any white man was bound to respect.

The impulse is probably natural to support these ancient and fly-blown contentions by keeping the Negro of the South still in a state of subjection, but the results have been disastrous upon whites and blacks alike. Nay, they have been worse upon the whites, and the best friend of the South today is one that seeks to free it from its self-imposed bondage of hate. Always the hater loses more than the hated. The Negroes in the South are deprived of normal status as human beings, denied opportunity, denied justice in the courts, denied the protection of the laws, but they have freer souls than the men that persecute them, immeasurably freer.

What race prejudice really has of substance may easily be shown by a single illustration.

In defiance of that Constitution we pretend to adore, in the South we exclude Negroes from the ballot. The ostensible excuse we give for this lawlessness is that they are low and ignorant and would be unable to use the franchise intelligently. Then to make sure that they shall continue in ignorance we scant their educational facilities by granting them only a meagre and wholly disproportionate share of the public-school fund. If we allowed them to vote they would be able to obtain their due share of this fund. So we refuse to allow them to vote, that we may refuse to allow them to be educated, that we may say they are ignorant and unfit to vote. And all this because we are still keeping alive the passions of a war that came to an end almost seventy years ago.

Around and around the stump, head in the air, each step on a Negro's neck, thanking God for race superiority.

If any one doubts that this is exactly what we do, one has only to turn to the records.

In eighteen states of this Union there were in 1930, 3,326,-482 Negro children of school age, of whom fewer than one-half were in any schools. Of these, more than a million were not even enrolled; of those enrolled, 75 per cent were in grades lower than the fifth. Most of these states provided inadequately or negligently for the higher education of Negroes, and whereas the average yearly expenditure for education in the whole country is $80 per capita of school children, the average expenditure for the education of school children in these states is only $15.

Most of these states have laws forbidding the teaching of white and colored children in the same schools. Colored children, therefore, can have only such facilities as are provided in the colored schools. In the state of Georgia, 43 per cent of the children of school age are colored, but only 9 per cent of the expenditures for education goes to colored schools. The value of the buildings used for white schools is $33,000,000; of the buildings used for colored schools, $4,000,000. There are regions where the Negroes pay the larger share of the taxes and of these taxes five dollars are spent upon the education of white children for every dollar spent upon the education of colored children. I am, indeed, understating the actualities to give an average. There are regions where the disproportion is ten dollars to one.

For these conditions the North is as much to blame as the South, and as ready to cry out against ignorant Negroes when confronted with the inevitable results of the ignorance we have fostered.

Yet for all men of any spirit of tolerance, out of this gloomy prospect comes one fact for rejoicing and the taking of hope. It is that despite all these barriers of a mad and stupid hatred, the Negro makes progress. Chiefly by his own efforts and in the face of every obstacle, he is winning to education and to achievement. Decade by decade, he reduces the percentage of illiteracy among his own people. Only those that have studied this subject have any conception of the sacrifices poor Negroes make in the South to wrest from terrific conditions an education for their children. Come, let us be reasonable. Tell us no more of that moldy fable about inferior races. Upon no people that have made the great progress the Negroes of America have made in seventy years will fit for a moment the badge of inferiority. Dig back into the history of your own human group, haughty Saxon, and if you can show me anywhere a similar period of equal development, I will admit that the blessed Constitution may properly be set aside to prevent Doctor W. E. B. Du Bois and James Weldon Johnson from exercising their guaranteed rights of citizenship.

But to return to the Association, it had been no more than launched when it was joined by a man to whom all these conditions had long been familiar and who had tried with conscience and energy to combat them.

This was John E. Milholland, an old-time newspaper reporter, next a political writer on *The New York Tribune,* at this time past middle life, tremendously energetic, tireless as a watch spring, wound tense on this subject of the Negro pariah. An eager, sanguine man, all Saxon in appearance, all Celt in sympathies and feelings; a blond man, with tawny hair, a tawny mustache, ruddy face, active blue eyes, a swift and spontaneous manner. Something of a politician, he had led a revolt in the Republican party, of which he was a member, against the devious methods of Tom Platt, the Republican Boss. Indeed, it was through the party door that he came actively into the race question. His party had made glib and eloquent promises to the Negro concerning the cure of disfranchisement in the South; his party had easily the power to combat this disfranchisement; his party quietly acquiesced in the wrong. He wanted his party to keep straight; he found that on this issue it was committed to go crooked. In response, he founded and carried on for some years a virtually one-man concern that he called the Constitution League, the object whereof was to direct attention to the violation of the Constitution practised in the South. This led him into many inquiries and at last to a knowledge of the actual race situation in America that few men of his time possessed. Of lynchings, shootings, burnings, and the like inflicted upon colored people he gathered a large and curious body of testimony. Incidentally, it included some matters of which the less said the better except this, that they were calculated to fill the average reader with fear and horror.

He had travelled widely and observantly, read much, knew history, loathed autocracy and aristocracy, had an innate urge for democracy. Few men could surpass him, I think, as an offhand narrator, and some of his stories of caste in England had a fine dramatic quality entirely aside from their significance. When the Boer War came on, that most miserable and abominable of all wars of modern time, he and I went about New York organizing pro-Boer meetings. At one of these that packed Cooper Institute he made one of the greatest speeches I have ever heard, a truly magnificent flight of oratory. It dealt with reasons, was fortified with facts, and without vituperation laid bare the filthy and shameful motives behind the attack upon the South African republics. At other meetings of ours, Robert B. Roosevelt and the mayor of Grand Rapids, Michigan, were speakers.

Milholland's view of this war may be worth detailing, as it shows the man and his mental processes. It seemed to him that this was an assault of a powerful and greedy nation upon weak people struggling for their rights, and that it had a peculiar significance to the United States. The old American tradition was being put to a rigid testing. Two little republics were contending against a great monarchy for the principle for which the American Revolution was fought. On the side of the British were arrayed all the forces of reaction, the powerful financial interests, what is called "society," all the latent snobbery, all the crawling sentiment that felt this country to be only a colony or a division of the British Empire. Milholland maintained that the American attitude would show how much of the American tradition remained alive and how much had been atrophied by materialistic aims, money-grubbing, and the propaganda of race. If America no longer cared for fundamental principles here at stake, one might date fairly well the beginning of the downfall of the Republic.

He was destined to a sharp enlightenment about these things and in a manner totally unexpected. He had become the chief owner of a patent apparatus much used in the post offices. It was an invention of value and importance and from the revenues it produced he had most of his income. One day he came into my office, cast some papers on my desk, and said in a despondent way:

"Well, I'm through. I'll have to quit you on this Boer business. They've put the screws on me and I must stop."

"Who has put the screws on you?" said I.

"Washington. I hate to give up, but there's no choice."

He would say no more about it then, but I understood. He had received an intimation that his post-office contracts were in danger and that meant his livelihood. The administration was all pro-British. It refused to receive representatives of the Boer government, although the Transvaal was still an independent nation and entitled to international courtesy, and it allowed Great Britain privileges in the American ports and market that it would not have allowed to a nation fighting against a powerful foe. John Hay was Secretary of State. He had been Ambassador to Great Britain, which is enough to say of him in this matter. Few Americans have had enough fibre to remain American after entering St. James. Poor Mr. McKinley was President. He did not know what it was all about. Mr. Hay knew. That was enough.

The resulting disillusion was to Milholland the more poignant because he had gathered from some trustworthy source definite information that from the beginning of the quarrel the South African republics had looked confidently to the United States, sure of its support in such an issue. They were not idiots, the Boers; they knew that against the 25,000 or 30,000 men they could put into the field the British could easily muster a million; but they believed that America would intervene to uphold their rights. America never lifted a hand for them but only reinforced their enemies. Then the Boers put their backs to the wall and fought for liberty with a skill and courage that filled all the rest of the world with admiration. Except the United States. The Irish sent contingent after contingent to fight with them. From France came sympathy and brave soldiers. The whole thing left the United States cold. Britain waged the war to obtain possession of the gold mines of the Rand and thus complete her ownership of the world's greatest sources of gold supply. Against such a purpose the rights of the republics were just some more scraps of paper. We let it go at that.

The sequel of the Boer war is the supreme sardonic jest of history. Great Britain made the war for this purpose to round her gold supply. By propaganda, by incessant argument, by cajolery and by other means she had previously induced the United States and other nations to abandon silver and establish a single monetary standard of gold, of the supply of which she purposed a virtual monopoly. When the test came, she was the first country to abandon this single standard of "honest money" she had forced upon the world. If a fair sense of the ironic obtains on Olympus, there must have been hilarious times upstairs when this news came along.

Milholland's antecedents were of the North of Ireland, but his sympathies took in the whole island and all its variations of religion and interest. He once had a notion that he could bring together the contending factions after the establishment of what is called the Free State. He knew that in Irish history when Brian Boru had wished to unite the chieftains he prepared a great Irish elk or something of the kind and made a feast to which all the chiefs were invited. Milholland sent over to Ireland a great fat Adirondacks deer with instructions to have it prepared for a "Feast of Reconciliation." It was duly cooked and eaten but it could not make peace between the Anglicized Irish and the Irish Irish; nothing could do that.

Milholland was a warm and intimate friend of General Booth, founder of the Salvation Army, and championed Booth and his cause. He had a beautiful daughter who became a member of the Socialist party and a noted campaigner for

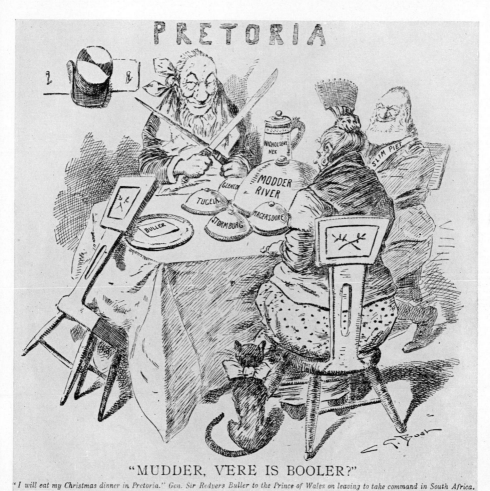

"MUDDER, VERE IS BOOLER?"

" I will eat my Christmas dinner in Pretoria." Gen. Sir Redvers Buller to the Prince of Wales on leaving to take command in South Africa.

Bush's famous cartoon on the Boer War printed in *The New York World,* December 25, 1899. Oom Paul, President of the Transvaal Republic, was still in possession of Pretoria, then and long afterward. The names on the dishes represent British defeats in the war

woman's suffrage. I happened to hear her the first time she attempted a speech in public and she nearly perished of stage fright. I have seldom seen any one so terrified. A few months later she was addressing great audiences and doing it with a perfect aplomb and magical success. She died at almost the beginning of what would have been a brilliant career; and the people of upper New York State have named a mountain in her honor.

Milholland consolidated his Constitution League with the National Association, of which he became a vice-president. His interest in it continued to the end; his bust stands now in the chapel of Howard University, the great colored educational institution at Washington. Few men are more gratefully remembered by the submerged people he tried so gallantly to help.

So again to the battering against this particular stone wall and the impression thus far made upon it. I recall an incident.

Carl Schurz and David Graham Phillips were talking at Schurz's house and not long before his death. Schurz in philosophic mood was recalling experiences.

"No reform ever gets what it sets out to get," he said. "Often it seems to win nothing and to prove just another disappointment. But it always gains something."

He spoke of the German democratic movement of 1848 which caused his own hurried exit to America and safety. Apparently it failed, that splendid dream of revolt. With the reaction came imperialism and the Franco-Prussian war. As a matter of fact, the futile revolt had sown its seeds. Eventually, it would flower into something notably fine. Besides, things after 1849 were never so bad as they had been before. If there was lèse majesté in Germany men did not go the road of thorns that Robert Blum trod.

"No just revolt ever totally fails. We do not get all we want but we get something. Take the Abolition movement in America. We thought that when we had destroyed slavery the Negro would be in all respects as free as a white man, a citizen like other citizens, and endowed with the common rights. When we think of the terrible condition of the Negroes in the South today we might be tempted to think the Abolition movement had failed. It did not fail. To abolish slavery was a tremendous gain. The emancipation of the Negro from the savage conditions imposed upon him by hatred and prejudice will take time but it will come. Think how long it took to end slavery!"

Chapter XV

TRUST-BUSTING AND OTHER INDOOR SPORTS

ONE would say now that forty years ago any person really pausing to think about the matter might have seen that industrial evolution meant industrial consolidation. The system by which mankind was supplied with its daily needs, the system of production for profit, was generating within itself a centripetal power that was dragging the units together and must keep on thus dragging them. As simple as syrup, as irresistible as fate, was all this process. Production being for profit, the cheaper the production the larger the profit, the larger the unit the cheaper the production. Why not?

Greater economy, greater efficiency. It was the force unturnable. Nothing could be more natural, nothing more reasonable. Yet in its looming shadow men saw coiled the serpent folds of another minotaurus seeking to devour us, and forth went many a stout champion all armed to do combat for our salvation, as St. George smote the dragon. For once more Monopoly was raising its head in what the English would call our midst.

Curious to the reflective philosopher is the natural history of monsters in America. Looking back, it seems to be the fact that the country has scarcely ever been free from the lethal approach of some hideous demon of destruction. The rum fiend, or the tobacco habit or Tammany Hall or Anarchism or the Red Flag or the Single Tax or the Hordes of Europe—there has always been something horned and horrible to disturb our slumbers with its stealthy approach. But of all these, not even excepting the demon of rum, none had at the time I speak of so great a power to shake us with alarm as this same Monopoly.

The very name countered upon our traditional prejudices and, no less, our present security. As the consolidating process went on and corporations became greater, richer, and therefore more powerful, out came the battle bell and sounded its alarums up and down the West. A National Anti-Monopoly League was formed; it spread its gospel of freedom to the less responsive East; Francis B. Thurber became its president. The Grange movement (strictly speaking, the Patrons of Husbandry), went into politics, organized for election, and for once banded together in one resolve the individualistic farmers, terrified the politicians, routed the railroad cohorts, fashioned a new adjective and planted it permanently in the American language.

One of their demonstrations was staged in 1873. It was a line of springless farm wagons banging over the clay roads to the macadamized highways of our town. Four miles long, that parade was said to be. Through the astonished and rather awestruck streets it went, almost every wagon adorned with banners shouting revolt and defiance to the money lords. "No More Monopolies," "Down with the Currency Monopolists," "We Demand Fair Railroad Rates," "Farmers Insist upon their Rights," and so on. All the morning the line hammered along to the Fair Ground, where these amazing insurgents filled the grand-stand while a candidate for Governor, in whose face shone still the sudden fear of God, promised them implicit obedience.

Promised it and gave it. There were similar processions in most of the ninety-nine counties of our state, and when the ballot boxes were opened in November, behold the grim-faced and stern-lipped farmers had swept the state and proceeded at once to enact the laws that the railroads anathematized as "granger."

Against the assaults of the Monopoly demon the sure defender and powerful champion was believed to be Competition. Monopoly, of course, sought to strangle Competition. Blessed

Competition must be rescued from the claws of Monopoly. Well, but how? Easy was the way. The farmers complained most bitterly about the monopoly of transportation effected by the railroads. As soon as this was clear, new railroad companies were formed all about the country to build competing lines and thus beat off the demon's talons. Towns and cities supposed to be undergoing asphyxiation subscribed with hope renewed to the stock of these competing ventures. It became a patriotic duty and a public service to subscribe; a fervor as of a religion went over the Middle West. Public meetings were held; certain newspapers flamed and thundered. Hundreds of companies were formed, thousands of miles of unneeded track were laid. Some communities were drained to form the capital stock; many men gave beyond their means. I recall some that were ruined.

All of these brave adventurings had an identical sequel. The lines were built, the trains began to run, more or less, the monopolistic railroads went their way serenely monopolizing, and the competing lines passed into receiverships whence they were absorbed at a fraction of their costs by the monopoly they were created to destroy. One identical end for all.

Some thoughtful genius then discovered that the reason for these failures was the great expense of building, equipping, and operating the standard-gauge railroad of four feet, eight and a half inches, and showed that with a gauge of three feet the cost would be less than one half. This chapter in railroad history (and of human folly) is now forgotten but once it loomed large upon the horizon of hope. People became convinced that the narrow-gauge railroad offered the true solution of the rail monopoly problem. Again a wave of rebellion swept over the country. More public meetings, more companies formed, more stock subscribed, more communities drained. Narrow-gauge railroads appeared, threading the Western map with marks of beneficent augury. Then it was discovered that they too were but another mirage. There could be no through shipment;

freight shipped by these lines must be transferred at junction points to the standard lines and transhipment was too costly. Short of paralleling every standard-gauge line in the country with one of three feet the narrow-gauge idea had no chance. Such a gigantic paralleling project was actually urged. Fortunately it was never attempted.

Still blessed Competition continued to be the panacea for all monopoly ills. Combinations began to be called trusts and the new word was loaded with new terrors. Strictly speaking, if it meant anything, it meant a super-holding company that knit together many units. Presently it began to be applied to any form of co-ordination in business. Then it grew so hateful that it was dropped from any legitimate use and became a sign of abhorrence and of public wrath. The more the consolidating process spread the more the generality of men denounced it. One that did not go through that period cannot now readily grasp the intensity of the feeling—in some quarters. The trust problem came at times to overshadow everything else. The national life was being sapped. The process must stop or we perish.

All political conventions declared against the ever advancing, ever devouring octopus. Most public men denounced it, or pretended to do so; sometimes with burning eloquence they denounced it when they were the beneficiaries of the thing they cursed. The nation clamored, and finally Congress bent to the storm. John Sherman evolved the celebrated Sherman Antitrust Law that made what were called combinations in restraint of trade criminal offenses and provided punishments for all persons guilty thereof.

With this the problem was believed to be solved and the nation drew a long breath of ease. The Federal government had taken in hand the evil-doers and would break across its knee the besom of destruction wielded by the depraved trust. It was but hope in vain. The law was on the statute books but now the difficulty seemed to be to have it enforced. When the second Cleveland administration came in it was fondly expected, because of Mr. Cleveland's declarations, to make vigorous application of Doctor Sherman's celebrated Hot Drops for Bad Trusts. In a short time Joseph Pulitzer in his *New York World,* then the leading Democratic journal of the country, was accusing Mr. Cleveland of violating his platform pledges by allowing the wretched trust criminals to live outside of the jails wherein they belonged. At Mr. Pulitzer's direction, David Graham Phillips wrote a series of articles reciting the misdeeds of trust after trust, sternly demanding thereto the immediate attention of Mr. Cleveland's Attorney General, Mr. Richard Olney, and notifying the citizenry that it had been betrayed. Every article concluded with these resounding words:

"Such, Mr. Olney, are the facts, and here, sir, is the law," whereupon the same quotation from the Sherman act "every combination in restraint of trade," and so on, all duly set forth.

But Mr. Olney did not move, the trusts continued to multiply and grow in power. The Presidential election of 1896, turning upon the money question, for a time diverted the general thought, but when that was over, the newspaper trust hunt was resumed with avidity. It figured largely in the campaign of 1900, in which that eminent philosopher, Mr. Richard Croker, evolved the theory that trusts were bad because they deprived young men of a chance to go into business for themselves. Wreck was the threat held forth to any party or public man that did not stand rigid against such wickedness.

The cartoonists of that day did manful service against the Trust peril. Homer Davenport pictured it as a giant with huge muscles and small head, a cruel eye, a mocking smile, and carrying a whip that at the order of the Money Power, his master, he wielded upon the shrinking person of the Common Man. Opper made a series of brilliant cartoons showing the callous mirth of the evil-minded reprobates that formed the trusts. They were indeed the villains of the piece. Everybody took a whack at them.

Now and then some public officer would make a feint at enforcing the law and prosecuting its violators. He became for the moment the popular idol. Curious results sometimes followed. Men that believed in the trusts, drew great fees from the trusts, went along with the trusts to do their bidding, were chosen to the United States Senate or some other high place by reason of one anti-trust gesture that they never meant, and for which they were paid.

There can be no doubt that some of the great combinations exercised in a tyrannical and arbitrary way the power with which they had clothed themselves. Often the bitter complaints made against them were abundantly justified. Miss Tarbell's revelations, and Henry Demarest Lloyd's concerning the oil industry, what Lawson brought forth about copper and other great enterprises, the facts revealed concerning the ruthless satrapy erected in the tobacco business, came now to one exact interpretation. In the pursuit of the great profits made available by these combinations, men, blinded by the possibilities, hesitated not at fraud, oppression, assaults, arson, and murder, and would therefore hesitate as little, or less, to reduce the population to the condition of hired servants and the government to that of an obsequious lackey. But no revelations seemed to check the process nor free the small dealer or small producer from the boa constrictor wound about him. In the oil field, for instance, Dan Rice of Marietta, Ohio, put up a fight for his business independence and right to live that if it were fully told would rank as one of the great epics of commerce. In the end, he went down to defeat with the rest, and the octopus swept on.

The government was at last moved to proceed against some of the law-breakers and prosecuted, with others, the Standard Oil Company and the American Tobacco Company. In both

THE NEW ANTHEM AT PHILADELPHIA.

Ring Out and Proclaim Trust-Imperialism Throughout the Land.

HOMER DAVENPORT'S TRUST MONSTER

(The figure at the extreme right is Mark Hanna) *New York Journal*, May 10, 1900

instances it won decisions that were sustained by the Supreme Court. Not only were they sustained but Mr. Justice Harlan delivered from the bench a scathing denunciation of the tobacco dragon such as had not before been heard in those conservative precincts. But the practical futility of prosecution and denunciation alike was quickly shown. These companies, convicted of an illegal combination in restraint of trade, merely resolved themselves into smaller companies that worked together for their former ends and the situation was not really changed. It may be true that because of the decision the oil field became open to companies that otherwise would have been excluded from it, but this was of no advantage to the public. It merely meant three hideous filling stations instead of one with the same prices at each.

In point of fact, the only combinations against which the law was enforced with distinguished success were labor unions, which were never contemplated in the original design.

But the agitation went on independently of the law's failure and tended rather to broaden as more and more people surmised or saw that back of the trusts was Accumulated Wealth and its problem of perilous power. To run back over the files of a trust-fighting newspaper of those days is to have a singular sensation of the strange and total disappearance of a great army, as if swallowed by quicksands, and the elimination of what was once an absorbing interest in that army's movements.

The whole avid pursuit dove-tailed into the muck-raking industry, which was really part of the same impetus. The other side sometimes responded with a manful blow and sometimes with one not so manful. Gentlemen that had been long the objects of the admiring plaudits of the public were not to be hunted to the grand jury without striking back. The spirit of caste was strong upon these persons; papa might have begun life as an ash-heaver in the gas works, but we are now of the superior order, was the typical thought. The furious personal attacks that used to be made upon William Randolph Hearst were largely of this inspiration. He was a conspicuous leader in the anti-trust campaign, but the gravamen of his offense went still beyond that. He was a rich man and had deserted his class to side with the mob.

Another interesting case was that of Stuyvesant Fish. He was of aristocratic birth and universally supposed to be of the rich men's guild. But it happened that in his early experiences, when he was learning the railroad business from the ground up, he had swung a lantern as a brakeman on the Illinois Central Railroad. Perhaps this experience, perhaps a native instinct for democracy in the man, took him out of the least sympathy with the class into which he had been born. He was now president of the railroad on which he had been a brakeman and also he was a director in the Mutual Life Insurance Company. The highly successful farce-comedy entitled Insurance Investigation, of which we have spoken in a former chapter, had revealed the Mutual in a most undesirable light. The other directors were in favor of standing by their class and bluffing out the storm with no compromise. Mr. Fish issued a perfectly frank statement in which he denounced the course of his company and the others and declared he was in favor of a new deal and the straight walk.

The sirocco of wrath that blew about his head in consequence of that statement has seldom been equalled in the corporation history of America. One would have thought he had committed some low and dishonoring crime that made him unfit for decent society. He was a large man with a big, strong body, big, hard hands and cool, hardy nerve; with composure he took the vituperation heaped upon him by his associates, who regarded him as another and viler traitor. The pride and joy of his life had been Illinois Central, which he had brought to a high efficiency of service. In his office one day while the cyclone was howling I suggested to him that the first move of

MR. COMMON PEOPLE AND THE TRUSTS
An Opper cartoon in the Hearst papers in 1904

the men he had offended would be to oust him from his presidency. The notion struck him as merely comical. He had been there so long, he had such a strong following, he knew how to handle his enemies. All of which was pleasant but not reassuring. The order had already gone forth to hamstring him. At the first meeting of the directors he was deposed. In the surprise and anger that came upon him he violently attacked the men that had undermined him. One responded with a blow and Mr. Fish rejoined by knocking his opponent down. Cornelius Vanderbilt, attempting to be peacemaker, danced about the combatants in agonized distress.

"Gentlemen," he shouted, "gentlemen! Remember what you are!"

Which always seemed to me a mot worthy of historical preservation, considering the occasion, the thing that had been put over, and the reasons for it. Mr. Vanderbilt would not have said, "Remember you are a collection of marionettes under the control of the central money power," but he might as well have said so.

The fight against the trust and monopoly went on with much valor and small results worth mentioning. On the side of what were called the predatory Interests was about this time developed the interlocking directorate, which greatly strengthened the defense. It was in fact no new thing, but the public had not before heard of it. The effect was to bring into one line many corporations of diverse interests but much potency. The trust fighters generally denounced it as a designed development of pure deviltry. In point of fact it was merely another manifestation of one process of evolution. As the wealth of the country tended more and more to be absorbed into a few hands, it was certain that these hands should reappear in many organizations. Men that controlled banks also controlled railroads, packing houses, coal mines, and oil supplies. At every fresh revelation of this fact, a fresh outcry arose. Then Congress, supplementing the radicals that from time to time had been pointing to these conditions, did one heroic job of muck-raking that surpassed all others. The Pujo Committee, now forgotten, placed under the limelight for all mankind to see the fact that the wealth of the nation was passing into the hands of a small group of men and with the wealth, of course, the attendant power. Accumulated Wealth—illimitable power. The barony of St. Johnsbury was but the microcosm of what had come to be a national condition.

But we were speaking of the efforts of the government to enforce the noble Sherman act, batter the Trust minotaurus and at the same time not fall from the slack wire. When Mr. Taft became President in 1909 there was for a time a lull in these entrancing gyrations. Then they came to an end in a way nobody could have foreseen and with a scintillating burst of fireworks.

Colonel Roosevelt returned from his lion-killing diversions in Africa and was naturally a figure of surpassing interest, especially to the increasing number of Republicans that did not like Mr. Taft. And among the dissatisfied was one element of great and almost determinative power.

So far as I know, the inside history of this remarkable episode in American life has not before been put into print. It seems highly appropriate to the occasion.

Mr. Taft had been elected in 1908 over Bryan, who for the third time was the Democratic candidate. With the President, the Republicans won a majority in both houses and proceeded, as usual, to celebrate and pay for victory by putting an unnecessary coping upon the tariff wall. This and other causes produced a reaction, so that the Congressional election of 1910 went heavily in favor of the Democrats. Experienced political observers are accustomed to give weight to interim elections as forecasting the trend for the Presidential voting two years later. The Republicans were chagrined and alarmed by the result in 1910 and made diligent effort to better their affairs. In the Congressional campaign the trust issue had figured with the tariff. The Republican party was always pictured as the party of privilege and the friend of the trusts. Taft's administration was assailed because while it was armed with the lightnings of the blessed Sherman act it loosed them not a bit against the audacious offenders although they were growing always in wealth and power while the poor sank to lower levels, or words to that effect. It was necessary to do something to show that the Taft heart also beat true to the glorious principles of no monopoly and an equal chance for all, and a policy was adopted of vigorous prosecutions of these concerns, represented to be depraved and lawless.

Among them, the battle-axe of wrath (for show purposes) fell upon the International Harvester Company.

Now this corporation happened to be directed by men that sincerely desired to be law-abiding and reasonably upright. Whether we like Big Business or abhor it, such was the fact. But in the course of their operations and development, being producers for profit, they had encountered a condition that forced them toward consolidation. The case is notable and illustrative of the principle involved. Competition, argued the leaders of the last generation, is the sure remedy for the evils of monopoly. Is it? Competition had ruled for years in the business of making harvesters and brought it almost to bankruptcy. It is a mad story and yet legitimate and unassailable. Two great concerns locked horns in competitive strife. At last their agents were going about the country almost side by side and almost forcing their machines upon farmers. But this was no real advantage to the consumer. If the machine of one kind that he bought last year was replaced this year with a machine of the rival concern, he had merely incurred another load of debt and was no better equipped, for one was as good as the other. But meantime, the two producing companies were spending money like drunken sailors and heading for ruin. So they combined into the International Harvester Company and returned to the ways of sanity.

Being conscientious men, they desired that they might not overstep the law. They took all their plans to Washington and laid them before the Department of Justice, cards on the table, face up. "This is what we wish to do. We leave it to you. If it in any way contravenes the law or is objectionable, say so and we will be guided by your decision."

The law department took the matter under advisement and rendered an opinion that the company's projects were wholly lawful and unobjectionable. With this clean bill of health, the company proceeded confidently upon its plans.

When there came the grand revival of prosecuting virtue on the part of the next administration, the company suddenly found itself indicted for doing the thing it had been told by the same department, though not by the same officer, was lawful and proper.

The International Harvester Company was closely allied, let us say, with great financial and industrial Interests, including Steel. It was often referred to as a subsidiary of Steel, though to what extent this might be true was not disclosed. The officers of the Harvester Company felt that they had been badly used. Some of their allies shared that resentment and believed that if such shifts should continue there would be in the country no such thing as business security. They determined to compass Mr. Taft's defeat. That meant of course the nomination of Colonel Roosevelt, who had declined a nomination in 1908 and gone off to Africa to kill lions and things. Some of the men in the steel business were intimate personal friends of the Colonel; others maintained that he had always been fair to their Interests, which was true.

On the other hand, other great Interests, including Oil, which might be described as the right wing of the Republican bird, Steel being its left, were entirely satisfied with Mr. Taft and content to have him reinstated. Dissension thus entered not so much into the ranks of the party as into the inner councils that were its life and being and sinews and success.

The first step by the seceders must be to try to obtain a majority of the delegates to the Republican national convention and so prevent Taft's renomination.

A President in office always has a preponderative advantage in such a contest. The insurgents failed to get the majority they sought.

The next hope was to frighten with a threat of a split and of withdrawal. For this demonstration the choice of an issue was not happily made. The Rooseveltians, who called themselves the Progressive wing of the party, vehemently asserted that fraud had been committed in the make-up of the convention because their contesting delegations had not been seated. There was no fraud, there was nothing on earth to complain about. The sergeant-at-arms, in accordance with an immemorial custom, had made up the temporary roll from returns sent to him by the state organizations, leaving the work of determining between contesting delegations to the convention itself, which is always the custom, and right.

Nevertheless the Progressives yelled their imaginary wrongs to high heaven, made a deafening clamor, and finally marched out of the convention. Then they hired a hall where they could relieve their chests of an apparently insupportable pressure and sing together like the morning stars the surpassing genius of their chief.

Next, backed throughout by the offended Interests and financed by the same delectable source, they proceeded to organize the Progressive party, to call a national convention thereof that should meet in August at Chicago, and to choose in each state delegates to this convention.

To organize in six weeks this immense country for a new

political party is a gigantic and extremely expensive task. Nobody seemed to inquire where the money came from that paid the bills.

Nevertheless the new movement went its way with swelling port. Besides Colonel Roosevelt's personal admirers that would have followed him anywhere and blindfolded was a large, interesting, intelligent, conscientious element that without being passionately fond of the chief, sincerely believed many conditions to be bad and the country to need penitence and a refreshing of faith. With heart-felt joy these looked upon the Progressive movement as the fulfillment of a hope deferred, as a reform, as an uprising for righteousness. They felt this; they said it; they meant it.

It is odd now to recall that among these were newspapermen that should have known better. Newspapermen as a rule are too sophisticated and too wisely cynical to be swept away by any such emotionalism. But Colonel Roosevelt had with newspapermen ways that were quite unusual and to some persons irresistible. To be slapped on the back by the President of the United States and called "Billy" by those august lips was doubtless to some minds an exalting experience; we Anglo-Saxons have not yet lost all the traits of the Cymbrian tribesman. But aside from these classes were millions of men and women that honestly regarded Colonel Roosevelt as the savior of the nation and our one remaining hope. He was the foe of the trust and of the plutocrat; he had affixed upon what was believed to be the oppressors of the poor the name of "malefactors of great wealth"; he was conspicuously of the order of Americans that "do things." Some of the things he did had to be undone or paid for at a high rate, such as his raid upon Colombia to grab the Canal Zone, but small eccentricities of this kind have never daunted the souls passionately hungering and thirsting to be led. It seems never to have occurred to these good but slightly naive beings that the pursuit they pro-

GETTING DOWN TO BUSINESS

THE COLONEL'S HAT WAS IN THE RING BUT THE MACHINE ROLLED RIGHT OVER IT

Famous cartoon by Tom Powers in *The New York American*, June 8, 1912

claimed constituted a reproach upon their nation and form of government. For certainly, if after 127 years of a form of democracy it had not developed in its citizens the beginnings of a capacity to manage their own affairs, either the form of government or the nation under it must be essentially futile. But for a people with their history, it must be admitted that the modern Americans are singularly diffident, a fact possibly to be explained because they do not know their history. Indeed, they are hardly in a way to know it since it is no longer taught in their schools.

But about the convention. It was duly held in the Chicago Coliseum, and was a grand and inspiring affair. Delegates were present from every state in the Union. I think I have never seen a great assembly that manifested a happier spirit. The fiery ardor of a crusade seemed to animate the mass of the participants. They felt that they were inaugurating a movement that would emancipate the nation from the grip of the terrible trust monster and the workingman from his state of virtual servitude. They were the heralds of a glad new day and let joy be unconfined. Even old-timers in the press seats felt the reflex of an unusual zealotry. Not like this had been the national conventions of their experience.

An apostolic aura seemed fitted to each face—perhaps it was even Pentecostal. Recourse was had to the scriptures as alone adequate to meet the spiritual requirements of the occasion. Colonel Roosevelt himself led the way in this pleasing excursion into Holy Writ. To an assembly that packed the Auditorium one night he delivered the mighty trumpet call to arms for regeneration's sacred cause. It was a carefully prepared and vibratory speech, delivered in his most exhilarating manner, à la staccato, and with perhaps a thought too much of gesticulation, for which his short arms were not the best vehicle, and of vehement utterance, for which his high, harsh voice was ill-fitted. But it was a good speech and galvanized the elect, which was the main thing. It closed with a quotation that immediately became classic and a potent summons to the clansmen of salvation.

"For I stand at Armageddon," shouted the Colonel, "and I battle for the Lord!"

Grand!

In the convention he repeated the speech and the quotation and thrilled every listener, despite the fact that the Lord he was battling for was one variety of Big Business trying to defeat another. "On to Armageddon!" became the battle-cry of the new party, sometimes shortened to merely "Armageddon." It is rather painful to recall that at first a part of the enthusiasts that spoke confidently about Armageddon did not know what on earth it meant, some confusing it with a brand of breakfast food, but this defect was soon remedied by those that had the advantage of a good Concordance.

A gathering with so strong a scriptural flavor must of course have a hymn. One was quickly found in "Onward, Christian Soldiers," which made a great hit. A choir was provided to sing it, but was soon proved to be unneeded. The whole convention sang the inspiring lyric, sang it with indescribable gusto, sang it loudly, sang it often. Men felt that it correctly described the new crusading. A brass band was stationed in the gallery at the farther end of the hall. Whenever there was a lull in the proceedings, the band would start up "Onward, Christian Soldiers," and the whole audience would spring to its feet and voice its enthusiasm and fervor by yelling its way battle-ward.

It seemed to have been thought that besides the Biblical selection favored by the great leader standing at Armageddon there should be some slogan of a more modern and practical kind, and that too was prepared and on the fire. "Pass Prosperity Around," it read and being displayed on many banners at once became as dear to the Progressive heart as the more hallowed line. Men repeated it with evident satisfaction; some shouted it. When the strains of "Onward, Christian Soldiers" had died down some one would cry aloud "Pass Prosperity Around," as if it were leberwurst on a platter, and the audience would cheer. Then it would sing again—the same dear old song. It was too lovely. There were in the press seats, I cannot deny it, coarse and unrefined souls that made scurril remarks when they saw an eminent Hebrew gentleman leading in the singing of "Onward, Christian Soldiers," but no such ribaldry shall flow from this pen to mar the record of a beautiful and touching spectacle.

Of course, there were occasional notes of discord even amid so much pleasant harmony. Such are always to be expected in this imperfect world. Some delegations of colored men from the South presented themselves and were rather rudely kicked in the face, no chances being taken on the possibility of carrying Southern states in the grand revolt against the malefactors of great wealth and others. There were also persons that said a political party sponsored by one set of Vested Interests against another was not exactly the best promise for the day of emancipation and the passing around of Prosperity. These were disregarded in the general happiness.

The convention had been called to nominate Colonel Roosevelt, which it did with tremendous cheering and satisfaction to all. For the second place on the ticket were many aspirants and much division of opinion as to the best choice. Not in the mind of the gallant Colonel. He knew whom he wanted and whom therefore the convention would choose. A large painted banner had been prepared and rolled up in the centre of the hall. As soon as the Colonel's choice had been ratified by the well-trained delegates, the banner was suddenly unrolled and behold!

For President, Theodore Roosevelt of New York.
For Vice-President, Hiram Johnson of California.

And with a final singing of "Onward, Christian Soldiers," a final reminder about Armageddon, and a final up-surge of pious enthusiasm the convention adjourned.

Newspaper correspondents that had kept their heads during this excitement asked themselves how far the Colonel had really deluded himself into the belief that he could win. It was a question interesting to philosophers and mental experts but insoluble. There is something about candidacy for public office that seems to unseat the reason and fill the mind with roseate mirage. Despite all indications, Colonel Roosevelt may have believed that the magic of his name would sweep the country. It did not, and I may say that no seasoned observer ever thought it would. If there had been no Progressive-Steel party that year, Taft would have been the only candidate to oppose Wilson, and Wilson would still have won. With a divided opposition he rode the wave of triumph. For, alas! the onward rush of the Christian soldiery went not far and he that stood at Armageddon stood not long.

Some of the Progressives, like Uncle Moses Clapp, wished to go ahead nevertheless and prepare for another fight with the octopus. The Colonel quickly put the quietus upon any such foolishness. With plain speech he declined to lead any more forlorn hopes, and after a few futile gestures from the zealots, the Progressive party came to a swift and inglorious end.

> If so soon it is to be done for,
> What in the devil was it begun for?

sang Uncle Mose and echo answered "What?" and "dass ganz melancholisch," as we say in the Potsdammerplatz. Prosperity was not passed around on a platter or otherwise, no one stood at Armageddon, and if there was battling for the Lord it was without the trumpet call from the Colonel.

And with that debacle the war upon the trusts came virtually to an end. Slowly, America, having passed out of its adolescence, began to perceive that evolution cannot be turned back with shouting or the making of grim faces. Slowly we began to perceive that we had trusts, not because the men that formed them were bad wicked men deserving of imprisonment, but we had trusts because trusts were an inevitable product of the system of society under which we live. It was a lesson worth while even at the cost of a futile campaign and much bitter disappointment.

Autopsy. The Progressive party died of rickets, megalomania, and ingrowing strabismus.

A hardened old cynic that sat next to me in the convention arose with the rest whenever the battle hymn was signalled, which was often, and sang

> Onward, Christian Soldiers, battling hard for steel,
> For its booming profits save the Commonweal.

But the occasion was not exactly one for cynicism. To see so many men manifestly desirous to help their fellows and to serve righteousness was something to think about. They might be deceived as to the trumpet that called them together, but there was a certain inspiration in the fact that they came.

Chapter XVI

THE AMATEUR DIPLOMAT

Cᴵᵀʏ of Mainz, Germany, River Rhine, September, 1896. German army manœuvres going on somewhere in the neighborhood stir the enthusiastic attention of all the burghers. In the morning the troops come in from somewhere to cross the bridge and go somewhere else. All traffic swept away far in advance. When they come, what a sight! Miles of men marching like a million machines, exact in step, identical in bearing, rifles at the identical angle, tramp, tramp. Stand at the side and look; a million legs going exactly together, and a million feet that keep exact time—whack, whack, on the pavement—wonderful! No break, no deviation, no human weakness, no fallibility. The most perfect co-ordination of human effort ever seen is a German military unit. What labor and thought to make it so!

A big and wonderful man rides at the head—a big man on a big black horse; a heavy-set man with a heavy, lowering face. The great spiked helmet on his head, the string of war-like decorations on his breast, the great sword by his side are not more disturbing to the quiet soul than his clenched lips, grim face, and scowling brows. With one hand, palm outward, resting on his hip he sits upon his horse and he glowers straight ahead as he goes and never so much as glances at the long lines of townspeople that gaze in fascination at the display of overwhelming power, the final proof of Germany's unequalled prowess. The perfect figure of Mars in uniform he is, the war god come to earth, Mars Omnipotens, riding to battle. Nothing is lacking except in the distance the thick black cloud of smoke should go up from the conquered town, and under his horses' hoofs should lie in rows the bodies of the slain. These may be lacking in physical fact; the imagination readily supplies them. Mars Omnipotens; a black and scowling Mars. And Deutschland über Alles.

Heidelberg, August, 1897. It is Sunday. A beautiful quiet on the grand old town. The river glimmering silver in the stirless air, rest and peace on all. The people are going to church. A mother walks with her children, boy and girl, nearly grown. Of a sudden an officer turns the corner ahead of them. He is in fullest regalia, marching along, head up, sword clanking. The sidewalk is wide enough for all. But when the three civilians see the officer they leap to the gutter and give him the whole walk, and stand in awe until he has passed, never having so much as glanced at them or been aware of their presence.

Trier, August, 1898. It is in a restaurant. In the evening. The town is garrisoned; many young officers are eating at the tables. A colonel enters. All the young officers bound from their seats and stand until the colonel is seated. Then one timidly approaches, salutes, and for himself and fellows asks permission to continue to eat their dinner in this colonel's august presence.

Carlsbad, August, 1902. There is a line of water-drinkers waiting at the Kaiserbrunnen for the first morning glass of water. At the end of the line are three old women, one with white hair and gentle bearing. An Austrian officer comes stalking along. The three elderly women are deep in converse and do not notice his approach. The straight line of his walk passes between the last two women. By deviating a foot out of his way he can pass behind the last woman and avoid a collision. He keeps straight on, bursts betwen the last two, bowls over a woman that might have been his grandmother and proceeds without so much as looking at her.

City of Frankfort, July, 1908. Great dining room of a noted

hotel. On the walls, on every pillar, printed in great black type, three inches high, this notice:

Jüdischer Besuch ist nicht gestattet.

Island of New Britain, Bismarck Archipelago, South Seas, February, 1911. In the six years since my last visit a great change has come over the natives. No more dancing, no more festivals, no more singing, the former dancers sit at the corners of the newly built town with their heads in their hands and weep. A German governor has come, a residency has been erected, German soldiers and German rifles, a German cruiser in the harbor. The town is rectangular, rigid, alien, built by forced labor of natives that never did such work before. In a field, a German sergeant is drilling and cursing a file of conscripted and miserable natives, each wearing a German cap and uniformed in a German handkerchief and a German cartridge box. Six years ago it was one of the happiest spots on earth. Now it is one of the most wretched and sorrowful. Terrible stories are told of the Iron Heel on all the archipelago, on the Pelews, the Carolines, the Ladrones. Imitators of Doctor Peters, brutal governors, floggings, incited insurrections that natives may be dragged into penal servitude for life, which is a euphemism for the return of the slave trade. Later, I land at Yap and Angaur, the slave island, and verify enough of such stories to give one forever a nausea of all imperialism.

But throughout the blighted island circuit, an immense development of the copra business, coming source of the world's fat supply. Vast ordered cocoanut groves where late was wild forest. And there is an immense development of the phosphate business on Angaur, late the loveliest of the Pelews and the most peaceful. Great profits are made from each as human lives are ground up under the advancing machine.

Machine—inadvertently I have hit the right word. Everywhere a vast, articulated, perfected organization, far-seeing purpose, ruthless determination, the echo of the tramp, tramp of the million feet moving in faultless precision, the organization of blood and iron, disdainful of obstacles, indifferent to all other considerations. Mars Omnipotens, translated into great wheels and engines, rolling on to realize Bismarck's doctrine of the eternally destined supremacy of the German race.

Angaur and Ponope, where the unsophisticated natives have been goaded into revolt that they might be subdued and turned into profitable labor. Angaur, where they work in the phosphate mines until they drop. Yap, the gathering place or depot for the "labor" thus "recruited" from ruined island after ruined island. All under the shadow of the steadily advancing machine and black scowling Mars.

The Earthly Paradise, Stevenson and Charles Warren Stoddard have justly called the South Seas. Now before one's eyes the grim machine is changing it to a hell.

I give these few sample scenes as indications of some results of the Grand Theory of Advance by Blood and Iron. The Germans, I tell myself, are in many respects, an admirable people. I know them well, esteem their good traits, like to visit their country. The system and ideals of their government are utterly incompatible with any faith in democracy or principle thereof. The system and the ideals are the system and ideals of a ruling class that is maddened with the lust of power, dominion, glory—and profits. They have dangled before the German people the great gilt bauble of imperialism at the sight of which most populations are likely to go mad. Except for going thus mad, and for tolerating an autocracy in the twentieth century, the German people are not to be blamed for the horrors of the South Seas or the incessant rumblings of their gigantic military machine, forever threatening the world with war. So I harangue myself, trying to readjust shattered ideals.

Almost every summer for more than twenty years I had been in Germany and under the spell of one insistent question studied it as well as I could. The question was, how long the spirit of militarism so ably fostered and nourished, and how long the lust of conquest, so persistently planting and watering a military arrogance, could go without an outbreak. No one could move attentively about the country without knowing well that exultation in the unapproachable military efficiency of Germany throbbed in almost every German breast. It was perfectly well known to every German that the army of his country had been developed by intensive study and effort until it was the most powerful the world had ever seen. What would be the inevitable result of that consciousness? Armies are not built, trained, perfected, for holiday show purposes.

The world has forgotten 1874 and 1884, it has forgotten Morocco and 1905, it has forgotten how the German Kaiser dictated the retirement of a French Minister of Foreign Affairs that had incurred Kaiserlich wrath by opposing schemes of this thundering German advancement. It has forgotten Zabern and the tailor with a sabre through his body. But those that from 1895 to 1914 observed Germany at close range and watched the European war barometer must still include these factors in the equation.

This and something else. Almost hand in hand with the development to perfection of the German military machine on land and sea went the unexampled development of the German colonial empire and of German industrialism and commerce. The population grew, the country was prosperous, capital multiplied from wise and profitable investments. As it multiplied it must have farther avenues for expansion; as it seized on these new avenues in South America, Australia, China, the Near and the Far East, it augmented its own volume and therefore its demands for more avenues and more expansion. The history of commerce has not seen in an equal period an equal growth of substance and of power. In 1905 and 1906 the prospect that Germany would Germanize the world seemed so imminent that more than one magazine article appeared in America explicitly setting forth the reasons for that alluring promise.

But they missed one element necessary to the fulfillment of the vision. The swiftly mounting trade of Germany was on the Atlantic or must start thereon, and Germany had no Atlantic port. All her ports looked toward the North Pole; all her shipping must pass through the bottle-neck of the Straits of Dover, exposed in case of war to modern guns within easy range. It was to get nearer to the indispensable Atlantic (although even then there would be no escape from the fatal bottle-neck passage) that the Kiel canal was built. But the Kiel canal was of small help to ease the constriction. As water power developed, more and more a wonderful dream took possession of many thoughtful German minds. There were endless possibilities of water power in the Rhine and other streams. Suppose one nation could manufacture with this power, ship easily to the Atlantic tide-water, transfer to steamers—with German technical skill, knowledge, science, energy, persistence, subsidies, what a prospect! The commercial world would be hers!—with a port or ports on the Atlantic.

The far-seeing Bismarck had perceived something of this when he proposed to Louis Napoleon that Germany should absorb Holland and France should take Belgium. In 1906-14 it was not possible to carry out any such benevolent scheme, but there was something else that might be almost as valuable. A war with France would result inevitably in German victory and another annexation of territory as indemnity, following the example set in 1871. Northern France had four good ports on the Atlantic. None of these was at the mouth of the Rhine, of course, but any one could easily be joined by rail with Cologne, for instance, and as the Rhine mouth would in time be surrounded by German territory its physical absorption would be inevitable.

And meanwhile the port on the Atlantic in full swing.

It was a German naval officer that first pointed out to me these pregnant facts. We were coming up from Sydney to Hong Kong. It is a long voyage, as voyages are in these times—twenty-eight days. There were few passengers; we were thrown much together. Each was relieved to find some one in that end of the world that could talk European politics, and whoever talked European politics then talked about the coming war. The naval officer was a splendid specimen of German manhood, exceedingly well educated, wise, courteous, sophisticated, honest. Hour after hour we sat on the deck and talked. He said the war was inevitable and not far off. Nothing on earth could prevent it. From his room he fetched a large map of Europe and pointed to the German ports and then to Havre, Cherbourg, and Brest. All the figures of Germany's phenomenal commercial expansion were like the multiplication table to him. He laid them beside the map.

"That tells the story," he said. "No one that looks at those figures and then at the map can doubt what is to happen. With all these colonies, all this mounting trade, all this increase in manufactures, Germany must have a port on the Atlantic. We shall have Paris three weeks after we start. Then the war will be over."

I asked if he thought it likely Paris would be annexed to Germany.

"Not so foolish," he snapped back. "We don't want that uneasy, restless, conniving population to deal with. Let it alone. All we want is Northern France with the harbors. Then Paris won't matter, for France will be reduced to a fifth-rate power."

Not long after I was in Germany and could not but notice phenomena that seemed to verify in every way the naval officer's prediction, and still more in 1913. With other literature I read the magazine published by the Pan-Germanic League. Its utterance left not the least room for doubt as to what was at

WANT
HUNGER
DISCONTENT
PEACE PLEAS
STRIKES
DISEASE
AUTOCRACY
GERMAN EMPIRE
DEMOCRACY

HOLDING DOWN THE LID.

Rollin Kirby in *The New York World*, May 3, 1917

hand. I went to Carlsbad, which was then a clearing house for the inside news of Europe. The air was tense, nervous, and charged with electric expectation. I had never seen the like there. All the talk was about the war. Grim fact, reluctantly admitted upon grim fact, drove down the last hope of any chance of peace. The thing that had been surmised about and dreaded for thirty years was about to burst upon us.

From Germany I went to France expecting to find a similar atmosphere. With the exception of one newspaper, *le Matin,* nobody seemed to have the least notion of what was going on. To the alarming articles of *le Matin,* the French Socialists responded with jeers. "Let the Germans come. We will welcome them with open arms as brothers." And the commonest remark of all, "We'd as soon wear a German helmet as a French kepi."

From France I went to England and found the nation absorbed in an issue that eclipsed any of these uneasy rumorings. For some mysterious reason there were few grouse that year in Scotland and the hunting season was largely a failure. At the height of this absorbing debate, *The London Mail* printed Bebel's fire-alarm letter, which might have been enough to startle the least excitable. Although its plain implication was war and German Socialist support for the war, and although it was as strongly nationalist as any Junker could have written, the English public gave it not the least heed but went on sedulously about the grouse.

But what I had seen and heard in Germany and Austria seemed conclusive and when I returned to America I offered to two magazine editors an outline indication of the coming storm, including the invasion of Belgium and the complete plans thereof. They laughed me to scorn. There would be no war in Europe; I was mad to think there could be. Their ridicule and confidence daunted me and I gave up the attempt. It was my only chance to appear as a prophet and I muffed it.

The war broke in the last days of July of the next year. I was on my way to Vienna via Rotterdam as a delegate to the International Socialist Congress. We landed at Rotterdam just as England decided to enter the conflict and while the German hosts were thronging upon Liege in the famous "hacking our way" trip through Belgium, and to the devil with treaties and neutral rights.

"The human race," said William G. Shepherd, as some months later we stood and looked together over a part of the Marne battlefield, "has gone insane."

I have never heard a better comment on the period from July 23, 1914 to November 11, 1918. In all of its phases and aspects and ramifications and implications it is merely madhouse. That anybody ever speaks of such a period as fated to return is proof of latent lunacy; from the first boom of the first shell there is nothing but a dance of maniacs. Everybody goes insane; it is the only form of insanity that is infectious. In times of peace I should deem no people on earth to be notably saner and cooler than the good people of Holland, but they went mad with the rest. Perhaps it was not so strange, after all. For many years Europe had lived in dread of this thing, imagining all black and yawning disasters to be in its wake, and now that it had come, behold, in scrambling panic Dutch bourses closed, the banks closed, business stopped, and the money-changing offices not merely closed but with boarded-up fronts. I do not know why, I wish some one would tell me; but they certainly were so. More wondrous still, silver currency magically disappeared overnight and the cities were forced to issue paper money to meet current needs. And the first introduction we had to a state of war was when the driver of our cab from the steamship pier refused to accept the perfectly good Dutch silver I had brought with me and I must get paper rags from the hotel porter.

The next phase of initiation was not so amusing. We had

done with dinner at the old Hotel Maas and were leaving the dining room when we were aware of a woman's hysterical shrieks coming from the street without. An open cab was passing and in it were a man and a woman, the woman stark mad, and appalling all men's hearts with her horrible laughter. They looked to us like Americans and we followed them to their hotel, where a doctor came and gave the poor shrieker a quieting potion. Nothing was to be learned that night, but the next day we found the man and had the ugly story. They were from a city in Ohio, but I will suppress the name, for the whole circumstance must be still inexpressibly painful to both of them. They had been travelling in Germany and when the war broke tried to make their way to Holland. Four times that day they had been stopped at stations, taken from the train, and searched. Each time the wife had been stripped stark naked in the presence of German officers. When she realized that she had reached Rotterdam and safety she collapsed.

Escaping Americans came on every train with stories of experiences that seem now like the fantasies of Bedlam: the war dogs, loosed at last, had run slavering and blind and drunken. Americans that were penniless because they had been stripped of money and letters of credit and aught else; Americans that had lost their baggage and had no notion of what to do or where to turn; Americans smarting under limitless arrogance and brutality—having a fair notion of what all this would mean in an American legation always about half equipped in the matter of staff, I went the next day and offered my services as a volunteer to Doctor Henry van Dyke, American minister at The Hague.

Doctor van Dyke knew me by reputation and most unfavorably. To him I was a wild-eyed Socialist, a rude unmannerly disturber of the peace of good men, and a dangerous character. His natural kindliness and courtesy checked him from saying these things but he looked them as he politely declined my offer. Four days later the legation being swamped and Mrs. Russell having appeared to guarantee moderation and restraint, the two of us went to work as volunteers to try to meet and deal with the flood of the unfortunate that now daily besieged the minister.

It was an experience with a fresh illumination every hour. At first the refugees had invariably tales of dreadful mistreatment by the German officers, strippings, searchings, confiscation of all papers and of money. Passports, position, respectability, counted for nothing. Mr. Archie Huntington arrived at Amsterdam one night without money to pay his porter or cabman; everything had been taken from him. Thousands of pieces of American baggage were scattered along all the lines of railroad. Much of it hopelessly lost, often with letters of credit or other valuables, so that most of the refugees were dazed and helpless as to their next movement. Hundreds of them arrived every twenty-four hours. Every morning when we went to our work at the Legation we found a long queue of them waiting at the front door, many penniless, some hysterical, all anxious and nervous.

In this emergency, Doctor van Dyke performed for his country and for humanity services that in any time of less chaos and welter would have earned him a lasting eminence. Surely few men in that time deserved so well of their countrymen. Like a general, like a born executive, he took in hand the turbulent situation, reduced it to order, organized the Legation for swift, effective action, calmed the excited, put upon everything a face of kindly sympathy and cheer, and so long as he had means, relieved the necessities of those that were without funds.

The money supply was his worst difficulty; the Legation's resources were almost nothing and his own but small. In these straits he determined to appeal to the people of The Hague, among whom he was exceedingly popular. He went to a prominent bank and explained his dilemma. The United States government, he had to set forth, unlike other governments, provided its legations and consulates with no emergency funds for the relief of its distressed nationals. His own means were exhausted and there were all these hundreds of people without a stiver to bless themselves with. What could he do?

At once and with one accord the bankers said:

"Doctor van Dyke, you can have all the money you want. Draw freely on us for all your needs and we will take the chance of being repaid."

He asked for $50,000 and they gave it, and with that sum he kept many a stranded American from despair and starvation.

He was tireless, indefatigable, patient, and thought of everything. The Holland American Steamship people, who also deserve a kindly word of gratitude, made superhuman efforts to get the refugees home. A steamer of theirs left for America every Saturday. They made their boats over, put up temporary bunks in the cargo holds, took on board four times the full normal passenger capacity and managed to feed them. Service in the dining rooms went on all day long with the passengers eating in detachments. Doctor van Dyke kept in touch with all these arrangements. Every Friday he went down to Rotterdam to see if all possible care had been taken of the passengers and stayed always until midnight inspecting the vessel and its outfitting.

The Legation under his direction performed also an international service that was indispensable at that juncture. Scarcely anybody has stopped to think of this, but all communications between England and Germany, Belgium and Germany, and to some extent between France and Germany had to pass through Holland and the Legation. It had become the great switchboard of Europe, that same little Hague with its unpretending legation house. Many Germans were in England when the war broke, more English persons were in Germany. English girls were at German schools, German girls were at English schools. Belgians were in Germany, Germans were in Belgium or France. The anxieties of parents and relatives were insupportable and there was no way to make inquiry except through the American Legation at The Hague. Every despatch must be translated before it could be forwarded. Mrs. Russell and I were the official translators. We had no lack of employment. Every morning lay on my desk a green bushel of telegrams from agonized relatives asking about the lives and safety of the marooned. These must be translated and forwarded, and when an answer came it must have the same treatment. To keep track of these thousands of inquiries was in itself a huge task and never could have been performed but for the timely appearance of another volunteer worker, Mr. Alexander Gulick, a New York lawyer with a genius for organization and method. He installed a system of card indexes by which we were able instantly to classify and handle every inquiry.

About five hundred German girls were at school or in service in England. Doctor van Dyke arranged for the chartering of a special cross-channel boat that brought them to Flushing whence they went homeward rejoicing.

Another volunteer, Mr. Merle Smith, a young broker in Wall Street, took charge of the financial operations and handled the money. The Reverend Tertius van Dyke, the minister's son, temporarily in The Hague, was an indefatigable worker.

Two other figures of those hectic days stand out in my memory. One is George Grafton Wilson, professor of international law in Harvard Law School, whose wise counsel and cool head kept us always straight and steady. When Doctor van Dyke was out of the office, as he must often be, Professor Wilson acted as minister. In a few days the whole establishment was running like clockwork. A rule was made that all applicants should be dealt with in the order of their coming and all treated exactly alike. One day a certain well-known millionaire or multi-millionaire of New York came to the door, pushed past the line and demanded to see Doctor van Dyke. Professor Wilson is officiating as minister.

Millionaire, impressively—I want to see Doctor van Dyke.

Professor Wilson, suavely—I am sorry, Doctor van Dyke is at the Ministry of Foreign Affairs at the moment, but if you will take your place in the line I shall be glad to serve you in any way I can.

Millionaire—I am Mr. Gotrocks, and I have some matters that I want to have attended to.

Wilson—Yes, Mr. Gotrocks, if you will take your place in the line, we shall be glad to do all we can for you.

Millionaire—But I am Mr. Gotrocks; you don't seem to know me.

Wilson—Yes, Mr. Gotrocks, I think I have heard your name, and if you will kindly take your place in the line we shall be glad to do all we can for you when your turn comes.

The millionaire went away in a rage.

Other persons were enraged about that time, some by Doctor van Dyke's perfectly even holding of the scales and refusal to deviate from the strict line of his duty. One morning as I approached the Legation I saw a carriage and footman waiting before the door. As I started to enter I was almost overturned by a well-dressed gentleman who came tearing out, spluttering and muttering, so blinded with excitement that he did not see where he was going. Also he was saying things not meant for polite ears. It was Sir Charles Wilson, British minister to The Hague. He had been to ask Doctor van Dyke to do something that would assist the British and Doctor van Dyke had plainly refused.

The other volunteer I am to speak of was General Charles H. Sherrill, who had been American Minister to Argentina. With Mrs. Sherrill and her mother, he had been at a German watering place, from which when the war broke they had

started to make their way to Holland. General Sherrill carried
a passport that distinctly set forth his place in the diplomatic
service; also an official certificate of his identity and citizenship
from the chief of police of the town where he had been so-
journing. With these he was sure of going through easily to
the frontier.

The train on which he and his party were travelling had not
proceeded far when it began to meet troop trains filled with
yelling, cheering, riotously happy soldiers bound for the front.
"Hoch der Krieg!" was always the burden of their cheers. They
seemed to be going to the battle field as to a picnic. Many had
chalked upon the sides of the car statements of what they
would do to Marianne, which was the general name among
them for France. Some of the chalkings were indecent.

The first large station was filled with roaring young soldiery.
Many were drunk, some so drunk they were vomiting. A big
soldier, probably of the intoxicated ones, dashed into the Sherrill compartment, seized Mrs. Sherrill's mother and dragged
her out, yelling that she was a Serbian spy. With difficulty
General Sherrill rescued her.

When they reached Münster, which was a corps headquarters, all were ordered out for examination. General Sherrill
showed his papers, calling attention to the statement that he
had been American Minister to Argentina. He was much
astonished when instead of being allowed to proceed he
was detained, and presently informed that he was under arrest
as a spy.

Without more ado he was carried to a military prison, locked
in a cell, kept incommunicado, with a sentry, gun in hand,
watching him through the grated door day and night. He
attempted to send telegrams to Ambassador Gerard at Berlin
and others, and cable messages to Secretary of State Bryan.
For these he paid, but the messages were never sent. Meantime, his agonized family lived in a hotel unaware what had

become of him. He asked to see the commandant and then the chief of staff of the corps, and was assured in reply, as he had been many times before, that at any unauthorized motion or any attempt to escape the sentinel would shoot him. He finally succeeded in attracting the attention of the chief of staff who listened to him at first with contemptuous incredulity but at least with some heeding. Seven days this lasted, when of a sudden, on orders from some superior, he was released and allowed to proceed. I said that war was in all its respects mere madhouse. This chapter of evidence is only one of thousands that could be cited.

On arrival at The Hague, General Sherrill went to work with the rest of us at the Legation. About two weeks later, he received a polite communication from the Postmaster General of Holland soliciting a call. General Sherrill went as desired and the Postmaster General produced all the money that General Sherrill had paid to his prison-keepers for the telegrams and cables that had never been sent. The Postmaster General said he had been requested by the German government at Berlin to refund this money. General Sherrill promptly refused to accept it and went away.

Two things about this proceeding were extraordinary. One was the accurate knowledge displayed by the German government of General Sherrill's exact whereabouts and the other the use of a Dutch high government officer as an intermediary. The latter phase was internationally improper, but it showed again that the Dutch sympathies were on the German side.

Of this we needed no confirmation. Waiters in restaurants had refused to serve us under the impression that we were English, and in one place in the evening a proprietor under the same impression refused to turn on the electric light, leaving us to eat in the dark. Unfriendly looks as we went about the streets were common. I asked the porter at my hotel about this. He said it was racial, but I knew another reason. I had been in Holland while the Boer War was going on and I knew how deep and bitter was the resentment against England's brutal suppression of the Boer republics.

The knowledge of General Sherrill's whereabouts and employment was of course obtained through the German spy system. The Hague, with the rest of Holland, swarmed with the undesirable agents of this activity, and the workers at the Legation were particular objects of their curious regard. Some of them did their job in a manner to make an old police reporter blush for their clumsiness. One Sunday morning as I was going to work, I was aware, as often I had been before, that I was being followed. I stopped, ostensibly to look at a picture in a store window in the Passage, and promptly the sleuth fetched up along side; they always did. So he made the first play. He said he was an American, of German parentage of course, but an American, and he wanted to get back home as soon as he could, but he said all this in the kind of English one learns in a German gymnasium; which was also what I had expected. I listened to all his familiar rigmarole and then asked:

"Where did you live in the United States?" He said:

"In Wisconsin."

"And where is Wisconsin?"

"It's in Milwaukee."

I wished him good morning and went on.

A day or two later, one of them got into the Legation on the plea that he was one of the German fathers whose stranded daughters we were trying to bring out of England. He had come to beg for news of his dear Minna, and was shaken with emotion as he thought of what might have happened to the darling girl. He was assigned to my desk, where he tried to weep on my neck. It was a clumsy performance, but clumsy have been all the histrionics of all the European secret service men I have ever seen, including those of Scotland Yard. One defect in this gentleman's ensemble was that his spectacles were made of window glass and another was that he crudely overdid the parental agony business. This kind of thing demands an artist.

The comical reflection was that they went needlessly through all this elaborate pantomime. We had nothing to conceal; everything we did the world was free to know.

But the German government was not as dumb as certain of its hired hawkshaws. I have spoken of the stories of terrible suffering and abuse related by the first American refugees arriving at The Hague; stories of brutal strippings, searchings, intolerable insults, the seizing of personal effects, baggage, letters of credit, and the like. For a few days these were almost the invariable experiences of Americans fleeing from Germany. Of a sudden a marvellous transformation went over the whole process. Surely the German people are for team work the best in the world. Some magic signal went forth from Berlin, possibly from the Kaiser himself, possibly accompanied with the flaming reproof he knew how to administer. The next company of refugees had not a word of complaint about the treatment they had received. On the contrary, if you will believe me, officers of the German government made astonishing efforts for their comfort and safety, accompanying them to trains, obtaining for them seats, asking after their welfare and mamma's health, and finally presenting to each departing American a nice bouquet of flowers. No more wanton arrests on the route, no more stripping of women, but the utmost courtesy and helpfulness. Somebody in the mad dance of nations had experienced a lucid interval.

Not only so, but another development caused our wondering applause for its cleverness. Many of the American refugees were of the Jewish persuasion. The Jews, of course, had a natural antipathy to Russia because of a thousand pogroms and savage persecutions. Gentile Americans at that time had no love for Russia, regarding it as a pestilent relic left over from the Dark Ages. So now appeared in every stateroom of every steamship leaving Rotterdam for New York supplies of a pamphlet neatly printed in excellent American, entitled "Why Germany is at War with Russia," and placing all the blame for the conflict upon Russia's head. Nothing was said in this ingenious document about Germany's invasion of Belgium, its long-standing menace against France or any other phase of the conflict. Merely Russia, the arch-enemy of mankind, had needlessly and of its depraved instincts, forced the war.

One feature of the volunteer energies shouldering at the Legation's immense load seemed to me to be worth a permanent record. It was and is common for those that defend the capitalist organization of society to say that man must have the incentive of gain and selfishness or he will do nothing, human nature being as it is and utterly bad. This moldy fabrication I have resented before, and now offer the facts that shatter it. Every emergency proves that men will do for service what they will never do for hire. Take the persons that came to the Legation's help—to try to hire them for one day at the compensation they were accustomed to receive would have been beyond the resources of the place and still have been ineffectual. They would not have done the work for pay. But for the sake of service they did it as long as they were needed, did it without compensation and at a considerable personal expense, and were glad to do it. And I doubt if any of them ever did anything in which he took a greater satisfaction. Incentive, says the materialist—we must have incentive, meaning the chance to stuff a pocket-book. Well, the greatest of all incentives is nothing of the kind but merely the joy of being of use.

When the rush was over and something of normalcy returned, we went over to London, where there was another kind of a show going on.

One night in June, 1905, I had sat in a London newspaper's

office and the editor, an old friend, showed me the draft of a bill by which the existing Conservative government was contemplating to establish in England what had never been known there, which was a system of universal and compulsory military training. I thought it marked a backward step and hoped it would not be pressed.

But October, 1914—that was something different. The nation, in a way that has never been made public and probably cannot be in this generation, had been plunged into a war about which the masses knew little and cared less, and yet a war that meant life or death. She must have an army, Britain, a great army, an efficient army or she would perish. No other government ever made such efforts to obtain recruits. One hundred million dollars were spent in advertising, whole front pages of newspapers, whole bill boards, the front glass of taxicabs, every available nook and corner, re-echoing one great poignant cry, "Your King and Country Need You!" Great rallying meetings were held nightly, orators as powerful and convincing as T. P. O'Connor made their best appeals, hourly the peril was stressed, and the result was merely disheartening. A strong curiosity drove me to the recruiting stations; one was but a short distance from the hotel. No man could see what was going on there without seeing also that the old system of volunteer enlistments, then put to its sharpest testing, was for modern conditions worthless. England would never have an army until she should conscript one. Naturally, she was reluctant to abandon the volunteer system that had been for centuries her ample defense. But machine guns have no respect for traditions.

Not only were the numbers of the volunteers inadequate but the physique of those that offered themselves was something to start alarm in any impartial observer. England was paying the penalty for her long tolerance of the slum and the deep submergence of her working population. These thin, scrawny, undersized men, pasty of face and vacant of eye that issued from the East End, what would they be pitted against the sturdy battalions that I had seen so often in Germany? I had for years visited and written about Duval Street and the other horror centres of London slum areas. "The People of the Abyss," Jack London had called the dwellers there, doing an infinitely better job. His great work I knew well and, something, too, of the painful revelations that had attended enlistments for the Boer War; yet it was a Conservative London editor that now first called my attention to the startling fact about the physical weakness of the 1914 recruits. He could see nothing but disaster in sending such men to the front. The more I saw of them the more I was impressed with the same belief and the worse seemed the chances for England. Germany had battered her way through Belgium. Liege, Namur had fallen, the heroic resistance of the little Belgian army had proved all in vain, Germany had entered France, had menaced Paris, had for days apparently swept all before her, and yet there appeared no such response to the bleak danger as one would reasonably expect.

In a strange and memorable way that should never be overlooked by any one interested in the affairs of men here below, the existing social system had turned upon and gnawed itself. It had made this war; it had also undermined the physique of these toiling or starving millions until they were no longer able to respond to the demands the system itself imposed upon them. The supreme trial had come, the whole structure of modern society had been shown to be shaped toward a colossal disaster, and the same system had made its victims incapable of fulfilling its own requirements. A year and a half after the war began, the Belgians held 19 miles of the western front, the British 48, and the French 516.

I was in London when it was convulsed with the story of the passage of the Russian troops, which ranks with the belief in the fable of the angels of Mons as among the most curious episodes of the war.

The situation on the western front was at the time exceedingly precarious. France, although taken unaware, had pulled itself together and delivered the tremendous ripost of the Marne, but the strange fact is that this battle and its significance were virtually unknown in England and so far as any Englishman knew, Paris might fall any moment. In a time of tense anxiety, it seems, anything may be believed. Some one started a story that at night in closely curtained cars, a large body of strange-looking soldiers had been transported from Aberdeen to Dover, where they had embarked for the continent. Wise persons saw at once what this meant. A great Russian army had been sent to help beleaguered France and because of the German submarines they had been sent secretly through England. The story spread and grew. There were many trains of these foreign warriors, they were all tall men, heavily bearded, heavily armed; they had gone on into France and might speedily be expected to turn the tide of battle there. Hundreds of men had seen them; persons were even found in Dover that had seen them embark. I talked with some of the London witnesses. They described in detail how they had happened to behold this benignant vision and what the men looked like. Hope rose hour by hour as the numbers of the Russians swelled and their soldierly qualities were descanted upon. All London was tip-toe to hear of their valorous deeds on the battle front. And then the whole thing faded away into myth. There were no Russians, there were no secret transferrings. There was only a car of Scotchmen that had been recruited somewhere in the North and were on their way to a training camp.

One other delusion may be noted here. The newspapers were keeping up a front of admirable poise and assurance, but I was curious to learn the real inside official view of the situation. A. C. Kenealy, who had covered the Johnstown flood with me in 1889 and was afterward a reporter on *The New York World* when I was its city editor, was then editor of *The London Mirror*. He had close intimate relations with certain men in the government and I asked him to set his machinery at work and ascertain exactly how the government men felt about the war and its probable duration. He obligingly made the inquiry and returned me the result. It was this:

"By Christmas there will not be a German soldier left in France."

October 3, 1914, this was. He believed it himself. Human wisdom is a wonderful thing.

Chapter XVII

SOME LESSONS OF THE TRENCHES

IT was a staggered, astonished, and almost incredulous England in whose ears the blast of war sounded on August 5, 1914. Never went a great nation into a great conflict so ill-prepared. On the land side nothing was ready, not even, so far as could be discerned, the vestige of a plan. Only one Englishman had clearly foreseen the inevitable catastrophe, but Edward VII had passed, leaving no record of the basis for his singular pre-vision, and there was no one to succeed him. For more than two generations England's wars had been mainly against black, brown, or yellow men in primitive and far-away precincts and the average Englishman had ceased to think that war could ever land upon his front doorstep. Intelligent men read in their newspapers daily the darkening signs of trouble and assumed them to be portents for the dwellers on the continent, not for home consumption. When of a sudden the storm broke upon a typical Briton he had no psychology for the onset and floundered upon strange roads.

The muddling confusion that followed should be for the pondering of nations. It seems that if we are to tolerate wars we must accept all that goes with that tolerance, including finger-on-the-trigger preparedness. There is no picking and choosing about the competitive system; it is all or nothing. To believe that we can oppose or neglect armament and still retain the system that makes armament necessary is only half-way thinking. England in 1914 was without an equipment to carry on war in the modern way, without the machinery to create such an equipment, and but for the navy might in the first few months have been cut up like cheese. Even the needful over-ture was at first inauspicious. The war was not popular, the cause that had led the country into it was not well known, and the general ineptitude was painfully shown in the placard that appeared in all the London shop windows. "Business as Usual," it cried and reiterated. "If it is no more than that," replied the workingman, "why should I enlist? My job as usual."

The wheels of defense seemed stopped on a dead centre. I will give but one illustration. Recruits in the Midland counties were instructed to repair to Preston, in Lancashire. When they arrived they found no one to direct them, no barracks, no tents, no provender, no reception arrangements. Rain came and they wandered the streets shelterless except for the bounty of the kindly residents. An American citizen of English birth, resident of Massachusetts, came to the rescue. Having ample means, he hired a hall in which the recruits could sleep, and bought bread, cheese, and ham with which he fed them until the government was sufficiently articulated to take them in hand. It is a picture to be set side by side with the designate and perfect clicking of the German mobilization, where a single hour saw millions of civilians transformed into a uni-formed and equipped army, starting in trains for the front.

After the close of the titanic struggle came a long, joyous period in which the fascinating game called "Passing the Buck" attained with many writers to a great popularity. While it ran its course every nation in Europe except Germany, Austria, and San Marino was successively found guilty of the war. Serbia was the caitiff wretch; it should have surrendered its sover-eignty at the demand of Austria. Russia caused the war; it should have abandoned its old-time policy of protecting Serbia, its little relative, from the aggressions of powerful neighbors. Belgium caused the war; it should have allowed the German troops to pass freely and so cut France to pieces in two weeks. Italy caused the war; it should have adhered to the Triple

Alliance, invaded France from the south and enabled it to be ground between upper and nether millstones. France caused the war; Frenchmen had conceived a hellish plot to invade Germany by night and murder the peaceful Germans in their beds. And finally, England caused the war; if it had given notice of its intention to support France and Russia, the German order of mobilization would never have been issued.[1]

How gladly we leap upon conclusions that fit their cogs into our prejudices! This dictum about England's failure in the supreme crisis to give notice of its intentions has been so diligently repeated and generally believed that it has become encysted in the current theory of the first days of the conflict. But imperialism is hateful enough without painting in the tints of fiction. The truth is that England could not have given any notice to anybody of any intention to support France and Russia because at any time when such a notice would have been of the least avail England had not formed such an intention.

The facts about the period between July 23, the date of the Austrian note, and August 5, when England declared war, are not well understood in America and may be offered as a warning against too ready faith in retroactive genius that would refashion events to suit desires. There was no time from the Austrian note to August 2, certainly, when a proposal to go to war for France and Russia could have been passed by or even seriously urged in the British Cabinet, and no time when it would have been acceptable to the nation. What! To fight for France? Strange rallying cry would that be after nearly a thousand years of strife, antagonisms, and inherited hatreds! Let not thy discreet soul think it. Virtually nobody in England was ready for any such adventure in new-found friendship. Throughout these ten days, Sir Edward Grey, the Foreign Secretary, was wholly intent upon leaping from bog to bog with eyes fixed

---

[1] Conspicuously the former Grand Duke Alexander, in his book, *Once a Grand Duke*. But there are countless others.

upon the glimmering hope that he might avert the inevitable, and the rest of the Council reposed in the comfortable belief that in some way things would come out all right and the grouse shooting would be better this year. Even on the morning of the fateful Sunday, August 2, Prime Minister Asquith had planned a day of golf and with but two exceptions, the other statesmen were quite as amiably sanguine that England could keep aloof.

Yet on the night before, German troops had invaded France, had begun to pour over the Luxemburg frontier, at 5:15 P.M. had been issued the Kaiser's final mobilization order—as King George was sending his pathetic little messages begging everybody to be good and keep the peace.

With all these chilled-steel facts before it, the Cabinet still hesitated, and the report of its deliberations printed next day showed it as resolving "to make every honorable effort to keep Great Britain out of the war."[1]

But the purpose of this chapter is to relate the effect of the war upon the Socialist movement in America and the foregoing facts are cited only because they are necessary to make plain what is to follow. And first of all, two considerations.

When Germany, kicking to right and left her treaty obligations, trampled over the border of Belgium, she imperilled every international covenant in the world and shook all the foundations of international society. This fact, which came afterward to be conveniently ignored and obscured, is impregnable now, and was then pivotal with men that appraised the war with their minds and not with their prejudices. It forced upon them a poignant issue. The success of Germany would mean around the world that no agreement among nations had more validity than the heavier guns and the bigger army could give to it. Large nation and small nation would be but cat and

---

[1] See *The London Chronicle*, Monday, August 3. The two men that were in favor of action were battering away at the rest but had not yet convinced them.

mouse and a screaming shell would be the only code of ethics. But the case of Luxemburg was different. The treaties that guaranteed the independence and integrity of Belgium had al-

THE DEATH-GRAPPLE.

ROLLIN KIRBY'S CARTOON ON THE WAR ISSUE
Published in *The New York World*, April 4, 1917

lowed her to retain an armament; she had therefore something to strike with, something in the way of armed defense. The treaties that guaranteed the independence and integrity of Luxemburg, treaties as incumbent upon Germany as upon any other nation, stripped Luxemburg of all such weapons, dismantled her fortress, and left her dependent for life wholly upon the good faith of her guarantors.[1] Many conscientious pacifists had vigorously asserted that all armaments were as needless as wasteful, since the good faith of nations, the validity of agreements, and the force of the world's opinion were a stronger defense than guns and armies. It was a noble, alluring, and exalted faith. Would to God it had been justified! It came in the case of Luxemburg to its complete testing and crumpled in a moment under the rolling of the German machine and the trampling war hoofs of Mars Omnipotens. When in total disregard of its own pledged word, treaties, honor, world opinion, the German armies burst into Luxemburg, they brought home sharply to every lover of peace a most disquieting question. For if Germany's trespass should be sealed with the all-approving stamp of success, there need be no more talk or hope of disarmament, but every nation must arm to the teeth.

To the pacifist that was also a radical all this was infinitely worse than to pacifists that were of conservative faith. For it must be clear, if we stop to think, that Socialism as a scheme for man's life must rest upon international concord. That one nation in a world so interdependent could establish and maintain a lone Socialist state is most unlikely. Socialism is not for any one nation but for the world. It can be for the world only by virtue of covenants, and if all validity was to be beaten out of covenants under the butt end of a Mauser, again what hope might there be?

But of course the situation for the radical and the Socialist was not even so simple as this. Germany ought to be opposed for tearing up treaties and scoffing at agreements, but to oppose Germany was to be aligned with Russia, always our bête noir and sign of loathing, and it meant that for the time being we were to hold in abeyance the opposition to British imperial-

[1] Treaty of April, 1867. It should be carefully considered by any person tempted by propaganda to think lightly of Germany's guilt.

ism that had such red registerings in India and Ireland. Yet
on the first count again, to support the Allies was to strive for
the existence of France that had so long upheld in Europe
and against such odds the standard of republicanism. France
the Republic, Russia the autocracy, Britain the iron-heeled imperialist—it seemed too incongruous. Could one favor the
Republic without endorsing the autocracy?

It looked like a toss-up of evils and to a great extent it was
no less. But out of the mischmasch of relative drawbacks, two
or three things stood fairly clear. Russian autocracy did not
threaten with destruction the faith between nations by which
alone Socialist progress could be made. Russian autocracy was
well enough known to be crumbling within and doomed.
Russian autocracy loomed not so large and black as Mars
Omnipotens, New Britain, Friedrichwilhelmshafen, Ponope,
Yap, Anguar, the slave trade, the Kaiser's speech—and now
Belgium and Luxemburg. "It is to the empire of the world
that German genius aspires," said Wilhelm. This was the
way, and too much.

But because we hoped for Germany's repulse, that did not
mean that for a moment we lost sight of the last roots of the
whole terrific situation imbedded in the system of society that
we opposed; imbedded in it and springing directly from it.
The last and worst of the war culprits was and is and always
will be Capitalism.

The ablest of the English Socialist leaders at that time and
one of the most remarkable minds I have ever known was
Henry M. Hyndman. We had long been intimate friends,
carrying on a confidential correspondence. As the situation
finally cleared to me, I wrote Hyndman from The Hague
telling him of the position I felt compelled to take. It proved
to be so exactly his own that he published my letter in *The
London Telegraph*. I found when in October I finally made
my way back to the United States that knowledge of this let-

ter had gone before me and thus added nothing to my popularity, if I had any. I had nothing to conceal on the subject and that my views might have a complete exposition, I printed in *Pearson's Magazine,* with which I was then connected, an article called "Who Made This War?" in which I set forth my observations of many years as to the genesis of the conflict and the immediate responsibility for it.

An important election was due that fall and I had expected that with so tremendous a verification of the Socialist faith as the war offered there would be a campaign of great vigor and onslaught. Instead of unusual energy there was a wholly unusual lassitude and the apparent beginning of a split in the party. To get film reels picturing the savageries of the war (of which a supply was ready), to hire halls and to begin a widespread effort to impress upon the American public the inevitable consequences of retaining the existing social system seemed the obvious course for the campaign. The suggestion was overruled. A party meeting was called for a Sunday morning at Labor Temple. I tried to set forth what seemed to me the immense propaganda value to us of the events in Europe. Prominent members that had other views about the war spoke against me and the majority was of their opinion. The campaign, therefore, was fought upon the same lines as before. I still think this was an error, but can understand now better than I could then the reasons for it.

We could not at that time talk much about the war without emphasizing the responsibility of Germany and the black moral turpitude involved in her brigandage in Belgium and Luxemburg. The greater part of the Socialist party membership was composed of Germans and Jews. Naturally the Jews had a deep-seated hatred of Russia, and, because of the Dreyfus affair, many felt a strong aversion to France. To say that among all the German and Jewish members of the party the nationalistic impulse was stronger than the devotion to Socialism would be unfair. Probably most of them would have resented such an implication. Essentially, Socialism is international, not national. Yet it is true that a majority of our members sympathized with Germany and hoped she would win. They would probably have given other reasons than nationalistic or racial for their support and probably again would have caused themselves to believe in their reasons, but the result was the same. It was easier to understand how they felt than to go along with them. In nine cases in ten, residence in an alien country with an alien speech and alien ways will multiply the nationalistic instinct. Talking with one of the officers of our party organization, and one of the best, I ventured to urge upon him the moral debacle that would come upon the world if Germany's trespass in Belgium and Luxemburg should come to have the tremendous signatory of a German success. Not a treaty in the world would be worth the paper it was written on and there would be an end to the faith by which alone intercourse among nations can be carried on. He said:

"Oh, England has broken treaties, too. She stayed in Egypt after she had promised to withdraw."

I tried to point out that if there had been any disregard of covenants among nations that fact made it more than ever imperative that there should be no more of such tergiversation and that a nation guilty of an overt burglary upon faith and national integrity should be condemned by all the rest of the world. He was impervious to the argument. A Russian Jew, all he could see was that Germany's defeat would be Russia's victory. It was enough.

We made the campaign, but it was without a galvanic touch. I had been nominated for the national Senate. Many good Socialists felt that they could not support me after my comments on the Kaiser. Looking at it impersonally, this seems an interesting psychical fact. With the utmost sincerity these

men believed in Socialism as the salvation of the world, the release of the worker, the bringer of peace on earth. When the
pinch came, they could not eradicate from blood and mind
the old instinct of the tribe. I am aware, of course, that from
the beginning there had been those among us that professed
Socialism chiefly because it was of German origin and en-
dorsement, but these were few and discountable. We are
thinking now of the other and larger element that wished
Socialism to come but also wished Germany to win, impelled
to one wish by reason and to the second by instinct, and instinct proving the stronger.

It was in the course of this campaign, when we were on a
speaking tour together, that one of our most distinguished
members, afterward a brilliant Representative in Congress,
told me of an apt illustration of this curious atavism. At that
time Victor Berger was the most active and persistent of the
Socialist leaders, and the best known. He was Austrian born
and could never overlook the Teuton in his versatile equipment. They were talking about the war and Berger grew
excited.

"Comrade Blank," he cried, "you know I have always hated
the Kaiser, but when I see the world taking arms against him
I feel that I must seize a rifle and take my place in the ranks
and fight for him."

He had clear warrant for his feeling in the examples set
by the German Socialists, to whom most of the party in this
country looked for mentorship. After all the long-professed
faith in peace and reason, many of these men rushed away to
arms as soon as the tocsin sounded. Even men that were beyond the military age and exempt from service volunteered.
One of them, a conspicuous member of the Reichstag, who
had drawn upon him much censure and some applause by
publicly proposing that Germany should restore Alsace and
Lorraine, a man of sixty years or more, at the first order of

mobilization insisted upon volunteering, entered the army, and was killed at the battle of Longwy. I believe there were many German Socialists in America to whom he seemed adorable. At least, I never heard criticism of his course nor of Bebel's war-gong letter, a fact that seemed to me then inexplicable. And at one Western city I was shown the little bronze medal that had been cast in happy expectation of the day when the German armies should enter Paris.

These things are cited here in no spirit of reproach but only to point out how swiftly all the aspects of life are transformed when the war drum sounds. Principles of faith most honestly conceived and accepted go glimmering everywhere before that note. French Socialists that in 1913 had proclaimed their purpose to welcome with open arms their invading German comrades prepared a totally different welcome when the faultlessly moving gray-green machine rolled over the border. Gustave Hervé himself, who had gone to prison as a violent opponent of armament, became the most eloquent and fervent champion of France when von Kluck menaced Mauberge. It became the fashion afterward to ascribe these transformations to propaganda. I do not think propaganda had anything to do with it, nor had any natural fickleness. "When I said I would die a bachelor," says Benedick, "I did not think I should live till I were married." When the French Socialists proposed a picnic with the invading Germans they never thought the invaders would reach the door blackened from the destruction of Louvain.

The simple truth is that war is a thing so tremendous that nothing can withstand it. When most excellent peace societies assemble and solemnly denounce war and resolve to have no part in it they but waste their time. Every war when it comes seems in the eyes of nationals an exception to all other war. "We hate war, but this is different," is the universal thought. If wars are to be prevented upon this earth they are to be prevented only by removing their cause. So long as we insist upon retaining the cause we cut an exceedingly ill figure passing solemn resolutions against the inevitable results of that cause. So long as we keep imperialism and competition we shall have wars. Nay, we can pile knee deep the pious resolutions of our exalted societies. Still war will come and still men of pacific faith will be drawn into it.

Under the spell of this grisly spectre the Socialist movement in America languished and dwindled. In 1912 we cast 900,000 votes for our candidate for President; in 1916 but 600,000. Once the organization had seemed vigorous, buoyant, full of promise of a great growth; now it seemed to fall away. Division in the ranks was deadly to any effective work. The American leaders, men like William J. Ghent, A. M. Simons, Graham Phelps Stokes, Carl D. Thompson, felt that Germany's housebreaking adventure in Belgium and her shredding of treaties made her as much the foe of Socialism as of political liberalism. German and Jewish Socialists seemed to see nothing wrong in Germany's course nor any evil in her triumph.

Then the stalemate became evident on the Western front. The French turned back the terrific assault upon Verdun, where 600,000 men lost their lives to make, as the French President said, an everlasting monument to human folly, and the British failed in their offensive farther west. After repeated visits to the front and to England and France it seemed to me certain that the war would settle into a long-drawn-out contest of dogged endurance on both sides. Good souls often spoke of calling the conflict a draw and making peace on that basis. Any such suggestion was merely fantastic. After careful inquiry, I knew well it was impossible. The terrific problem that was beginning to face this country was whether it should allow the war to go on until there should come upon Europe and the world a devastation beyond anything ever imagined and out of which civilization should emerge gasping and impotent, or whether the United States should go in and end the strife. President Wilson had been tolerant enough to encourage me to write to him, and I now reported to him what I had seen and heard and the conclusions to which I had been driven.

The war as it stood was due to last for years, and to end then in the triumph of the ideals of German imperialism, treaty breaking, and the spirit since manifested as Hitlerism.

After the war was all over and done with, a saying became current among those that had not approved of the course of the United States, that we were propagandized into taking arms. If there were any truth in this charge, I suppose I should have at least this share in the guilt. From July, 1916, I was convinced the United States should enter the war to end it, being totally unable to see any other way by which it could be stopped.

But the charge is untrue, as untrue as the other assertion often made that Wilson was eager for war and wantonly thrust the country into it. Those that said these things did not know the facts or conveniently forgot them. Nations, like individuals, never do anything for but one reason. Two impulses drove the United States into the conflict. Germany, in total defiance of international law and the practise of civilized nations, was killing American citizens and refusing the least satisfaction to the continued American complaints. For more than two years the American government had continued its protests and been consistently affronted by such response as Germany deigned to make. A government exists to protect its citizens. The government of the United States had reached a point where it must either acknowledge that it was unable to perform its normal duties and functions, or it must with force vindicate for its own people and all the world the indispensable principles it had announced.

The sinking of the *Lusitania* in violation of international law and civilized usage with the loss of 114 American lives was an act of aggression that no self-respecting nation could overlook. It came afterward to be forgotten that President Wilson's protests against this piracy were unheeded, that it was followed by the sinking of more vessels under the same circumstances with more losses of American lives; that after many of these incidents, all eliciting futile protests, President Wilson gave notice that unless the practise should be abandoned diplomatic relations with Germany must be severed; that the answer to this warning was more sinkings and more American lives lost; that even when on February 3, 1917, President Wilson was driven to make his warning good and break off diplomatic relations he declared that there would be no hostile act by this country unless Germany continued her illegal and murderous practises and that at once Germany redoubled these practises.

There is no question that England wished us to enter the war. She had wished Italy to enter, and Portugal and Rumania. But to say, recalling the record, that our entry was the result of British propaganda is manifestly absurd.

It is no less preposterous to say that the American capitalists and financial interests inveigled us into the war. I was in Washington and observing Congress throughout the period when the war resolution was passed, and the capitalists had nothing to do with it. If they had, I should have known the fact. The sources of influence on Congress are not so easily hidden. Mr. John Skelton Williams, Comptroller of the Currency, furnished me afterward with a summary of the comparative profits of the chief munition makers in this country, and it showed that they made twice as much money before the United States entered the war as they made afterward.

The other motive upon which this country acted was the knowledge possessed by President Wilson and others, aware of the facts, that the entry of the United States would bring the frightful conflict to an end and restore peace to a torn and bleeding world, and if that object was not worth while nothing in life is worth while except a supply of bread and beef.

As soon as Congress had passed the war resolution, my duty, in view of what I had urged and believed, was of course plain. I wrote to the President offering my services in any capacity he might wish to employ me and he responded by asking me to take a place on the special diplomatic mission he was sending to Russia.

At once arose bitter complaint from certain elements among my fellow members of the Socialist party.

As this episode illustrates what I have said about the virtual impossibility of a dispassionate estimate of anything connected with war, it may be worth considering, the more that it came to be a matter of widespread debate far beyond the importance of the original participants.

In the first place, contrary to the all but universal belief on the subject, there is nothing in the Socialist creed that forbids a Socialist to take part in war; not a paragraph, not a sentence, not a word. On the contrary, part of the original Socialist creed was the creating of a citizen army to repel invasion.

I was not, therefore, as came to be so widely proclaimed, violating my Socialist professions when I offered my services to the President. Any Socialist was at perfect liberty to do this and retain his full standing in the movement.

In the next place, as my position had long before been set forth, there should have been no surprise nor resentment about it. In many articles in *Pearson's Magazine* and other periodicals I had stated it plainly. Writing in the *New Review* I said of peace made at that time, 1916, that it would fasten upon the world these principles as established by the war.

1. Treaties have no validity and can be broken at convenience.
2. Small nations have no rights that great nations are bound to respect.

3. A nation can reject arbitration and insist upon war and still suffer nothing in the estimation of mankind.

4. Absolutism is right, proper, and enduring.

These deductions were directly in line with the resolutions adopted by the Conference of the Socialists of the Allied Countries held at London, February 15, 1915, which declared that the invasion of Belgium and France by the German armies threatened the independence of all nations and shattered all confidence in all international treaties. Under such conditions, said the resolutions, a victory for German imperialism would mean the defeat and annihilation of democracy and freedom in Europe.

I go into these details now because they seem, on being recalled, rather interesting merely as psychological curiosities. When I had accepted President Wilson's appointment and was on my way to Russia, the Socialist party expelled me.

This action, which happened to be in violation of the party's constitution, was not based, as was everywhere believed, upon the fact that I had supported the entry of the United States into the war but upon my acceptance of a place under a capitalistic government—the place, incidentally, being one that carried no compensation.

Some of the next developments were of the order of unintentional humor. Many Socialists that had applauded their German comrades for adhering to their government in time of war condemned me although the worst that could be said was that I had followed the German example. Parlor Pink radicals that had never contributed to Socialism anything but their jeers and sneers were certain I had proved faithless to its first principles, not knowing anything about those principles, but cocksure, nevertheless. Most joyous fact of all, a large part of the capitalist press and many capitalistic gentlemen loosed upon me the vials of reproof because I had fallen by the Socialist wayside, of which they, too, knew nothing. The most reactionary newspaper in New York was good enough to say that I had joined the Socialist party only because I could get publicity in that way and I now left it that I might get more publicity, sweetly ignoring the fact that I had not left anything but had been flung out on my head. It may be cited as one more psychological curiosity that many persons of radical and pacifist sympathies actually caused themselves to believe that when the United States went into the war to end it the United States became responsible for the origin of the war, which is exactly as if a policeman that tries to stop a fight should be arrested for causing it or a fireman that holds a hose nozzle upon a fire should be accused therefore of arson.

Of course there were non-resistance pacifists that were also Socialists, just as there were Socialists that were also Presbyterians—a few. But the doctrine that when war has been declared a Socialist must sit with folded hands and see torn to pieces the whole structure of international faith upon which alone must rest the hope of peace and of all human progress— that doctrine was never more a part of Socialist creed than was the doctrine of infant damnation. In support of which statement it is only necessary to refer to the utterances of Karl Marx, Engels, Bebel, and of the Socialist parties in country after country.[1]

Afterward it seemed interesting to recall that the position I felt compelled to take was exactly that taken by Clarence Darrow and upon identical grounds. In a great speech he made one October night in old Madison Square Garden, New York, one of the most powerful of his many notable flights of eloquence, he set forth in white lights the true nature of the issue that confronted the world. As soon as the war was over, Parlor Pinkdom pardoned all his offense but declined the least amnesty for mine, which only (and humbly) duplicated his.

[1] William English Walling, in his valuable book, *The Socialists and the War*, has made a compilation of records and opinions on this subject that place it beyond the least question.

Whether this discrimination was due to his far greater general merit or resulted from some process of the Pink reasoning unknown to the lower orders, I am unable to state.

My old friend and comrade, Victor Berger, was furiously incensed by the course I had taken and in many attacks in his *Milwaukee Leader* declared that I was influenced only by the fact that I was of English descent. This in view of his remarks about the Kaiser should add another element to the collation of humor the whole episode afforded. As a matter of fact I did not give a hoot about England. Having been in India, China, the South Seas, and Ireland, I should have been glad to see the British Empire shattered by any power less reactionary. But the choice of evils included no chance of choice about the rape of Belgium and Luxemburg, nor about the results of a German success that was inevitable unless the United States should intervene; and that is the whole story.

Inevitable, after a long and terrible struggle the thought of which was unendurable. Repeated visits to both countries had convinced me that neither France nor England would submit without exactly such a struggle. The United States by intervening would be exposed to a heavy expense and a deplorable loss of lives, but all of its losses together of all kinds would be inconsiderable compared with the disaster that was certain if the war were allowed to go on.

I was of that opinion in 1917. I am of that opinion today. Nothing has happened that has changed in any way my conviction on this subject nor caused me to regret the course I took. The temporary erection in Italy and other countries of a dictatorship that cancels or obscures the democratic creed seems of slight importance in any large view of Europe. Any dictator is better than any king. You can at any time get rid of a dictator; you cannot get rid of a king except with long years of painful effort and recurrent defeats. Historically, the dictator is the pavement-layer for the coming republic.

It is of course obvious that in its last days the competitive system finds that it cannot coexist with the forms of democracy. But this fact again is not momentous. Since capitalism is doomed, its dying vagaries about Fascism and the like are interesting but not disturbing.

After the war there arose a taunting question among those that never clearly understood it and its genesis as to what the United States derived from it, since we gained no territory, no indemnity, and nothing in fact but a debt. To all these cynical queries it is answer enough that the United States brought peace to a war-shattered and despairing world and saved it from the illimitable disaster that threatened it.

Instead of that disaster, came advantage and civilization's gain. For there crashed to earth three old, mediæval, autocratic monarchies that had ruled to military madness the destinies of 300,000,000 people, and on the ruins of these monarchies, once deemed rock-rooted and eternal, arose a group of republics. That great advance signed the beginning of imperialism's downfall, and if our republican faith is now indeed more than a tradition, here is gain enough.

Oh, yes—I know. The dictatorships again. But how poor are they that read history with their eyes and not with their minds! Dictatorships! What are they? Nothing about this apparent wave of reaction is in any way novel. Exactly this process the world has passed through after every democratic forward surge. Its perfect prototype is seen in Louis Napoleon overthrowing the Second Republic and in the total collapse of the advance of 1848. But where is the Second Empire now? Where is the stony-hearted tyranny that put Robert Blum to death? The tide runs forward, the tide runs back. But never so far back as the line from which the advance started. With perfect philosophy one may view the Mussolinis and Hitlers, the black, brown, green, and other styles in haberdashery. When the giantess turns sunward again she will trample all this tinted lingerie into the dust and never know she has trodden on anything.

The war was the world's attained limit in murderous madness. How horrible it was only those know that saw it in the trenches and hospitals. To pay such a price for a modicum of wisdom seems preposterous. Yet it seemed also to be man's way and great as the cost was, I am not sure that another generation may not look upon it as for the world a turning-point of regeneration such as Sedan proved to be for France, terrible, stupid, mad, and yet with compensations.

Chapter XVIII

BEING AN ATTRACTION

MEN have said harsh words of the radio, of the unhappy metalism of its tone, its curious tricks with the human voice, its futile wrestlings with static, its loutish interposition of symphony movements and ballyhoo for tooth paste, and the like. Yet though its sins be as scarlet, they would be, to one wound-nursing element, in hours of bitter retrospect, as white as snow. Evil has the radio done, much evil; but glory be to it and praise, sing these sufferers, for it killed the Chautauqua.

The Chautauqua, that queer attempt to capitalize the racial instincts for culture and a bank deposit, that most curious manifestation of the irrepressible urge for learning and profits that combine in the Puritan to make him historically the world's wonder. The radio did for it, and among those that mourned at its bier were to be counted few of the hard-worked, under-paid and sorely tried men and women that were called its Talent.

A thing so typical, a development at one time so widespread and so powerful in influence, should have more than a casual obituary. What was it really like, this Chautauqua system? Nothing but excerpts from experience can fully tell that painful story, and thus I begin:

It is a Sunday afternoon in a town of the Middle West, a town of about two thousand inhabitants that lives upon the region farmers. There is a huge tent, like that of a circus, a platform at one end and a restless, sweltering, and unhappy audience. I am sitting on that platform holding a slip of paper whereon appear these cryptic notations:

Sunday, August 15—
"Leave Orkney 5:49 p. m.,
    Arrive Goshorn 8:23 p. m.;
Leave Goshorn 8:51 p. m.,
    Arrive Shawmut 11:22 p. m.,
Leave Shawmut 1:40 a. m.,
    Arrive Jena Junction 3:10 a. m.;
Leave Jena Junction 4:16 a. m.,
    Arrive Willesdene 6:55 a. m."

Plainly that was what he had meant, the fiend that filled in the blank spaces under the heading "Itinerary" here on the last page of these "Instructions to Talent" that with a growing suspicion of lunacy's first symptoms I had been studying for the last twenty minutes. He had not intended, as for a time I tried desperately to hope, that these flying leaps about my native land should be stretched decently over two days, with some Christian opportunities between for food and repose. In the depths of a depravity that seems now inhuman he had conceived the twisted horrors of this night's journeyings and then had satiated malignity by wishing them on me. One's head might whirl and buzz as one contemplated what was in store, but from its physical facts was no escape. Nothing could be more certain, for here in the next space below on the "Itinerary" appeared these fatal lines:

Monday, August 16—
"Willesdene, speak at 3 p. m.
    Treasurer, O. B. Jenkins
Leave Willesdene 6:30 p. m.,
    Arrive Eagle Rock 8:53 p. m. and so forth.

About this time my eye, horror-fascinated as is the dove's before the serpent, fell upon a "Special Notice" printed conspicuously on the first page of the "Instructions," headed in full-face type and ominously adorned with a margin of fists, all pointing to it their minatory forefingers. Often I had promised myself that I would read this awesome thing because I was almost certain it contained something I ought to know, but I had nevertheless managed to evade it because I was equally sure that it contained something disagreeable. As to the second attribute I seemed to have had a gift of prophecy or divination, for when that afternoon in Orkney I finally mastered the "Special Notice" it was with these unfeeling phrases that it sent a chill down my spine:

SPECIAL NOTICE

The Attraction must in every instance verify independently the information given here concerning the arrival and departure of trains. Consult the local ticket agent.

The Attraction will take notice that it is expected to inquire in each locality if there is any better or quicker way to reach the next engagement than that set down in the Itinerary. This firm will not be responsible for any failure to do so nor for the failure of any Attraction to fill its engagements.

THE SPENLOW & JORKINS CHAUTAUQUA BUREAU.

While with mind insurgent I was digesting this last frigid comment, I was also waiting for the local Platform Manager to find a terminal for his remarks concerning the superior quality of the coming week's offerings at his show. He seemed to have more to say than the 600 persons in that tent could hear and while he struggled with the terms of that problem the clock hands were advancing. After he had made an end, a local church choir obliged, apparently to the derision of a part of the audience, and likewise a traveling cornetist, both, of course, being encored. It was one of the peculiarities of the Chautauqua business that a musical offering of any kind invariably got an encore. The performance might have been so bad that one could hear the angels in heaven sobbing, or the selection so old and weary everybody in the county had turned against that tune summer before last, and yet that audience would sit there and clap with its hands and hammer with its feet until it won to hear again the outworn air it must have loathed. On a hot day, too, a day so blistering hot the paint peeled off the tent poles; or on a night when the mosquitoes came down in swarms thick enough to drive any other people home or mad, there they would sit and clamor a never-ending desire to be tortured again. Any old Chautauquan could tell about this, but not one of them could explain it. Robert Louis Stevenson once called the passion to encore public performances a beautiful trait in human nature. Stevenson was never on the Chautauqua.

It was past 4 o'clock that afternoon when all this dreary prologuing (preluding was the professional term for it) having been ploughed through, I got a chance to start on my own turn and illuminate the Orkney intellect. It had to last an hour and fifteen minutes or any Chautauqua audience would feel itself cheated and would complain to the management and get me discharged or blacklisted or something, and yet at that rate I stood to miss the 5:49 out of Orkney and bring down upon me the wrath of the "Special Notice" with all of its warning fists.

From the tent to the railroad station was nearly two miles, there was never a vehicle in sight that could be hired, and the manager or treasurer, or whoever he was, having disputed my account, gave me no other encouragement than the vision of his back. In this emergency the driver of a cement truck made room for me on the seat beside him and I landed at the station with six minutes to spare. I had there a small trunk to be provided for and the next stage of my initiation was reached with the fact that this seven-times accursed thing could not be checked beyond Goshorn. "Why not?" echoed the station agent, delighted to have somebody he could overlook from the heights of superior knowledge, "because it's the B.C. & D. and that ain't our road and that's why not and it's enough."

If I had doubts about its sufficiency they were due to be dispelled before the morrow morn. About two hours later I alighted upon a long open platform at one end of which arose a shed that I perceived to constitute the Goshorn railroad station. My drooping spirits were cheered by the sight of my trunk as it hurtled through the air from the baggage car and landed on the farther end of the platform, and then the train pulled out and left me standing there, a comical figure of lonely impotence, for I was the only human being in sight. The shed was deserted; being Sunday there was no station master, baggage man, transfer person, nor other sign of help and hope. On every side spread away the pathless wilds of Goshorn, revealing to my anxious eye nothing of animated habitation. I sat upon the trunk and held converse with myself, after the manner of Crusoe. By all accounts I had eighteen minutes to get to the other station, wherever it might be, and thus escape the vengeance of the Special Notice, and while I could easily conceive of myself as striding across Goshorn's bosky vistas looking for that station, the 106 pounds of trunk did not seem to fit into the picture. From this strait I was happily rescued by a native of the Goshorn tribe and in a manner that I aim to tell because it was so typical. He came swoshing along, smoking a pipe and so evidently on good terms with himself that I judged he was late come from a table such as I should not see that night. With benignance and pity he looked upon my misfortunes and heard my story.

"No, there ain't no transfer here Sundays," says he. "Other days Jim Green usually hangs around with his old go-cart, but not Sundays."

"How far away is the B.C. & D. station?"

"Why, it's right handy by. It ain't more than a quarter of a mile."

I wilted.

"How do I get that trunk over there?"

He drew on his pipe while he considered this question and the trunk. Then the oracle was delivered.

"Well, boss, I'll tell you, there just ain't no way unless you tote it, and I guess I'll have to help you."

So between us we carried and dragged and slid the infernal thing down one line of rails until we came to the crossing and then along another line of rails till we came to the station. There, before the train came (it was late) I had ample time to consider in one of its most absorbing aspects a dark mystery of the American railroad system that must have puzzled many a tortured mind. One town, two railroad stations and these set as far apart as ingenuity could devise; two stations to do the work of one and so multiply the sum of human woes and swell the tide of human profanity. And still I have heard persons express doubts as to whether a personal devil really goes around setting traps for human souls. They had never been on the Chautauqua—persons that talked like that.

At Shawmut this variety of his work was still more apparent and gloomier, for the stations were nearly two miles apart and placed on opposite edges of the town boundary, "for fear they quarrel," said the friendly brakeman that on the way down elucidated this and other matters, including the politics of his Congressional district. He said that on Sundays there was but one automobile that transferred passengers at Shawmut and urged me to waste no time about getting into it because there were always more passengers than the thing would hold. "If I was you, I'd be standing on the steps when we pull in," said he, "and make one clean jump into that machine before we stop. You do that and you'll have a chance to ride and it looks as if the walking might be right bad about that time."

He was referring to the weather, which was lowering. But when he talked about making one clean jump and that kind of thing he did not know about Nemesis the trunk. I knew about it, though, and how it was going to trip me, which it did. Before I got through negotiating about it the automobile was filled and I stood there in my favorite rôle of fatuous ineptitude, in which I may say I have few rivals since Moses was at the fair. "You wait here, I'll come back for you," said the chauffeur. He had seen and comprehended my distress and was quick to relieve it, and I should be doing scant justice here to my fellow countrymen if I failed to note that in a long and variegated experience with the difficult travel conditions prevalent in rural United States I seldom failed to find ready, generous, and unstinted assistance as soon as it was known that I was in trouble. The brusque American manner is only an outward flourish, or kind of defense against the aggression that seems to be expected of a stranger merely because he is strange. When as a traveler you can manage in some way to win through that tough armor plate to the human being within, happy you will be, for out in the country, anyway, they will do anything for you.

I sat me down within the station to wait. In ten minutes or so the station agent began to put out the kerosene lamps that by a disheartening fiction were supposed to illuminate the waiting room. I said:

"Not going to close up, I hope?"

"Sorry, boss," says he, not unkindly, "it's the rule. I gotta shut her up after this last train."

On the platform outside I found a small box on which I could sit and watch the coming storm, count the probable minutes until that chauffeur should return, or hold debate with myself if he would come at all. The storm was the more fascinating speculation because from the brightness and frequency of the lightning I could see it would be in its way up to the usual Western standard and likewise would probably find me without a shelter. The station stood alone, the nearest house was all of a thousand feet away, and if I should take myself that distance I should lose the chance of getting the auto—even if it should come, and about that I would not make a bet even with myself.

I sat on the train side of the old wooden shack, leaning back against the wall of it, and partly concealed in a shadow cast by the arc light that hung above the road crossing to my left. On a parallel sidetrack beyond the main line stood a row of box cars. An opening had been made in them where the wagon road went through, and beyond that the row of cars began again. At this place the side track was flanked with a clay bank four feet high, and above that a board fence, so that to any one on the highway beyond the crossing the cars were invisible. As I sat there on my box and fidgeting, I was suddenly aware of two men that issued from the shadow of the cars in front of me and moved like cats to the centre of the road crossing, where they stopped and carefully inspected the station building.

In the light of the arc lamp I had good chance to note them and the observation was not exhilarating. I had been too long a reporter at the Tombs police court not to recognize that order of face. One of the men carried in his right hand a hammer and some other things whose use in certain lines of trade unpopular with the law I could hardly mistake. That hand was on his shady side, but he swung around once to stare down the road and the light coming full upon his freightage added nothing to my happiness.

It was evident that in their viewing of the station they had overlooked me sitting in the shadow there and I was in no haste to call their attention to their error. I had somewhat more than $200 in my pocket, the net proceeds of my last three lectures, and I purposed to keep it if I could.

They now moved forward along the shaded side of the next car beyond the crossing, under which in the glare of the arc light I could see their legs. They stopped at about the middle of the second car and next I heard the sound of muffled blows with a hammer, followed by the sliding back of the car door. I could even make out their feet as they clambered into the car.

I saw my duty then and conscientiously I abstained from doing it. Every obligation of citizenship, law, order, and uprightness demanded that I should cast myself upon the malefactors and rescue the railroad company's property, or hang desperately to a robber's leg until a policeman should come, or with a stick disguised as a revolver confront the thieves at their work. I did none of these things. The precious thought occurred to me that if the business fancy of any strong-armed, beetle-browed gentleman ran to breaking into freight cars at a lonely crossing at midnight, who was I indeed to quarrel with such a taste? Furthermore, I had reason to doubt whether they belonged to my social set and felt opposed on principle to these promiscuous acquaintances. What I did therefore was to crowd myself still farther back into the shadow and give thanks that my skin was whole.

Presently one of them reappeared with his armful of goods, which he deposited under a car and returned, I judged for more. And just then the storm broke and the automobile arrived. I helped the driver hurl the infernal trunk into the rear seat, sat down in front beside him, and when we were well under way told him of what I had seen at the crossing. It seemed that he likewise had no irresistible urge toward personal contact with gentlemen in the car-breaking line. He said there was a night policeman on duty in the town and we had better hunt him up and tell him. So we hunted him up and he said he would go out there and look into it, but I have never been shaken in my conviction that the only thing he looked into that night was a beer mug, this being in grand old departed days to memory dear. Anyway, about that time my train was due.

As may be seen from the time table, printed at the head of

this epic of unrest, from Shawmut to Willesdene via Jena Junction is some ride. The only empty seat on the train was in the smoking car, which was reputed to be the first railroad vehicle ever operated west of the Mississippi River and exhibited nothing that belied its reputation. The going was bad and sleep being impossible in the Procrustean facilities provided by an economical management, I fell back upon the usual mental refuge of the harassed Chautauquan, which is to ponder the insoluble problem of the American social organization as daily thrust upon his pained attention, thus:

Why, in the Middle Western region of our proud native land, did the onward sweep of civilization stop short of the small-town hotel? Why was the small-town hotel always dark, damp, and moldy? Why did the proprietor always smoke a cob pipe, sit in his shirt sleeves behind his counter, and regard every guest as his mortal foe? Why did he invariably have the beefsteaks on his bill of fare cut right off between the horns of aged steers? What was his conscientious objection to soap, brooms, and dusters? Also, to disinfectants? Why did he view a question about train departures as a personal affront? Why was he so unthrifty as to fail to plant something in the rich soil accumulations of his office—garden truck or potatoes or corn? Why did he always choose for his clerk a youth that had been blighted in his affections and thereafter consecrating his life to a swooping revenge upon the whole human race? Where did he hire for his waitresses those scornful and bitter young ladies that brought me my coffee with the evident hope that it contained arsenic? Where did he find those lineal descendants of the Borgias that operated in his kitchen? Why did his convictions run counter to supplying sheets long enough to cover the human form and to having these clean and whole? What calamity did he think would follow if he were to remove the accretions of twenty years from the margins of the bowls in the wash room? Or if now and then he were to provide a clean towel?

The whole subject bristled with problems as perplexing and vital as these, and yet neither Congress nor the scientists had ever investigated it. Why did the waitress at such a hotel always resent the appearance of a strange traveler? You would think that now and then one might arrive that she had no impulse to slay. Why did she stand behind his chair and with every indication of contempt and loathing reel off icily "There's-roas'-beef-roas'-pork-an'-boiled-dinner" the while she inundated Harry, the star boarder, with her most gracious smiles? In at least nine cases in ten I am sure the unfortunate stranger meditated no campaign against her youthful affections and wished in no way to disturb love's young dream by rivalry with Harry, but only to get something to eat. "There's-roas'-beef-roas'-pork-an'-boiled-dinner" and might as well have added "and-I-hope-yuh-choke. Didn't see yuh at the dance last night, Harry. It was swell. Roas'-beef-roas'-pork-an'-boiled-dinner-whadda yuh say? Tea or coffee?"

Why does this fair nymph snort with disdain when I ask for another slab of the chilled dough they call bread and with her own lily hands and without asking, bear to Harry another piece of the solder-crust pie? Why does the whole establishment view the traveler as a hateful intruder in their otherwise happy home and glare upon him as if seeking only a good chance to throw him down the well? Why is the poor inoffensive Chautauquan a particularly obnoxious intruder in these charmed environs? Or does he only seem so? I thought for a time that some Attraction must once have cruelly and wickedly wronged a hotel proprietor and the whole guild was aroused to an implacable revenge, but after mature reflection I was obliged to give that up. There was a conclusive objection that I had not at first thought of. A man feeble-minded enough to go on the Chautauqua would not have wit enough to be wicked.

I do not know how to explain the fact, but even the disinterested seemed openly or covertly to have a grudge against every Attraction—male Attraction, anyway. One poor unfortunate lecturer found no key to his room in a rural Illinois hostelry. He was new to the business or he would have known, first, that these rooms never have keys, and, second, that no matter what may go wrong in such resorts never on your life complain about it or mention it or betray the least consciousness of it or of anything else. Silent submission for you, and a-plenty of it. He had about $300 in his possession, not all of it his because he had yet to remit the handsome percentage the Bureau gouged from him, and he thought he would rather have his door locked. The night clerk was reigning over the establishment, having succeeded to the insignia of office, which consisted of the cob-pipe, shirt sleeves, and seat behind the counter. Conversation with this potentate:

Guest. May I please have the key to 19?

His Majesty (expectorating). Ain't none.

Guest. I beg pardon.

His Majesty (annoyed). Ain't none, I told yuh.

Guest. Well, I have a considerable sum of money. May I leave it in your safe?

His Majesty (glaring). Safe? Whadda think this is? A bank that's open night and day? Old Man's got the keys and gone to bed.

Guest. Then I think I ought to have something to fasten the door.

His Majesty (annoyed now to the point of sarcasm). There ain't no key but if yuh're afraid to stay in yuhr room alone here's the dog yuh kin take up there to pertect yuh.

A sextette of players from the Boston Symphony put in one summer on the Chautauqua. From conversations we had when our paths of misery chanced to throw us together I judged they deemed one such summer to be enough. The first

violinist was an accomplished soloist, a slender, rather undersized young man of polished manners and conscientious
devotion to his art. As I am about to relate a painful circumstance I think I will withhold his name, which was well known
in Boston and in musical circles elsewhere. At a town in the
Southwestern country the sextette was programmed to perform at the afternoon session of the local Chautauqua. The
violinist in his hotel room devoted the morning, after his custom, to practise. While thus engaged the door of his room
was suddenly kicked open and before his petrified gaze strode
in a tall and brawny native.

"You stop that damn' noise," said Husky, standing over
him and glowering.

Violin, when he got his breath, explained deferentially that
he was engaged to play at the Chautauqua that afternoon,
that he could not play without practising, that he must keep
up his practise for the sake of the public.

"Cut that all out," says Husky. "Are you going to stop?"

"I am sorry if it annoys you, but you see I must practise."

Whereupon the native ended the debate by knocking the
violinist down.

The local management, to whom Violin complained, advised him to have his assailant arrested. The case was tried
before a local justice of the peace, who dismissed the complaint. The native now swore out a warrant against the violinist and Dogberry on the spot fined him $25 and costs. What
for? Oh, for disturbing the peace by playing the violin. Besides he was a foreigner.

The burden of my own song as I leaped furiously along
the dizzy Chautauqua way was about the Unconsumed Surplus. I might better have taken James L. Ford's advice and
recited an essay of Emerson's backward. No doubt the fault
was all in the telling, but after three summers spent in these
laborious pursuits I think the theory of the Surplus remained

unexplained. Part of the time I was engaged in joint debates with that delightful man, charming traveling companion and powerful orator, Doctor John Wesley Hill. He always had the last word, and after I had spent my hour laboriously explaining the origin and results of the Surplus as I understood it, Doctor Hill would overturn the whole structure by inviting me to produce my Unconsumed Surplus that it might be consumed on the spot. This invariably brought down the house and erased my feeble efforts. As long as I can I will cling to the soothing thought that I might have had more heeding if I had not urged the Socialist commonwealth as the only possible remedy for these perilous operations, Socialism being at that time rather less esteemed than smallpox or hog cholera.

Some of my fellow Chautauquan sufferers made a new geography. They divided the country into the Bed Bug Belt, the Cyclone Belt, the Broiling Belt, and the Hellish Hotel Belt. Which of these an Attraction deemed the worst depended upon which he happened to be in at the time. In point of interest, however, the Bed Bug Belt and the Cyclone Belt had the others at a disadvantage. As to the first, I have sat up all night in some truly battered caravanserai not daring (for sufficient reasons) to go to bed. For a time the antics on the walls cut by these sociable little creatures were diverting, but it is an amusement that can be overdone.

Interest in the Cyclone Belt is still more vivid because most of the Chautauquas were held in tents and the results when a cyclone hit a tent were so various that there was always ample room for that speculative uncertainty best adapted to the real allure. The tent might be swept up into the air, taking you with it, or it might merely fall over upon you. Cyclones prevent stagnation and monotony, but there always seemed to be a surplus of them where I was. An average cyclone, even when viewed from a distance and a car window, will keep off that drowsy feeling, but a seat in an automobile while traveling along a country road affords a more commanding view of the event, particularly if the automobile be of the open-faced variety. I can furnish testimonials on this, having tried them all. As many Chautauqua jumps had to be made in automobiles, the Attraction was often able to avail itself of the best location for sight-seeing.

An itinerant but excellent concert troupe with which I was often a fellow-traveler, had occasion to go thus from Momus to Mortuary, two towns on the circuit that I am sure will be readily recognized by all really experienced Attractions. No railroad train was available and the only automobile to be found in Momus was without a cover. But the sky was clear, the portents declared by experts to be good, and the company piled merrily into the machine. Although Attractions tutored by many campaigns, the members were naive enough to have confidence in weather forecasts in the Cyclone Belt. No one should do this. The weather there has a depraved way of putting on a face of cheer and an inviting smile in the early hours and then turning loose a cloud-burst or an electrical storm when you are at its mercy. The concert company did not know this when it started but was better informed before the day was over. It had made about half of its journey when there burst upon it what was by all accounts one of the dizziest cataclysms the Belt had ever seen.

There were umbrellas under the seats but the gale quickly wrecked them when they had been seized and opened, and the whole carload of the choicest Attractions sat there deluged with the rain that came down like Noah's flood. All about cracked the lightning, every minute they thought to be struck, and the incessant bellowing of the thunder and roaring of the wind made up a combination of perditions not often equalled. They could see no dwelling anywhere, but after a time made out a school house on the top of the next hill, and pointed for it. The season was midsummer; the place would be closed, but they thought they might force a window and crawl in. They found the door locked and every window spiked down. And then an odd thing happened. One of the men in the party spied a bent nail lying in the pathway and with it managed to pick the lock of the front door. I make no comment on his probable vocation before he became an Attraction because he was a friend of mine and the sparks of gratitude still glow within me, but you can judge for yourselves. The bedraggled company had scarcely tripped over the doorsill when a bolt of lightning struck the tree under which the automobile stood.

It was then after 12 o'clock, the troupe was scheduled to prelude the afternoon session at Mortuary, 2 o'clock was the starting time, and they were thirteen miles from the town, as wet as drowned cats, and outside a storm was raging fit to make one think of the end of the world. It merely shows how Attractions developed in these emergencies their resources of ingenuity and self-command. When the hubbub relaxed, one man got to the automobile and fetched the hand baggage and a carriage robe. They hung this across one end of the bare school room and behind it the women changed their clothes and made up for the concert. The men likewise got on dry attire, or partly dry, from their valises, and behold at 2:10 that afternoon the Dulcetta Concert Troupe, an Attraction justly famed from Mouse River to Waco, walked smiling out upon the platform at Mortuary and sang "Oh, listen, love, to me" as if nothing had happened.

One Sunday at New Washington, Ohio, I judged that my time had come. All morning the storm had been steering up for that handsome and thriving little town, advancing upon it from four directions at once, which is unfair. The Chautauqua was held in a tent about a mile away. The people were nervous and uneasy, as might be expected, and the worthy

Platform Manager went outside and had a look and came back to report that the danger was over, the storm had passed. I don't know where he got his information, but the event proved that it was poor stuff. I went on about 3 o'clock and had been going ten minutes in a determined but probably futile effort to interest New Washington in the Unconsumed Surplus when the storm fiend must have concluded that he had heard enough for that day, for he turned on the uproar all at once from the four directions. When I came to myself I was lying on the ground with about three tons of wet circus tent over me. The thing had gone down before the blast. The next moment the real cyclone took hold and blew the canvas away and then came the deluge. I managed to crawl under the platform, which still stood. An upright piano had adorned it and the wind blew the piano over while I was crouched beneath. The roaring was so great that I did not hear the sound the toppling piano made but felt the jar. A woman refugee crawled in beside me. She had an umbrella and raised it against the water that was spouting through the cracks above us. I remember she asked me in the coolest possible way if I thought the platform over our heads would withstand the wind and when I answered her my voice sounded to me like the voice of a man in a dream. After a time a river came flowing under the platform and drove us out, but now the wind had gone down and there was nothing but huge dashes of rain in which we made our way back to town, drenched. It is a remarkable fact that only one person was killed when that tent went over, though more than six hundred were caught in it.

Once I was scheduled for the chief afternoon turn in a town in Southwestern Missouri, being preluded by an excellent traveling orchestra that I had often met in my perambulations. Its youthful leader, C. C. Cappel, was afterward a noted figure in the music world. By this time I had learned a little of the significance of the skies and the atmosphere and that afternoon I foresaw trouble. Black clouds were whirling up towards the centre in a way I did not really care for, and the behavior of the natives struck chill into my bones, for they were out on the streets gazing upward and shaking their heads. The town had been through three cyclones and might be supposed to know something about this form of entertainment. I noted without delight that in the front yard of practically every residence in that place was a cyclone cellar.

Soon after we went to the tent the sky grew so black they had to turn on the electric lights and all the time I could hear the mischief brewing outside. The tent stood near the railroad line. As soon as the show was over I took one look at the prospect overhead and sped along the track to the railroad station, which was less than half as far as the way through the village, and arrived in time to catch my train for St. Joe. Ten minutes later old Aquarius upset the rain wagon with a tornado and fireworks, part of which I was able to view from the train. The orchestra was less lucky. It had a town to make in the other direction and traveled by automobile. After a few miles the road had become impassable. They ran into a farmer's barn for shelter and when the storm let up, made out to follow the road again. At night the storm came back, which is a habit storms have in that part of the world, and was worse than before. A flash of lightning revealed a bridge just as it was sinking in front of them. But for that illumination they would have plunged into a raging river. The chauffeur knew no other road. They sat there all night, most of the time debating whether their machine was likeliest to be blown away, washed away, or smashed by falling tree trunks. But with the morning they found a road and got to the next town in time to dry themselves out and fill their engagement. The fidelity of the Attraction to his engagement always struck me as truly remarkable and reflecting honor upon the profession.

Any of these people would wade in mud to their waists, brave floods or wreckage, and risk pneumonia any time rather than disappoint an audience.

I learned many things besides the peculiarities of the rural hotel in America and the way to foretell a cyclone. I learned how to make a success on the Chautauqua; learned it from one of the greatest of all successes, who had been nineteen years on the circuit and knew every blade of grass in every town street in Kansas. He gave me the prescription, and invited me to come and watch the audience take the dose at his hands, and I went, and it worked perfectly. I do not see how anything could be better. He explained that the first thing to remember was that no audience really wanted to hear anybody, but only went because it had to go. Now, he said, the man that could make all those people forget the miseries of the hard benches and the heat could have their support and money every time. My friend had managed to figure this out for himself and from his rich experience he had made rules for success, like this:

"Limit your talk exactly to one hour and fifteen minutes. If you go beyond that they will be dog tired and mad at you and if you cut it shorter they will think you have cheated them.

"Talk for ten minutes about the old red school house and the happy days you spent there. This will set them to recalling their own youth and please them. Nothing goes like reminiscences of our youth. At the end of that passage, tell a story. I will explain later about the stories.

"Now branch out about early education, the value of training, the wisdom of church attendance and just as the twig is bent the tree is inclined. About ten minutes of this and then another story.

"Now weave in something about the dear old parson of the little old church on the hill and how his admonitions to piety have helped you all your life, and follow it with another story.

"Next get into the principles of success. This is what snatches them every time. Honesty, fidelity to duty, industry, especially industry, (go heavy on industry—every farmer has his hired man) have been the touchstones of your own success. Tell about early struggles and privations and ring in a lot about the poor farm boys that have become millionaires. Then another story.

"Come now to the climax of your effort, which we'll say, is the value of home training and the influence it exerts throughout one's life. Show that it is the American home that has made America great. You have only then to explain how great it is and you have got them by the hair every time and they will want you to come back next year and do it again.

"But about the stories, let me give you one hint that you will find to be invaluable. Stories must be old. Never by any chance tell a new story. The temptation will often be strong, but strive against it, my son; strive hard. Remember what the Good Book says about resisting the devil and he will flee from you. Try some of that when the hour of temptation comes. Provide yourself with a stock of sound, matured, ripe old chestnuts that have stood the test of ages and can therefore be depended upon. There is nothing an audience resents so much as a brand-new story. You see when a man hears you working along up to a bearded old anecdote that he knows well, his vanity is gratified. He knows as much as the speaker and he thinks that he has one on Jake Potts, his neighbor over there, because there is hardly a chance that Jake ever heard this thing that is coming. So he listens and when you are through he pats himself on the back and says, by jinx, it is a good story, isn't it? only you didn't tell it as well as he can tell it, and so he goes home perfectly happy. But if you ring in a new story on him he feels that he isn't as smart as he ought to be because he never heard that one before, and goes home sore and like as not will refuse to subscribe next year, being convinced that the Chautauqua is deteriorating."

But above everything else, said my friend, deal in optimism and lay it on thick. One of the most popular men on the circuit was the Honorable James E. Watson of Indiana, known everywhere as "Sunny Jim," and he brimmed over with smiles and the assurance that everything was fine and going just right. The people loved to have him come around. They might not remember anything he said but he soothed them and made them feel happy and they insisted upon having him on the program every year. My friend said that for himself he always preferred the home-and-mother line because it brought the best results, but if I couldn't manage that the next best thing was to be optimistic and reassuring. The banks liked that and the banks ran most of the Chautauquas.

He must have been right about this, for he showed me his engagement book and he had been to some towns as many as seventeen times and they still wanted him to come back.

But the incomparable Chautauqua pet and favorite (with the public) was William J. Bryan. The audiences that he drew made all others seem comic. When he was to address a Chautauqua the railroads ran excursion trains and in all the near-by towns if it was a week day business was virtually suspended.

At Ashland, Oregon, for instance, the Chautauqua grounds made a natural amphitheatre of singular beauty and great size. The spectacle of the crowd that sat there on the grass, tier after tier, rising far up the hillside, waiting to hear Mr. Bryan for the nineteenth time has not often been equalled in our day. Being at pains to inquire, I learned that many admirers had traveled more than a hundred miles for that peculiar pleasure. I remember well a Sunday when he spoke at Shelbyville, Illinois, and I estimated at 30,000 the crowd that filled the vast Chautauqua auditorium there and stretched far and far beyond it. Most of the persons that heard him that day had heard him before in the same identical address, and hoped and expected to hear it again the next year and the next. Yet they hung rapt upon every word as if it were a jewel of inestimable price. I have talked with experts about this mystery, including some alienists, and none has ever offered an adequate solution. If anybody else had spoken the same platitudinous melange the same people would have fallen asleep.

I said he was a great favorite—with the public. Not with the Talent. The Talent regarded him with loathing. Not because he drew these great crowds, but for another reason. The rest of us were routed six months or more in advance of the season and must take what the lordly managers were pleased to give us, being tonight in Ohio, tomorrow in Iowa, and the next day in Indiana, hopping to and fro across six or seven states like some form of maddened human flea. Mr. Bryan would make no engagements until a short time before he was ready to start. Then he took a map and selected the towns at which he was willing to speak and upon what dates and everybody else had to get off the track. All engagements that interfered with his selections must be cancelled. After an Attraction had been ditched in this way three or four times in a season, sitting in a horrible hotel and biting his thumbs while he heard of Mr. Bryan's wondrous success, he accumulated enough ill will to choke any orator but one with a thick hide as well as a silver tongue.

A native was extolling to me the marvels of the Peerless One's address of the day before.

"What did he say?" said I, full of bitterness and verjuice, having just been muscled out of three good engagments.

"Well, I don't just remember what he was talking about," says Lusty Juventus, "but it was a grand speech."

I did not have 30,000 people in my audience when my turn came, but in one respect I had the edge on Peerless.

The people remembered what I said, or some of it—long enough to write to the management complaining about it.

Poor harassed management! I think it resisted as long as it could but the banks were too potent and generally of the opinion that my contributions to forensic lore were subversive of the best interests of our nation and calculated to foster class antagonism. Plainly it was intimated that my place, if any, was with the degraded hordes of Europe, whereto I was kin, and thus, scarce with glory, I made my exit from the Chautauqua.

"The banks run most of the Chautauquas," my old and learned friend had said. He spoke true; the Chautauqua was at bottom a branch of the banking business—rural. It was the local bank that financed the local Chautauqua, supervised it, dominated it, and put the kibosh upon all Attractions of a disturbing nature. The modus and reason were alike simple. Chautauqua meant that many farmers would come to town and spend money with the town's tradesmen. It took the place of the old county fair and was more orderly. Sometimes the farmers came and stayed out the week, sometimes they went to and fro between the town and their homes. In either case they left money.

Culture and profits. In no other country in the world could you find them thus going sweetly hand in hand. At the height of the fashion there were 22,000 Chautauquas in the United States and Canada. Bishop Vincent when he began all this at his famed resort on Chautauqua Lake, New York, could hardly have thought how tremendous an engine he was loosing. Attempts were made to make it take root in alien soil, in New Zealand and Australia. They failed. It was only America that would respond to the mixture.

It is not to be denied that often the Chautauqua was a great educational factor. Some of the shows had programs that involved and compelled study and research of a high order. In many instances there was excellent music. Often, again, the lectures were informative or of substantial value. I remember, for instance, a scientist named Williams that traversed the country with an illustrated lecture on electricity and packed into an hour and a quarter more valuable facts than I have ever heard in a similar period. For sixteen years Robert Seeds of Pennsylvania gave to the farmers priceless scientific knowledge about soils and tilth. The better Chautauquas maintained classes of instruction along many lines. Amusing the movement might have been to a foreigner, but under its least attractive aspects was often a rather fine impulse to be of use and to further knowledge. As a rule the spirit was wholesome and the aim high. Sometimes the banks with their money-grubbing mixed a genuine purpose to serve, sometimes they showed that they cared for nothing but to attract crowds. In either event the social contacts were salutary and the break in the monotony of farm life must have been a boon. The Butchery of an Attraction to Make a Chautauqua Holiday was probably unavoidable though there is no denying that it was done to the muffled shrieks of the sufferer.

Chapter XIX

STONE WALLS IN THE HEARTBREAK COUNTRY

O NE day in the fall of 1919, a truck-load of scale-weights
was driven through the streets of the city of Fargo, North
Dakota.

Scale-weights—they are no great matter. Yet the sight of
that truck-load filled many citizens that looked upon it with
an exuberance of satisfaction, for it was the sign of their great
emancipation from a serfdom that for many years had held
them as if with gyves and handcuffs.

Serfdom—that is a strange thing anywhere in the modern
world; in the Land of Opportunity, strangest of all. Let us
have a look at it.

It was 1915; summertime. I was flitting across the state by
automobile from one Chautauquan lodge of sorrow to another.
The first leap was but forty miles or so, up in the Mouse River
region. Only forty miles, but it supplied me with an initiation about serfdom I was not likely to forget. The start of it
was this, that as we bumped along over the gumbo road across
the level plain, there fell upon my attention two or three farms
that were obviously not under cultivation, for the houses and
barns were falling into disrepair, the fields were given over to
weeds, the doors and windows gaped. All abnormal, most
abnormal, for the soil was black and rich, the region perfectly
adapted to the prosperous raising of the materials for man's
daily bread.

The driver of the machine was a typical young Western native, keen, affable, intelligent, and I gave over to him the puzzle of the idle farms. He said:

"The bank hasn't found a tenant yet."

"The bank—how the bank?"

"Foreclosure—man couldn't pay his interest."

I said I supposed that seldom happened. He said:

"The banks or some loaning agency own one farm in five around here. If they keep on, they'll own them all."

Before long arose upon the level edge of the plain a strange hovel-like structure, with walls crumbling and irregular; in some places black, in some streaky yellow, mixed with scattered tufts of growing grass. It was so low a tall man could hardly stand upright in it. The roof was of boards. In the walls, a door and a window had been set. From one side stuck forth in lieu of chimney a joint of stove-pipe with an elbow. The thing had been built of sods cut from the prairie and piled one upon another like bricks. Rains had channelled and suns parched it until it looked like something with eczema. Considerate men would not wish to house beasts in such quarters, but here it was the dwelling of human beings. Truly, it was. What? The mud hut of India transferred to free, happy, prosperous, glorious America? What could be stranger? The size of it might give space for two tiny rooms, maybe three, if the inmates could live mole-like and burrow. As we passed, a man came to the door and looked out. In his arms lay a baby—what a hole for a human being to be born into! Behind him was a glimpse of a dark and dismal cavern and of a work-weary woman looking out over the man's shoulder. The whole prospect seemed cursed and blighted with the extreme of poverty; hardly on the East Side of New York had I seen anything so depressing; and I wondered if the ragged man I saw in that doorway, traditional free yeoman, dweller near to nature and so on, might not envy the average inmate of a New York tenement.

They called this country North Dakota. It should have been called the Land of Broken Lives.

Broken by a system. The case of the ragged man with the baby on his arm, as told by the driver, proved to be typical. He was the son of a farmer in Illinois, he had been lured to North Dakota by reports of the wondrous fertility of the soil, the healthfulness of the climate, the size of the crops, the cheapness of the land. To obtain the purchase price he had given a mortgage. All his money being gone, he and his wife had built the hovel of sods, hopefully expecting that the first crop would bring them enough to build a decent habitation. The sods nature had provided, ready at hand for the cutting; the window and door frames he must get on credit. With backbreaking toil he had opened the prairie turf and sown his seed and reaped his harvest. When he had sold it he found he had barely enough to meet the interest on his mortgage and keep his family and his horses alive through the winter.

The reason was that with the rest of the farmers of North Dakota he had been the victim of a vast complicated racketeering that at every turn snatched away the reward that should have been his for his labor.

To begin with, a series of ingenious devices had loaded upon him an interest burden far beyond the limit supposed to be provided by the paternal laws against usury. He must pay commissions, he must pay bonuses and he must give a pre-dated mortgage. Instead of paying 8 per cent for his money he was paying nearer to 18.

In the next place, he was raising wheat upon some of the best wheat soil known to man, raising an excellent quality of wheat, but he must sell it to or through a near-by elevator and all the elevators in his part of the world were owned in chains by companies in Minneapolis that worked together to exploit the producer and make money for themselves. The price at which he must sell depended upon what was called the grade of the wheat, supposed to be based upon quality. But these grades were determined arbitrarily, determined in the sole interest of the buyer of the wheat, and over the determination the farmer had no control nor influence.

Suppose, first, that he decided to sell the wheat outright to the elevator. In that case the buyer took a sample from the wagon, looked at it, and pronounced its grade as he pleased, and the farmer must accept that rating or take his wheat back to the farm.

The high grades of wheat commanded prices much higher than low grades. If what was rated as No. 2 was selling at 78 cents a bushel the lowest grade might be priced at something like 60 cents a bushel. If therefore the elevator man should grade as Rejected (the lowest of the grades), a load of wheat that was actually No. 2 he would make 18 cents a bushel. Since the fixing of the grade was, in such instances, wholly in the discretion of the elevator man, one that could resist the temptation to undergrade would be of angelic virtue, in which case he wouldn't be in the wheat-buying game nor anywhere near it.

The mere existence of such a jug-handled process was an incentive to fraud and a manifest injustice to the wheat grower, but it went on year after year unchanged.

In addition to undergrading, the farmer was preyed upon in other ways. The wheat he sold was subject to an arbitrary deduction called "dockage" for the impurities it was said to contain—wild oats, cockle, other seeds. Like the grading the percentage of this deduction was wholly in the discretion of the elevator man; the farmer had nothing to say about it. His wheat might be perfectly clean, be docked at 8 per cent for impurities it did not contain, and he must submit. What else should he do, being a serf? If extraneous material was mixed in his wheat this often had a considerable value. It was annexed by the elevator man; the farmer got nothing of it.

But the trimming of him was not yet at an end. He brought

his wheat in a wagon. The amount of the contents was determined by weighing—so many pounds to the bushel. The full load was weighed first, then the wheat was taken out, the empty wagon weighed and the net amount supposed to be ascertained. The elevator man or his employees did the weighing, the farmer had nothing to do except to sit still, take the card that purported to show the results, and trundle dutifully homeward. Some of the scales were of the order of the false balances said to be abominated by the Lord. They were not abominated by some men that exploited the farmers, certainly, but beloved and esteemed. Yes, and used to such an extent that in the year 1914, which was the year before I was drawn into this fight, it was estimated that 500,000 bushels of North Dakota wheat mysteriously disappeared on its way to the flour mills.

But if the farmer distrusted his elevator man he could always ship his wheat to Minneapolis to be sold there on commission. True. And what happened to it there?

The car arrived, the official grader came along with a kind of pump that sucked up a handful of wheat from the load. The grader looked at it, called it No. 2 or No. 4 as the case might be and went to the next car. What did he mean by No. 2 or No. 4? Nobody rightly knew except that he had affixed the name to it. If he thought he found moisture in the wheat, he called it No Grade, whereupon it went to the Chamber of Commerce to be sold on sample. If called No Grade it might be sold for 60 cents a bushel, which when the brokerage commission, terminal charges, and other deductions had been taken out, would be remitted to the farmer. He had already paid the unreasonable freight charge to have it hauled to market.

The wheat would then go to what was called a "mixing house," which was merely a kind of elevator or storage place from which it would presently emerge, and be regraded, when it would be found to be No. 2 or No. 1 and to be worth not 60 but 80 or 85 cents a bushel, nothing having been done to it meanwhile except to dry it.

The railroad rates were excessive and unreasonable because the railroads had been loaded down with watered securities to make fortunes for the gentlemen that controlled them, these securities requiring extortionate rates that interest and dividends might be had upon an investment never made.

On every car of wheat there was levied a "switching charge," although often no switching was done and it was never worth the amount charged for it.

Honest business. It is and was then the grand talisman of our commercial, social, and educational organization. Forgers, check raisers, three-card-monte men, bunco artists were not honest business men and were ruled out of our social horizon. It would be difficult to show wherein their activities differed from those of the exploiters of the wheat growers. Except possibly second-story men and the yeggs. Farmer exploitation might be deemed to stop short of breaking and entering. Sometimes.

I would have you note that the gentlemen that profited by these forms of picking and stealing, were highly respectable members of the community, named among our leading business men, looked up to and admired. They lived in beautiful houses in the choicest residence regions. They went to church, too; regularly, with pious mien. They went to church and prayed on Sunday and the next day donned the black mask and went upon the road, pistol in hand and riding Black Bess. It was like the seventeenth century and Tom Faggus. Praying on Sunday and preying the rest of the week.

There were no sod houses in Minneapolis, please also note. The men that lived in sod houses in North Dakota built many an elegant mansion in Minneapolis. Built it out of their own sweat and the privations of their children. But anyway the

mansions arose and the city was beautiful and proud and happy.
Viva la bagatelle and on with the dance!

Shall you suppose then that the victims of these performances,
being free Americans or Scandinavians of sturdy stock, submitted docilely to such extortions? They did not. But what
could they do? The exploiting corporations were tied up
through interlocking directorates with the banks, the banks
with the railroad companies, the railroad companies with the
great financial syndicates of New York. The banks had the
strangle-hold upon the department stores, the department stores
upon the newspapers. The stone wall upon which beat the
North Dakota farmer surrounded him on all sides, adamant
against attack, carried so high he could not climb over. Many
a pair of hands had been macerated on that wall and left no
mark except streaks of blood.

Some of the facts about these operations I heard that day
from my driver as we worked our way over the gumbo. The
rest I gathered as I sped from Chautauqua torment to torment,
pursued by the terror of Spenlow & Jorkins. But with never a
surmise that the gained knowledge had any personal interest
for me.

About such things "the ball no question makes of Ayes and
Noes." I was speaking one night at Devil's Lake, a place that is
entitled to another name, for the lake is beautiful and the town
sightly and good. Before I went upon the platform a man
I did not know came to me, called me by name, and said:

"Wait for me after you get through, I want to see you."

He was about five feet, ten inches in height, sparely built,
angular, with good features, lean in the powerful jaws, the nose
of a thinker, a pleasant voice that somehow gave one confidence in the man's sincerity, a direct, brief, pointed style of
speech, and a coolly inquiring manner of looking at one
through keen gray eyes. All in all, the Yankee, if ever I saw
one; no other nation could have produced his type.

As requested, I waited after I had performed my stage stunt and he took me in his automobile back to the hotel while he began to unfold his business.

He said his name was Townley and he had formerly been an organizer for the Socialist party, whereby he had come to know me. He had left the Socialist movement because he believed he had something better and bigger and he wanted time to tell me about it. He knew I was to speak the next night at Valley City and proposed that instead of the train I should travel with him in his automobile so we could have plenty of time to talk.

Long automobile rides have no charms for this old traveler, but there was something about the man so engaging and I was so curious to know why he thought another movement was better than Socialism that I agreed, and the next day we plowed into the gumbo while he told his story.

It seemed that he had had his own individual bout with the grain octopus and had been worsted. He and his brother had taken a tract of land, sowed it to flax under the allure of a grand market promise, worked upon it literally day and night, raised their crop, and then lost their investment through market manipulation and a condition provided for them by agencies they could not touch nor know. The experience had enlightened without embittering him, which I deemed remarkable. He saw that the system of production was framed against the farmer from the time he sought his first loan until he received the last check for his crop, and that farming would never be anything but serfdom until the whole process of financing and marketing was remade. He knew that Socialism would do this but Socialism was too far off, the prejudice against it too great. He believed he had hit upon a short cut.

The farmers were in overwhelming majority in North Dakota as in other Western states. But the farmers never had anything like a fair share of government attention. On the contrary, the bald fact was that the government was conducted by and for the exploiters, who were a minority. This abnormal condition came through blind adherence to the fetich of party loyalty on one hand and the adroit manipulation of party machinery on the other. He said that when the people had revolted against the Republican machine and installed the Democratic nothing had been changed but the label, since the exploiters controlled one machine as easily as the other. What he purposed was a farmers' party that should have no connection with either political machine, should allow a Republican to remain a Republican, a Democrat to remain a Democrat and still the farmers to vote for themselves and their own interests. He had already visioned this party and had a name for it. He called it the Nonpartisan League.

In the frankest way he told the whole story, good and bad, and then asked me to join him in the attempt to put the League over.

I reminded him of the collapse of every effort to unite the farmers and make them a power in politics. The Grange, the Farmers' Alliance, the Populist party had arisen in promise and fallen in ridicule. There was no news for him about any of these episodes; he knew them as well as anybody else. But here he had something different. Here he proposed no defection from the grand old parties of the fathers and that sort of precious imbecility, but only a non-partisan movement to secure control of the state government for certain specific ends of farmer relief.

How far had he gone with his project? Strange as the fact seemed, already he had well laid the foundations for a statewide movement.

He had a gift of singularly terse and pointed expression, a mind like a steel trap for alertness, a perfect knowledge of his subject, a practical knowledge of the ways of men. He left no more room for doubt of his energy than of his capacity. It appeared that the work of organizing his League had been started by himself and single-handed under conditions that would have daunted the hardiest. He was without funds and without standing except the highly doubtful warranty of a Socialist organizer. He had started out on foot and walked from farm to farm, explaining his plan and asking support for it. At night he would be sheltered and fed by some kindly farmer and the next morning trudge upon his way. Many counties he had virtually covered in this lonely evangelizing. Sometimes he had a favorable hearing; sometimes the farmer, terrorized by the ruling powers, backed away as from high treason, but would give him a lift to the next isolated dwelling.

The turning point in his heart-breaking campaign came one evening when he fell into the home of a farmer with a big, open mind, a broad vision and much study of the agricultural problem in America—F. B. Wood, a name worth remembering. He saw at once the great possibilities of Townley's project, enlisted for it with his stalwart sons, and from that time it began to take root.

But back of all the evolutions on this picturesque stage, moves one most singular figure, never much known to fame, yet at one and the same time the fountain-head of all the revolt, its intellect, and its conscience.

He is gray-bearded, compactly built, short-bodied, spectacled; reticent of speech, abstracted in his bearing, having all the marks of the classroom and the student's cell. Naturally. He is president of the North Dakota Agricultural College at Fargo and all his life has been in the teaching and studying way. He is an Analytical Chemist. Not alone of materials. That is the remarkable thing. He is an Analytical Chemist about deeds, actions, laws, institutions, and their morals, about public policies, programs, characters, whatever may be pertinent to the Common Good, of which he is one of the strangest but most effective soldiers.

He, too, is a Yankee, coming from Maine, of an old American family, one of the oldest. He begins life as professor of chemistry in the Agricultural College of New York; then he is drafted to take the same chair at Fargo; finally he becomes the institution's head.

In that capacity he interests himself in the food sold in the state, analyzes much of it, lands upon articles that do not come up to the standard, brings about their exclusion. In a short time he has angry hornets darting at his head, while the name of North Dakota begins to go around the world as one region where one cannot for food sell rubbish or unwholesome concoctions. Tremendous efforts are made to oust him from his position. The state is governed by a political ring, but the ring does not dare to touch Doctor Edwin F. Ladd, president of the Agricultural College; the people would rise in wrath and with arms in hand to defend him. He rules out of the state the products of a baking-powder company with a powerful corporation and much influence back of it. The company puts forth all its strength and is foiled by the simple faith of the people. Then it sues Doctor Ladd for $200,000 libel. Above everything else he is imperturbable. He is not enough concerned about this suit to tell his family of it. The trial comes on, he goes cheerfully upon the stand, exhibits his proofs, in a few minutes has the verdict.

He is the strength of the fight for pure-food laws in this country. Great Britain hears of him, invites him to come there, he spends three months in London at government expense and helps to frame the British pure-food law. At the time of the Peace Conference of 1919 he is again wanted abroad, and the talented gentleman then Attorney General of the United States will not allow him to have a passport on the ground that he is a radical, a red, a dangerous person. Wise Attorney General.

When he is in the United States Senate he is heavily attacked by men of great eminence, by Charles E. Mitchell, president of the National City Bank in New York, and by one of the most eminent authorities of Columbia University. To every public attack he replies publicly, but always in this strange manner of a perfect detachment as if it were nothing on earth he was personally interested in, but something to do with H_2O_4, or exactly as if he were talking about permanganate of potash—the only man I have ever known that could do this at all times and under all conditions and do it perfectly.

But this is to run far ahead. At the crucial time of 1915, Doctor Ladd is the strongest man in North Dakota. He is not in politics, not in business, has no money, has no social backing, is no kind of a mixer, has no skill to please, sticks, head down, to his job at the college, and yet is the strongest man in the state. Well, why? For a reason so strange it should be emphasized and celebrated. He is strong because he does not care a rap for anything except to have it right and straight. About everything he is the Analytical Chemist: he has his formula reached after repeated tests. He never says anything he has not submitted to test tube and blow pipe. People look upon his lightest word as gospel. He is no orator, no leader in the usual sense, speaks not often, nor at length, but then deliberately and finally, and the state has formed a habit of looking to him for the truth.

He keeps on saying in his quiet sure way that the existing method of grain grading is unsound, untrue, illogical, and predatory. The only basis for the price of wheat should be its value in milling, what it will yield in consumable products. In the college he sets up a miniature flour mill and bakery, grinds wheat, bakes bread, shows by infallible analysis what each handful of wheat will yield in actual commodity, shows at the same time how monstrously the farmers are plundered by the grading methods imposed upon them. For he takes the lowest grade of wheat and proves that its actual residuum in value is better than that of many grades placed above it.

His quiet, unwavering insistence upon these facts stirs the farmers. Townley comes along and on the foundations thus created builds his Nonpartisan League.

What would the Nonpartisan League do for the plundered farmer, if it should by chance win to control?

It would abolish the grading fraud.

It would cast out the false weights.

It would build elevators to be owned and operated by the state—and therefore operated for use and not plunder.

It would provide at cost insurance against hail and fire.

It would establish state-owned flour mills so that the wheat raised in Dakota should be ground there—for truly the hauling of wheat to a far-off grinding place is as much an economic waste as a financial brigandage.

It would regulate freight charges within the state and relieve part of the burden imposed by the water-stock railroads.

It would release the farmer from the grip of the loan shark.

All these things seem possible, if the movement can oust what is called The Old Gang that with the aid of the railroads, the banks, the commission houses, and a kept press has long ruled the state. As about nine-tenths of the voters are farmers, nothing is needed but a sense of union and some weaning from the wet nursery of party devotion.

We left Devil's Lake about ten that morning and reached Valley City about five, having stopped on the way to visit two or three farms that I might see for myself the actualities of life on the prairies that Townley expounded to me as above set forth. Before we were done, I surrendered, undertook to join the movement and to serve it so far as I could without interfering with my obligations to the Socialist party.

As soon as I was done with the horrors of Chautauqua for that season I trailed back to North Dakota where the first job assigned me was to start for the League a newspaper.

In one of the residence streets of Fargo was a church building that had been abandoned. We took it over for our printing office. The entrance had been dismantled and carried away and for some reason unexplained an excavation like a great trough had been made around the building. We gained entry by lifting two planks to form a bridge to the sill of the side door. Next we commandeered a stove and set it up. We leased two type-setting machines, and bought (on time) some head type. We found an expert foreman and make-up man and two good printers. And thus in September, 1915, we launched *The Non-partisan Leader,* official organ of the Nonpartisan League.

Meantime the League was spreading in a way to give its projector joy. Membership carried an initiation fee of $6, of which $2 was for a year's subscription to *The Leader,* $2 for a year's subscription to *Pearson's Magazine,* the last remaining exponent of magazine radicalism left alive in the country, and $2 for the expenses of the League. For these, post-dated checks were accepted, and the first thing I saw when I entered the League office was a long white windrow of bundles of these checks, to which hundreds were added daily.

At first the railroad, elevator, and commission-house Interests looked upon the movement with amused contempt. So often dreamers had imagined a vain thing about the possibility of united action from the farmers. But when the formidable nature of this revolt became too evident, there was first let loose a stream of ridicule, then of denunciation, and then a furious clangor upon the alarm bell. Newspapers over-ran with jibes about the "Six Dollar Suckers" that were being victimized by clever impostors. Then with solemn warnings against a hoax and swindle. Then with expositions of the bad character of the men engaged in the huge fraud. Then with frantic appeals not to be led away into costly and impossible schemes of state elevators and the like. All experience had proved that every-thing done by any government was badly and extravagantly done and ended in failure—everything, always.

Most of the newspapers in the state were at that time owned or controlled in the interest of the existing order. The League fought almost alone. I think it is interesting to record that straight in the face of the enormous power the press ordinarily wields, despite every form of argument, appeal, warning, and denunciation, the League grew. Farmers read in their journals that it was a disguised Socialism, Anarchism, concocted by depraved men for the worst purposes, a swindle, a fraud, a crime, and went to the post office to send in their membership checks.

Other powerful influences than those of the press were enlisted on the side of the existing system. Minneapolis corporations or firms owned these long chains of elevators that crossed and criss-crossed the state. Every elevator was a dynamo of political power, if the manager cared to use it. The elevator man bought the farmer's wheat; he had only to intimate to the farmer with due significance that activity in the League was exceedingly bad for business and tended to lower wheat grades, and the effect was likely to be magical. Similarly, the banks were then, as later, a tremendous power. Most farmers must have loans to carry them through the season when the crop is growing, or must have advances to get seed. The banks were as a rule lined up strictly with the existing modus. Suppose a banker to intimate to the applicant for credit that the League was a dangerous thing and so threatening to business stability that he could make no loans to any one that countenanced it. With perfect propriety he could do so; the granting or withholding of loans was entirely within his volition. But thereby a League farmer might be confronted with a hopeless situation. Money he must have and money he could get only on condition that he should abjure the League. Case after case of exactly this form of hi-jacking came to the knowledge of the League. Townley only gripped his long jaws and worked the harder.

He came afterward to be bitterly assailed as are all men

that make headway against Vested Interest. Let us do him justice. He was one of the best organizers this country has produced, a man with a genius for organization, and up to a certain point an excellent leader. He was perfectly cool, never flustered by any emergency, expert about men and their motives, sophisticated, clever, discerning. In his youth he had knocked about the country in various capacities, including that of a journeyman plasterer, had ridden the brakes, mixed with all varieties of the human species and learned to view with good-natured contempt the political methods of the day. He was not much of an orator; yet on occasion he could make an exceedingly telling speech, short, incisive, and direct. One thing about him that was invaluable was his courage. He had the best variety of that quality, quiet, reserved, not a word of bluster or show, always sure of himself and his position. Men came to him shaking with fears as to what the Interests would do. Townley, a tooth-pick in the corner of his mouth, would listen silently and then with two or three words dispose of the matter and send the timid soul forth with strength renewed.

In North Dakota, the primary is a great institution. Townley's plan was to have the League pick its candidates for all administrative and legislative offices, recommend these to the voters at the primaries and thus virtually assure the control of the state without disturbing the existing parties. Wonderful plan—if only the League could develop enough strength to swing it. Townley knew this without being told. All that winter bands of organizers were threading the state, registering Six Dollar Suckers, while public meetings were held and appeals uttered; one that I remember particularly well on Christmas Eve with the thermometer 42 degrees below zero.

Early in the spring of 1916 it was evident that the League was in a position to name its candidates. An election would be held that fall. A delegate convention was called to meet at Fargo. It packed the large auditorium there. Many speeches

were made, some of an unusual kind—for a political convention. They had meaning and were of other content than hot

THE SLOGAN THAT WILL WIN!

WE'LL STICK

JOHN M. BAER'S FAMOUS CARTOON IN THE NON-PARTISAN FIGHT

air. John M. Baer, the cartoonist, afterward a member of Congress, was there and made on the stage a series of his lightning
cartoons. One of the speakers, the editor of a weekly newspaper, unknown to fame, made a speech that deserved to become
a classic. It was a closely knit and swiftly mordant historical
sketch of the struggle for human liberty, first against absolute

monarchy, then against limited despotism and now against the absolutism of Accumulated Wealth. He used the American Revolution as one of his powerful illustrations and drove his point home and home to the creating of a tremendous enthusiasm. It was the most effective speech of the convention or the campaign and lifted the League to a new level of serious endeavor.

This reminds me that in the course of a long experience I have known reformers to do many foolish things, but nothing else so foolish as when they allowed themselves to connive at the destruction of the American tradition. A cheap and silly notion got abroad among them that in some way it was smart or showed emancipation to join in the discrediting of the American Revolution and of the men that took part therein. If they had known the origin of the movement they were assisting they might not have been so ready to echo its prepared flippancies. To all persons really believing in the forward march of man, every struggle for his emancipation is an instruction and an inspiration. The name and the shape of the enemy he confronts will change from century to century, but the substance within is one principle. The men of the American Revolution fought it in one shape; the Nonpartisan League confronted it in another. All the men that have stood against it in whatsoever shape are worth respect. The obvious reflection about reform movements in America is that if they have merit they consciously or unconsciously seek to complete the ideals of the Revolutionary fathers. The fathers started; it is for the sons to go on.

The convention was a booming success. It was to nominate a state ticket and much speculation was going on as to who should be the candidate for Governor. It is to an old convention-goer proof enough of the unusual quality of this one that there was no log-rolling and no secret bargaining for that or any other honor. Many men were mentioned. Townley had already made up his mind. He had looked the field over and weighing men and men, picked the likeliest.

Near the little town of Hoople in the Red River valley was a university graduate and former football star that was conducting a farm, fighting the obstacles that all farmers combated and doing a good clean job. It was like Cincinnatus at the plow. A delegation from the convention went up to notify him. He was not at home and the delegates met him bringing in, with a team, a load of fence poles, and dressed in overalls. He had never an inkling of the fate in store for him. The delegation whisked him down to Fargo and that night before the convention he made his first speech. He was badly frightened but carried it off well, so well no one in the audience knew. Only, sitting directly behind him on the stage, I could see his knees shaking. One might not have surmised that night that Lynn J. Frazier was to become one of the easiest and most graceful speakers in the United States Senate.

He was nominated by acclamation, made a great fight and won. He introduced a new style into political campaigning— no flub-dub, no eagle flights, no fantastics, but plain common sense directly and forcibly put before his fellow citizens. Besides, there was one thing about him that was to the observing soul irresistible. It was evident from the first word he uttered to the last that he was absolutely and unswervedly and everlastingly honest.

The whole state ticket was elected except one candidate. There is a fly in most of these political ointments, however delectable otherwise. The excellence of the victory was marred by the fact that the candidate for State Treasurer was beaten merely because he was a Catholic.

With the rest went the control of the State Supreme Court, a highly desirable possession, and of the lower house of the Legislature. Only one-half of the Senate was elected that year. The League carried nearly all the seats voted for, but the holdovers gave the control of the upper house to Exploitation and the League was balked.

Balked the more effectually because of a strange development. The man chosen for Lieutenant Governor by the League turned against it. In North Dakota the Lieutenant Governor made up the Senate committees. This man made them up against the League that had elected him.

Yet it forced or wriggled through the reactionary Senate some excellent laws that showed what it might do if it had full power.

The state-owned elevator had been one of the issues in the campaign. For the third time the people had voted for it. The Senate reactionaries and valets ignored the popular vote and defeated the elevator.

But the atmosphere was cleared, the League had gone off to a good start, the work of organization and agitation marched on, and at the next election, 1918, the League swept the state, won both houses and for the first time the farmer ousted the lawyer, kicking to pieces the hoary old anomaly that one-half of one per cent of the population should have a greater representation than all the rest.

The full League program was now greased to go through and much of it was enacted in the shortest, least expensive, and most business-like session the Legislature had ever held. It passed laws:

To oust the loan shark by establishing a state-owned bank to lend money at reasonable rates.

To end the grading swindle and the false weight thefts by establishing a State Inspector of Grades, Weights, and Measures, with full authority to establish and regulate grain grades.

To compel elevators to end the dockage swindle by paying for all dockage that had value.

To abolish the mixing-house swindle by establishing state-owned mills and elevator—at last!

To mitigate the railroad-rate swindle by reducing freight rates within the state, which was as far as the Legislature could go.

To help the farmer by establishing state hail insurance.

To relieve him of part of his taxation burden by taxing high incomes and inheritances.

To provide a system of compensation for injured workingmen.

To amend the constitution so as to provide for the recall of public officers.

To restrict the right of courts to issue injunctions in labor disputes.

To give state help to the building of homes.

Then Doctor Ladd was made State Inspector of Grading, Weights, and Measures. He installed his scientific system of grain grading and conferred an inestimable boon upon the farmer. He sent an expert to test the weights used at the elevators and the truck so significant to Fargo that fall day of 1919 was filled with false weights that had been detected and seized by Doctor Ladd's agent and were now on their way to be destroyed. The 500,000 bushels of missing wheat were not to go astray again.

All of these laws and others passed at this session were subjected to a terrific and ceaseless assault, not only in North Dakota but from all parts of the country. It was felt everywhere among the Respectable and the Right Minded that here was a menace that must be crushed before it could go farther. To crush it the state was flooded with adroit propaganda, the country with concoctions about the peril of Townley Bolshevism.

I cannot deny that the League helped its enemies by slipping and slopping. It allowed itself to be manœuvred into a position where the reactionaries could accuse it of disloyalty in the World War. It went out of its way to engage in activities that it should have let alone, co-operative business enterprises, newspapers, banks. Besides misfortunes that it could have avoided it received wallops that were inevitable, in view of the Interests it had antagonized. It suffered from a colossal and relentless assault upon the credit of the state to prevent the building of the public elevators and the success of the state bank; it saw law after law for the relief of the farmer negatived by the United States Supreme Court. Its unwise business ventures exhausted its treasury and left it heavily in debt. Slowly it shrivelled from the full measure of its power and glory.

At the summit, it had been organized in thirteen states; it had all told 245,000 dues-paying members. That day it stood to go through all the nation, to uproot the old partisan superstition that had been so serviceable for Exploitation and to bring in the practise of independent and intelligent voting. Under the skilful and incessant blows of its frightened enemies it mussed its destiny and thereafter it steadily lost ground.

At last came a day when it seemed to have suffered the final blow. Among the enterprises in which it had unwisely launched was a bank in Fargo. Privilege now so manipulated things that this bank was ordered to be closed as the result of a decision holding the League's post-dated checks to be illegal. Then indeed was joy unconfined in the caves of Reaction. Mossback newspapers gave first-page features to the collapse of Townleyism and of the Bolshevik League. All was over and done, the funeral would be soon, and held without mourners, if one could judge from the Eastern press.

But in this case the Autopsy was prematurely ordered and the funeral festivities were superfluous. A few days later the Supreme Court of North Dakota stepped in and destroyed all the sport by declaring the post-dated checks to be legal while it found the bank to be perfectly sound and its closing indefensible.

The league neveer recovered from the blows it had suffered

in its unwise business ventures, and the adverse decisions of the Federal Supreme Court. Its ambitious programs and plans were largely abandoned. Yet seventeen years after its founding it was still a vital force in state affairs. It still held its conventions, picked its candidates, and elected them. In the election of 1932 it swept the state with every candidate upon its list.

And again, no one can say that it has not bettered the condition of the farmer. Because of its efforts, there is less oppression and less robbery. Its grain-grading law, which might have revolutionized farming, was destroyed by the Federal Supreme Court; but the false weights are gone, the mixing-house evil has been mitigated, the dockage swindle has been largely abolished, the loan shark no longer has full opportunity to extort. Not all of the Townley dream came true. The Stone Wall was too strong and too well buttressed. As so often before, the bare hands came back from it having smitten in vain.

And yet the whole thing was worth while. For observe this well, that the Nonpartisan League made North Dakota the most independently minded constituency in America. The old partisan fetich is there dead as a coffin nail. The intelligent people of that state vote as they please, irrespective of party. In the election of 1932, Franklin D. Roosevelt, candidate for the Presidency on the Democratic ticket, carried the state by about 70,000. Gerald P. Nye, candidate for the United States Senate and endorsed by the League, carried the state by almost the same plurality on the Republican ticket.

Or for another test, take the questions that now, because of the League's work, are submitted at every election to the popular vote. Entirely upon independent judgment, the people vote about these. One proposal they accept, the next they reject, and they take no direction or instruction from anybody. Progress is slow, but surely there is something gained.

Chapter XX

MORNING SKY IN RUSSIA

Iт had been a school, club house, and dormitory for young
army officers in the old dark, hateful days of the Czar, this
Kadetsky Korpus that had become the capitol of the glad new
Russia. In its huge plain hall met now the first Russian national
assembly,[1] elected by the votes of all the people in all parts of
the new-born democracy. Close upon a thousand sat there,
men and women delegates, peasants, former soldiers, rough
fisher folk, unlettered, unskilled, with government, of which
most of them had never dreamed, suddenly thrust upon them.
The hall was bare as a barn, and flat-floored. From the rear
seats it was not easy to see what was going on in front.

On the back walls were home-made posters setting forth
sentences in Russian from Karl Marx, among them conspicuously and oft-repeated, "Workers of the world, unite; you have
nothing to lose but your chains." In a day, the prophet despised
had come into his own. Outside the door, were stands at which
were sold Russian translations of the works of Marx and other
Socialist leaders.

Signs and posters were all in red. Everything was in red.
All the way from Vladivostock the rail stations had been
adorned with banners, streamers, joyous announcements all in
red, usually a kind of crimson shouting to the world that the
new day had arrived and tyranny was dead.

Its death had long been overdue. The whole Russian system
had become an intolerable anomaly, a kind of autocratic putrefaction thrust into the body of a Europe that was always becom-

---

[1] Officially, the Council of Soldiers', Peasants' and Workmen's Delegates.

ing more democratic. In its last stages absolutism had made
desperate efforts to sustain itself in Russia, apparently by re-
doubling its horrors; more espionage, more eavesdropping,
more agents provocateurs, more arrests, more executions, more
men and women herded into the living death of Siberia. And
now, in the heart of what was then Petrograd and is now
Leningrad, stood, as a grisly memorial of all this, the blackened ruins of the building that had been the most hateful object
in Russia, the depository of the secret records and reports of
the vast system of gimlet-holing, gum-shoeing, and trap-
laying upon which rested the quaking throne of the last of the
Romanoffs.

The lifting of the black pall that had weighed upon the
country so long had not wholly changed the mental habits and
instincts of the people. It was now June, the Revolution that
had set them free had taken place in March; they were still
from custom awe-struck before certain symbols of the lost
dynasty. We were quartered at the old Winter Palace, one of
the largest buildings in the world, a vast red symbol of the
waste and insanity of monarchy. The Czar was gone with all
his tribe, the palace had been taken over in the name of the
Russian people, but still the drosky drivers of the city could not
be induced to drive within the precincts that once had been forbidden to all except imperial vehicles, and in the palace the
guards and servants looked with horror upon me because I
whistled where once imperial majesty had moved.

But at the Kadetsky Korpus, all these new-made legislators,
snatched almost in a day from plow-tail and fish-net, how do
they carry it off?

Here is the point on which I would dwell; it is one of the
obscured pivots of the Russian story. How do they carry it
off? Exceedingly well, no one can deny or doubt that fact;
exceedingly well. The order in the huge hall is perfect, seldom
must the chairman tap his bell for silence. Hour after hour they

sit there, absorbed in the proceedings, listening to every word. Those in the rear make ear trumpets of rolled-up newspapers that they may miss nothing. No conversation, no restlessness, no shifting about. It is amazing. They come early, they stay late, they seem incapable of weariness. And they are not dumb, driven cattle, either. They watch for points and applaud liberally. If a speaker says something they do not like they show dissent. They are insatiable of oratory, consume it, consider it critically, relish it, want more of it. An old Washington correspondent may well compare all this with the American House of Representatives and be instructed. But not in the boasted superiority of the superior.

The hall is oblong. At the end opposite the entrance is the high stage where sit the chairman and some secretaries. Tschaidze[1] is chairman, the redoubtable Tschaidze. As a presiding officer, I think there never was a better. He guides the whole assembly easily and steadily, keeps it working and never loses for an instant his air of unruffled command. One can see that he rules by prestige and his powerful mind; his physique is by itself not impressive and he has chosen to hide his strong, resolute, intelligent face behind a mattress of tawny beard. He can give thanks for a powerful voice; when he speaks the last row can hear and needs no ear trumpet.

I am sitting on the platform near him and looking out over the delegates. What a scene! The great silence, the earnest, eager faces all gazing one way, the rapt attention that never seems to slip. Let the proceedings be purely routine and perfunctory, every detail is precious to these people; they will not lose a word.

But the proceedings are seldom tame even to the sophisticated. One afternoon a man is speaking from the rostrum. Roughly clad, heavily bearded, great handed. They tell me he

[1] Also spelled Chkheidze. Russian names are the best. You can spell them any old way. The French could see no sense in spilling the whole alphabet on one man's name and adopted the spelling I have used here, which is as good as any other.

is a fisherman from Siberia and can neither read nor write. It is astonishing and I can scarcely hope Anglo-Saxons will believe me, but his speech flows on without a break, perfectly smooth, never an instant's hesitation for a word, a voice with modulations for effect, no hemming or hawing, and no affectations! The interpreter translates as the delegate goes on. It is a good speech, it has ideas, the man knows what he wants to say, knows how to say it. He has wit, too. He cracks a joke. The assembly catches it on the fly and laughs. He speaks his full time out, the chairman's bell rings as he ends what seems to be a flight of eloquence that echoes into thundering applause as he leaves the rostrum. A bearded fisher from the Siberian coast and illiterate! But unabashed and unsuppressed after all these years of the heavy hand upon him. Are not these a remarkable people? The stuff they must be made of to be still unsubdued! The world may well take note of them and their acts.

What faces! One sitting here on the platform and looking straight into them is likely to have impressions about his fellowman such as he has never had before. The bodies may be uncouthly clad or distorted with toil, but the minds shine out like strong flashing lamps. There, just below, near the front, sits a woman, big burning melancholy eyes fixed upon the speaker. What a face and what eyes! With those deep furrows torn into forehead and cheeks, and an air as if she had been beaten down by the years, how old do you think she is? Sixty, at least. But they tell me she is about thirty-nine. Eighteen years she has been in Siberia and it is the slow torture she has borne and the cruel graving of a life without hope that has scored all these wrinkles as it has grayed and thinned her hair. Eighteen years in Siberia. What for? She had written something the government did not like. What was it? An argument for universal education. She was a member of the Social Revolutionary Party, and the police spies had been boring holes and listening at keyholes, and so to Siberia with her.

Where in Siberia? For there are different circles in that Inferno also. At Irkutskh they keep the intelligentsia and the plotters of small guilt and much wealth, and there they are in exile but no great misery. But this woman, she was in a prison settlement somewhere near the Lena River, says the interpreter.

The Lena River! My mind goes back ten years to a time when I was managing editor of the old *Morning Journal* in New York. William Sulzer was a member of Congress. It was his custom to spend his vacations, when he could have them, in roaming about the untrodden Arctic regions, for he had the call of the North Pole, I do not know why. One day in the late fall, a short time before Congress was to reassemble, he came into my office fresh returned from one of his long, lonely jaunts northward. This time he had gone on new paths and had come upon one of these Russian penal settlements. It was on the Lena River, near the outlet, far inside the Arctic circle. The horror of the thing was still upon him. He said the inmates, insufficiently fed, dwelt in wretched stone hovels insufficiently warmed, men and women of culture banished to the last verge of all the world. So far north they were they had but two days in the year and the long night so weighed upon them that soon or late they went mad. He had come back with a noble thought, sprung from a burning indignation, that an expedition should be organized to take ship, suddenly descend upon the camp, and rescue the prisoners. He said the place was lightly guarded because the wretched victims were deemed to have no chance to escape, and a few resolute men could overcome what soldiers were there and be far away before St. Petersburg could learn of the dèmarche. He pointed out that as the prisoners were all political they could be brought to the United States with safety and while Russia would certainly rear aloft with furious complaints she could not recapture her prey in America. He wished *The Journal* to undertake such an enterprise. Perhaps we should have done so. At the moment we were busy in an attempt to track down a murderer and rejected the chance to free prisoners in Siberia as too far from the Bowery.

This woman had been in some such place and had escaped with her reason intact—wonderful to say. But not with her health. Not all the profound exaltation of the scene around her nor the sudden realization of her dreams could lift her far above her shattered frame. She had been trampled, wrecked, and battered, like a million others, that the Czarist system might go on.

The people had elected her a delegate even before she had come back from her place of torment. I said before that these were good people.

In that Assembly sat with her more than a hundred men and women that had been rescued from the Siberian perdition. One such victim was in the cabinet—Tseretelli, a grim, hard-featured man, taciturn and unapproachable.

Down at the left of the dais, about a third of the distance back, sat the renowned Bolsheviks, the uncertain quantity in the situation, the element that Trotsky and Lenin commanded. General Judson, who was assigned to accompany our mission, and had been much in Russia, assured me that Lenin was a great man. No doubt the fault was wholly in my observation, but he did not make that impression on me. Rather he seemed an obstinate fanatic bent upon making trouble and without clear notions as to what he wanted beyond the promptings of a lust for power and the fact that he did not want what was going on about him. Of this he plainly disapproved at every step, observing the proceedings with a sinister frown. In his newspaper, the *Prahvda,* Trotsky had revealed to the world that I was a secret member of the firm of J. P. Morgan & Company and had come to Russia to betray the Revolution and restore the Czar, but for all that I thought he was a much more likable person than Lenin, more human and wiser.

In its less fantastic and more workable aspects, the funda-

mental theory of Lenin's philosophy was that democracy everywhere and in all respects had failed and that the new state in
Russia should be all an autocracy, but conducted in the interest
of the workers. If one asked particularly as to what would be
in the interest of the workers, it appeared that this was a matter for Lenin himself to determine later. Perhaps the state he
visioned was not so much an autocracy as a theocracy with
himself as the titular deity. In his view, the Assembly and all
its ways and works were merely absurd. All elections were
farcical. I think there were in the Assembly only 166 Bolshevik members in a total of nearly a thousand. It was quite in
accordance with Lenin's theory that these 166 should dictate
to the rest.

Wherein these views could be adjusted either to history or
the plain trail of the human advance, no one could say. If so
far the story of mankind has taught anything it is that a people's progress must be self-achieved. You cannot take them by
the throat and jab progress into them as a cook stuffs a turkey.
The doctrine of doing good to the people because they are too
incapable to do anything for themselves is bearded with age.
It has been the excuse of every tyrant and bloody-minded murderer that ever sat on any throne. Caligula would have urged it
as the sufficient reason for his performances; satraps, czars, and
kings had always advanced it. To William English Walling,
Lenin had pointed out that the republican form of government
in France and the United States had not benefited the workers. At that moment the Czaristic scheme of things was in full
swing in Russia and workers that objected to it were being
shipped to penal camps in Siberia, such as Mr. Sulzer found.
Granting that the workers in France and the United States
were not yet exercising for themselves the full measure of the
power that lay in their hands, comparison between their state
and that of the workers under an autocracy seemed a sufficient
answer to his theory.

I was told, I know not how truthfully, that he was an ardent admirer of Louis Napoleon, a statement most interesting because it was the first time I had heard of anybody that admired that greasy mountebank and shell gamester, but at the same time disturbing. For was it not difficult to see how anybody that found tricks, bombast, and treachery admirable could have the essentials of greatness?

But the man in the assembly that interested me most was the chairman. He seemed of extraordinary force of character, perception and capacity. The manner of his handling of the delegates would have forced the admiration of any old political reporter. He had tact, wisdom, prescience, understood the parliamentary game and played it faultlessly. He was reputed an extreme radical and wholly hostile to the American Mission; certainly the night I spoke before the Assembly his reply might seem an equivocal welcome; but he was sincere, and I think, placed the common cause above his personal fortunes. He was then the greatest power in Russia and I looked to hear of his swift advance.

Interesting men stalked daily across that vivid stage, chief among them of course Alexander Kerensky, then a minister in Luvoff's cabinet but soon to be endowed with the first place in the government. In appearance, a typical Russian of the intelligentsia, rather pallid, clean-shaven, gray-eyed, with large and regular features, his brown hair cut short and brushed straight back, a good head, and an impressive poise. He went always carefully attired in a plain business suit of dark bluish gray, with a sack coat, and yet he always looked, I cannot tell how, more like a poet than a business man. It must have been his big dreamy eyes. His face was interesting but not strong; indeed, it had a certain meditative cast that suggested trouble, a suggestion justified by subsequent events. There was about him none of the relentless, hard-boiled, inflexible crispness of Tschaidze. Yet Kerensky was by far the more popular. The first time I met him and for a long period afterward he must carry his right hand in a sling and offer a visitor his left, for his right had been disabled by handshaking with his delighted followers. The chief nerve of his power lay in his oratory, which I think excelled anything I have ever heard. Certainly he must be placed near or at the head of living masters of that art. The test is the effect. Well, many a time 30,000 people have stood all night to hear him, and have felt, I am sure, amply repaid.

Men of this gift are seldom of the executive order. Kerensky's great popularity carried him into the place of premier of Russia but he lacked iniquity to do him service. Among his convictions was one against capital punishment. All reprisals for political offenses seemed to him inexcusable; everybody must be allowed to speak his thought whatever it might be and then to act as the thought indicated—politically. Anything might be deemed possible in a state so lately in revolution, but when we bade Kerensky good-bye not one among us imagined that three months later he would be another hunted fugitive, making his way in disguise with a price upon his head, dodging along lonely roads by night and hiding by day like a runaway slave before the Civil War, and so over the border.

Another interesting figure in the cabinet was Tereshchenko, the Minister of Foreign Affairs. Young, lately graduated at Oxford, able, alert, quickly adaptable to the occult methods of modern diplomacy, but personally frank, cordial, wise. A well-built young man above the average height, and suggesting in the swing of his shoulders and his long stride much outdoor athletics and wholesome living; fluent in English, French, German, one of these steady-eyed, clean-complexioned young men that are the best products of the university. His father had made a fortune in the sugar industry; for this reason he was himself with the masses the least popular of the cabinet officers and with the Bolsheviks an incessant target of attack and abuse.

Six months later he was groping his way about an underground prison, his beard grown and his raiment ragged. In the dim light of the old Czarist dungeon he met one that had been closely associated with him in the government.

"Don't you know who I am?"

"No. I never saw you before."

"I am your old friend, Tereshchenko."

So went the shuttlecocks flying when the Bolshevik battle-dore began.

It has often been said that Kerensky paid for his lenity with the fall of his administration; for after the first Bolshevik attempt if he had hanged Lenin and Trotsky, as they expected he would, Russia would have continued to tread conventional paths and he might have been for years its guide and commander. I do not know that this is so, but at least Lenin and Trotsky came back and began to prepare for the next outbreak as if the first had been not.

But the person I was most eager to see was Marie Spiridonovo, the fame of whose deeds had penetrated to America and, not without reason, had been celebrated in verse by Witter Bynner, as by another less renowned.

She had been a school teacher in a town about twenty-four hours from St. Petersburg, the capital of some state or province. When the futile Revolution of 1905 collapsed and the authorities were relishingly destroying those that had taken part in it, the governor of the province where Miss Spiridonovo lived distinguished himself even above his compeers by a savage brutality. For the first time the real nature of the government under which she lived came home to her and filled her with horror. As no one else seemed to have the courage to deal after his deserts with the governor beast, she determined to take that task upon herself. She learned that on a certain morning he was to arrive by a certain train from St. Petersburg. She bought a ticket for the same train and waited on the platform. When the governor appeared with his retinue and guard, she kept her revolver hidden in her muff until she had a fair chance at him and shot him dead.

All official Russia was aroused to make of her a memorable example. The tortures that were ingeniously studied and fiendishly executed upon her are better left unrelated. At the end of months of such sufferings that it seems strange the human frame should endure them, she was shipped to one of the worst of the Siberian prisons and virtually buried alive. Eleven years she spent in that dungeon and never expected to leave it until she should be carried out dead. When the Revolution of March, 1917, ended Czarism forever, the new government ordered all political prisoners in Siberia to be released and brought home. The governor of the prison house where Marie Spiridonovo was immured refused to obey the order. Then the Revolutionary government, hearing of this, gave the governor one hour to release his prisoners or be stood against a wall and shot.

She was now living in Petrograd but to find her was strangely difficult. So strong was the old habit of mind upon the population that every inquiry about anybody was taken to mean some sinister purpose and was met with evasion. At every mention of Marie Spiridonovo's name every face shut up like a nutcracker.

She proved to be the merest wisp of a woman, about five feet in height or less, and so slight she could not have weighed ninety pounds, but oh! the spirit that blazed and lightened in her blue eyes! The most interesting part of her talk, when she too had become convinced that we had come with no sinister purpose, was about her prison experiences. It was a prison for women. She said that some of the inmates had been there so long they had become mechanically adjusted to the surroundings and had forgotten any other life, having gone mad, no doubt. When the final order for release came, these refused to leave their dungeons and being brought out by force, one of them broke from the arms of the men that were carrying her, ran back and cowered in her cell.

Upon her restoration to life, light and the blessed air of freedom, Miss Spiridonovo became absorbed in the cause of the peasants and became their champion. After the successful Bolshevik coup of November, 1917, she at first followed Lenin, believing that he would solve the poignant land problem that was confronting and overwhelming the peasantry. Lenin assured her that he had the correct solution and in due time would announce it. The essence of the problem was that with the peasant population increasing rapidly, there was not enough arable land to support it. While this may seem strange in a country so sparsely settled as Russia and with such vast areas of unoccupied territory, two great difficulties are to be remembered. The unoccupied land was useless in existing conditions because it was out of reach; there were neither railroads nor wagon roads to make it available. And next, Russian peasants will live only in villages; they will not accept separate homes upon the soil they till.

At last Lenin announced that on a certain night in the Moscow Opera House he would make known his land policy and report also his negotiations with the German envoys. Marie was there, expectant, and occupying a proscenium box. When the time came, Lenin stood forth and in a speech disclosed his long-expected agrarian remedy.

It was simplicity itself. Between village and village through the country were still left many large individual estates. The villagers were to arise, drive out the occupants of this land, and seize it, killing anybody that objected.

Aside from any ideas of conventional morality that might be traversed by this project, it had a fatal defect because the total amount of land that could thus be had was not enough to meet the demands of the situation and Lenin must have known that it was not.

When she had grasped the significance of the whole design, flaming with anger, Miss Spiridonovo bounded from her box upon the stage and launched into a furious attack upon Lenin. It was said to be the only known occasion when he lost his poise. As he arose to reply, one of his lieutenants shouted an insult to Miss Spiridonovo, an insult based upon some of the tortures she had endured, an insult to cause the blood of all decent men to boil with rage, such an insult as in some parts of the United States would insure the lynching of the insulter. Lenin made no effort to repudiate the hideous taunt. His rejoinder to Miss Spiridonovo's attack signified little. Almost at once she was arrested and locked up in the Kremlin prison. Doubtless she would have been taken out and shot with the rest but for the furious outcry that arose from the peasants. To save the face of the dictatorship the pretense was made that she was insane and she passed many months confined in what was called an asylum, whence she was quietly carried into exile. For a long time it was generally believed outside of Russia that she had been assassinated—strangled, may be, in the name of the dictatorship of a proletariat that never existed.

Her fate was far better than that of many another former victim of the Czarist Terror that now fell before one still more cruel. For the slightest dissent, real or imagined, to the new form of the Iron Heel, swift arrest, a farcical inquiry or none, the firing squad in the dim morning twilight and maybe a line in *The Prahvda,* "Catherine Sofanoff was shot at the prison this morning"—after twenty years of horrible suffering for liberty in a Siberian prison camp. Many strange things have passed within the ken of this observer but nothing stranger than that progressive men and women, once shuddering at the cruelties of Czarism or of war, should view with complacency the horrors of the Bolshevik autocracy.

But to return to the Mission, rumors of outbreaks by the Bolsheviks were common. One day it was announced that at

noon they would march in force upon the Kadetsky Korpus,
drive forth the deputies and proclaim Lenin's Dictatorship of
the Proletariat. So on that day we met instead at the palace
Empress Catherine had built for her lover Potemkin. No
Bolsheviks appeared. Peace reigned undisturbed and the next
day we treked back to the former quarters. I wondered people
were so jumpy; later I lost that particular wonder.

The next onslaught of the terrible man-eating Leninists was
fixed for a certain Sunday. A great demonstration of workers
and peasants had been planned for that day with a parade
through the principal streets and a grand feast of oratory on
the Field of Mars, the old parade ground of the empire. Oratory! All Petrograd brightened with joyous expectations. Oratory, the breath of life, the food of the spirit, the last delight
of the emancipated! They soaked their souls in it, these people;
never could they have enough of it. All night they stood at
street corners to bathe in it, drink it in, rejoice in it. For the
first time in their lives they had the opportunity to speak without fear of eavesdroppers and police agents, prison, knout, and
Siberia. The joy of it swept them from their feet into un-
traveled ways of forensic ecstasy. So they were to have speaking all about Mars's Field and all the rest of the day, when
they had marched the streets long enough to impress everybody
with whatever it was they wished to impress. All would be
well, then, if only the Bolshevik wolves came not down upon
the fold.

The report went abroad that the demonstration was to be
too much for Bolshevik restraint, if any, and the long-expected
assault upon everything in sight was to be pulled off at noon
on that glorious day. I should remark here that from the beginning the Mission had been the bright particular mark of
the Bolsheviks' hatred. At Vladivostock they attempted to
prevent us from landing and came near succeeding but for the
commandant of the post, who interfered with a detachment

of infantry and got us ashore. Then they hired a train to follow us to Petrograd and at every station where we had stopped
they flashed forth their orators to tell the people what scoundrels we were and with what a devilish purpose we had come
to restore the monarchy. It was now declared that on this Sunday they would begin their jubilee by assaulting the Winter
Palace and wiping out the Mission.

We were strongly advised to leave Petrograd Saturday night
and spend the fateful Sunday in Helsingfors, Finland, which
was described as a nice place and perfectly safe from Bolsheviks.
Some of the Mission viewed this as sound. The two representatives of the hoi polloi and the horny-handed objected, not because they had any greater resource of courage but because they
happened to know that the demonstration would be wholly
harmless and there would be no attack from the fierce, fiery
Bolsheviks.

It was a beautiful day of sunshine and peace and the march-
ers marched for hours to their infinite delight and the applause
of the spectators, vast throngs of whom came in from the country to enjoy the festival and hear much oratory. Many banners
in red were carried, all valorously declaring in favor of the
utmost democracy, more power to the people's representatives,
and down with the sugar exploiters, meaning Tereshchenko.
There were many bands and no end of singing, the Interna-
tionale being the favorite air, and sung with an immense gusto
that never tired. After which a thousand orators eased their
chests and minds on Mars's Field to the great delight of other
huge throngs, and so the day ended. Duncan and I walked
along the sidewalks viewing it. While we were so engaged, a
figure went by that for us had more than a passing interest. It
was a man above medium height, rather florid, a trifle stout for
a Russian, wearing a derby hat on the back of his head and no
insignia, going quite alone and unattended. He was the Grand
Duke Michael, the man the British had plotted to push into the

seat of poor Czar Nicholas. Although he might be regarded as in far greater danger than any of us he passed unmolested and wholly unconcerned along the sidewalk back of the throngs viewing and cheering the paraders. I cannot but think he had his courage with him, in view of the fate that befell the rest of the imperial family.

The Czar, the Czarina, and their children were then prisoners on the imperial estate at Sarskoie Seloe, about twenty miles from Petrograd. They could walk about the estate but not leave it. I asked some of my Social Revolutionary friends what disposition was to be made of these troublesome guests and was assured that nothing more drastic was contemplated than exile. A deposed monarch in exile made sometimes a perilous condition to the state that thrust him forth; they knew that well enough but had resolved that the Revolution should be stained with no blood or violence. Within six months it came to drip with blood and be stained with such cruelty as would have ruined its fame if the world had not agreed, in this case, to look tolerantly upon all its excesses.

Most of the men in the government were members of this same Social Revolutionary Party, of which Kerensky was the conspicuous leader. It was an old-time secret organization that had been under Czarism the most effective motion toward freedom. To it belonged many of the intelligentsia, most of the men and women that had suffered for the cause of Russian liberation, and most of the advanced thinkers. Some of its leaders had been recalled from Siberia when crumbled at last the ancient, blood-wrought, tear-cemented citadel of tyranny, and some bore plain marks of their martyrdom. All were what would be called in America extreme radicals. Political freedom they had passionately yearned and striven for as the first indispensable requisite to man's emancipation; but their thinkings went far beyond that stage of progress, at which incidentally ours seemed to have stopped.

So went the general thought of the nation—that was the strange thing. A marvellous and unforgetable transfiguration had come over the visible face of Russia. Such an upsoaring of the general mind has hardly been known or knowable on earth as took place among these people between March and August, 1917. Only to see it and feel it made profitable any journeying, however long. There was in it a new sense of the possibilities of the human mind to see and be enamored of good things. All their previous days these people had borne the heavy black load of a conscious suppression and the mental canker of an indomitable distrust. Scarcely could a man have faith in his own brother, his own father, his own son. Everywhere about him was spread the subtle, mysterious, irresistible network of an espionage that seemed omniscient and supernatural. Even in the seclusion of one's home one dared not speak lest there should be gimlet holes behind doors and unknown ears glued to keyholes. From earliest consciousness to the last gasp of life, there was no relaxation of the deadly presence. Friends could not even stand in the street and discuss the weather.

There is in human history no more wonderful fact than that in the teeth of these conditions, despite a horde of agents, spies, traitors, agents provocateurs, police in uniform, police in black coats, the agitation went on and brave hearts managed to meet and to plan bold deeds. Fresh drafts of the discovered were dragged week by week to Siberia: as fast as one disappeared into that black and awful cavern, another arose to take his place, arose without shrinking and without fear. Police, scaffold, firing squad, exile decrees could not work fast enough to stamp out the eternal spirit that led on these men and women. Surely if there is any grateful remembrance anywhere for those that immolate themselves for the liberation of their fellows, none is better to be held in affection than the men and women that year after year, delving in cellars and going close brothered to death, kept the flame alight in Russia.

And now they had come upon the thing of which they had dreamed but never dared to hope. Gone were the secret police, the scaffold, the exile, the Azeffs, the terror, the darkened lives, and suddenly light shone everywhere.

It was astonishing to observe how widely ideas of a far advanced social state had spread among the masses of the people that are called common; spread with a competent understanding and a general acceptance. Once more, surely these are remarkable people. It was usual in the old days of darkness for the ruling class to excuse to the world the hideous state of Russia by averring that autocracy was necessary there because the people were so stupid they could not grasp the ideas of self-government and self-restraint that the rest of civilized mankind was familiar with. So I had heard them say many a time in many climes. Stupid! Why, the average unlettered mujik of the village had gathered in some way a grasp of the most modern conceptions of social philosophy and could talk Karl Marx by the yard!

Of what use are attempts to suppress speech and discussion and agitation? Do but look at this example. For years the Iron Heel had been driven down hard upon Russia to stamp out every revolutionary spark. Never had it been, never could it be, more relentlessly driven, more skilfully directed. The gallows gorged, the firing squad busy, the exiles in endless procession moving to Siberia, all to keep from the Russian mind the least knowledge of revolutionary ideas, and under it all the whole nation, you might say, so permeated and steeped in Marxism that the moment the Heel was displaced, up shot a movement informed and determined for the co-operative commonwealth! In our own country, how did it profit the Interests to suppress the free-speaking magazines? Yet a few years and everybody knew that the business methods the Interests protected were rotten. What was it the old town clerk said some two thousand years ago? It might well be paraphrased for the Red Hunters of a later day. If a thing is true it cannot be suppressed; if it is false it will suppress itself.

All the first manifestations of the new day in Russia were idyllic. The released masses reacted not into excesses but into grandiose dreams. For the first six months of the Russian Revolution no nobleman's life was in peril, no mass movement for revenge was observable. The restraint of these freedmen was something to ponder; from only an unusual depth of character could such a manifestation come. No life in danger, no property rent violently from its owner's hands, no reprisals, but virtually a whole nation betook itself to dreaming—and oratory. We haughty Anglo-Saxons that vaunt us of our Websters, Clays, Chathams, believe me we are but bunglers in public speaking compared with these natural masters of the art. Such fluency, such command of language, such knowledge of the surest appeal! A Russian that should speak after the current English fashion, with interjections of "ah!" "ah!" "ah!" every ten words and a painful searching for the next phrase would have no listeners. The Russians' notion of an orator was one that could lift their imaginations and soar away on unflagging wings out into the boundless regions of their hopes and visions.

And the men that seemed to have the best of these visions were the Social Revolutionaries. They saw an ideal state for Russia that should give the model to a world about to be remade after a new fashion, the universal brotherhood come at last, no more wars, no more hatreds, no more competitions, sufficiency and light for all, the grand utopia made real—in their imaginations. The Terror had been banished from Russia; any good thing was possible anywhere!

I do not exaggerate. It was impossible to escape the exaltation that possessed the generality of the people and was reflected in their faces, most to be observed in the faces of these that sit in the National Assembly.

"In their eyes the light and fire of long pain ended"—and the dream of the Golden Age to come at last. But on that dream the black shadow and blight is the war. In the glad New Day there must be no more war, and yet there is the long eastern front held by millions of Russians under arms. What shall be done about these?

The Allied governments, gravely upset by the revolution, which none of them had foreseen, are frantic lest the New Day shall mean the crumpling of the Eastern line and the release of two million German and Austrian troops for the Western front, where the Allies are already desperately beset. To fortify the Russian spirit and keep the new government in just heritage of the engagements of the old, delegations are sent from England and France.

Not happily from England, certainly. Members of the British Labor Party come and stare dazedly at the whirling exaltation and have for it little sympathy; indeed, little understanding. They make some speeches and go away, leaving behind them one comment that rankles in the Russian breast.

"If this is democracy, we don't want any democracy in our country."

Albert Thomas, the wise and perspicacious French Socialist, comes and understands and makes kindly and sympathetic addresses, but the situation is too big for any one man, and Russia is wavering whether to go on or to give up, there on the front.

It is odd to reflect now how great a part in that crisis was played by a thing so simple as the congenital British inability to understand the other man's point of view. The Golden Dream meant nothing to the practical minds of British diplomatists. They felt that Russia had entered into certain treaties that bound her to keep on. The best way to make sure that she would keep on was to remind her of those treaties. They could not understand that the New Russia cared not a cent for engagements made by the Old Russia because it believed the government of the Old Russia had not the slightest right to exist and that all its acts were void. The Russians in the mass, and theoretically, yearned for peace, but they were willing to fight, as they showed afterward, fight like tigers, if they saw anything to fight for. The trouble was that in the existing war they could see nothing to fight for. The causes of the war had never been told to them; all they had known was that the Czar ordered them out to the firing line and they had been compelled to go, but they had no thought to stay there unless some one should show them a good cause to stay. And that good cause to be really good in their eyes must be something connected with the survival and progress of democracy. Otherwise, you but waste your breath.

The British had no idea of supplying such a reason; indeed, they were hardly in a position to do so. Men that lived under a monarchy could hardly preach with sincerity or conviction the gospel of the democracy the Russians believed in. And again, the Russians were all for idealism and the idealism of Britain in the war was that a pawnbroker exercises in his calling.

Unluckily, for the Allies, the British conception of effective propaganda was allowed to prevail and the harping was always upon Russia's engagements and treaties. If anybody wishes to know now why Russia faded out of the war this is one great reason. She never knew why she should stay in it.

The British sent over a lot of films to stir the drooping Russian spirit. What were they? If you will believe me, pictures of British troops in battle being shot to pieces and that kind of thing. The Russians knew too much about battle lines; what they did not know was a living reason why they should offer themselves to be shot.

Woman suffrage had triumphed in Russia with the Revolution and Mrs. Pankhurst was sent from England with the notion that she would appeal to the women. I had campaigned with her for woman suffrage in America and greatly admired

her, but obtusely hurt her feelings by laughing at her notion
that the way to win Russians to stand by the Allies was to
remind them of Serbia. Serbia? One might as well have reminded them of the great Cham's beard. They cared nothing
about Serbia. What had Serbia to do with the regeneration of
mankind?

Kerensky wanted to go on with the war, even with a reluctant populace. He tried it and failed. The Bolsheviks, jeering
and shouting, promised peace, Russia was dead weary of a war
it did not understand and Kerensky succeeded only in strength-
ening the hands of his Bolshevik enemies that had sworn his
ruin.

And again, while the Social Revolutionaries dreamed of the
ideal world to be, the inhabitants of Petrograd stood in lines to
obtain rations of the most necessary things. It was summer and
warm; common sense suggested that when winter should come
they would not so patiently stand there and the awakening
might be ill for the golden dreamers. I ventured to urge this
view upon certain of my new-found Russian friends.

They did me the honor to invite me to come one night to the
large, bare dining room, once the cadets' refectory, under the
Kadetsky Korpus, and drink tea with them and hear their program. We sat around one of the great plain tables and they
told what they had seen in their golden dreams. Not mere
visionaries; most of them were members of the Assembly, able
young men. In all good things they seemed to have an invincible faith; a perfect democracy in which all men and
women should share on equal terms, all power in the hands
of the people, the socialization of the sources of supply, no privileges, no private monopolies, no imperialism. And how about
the ever present land question? That to be settled by building
good wagon roads and extending the railroad system so as to
open up new regions for agriculture; also by draining swamps
and felling forests. Then villages were to be built in the newly

opened regions and the pressure on the old villages was to be relieved by voluntary migrations to the new lands. The great estates to be broken up, the vast areas of crown land, all to be given over to the farmers. Russia to be made so far as possible self-sustaining by the developing of her agricultural and other resources. No capital punishment, a whole scheme of prison reform, and of course a complete system of free education for all.

What men had brooded over and imagined in the long, dreary Siberian nights was to be real.

It was an entrancing program. I called attention to the fact that while it glowed and glittered in so many ardent minds the bread lines and the meat lines were there and furnished no flattering augury. While the leaders dreamed, the railroad facilities of the country remained inadequate, the wagon roads nothing. Not dreams but action was the prescription if the state was to live.

To this they gave a cheerful assent but pointed out that until the wretched war should end, their full program could not be carried out. But they could make a beginning. The rest would come.

So many ardent young minds, so many capacious heads, so many self-forgetting champions of a world to be made anew, pathetic it is to recall the sequel. Undeterred by the failure of the first attempt to break up the Assembly with arms, the Bolsheviks tried it again more boldly and this time succeeded. The non-resisting Social Revolutionaries fled. Some got in safety over the border, many were captured and summarily shot, the old systems of espionage, killings, and exilings came back. A few of the golden dreamers made their way to Paris and ended their dreaming in melancholy exile and often in want.

Tschaidze the redoubtable, the wise, on whom mostly my own hopes had been set, escaped to the Russian province of Georgia, where he created the Georgian Republic and became its president. The Bolsheviks invaded and suppressed it and Tschaidze was again a hunted thing fleeing for his life. He got through the frontier and so to Paris. For some time he managed to live obscurely in a suburban village. At last in despair he cut his throat. Twenty-four hours later he was dead and it became my melancholy duty to attend in Père la Chaise the funeral of the man that I had picked as the coming leader of Russia. Among the mourners that day were men that had suffered long imprisonment, exiles, tortured of body and mind for a free Russia, and were now again exiles from the country they tried to save; Georgians that had fled from the destruction of their promising republic; kindly, sympathetic Frenchmen that had tried to succor these fugitives, and one lone American that had known the dead man at his height of power and glory. These made up the little company of mourners. It was a singular commentary on the football nature of human existence.

Without leaders, the rank and file of the old Social Revolutionary Party abandoned the organization and the Golden Dream dissolved. Nothing finer has been conceived among men. Perhaps it will come again. Perhaps the great potentiality of idealism revealed among the Russian people after the Revolution of March, 1917, is still to stir and inspire the world as those bright-eyed young men believed that night in the basement of the Kadetsky Korpus.

Autopsy. The Social Revolutionary Party of Russia was shot to death by the rifles of men that professed to want the same things but insisted upon getting them in a different way.

We of the Mission were not quite through with the Bolsheviks when we had completed our errand and started homeward. Senator Root, who was the Mission's head, had been from the first their chief target of attack. The charge was made that when Secretary of State he had tried to return to Russia political refugees on whom the Czar's government wished to take vengeance. I think the charge was baseless, but in the state of the Russian mind, filled at the moment with kindliest sentiments toward the old revolutionaries, it was good ammunition for the Bolsheviks. One may remark that a few months later, they themselves were to treat even worse than the Czar's government had treated the same men and women they then haloed with glory, but at the moment no one guessed that this could be. From the violent attacks upon him translated to me on Mars's Field I doubted if Senator Root's life was safe and I am sure he was himself fully aware of the danger he ran, but he bore himself throughout with a dignified and tranquil composure that moved us all to admiration. Mr. Root's social creed and mine were irreconcilable and as far apart as the poles. But I should be unfair if I were to touch upon this theme and say nothing of the conspicuous ability and flawless fidelity with which he discharged every duty that fell to him. His addresses in Russia were models of argument and eloquence and his personal kindness, unfailing wit, and genial acquiescence in whatsoever hardship or difficulty won all our hearts, however we might differ from his views.

I think it was chiefly with animus against him that the Bolsheviks on our way back burned a bridge in front of us with the pious hope that we should be wrecked, and when we were blocked at Viatica by this incident, tried to set fire to the train. Exactly how either attempt, if successful, would have furthered the emancipation of man is a puzzle not for my solving.

Chapter XXI

DRUMHEADS AND FIRING SQUADS

Two figures, supposed to typify Ireland, are familiar to readers of English literature and no less to observers aforetime of the work of English cartoonists. One is called the Irish peasant, and well you remember him, ragged clothes, shapeless hat with a clay pipe stuck into its band, ragged whiskers, prodigiously long upper lip, stupid face. The other stands for the Irishman that has managed to get a smattering of education, impulsive, erratic, hot-tempered, emotional, given to whiskey, quarrels, and bad tobacco, gifted with a flow of words and superficial eloquence, but untrustworthy.

Diligent repetition fastened upon the English-speaking world a general acceptance of these creations as representative and substantially correct. Of course, some of the Irish had a certain kind of wit, but in the main they were either hopelessly ignorant or hopelessly temperamental and so addicted to brawling that we must keep them under incessant watchfulness and restraint. But for the wholesome supervision of English wisdom and English arms they would be ever cutting one another's throats.

Go back over English literature and English newspapers prior to the World War and see if this is not a just summary of the English view of Ireland and the Irish. Try to recall in English fiction, English history, English verse, English caricature any reference to Ireland that is not essentially derogatory. Captain Costigan, Captain Shandon, Macaulay's account of the Armada, of the siege of Londonderry, even Swinburne calling Ireland "Liarland,"—it was the common practise. When the Home Rule agitation was on in 1886 and 1887 the assertion was openly made by the English press that the Irish were so congenitally incapable and riotous, any attempt to restore to them a local parliament must end in ridiculous failure and broken heads, with the English stepping in to prevent annihilation. The fact that as soon as Irishmen left Ireland they seemed to take on a rather unusual capacity not only for government but for large affairs and successful business management counted for nothing. Incapable they were, incapable they must remain. Praise God for the benevolent intervention of England that alone kept them from relapsing to the native nakedness!

Emotional, incapable, extravagant, voluble, untrustworthy. Bearing well in mind this traditional estimate by English writers, come with me to a public meeting in Ireland today. There is an open square, let us say, in some interior Irish town. A platform is erected in the centre, an immense crowd is gathered about it, peasants, workers, all classes.

The first thing you will notice is that the people are at least as well dressed as a similar gathering anywhere in England would be, the women with better taste and less dowdiness. Next you will look in vain for any figure that in the least resembles the familiar creation of the clown with the dudeen pipe. Next you will make note that the proceedings are as orderly as you are accustomed to see in other countries and the people no more excitable or emotional.

But now the principal speaker comes forward, a tall, slender man, wearing eye glasses, carrying himself with the student's stoop, a grave, cold man, that you would take anywhere for a college professor or perhaps an advanced scientist. The crowd cheers. Then he begins to speak. Where is all this fiery eloquence and extravagance of diction? Not here. He stands with his hands behind his back and never makes a gesture. He speaks in the slow, deliberate, unimpassioned manner of a judge delivering a sentence from the bench. He deals with facts and figures, bald, unlovely, angular. At will, he gives you the dull and uninspiring details of a budget. He speaks of the country and its right to be free as one might read an editorial on the trend of the stock market. There is no more emotion in his voice than there is in a street-car conductor's and no more appeal to sentiment than you can find in a seed catalogue. He never varies his manner, he never cries to high heaven. He deals in nothing but fact, fact, and the stony chill inferences therefrom. He does not smile, he does not smirk, he does not talk to climaxes that there may be applause, he does not seem to care how his remarks are being received. Above all, he tells no stories and intersperses no jokes. It is all dead earnest from beginning to end, the serious expostulation of a serious mind.

The people listen in rapt attention. From time to time they interrupt him with applause when he makes a particularly strong point in his calm reasoning. For two hours he can hold them thus intent. He is the most popular speaker in Ireland and there is no more heat in him than there is in so much granite.

He is Eamon de Valera, leader of one of the chief political parties of Ireland, a strangely gifted man with a strange career, a mathematician, a student plucked from the classroom to assume a military command in the revolt of 1916, condemned to death before a firing squad, having his sentence commuted to life imprisonment, escaping from prison by sheer hardihood and invention, a fugitive in America, coming back to be President of the Irish Republic, commander in chief of Irish forces in a civil war, proscribed, hunted, a price upon his head, to emerge with nothing changed as the foremost politician in Ireland, then before the world suddenly appearing as thinker, wise statesman, chief administrator of the country whose government had tried to get him to the scaffold—here is the most remarkable career of modern times. And all the while as cold as granite, with no accepted symptom of that magnetism supposed to be indispensable to every great political leader, most of all in Ireland; successor to Daniel O'Connell, and in method, manner, appearance, psychology, O'Connell's antithesis.

Behold, then, what changes the modern university has wrought, even upon the hustings. Ladd and de Valera, analytical chemist and mathematician, flung into the vortex of politics, and what is their bearing and what is their power!

Before such a man and such a career, the lay figures created so laboriously through so many generations by tribes of sweating English writers and cartoonists disappear like mist. Here is another Ireland, here is a totally different psychology, and here is a force the world cannot ignore. If so small a population can occupy so large a space in the thought of mankind, we may be sure the fact is not without due cause.

For as he is, so in less degree are others of his day. Their prevailing and dominating manner is not untrammeled expression but the stress of an impeccable restraint. It is his practise to emphasize by understating. The young men that follow him are of his conviction about this, also. Listen to Stephan O'Meara, once lord mayor of Limerick, a man of sage, considered counsel and long experience in public affairs. As with set jaws and the power of silence he underwent savage persecution for his republican faith, so he would not in his public addresses before or afterward vary a particle from the one manner of rigid and almost icy command upon himself. Or Frank Aiken, once chief military leader of the Republican armed forces, a wonderful strategist and the darling of his men; he speaks in public with the calm deliberation of a man appraising lumber or Abraham telling sheep.

So are the young Irishmen generally of this time. It is their practise and fashion about all things. Take this collection of poems written by men condemned to death for striving to free their country from an alien and hated yoke, this book called *Poems of the Revolutionary Brotherhood*. Through all their singing is the identical note of a noble self-discipline. Where is this old spirit of reckless bravado that was supposed to expend itself in one hot charge and then give over? Where is the pulsating Celt of English fiction? You will not find him here, certainly.

In a measure, vehemence has been subdued by the greatness of a great cause and of great spirits enlisted in it. Seven centuries of it this generation inherited; the dignity of it as well as its unassailable truth and worth has sobered men's thinkings but it has not daunted their devotion.

And as for the cause, there is none better in all this world; no, and none has been. Concerning one revolt elsewhere men may say it was prompted by undisclosed economic aimings; of another that it sprang from one man's ambition. About Ireland there is and has always been only the one straight question fundamental to the existence of democracy, as vital to dwellers in Jehol as to dwellers in Waterford, whether the basis of human government shall be the bigger gun and the harder conscience or be the consent of the governed. To that issue there have been so far in this world, two answers. One is the emancipation of the people that groaned against the Iron Heel and the other their annihilation.

This is one phase of the long drawn-out Irish question that has never been well understood in America. Often I have read in American newspapers, editorial and other articles speaking of "Great Britain's rights in Ireland." Rights, say you? What rights? The rights of Great Britain in Ireland are in all respects the rights of a burglar to the plate he takes in the dwelling he has entered; no more, no less, but so.

To this conclusion we are driven not emotionally but logically. If Great Britain has any shadow of right to possess Ireland then all wars of conquest are legitimate and no nation has any rights except those it can successfully defend upon the battlefield.

In but two ways can governments be erected in this world,

One is on the consent of the governed, the other on the preponderance of brute force. If any American is willing to accept the second as veritable or tolerable, then he rejects with the same motion the sole basis of his own government.

Probably in these days, no one will be hardy enough or ignorant enough to adduce the fraudulent Act of Union, passed by hand-picked English agents and totally without authority to speak for the Irish people, but others may possibly urge the Treaty of 1921 as some justification for Great Britain's claims. In point of fact, the Treaty of 1921 has the validity of an agreement given to a highwayman that holds a pistol at your head—this and none other.

History wonders at the unparalleled length of the Irish struggle and English writers ascribe it to the stupidly stubborn and unreasonable Irish character. The real origin and cause is the fact that deep planted in the Irish heart is a sense of the perfect justice of Ireland's claim to freedom.

It is not to be denied that in these centuries of enforced subjection England has succeeded in Anglicizing a certain element of the Irish people. With her proximity, her power, and all the opportunities of uninterrupted rule the wonder is that she has Anglicized so few. But the heart of Ireland remains as Irish as when the alien domination began and there is no record of a greater failure of imperialism.

Against this profound faith and this conviction have been marshalled all devices and expedients that ingenuity could conceive and skill or brute force execute. Not scaffolds nor firing squads, exile, prison cells, on one hand, nor cajolery and flattery on the other, have moved it. The world has come to accept it as a matter of course, looking upon it often with amusement and seldom with the curious attention it deserves; for it is the most remarkable phenomenon in the human story and in some ways the most instructive.

Irish history is imperfectly understood in this country; Irish events are seldom fairly reported in the American press. If we know at all of an Irishman that gives up his life for his cause we customarily think he is some wild-eyed fanatic or half-crazed enthusiast that, led by the national spirit of insubordination, has flung himself against the stone wall of some law and perished.

To see how justly we deal in such matters, let us take one case of our own times, that of Erskine Childers.

Here was a man emerged from an English background, who became so overwhelmed with the facts about the English occupation of Ireland that he was transformed in spirit into an ardent Irishman. A student, highly educated, naturally a gentle and retiring spirit, of so lofty a character that even the enemies that dragged him down to death acknowledged his rectitude, the sheer moral force of Ireland caught him and swept him away to surrender all else for her sake.

He was born in England of an ancient English ancestry, but certain relatives being possessed of a handsome estate in Ireland, he was sent there when he was still a boy, to be bred. It was his early studies and observations, his knowledge of Irish history and his sympathy with the struggling people around him that did the business for him. He grew up a kindly, reserved, somewhat diffident, studious youth, rather tall, blond, with light-blue eyes, light-brown hair. He traveled much, met and married a beautiful and brilliant American woman, descendant of the famous John Alden of Massachusetts Bay, and settled in Ireland as a landed gentleman. When the World War broke, he enlisted in the British army, went into aviation, became a noted flier, achieved a great success, and was decorated, cheered, and honored. But the Irish that was not born but only seeped into him, was still dominant. At the close of the conflict, he walked into the War Office at London, unpinned from his breast the medals that covered it, laid them upon the desk of his superior, and said:

"I have done my duty by the country of my birth. I am now going back to the country of my adoption," and resigned.

Things were not well in Ireland and he was bound there to take his part in a new phase of a long struggle.

To understand why he was moved to this enlistment we must go back to the Easter Uprising of 1916.

Strange it must seem to the philosophic reader of history that men and governments are so dead slow to learn one fact that most protrudes from the tangled records. It is that revenges do not pay. The Easter Rebellion was the surging of a people long and passionately devoted to their liberties and determined against all odds to attain them. The attention of England was absorbed in the war where she had all she could do to prevent her own annihilation. It seemed a propitious time for Ireland to strike for freedom. The revolt was quelled after hard fighting, and the English authorities that had been startled and alarmed by this blow in the rear raged for a notable punishment. With inconceivable folly they believed punishment would deter other patriots from similar restlessness and make of them patient, docile subjects to be led by the nose as asses are. So with revolting cruelty they drumheaded the leaders of the uprising and shot them, one after another. I will not go deeply into the horrors of this beef-witted performance, but merely remind the reader that one of the victims was so badly wounded that he must be carried in a chair to the place where he was shot. Among the men put to death that direful day were some of the greatest scholars and finest spirits in Ireland, poets, teachers, intellectual leaders, men like Padraic Pearse, one of the world's greatest educators, Thomas Macdonough, the brilliant historian of Ireland's literature, Joseph Plunkett, the gifted poet.

What followed was exactly what follows every such slump backward into the times of claw and fang. Temporarily, the revolt was quelled but only to break out again with an immeasurable augment of violence and hatred. The ruthless cruelty of Sir John Maxwell's drumhead achievements drove all of Ireland's young men that were not atrophic into the Irish Republican army and when the World War ended the Irish War started anew.

The fresh revolt was accompanied with features never before known in such motions, Ireland or elsewhere. What was virtually an independent government was set up inside the tegument of the British governing machine, a secret and intangible government but one that was complete and functioning. A British parliamentary election came on. The Irish people used the occasion to elect a parliament of their own, called, in their Gaelic speech, the Dail or assembly. This created an Irish Republic, with a president and a full set of cabinet officers. Still more remarkable, there were also created native courts with jurisdiction over all cases of civil action, which operated so successfully and ably that the courts constituted under the British rule were ignored and the judges sat with nothing to do, while almost under their noses existed again a genuine Irish parliament and a fully equipped national government, this slender, student-like, and reticent person, Eamon de Valera, being President thereof—granite-cold and all the rest—and Erskine Childers the head of this extraordinary system of justice.

But if outmanœuvred, Britain was not idle. At the start it had ordered troops to subdue and overawe the insurgent Irish as so often before. But this time the case was different and the overawing proceeded not prosperously. The Irish Republican army, ably commanded, was in the field, a secret, desperate, and dangerous foe, carrying on guerrilla warfare by night and invisible by day. To produce an effective state of terror so that peasants should fear to conceal the native fighters and thus the hidden coverts of rebellion might be unearthed, a campaign of frightfulness was ordered. The British troops engaged upon it were found to be ineffectual. They could not easily be induced to burn, shoot, torture, and maim. To do what they were too decent to do, troops called "auxiliaries" were introduced from England, and because of their distinctive uniforms became known as the Black and Tans, a name that will not easily be erased from Irish history.

The contention of the Irish was and is that these men were criminals taken from English jails or enlisting as an alternative to a term of punishment. As to this, I have no information, but the recorded deeds of the "auxiliary troops" will sicken all sensitive readers so long as the records last. The savageries on one side produced upon the other a reckless impulse of revenge. They always have this effect; why dwell upon the fact? I will give but one example.

It was the practise of the Black and Tans when they were able to come up with any of the elusive Irish soldiers to torture them first and then kill them out of hand. Often no effort was made to discover whether the captives really were connected with any insurgent band. After a particularly flagrant case of this kind when boys had been wantonly tortured and slain, three of the officers that had commanded the squad engaged in this work were lying in their barracks peacefully sleeping when secret foes managed to steal in and cut their throats as they lay.

After some months of bush warfare in the country and passive resistance in the cities, the acknowledgment was made in the British House of Commons that the British writ did not run in any part of Ireland.

These manifestations were made known, more or less, to the people of Irish descent in America. A strong organization was formed to assist the struggling patriots in Ireland. Millions of dollars of the bonds of the Irish Republic were sold here. A committee of prominent Americans was formed that took testimony about the outrages of the Black and Tans and rendered a scathing verdict against the perpetrators.

This was touching Great Britain on its tenderest nerve. Since the close of the World War the fixed British policy had been to put forth every effort to draw the United States into a virtual Anglo-American Alliance. The large element in America that was of Irish descent was, as it had always been, a serious obstacle to such a design, and the obstacle now promised to have unexpected reinforcement.

Lloyd George was then the controlling influence in British affairs. He had declared many times that he would never negotiate with "that band of murderers," meaning de Valera and his followers. He now made overtures to that same band; made them at first covertly and indirectly, made them when forced to do so directly and openly, and out of the dealings between commissioners appointed by the new-born Irish nation on one side and Lloyd George's representatives on the other came the celebrated Treaty of December, 1921, which eventually created what is called the Irish Free State. But its main purpose was to silence opposition in the United States, convince American opinion that Ireland had won to a virtual freedom, and thus allow the grand design of the Anglo-Saxon Alliance to swim on, aided by an indefatigable propaganda.

The Treaty contained features extremely repugnant to de Valera and his companions. Those that came afterward to review the facts were compelled to admit that the manner of it was as bad as the matter. Five commissioners represented Ireland. Late at night, after long discussion, the Treaty was brought out. Two of the Irish commissioners, who had been in secret conference with Lloyd George, at once declared their willingness to sign. The others demurred. Upon these Lloyd George brought to bear the menace of "immediate and terrible war" as the alternative of refusal. For every man, woman, and child that would be killed in that war, for the devastation and ruin of the country, these three commissioners standing there would be solely responsible. Still the three hesitated.

"Sign all or sign none!" cried Lloyd George. "Immediate and terrible war and all the bloodshed on your heads."

It was almost daybreak when the last man signed, virtually with a pistol at his head.

One in that company utterly repudiated from the first the whole arrangement. He was not a commissioner, he was present in only a secretarial capacity, but he did not hesitate to express his opinion and when the last commissioner yielded to coercion he stormed out of the room in a manner so violent and angry that Lloyd George strongly objected and afterward described the incident as dangerous and disruptive.

The man that protested thus was Erskine Childers.

He had joined the Irish Republican Army when he returned from the World War. Arms for the Republican soldiers he had brought in from Germany, brought them in a small yacht, steering through the British Grand Fleet, he and his brave American wife, operating at the imminent risk of the seas and of capture, landed them safely after adventures and escapes that would be priceless for the fictionist. He now went back to Ireland to denounce the Treaty and found that de Valera had unerringly discovered its evils.

Michael Collins, head of the secret service under the Republic, had been a commissioner and one of the first to sign the Treaty. He busied himself to obtain the approval of the Dail, as a vindication. By a close margin, he won it. Yet it was in truth nothing. The Dail's consent was not even a gesture. The Treaty contained no stipulation for it.

De Valera and his followers walked out of the hall in protest.

One point that he made was that the Dail had on this matter no mandate from the people. As to this he split with Collins, who had been one of his aides. Harry Boland, a daring spirit, who had helped de Valera to escape from an English prison, undertook to heal the breach, and locked the two into a room with the information that the door should not be unlocked until they had reached some agreement. They reached one known in history as the de Valera-Collins pact. De Valera had contended for the election of a new Dail upon a new registry or list of voters. Collins acceded to this and the two farther agreed that in every district where one had a known preponderance of strength, the other would make no contest.

The Irish Republican Army from the first repudiated the Treaty and when the Dail gave its approval, withdrew all support of the government. It had its headquarters in Dublin on the left bank of the Liffy in a building called the Four Courts. There Collins negotiated with it on the basis of an expedition to the North. Negotiations were still pending when Collins received an abrupt order from London to root out the Republican Army and be rid of it. That same night at 11:30 he sent an order that the building should be vacated before 12 o'clock or he would attack it. The Republicans did not go, protesting that they did not understand the order. Meanwhile English troops had been brought up, with English artillery and English gunners, and promptly at midnight fire was opened on the building, which was wrecked.

Many Republican soldiers were killed. The bravest and ablest, Cathal Brougha, their commander, issued from the front door with a revolver in each hand, firing into the troopers that surrounded the building. The next moment he fell, riddled with shots.

This was the beginning of a new civil war that raged for eighteen months.

Meanwhile the Free State government had been set up under the Treaty and a constitution prepared under the direction of Lloyd George. Collins and Arthur Griffith were at the head of the administration. They waged active warfare against the Republicans that had declined to accept the new form of government. Ammunition and guns for the Free State Army were supplied from England. Acts for the suppression of the rebellion were passed by the Dail, from which the Republican element was still absent. These acts were of an increasing severity and some of them unusual even in a state rent with civil war. One made the possession of a weapon by any unauthorized person a capital crime.

Erskine Childers was visiting at the country house of his near relative, Robert Barton, southwest of Dublin. A file of Free State soldiers descended upon the house and arrested him. They found a pistol that had been given to him as a souvenir by Richard Mulcahey, head of the Free State Army. On the charge of having it he was tried and convicted under the arms act. His attorneys appealed the verdict, alleging that it was grossly unfair. While the appeal was pending Childers was kept in prison. Four nights in succession he was notified that he was to be shot the next morning; four nights in succession he wrote tender and touching letters of farewell to his agonized wife. On the fourth morning, a guard came to his cell, marched him forth into the prison yard and shot him—on the order of Mulcahey.

You can gather what kind of man he was when I tell you that he shook hands with each member of the firing squad that a moment later ended his life.

In eighteen months, seventy-five other Republicans, some of them mere boys, had shared the same fate. Thousands of others were in jails or prison camps.

In Mr. Cosgrave's own expressive phrase, "We beat hell out of them."

De Valera, as President of the Republic, was in control of the Republican troops. His whereabouts were unknown, but from time to time he was reported to have been seen at one place or another. The Free State authorities were exceedingly eager to lay hands upon him, as they felt that armed opposition would cease with his capture. For months he eluded their utmost vigilance and infinite searchings. When you consider how small a country is Ireland and how great a reward one might expect that would betray him, the exploit seems to belong to romance.

One night I drove out to see him in his place of concealment. Even now, I do not purpose to say where it was, but when I saw it I wondered no longer that the swarming spies and scouts of the government were never able to come upon it. A young woman of the Republican forces took me in an automobile without other escort. We started at sundown and rode until nearly midnight and it was a wild and occasionally a weird journey. I think I will not describe to you how this hunted President was disguised, but I doubt if his mother would have known him.

We sat and talked until near daybreak. However changed his appearance, he was in spirit and manner exactly the same as when he sat in the Dail as the head of his singular government. I mean he was the same calm, steady, reasoning, unemotional, iron-nerved man under the hazardous conditions of hiding as he was elsewhere. He had been a professor of mathematics. I found that in exile he passed his unoccupied time in the solving of abstruse problems of algebra. He talked about the situation of his affairs exactly as he discussed mathematics. I had known him in America, and one peculiarity I had noticed then seemed still more observable now. It was his precise manner of speaking and his curious fidelity to a rigidly exact expression of his idea, whatever it might be. On this occasion he was talking chiefly economics and if he had none of Arthur Latham Perry's power to make the subject alluring he knew how to formulate its intricacies with expert equipment of knowledge. Erskine Childers had coined about him a phrase singularly apt. He said that what most impressed one about Eamon de Valera was his "crystalline integrity." It was so. I have not known another man that seemed farther removed from pretense. The most rectangular of politicians are allowed by common consent a liberal leeway in compliment and gracious speech. It was a prerogative this man never used. In after years he proved himself to be one of the shrewdest of the politicians of his age and the idol of his people and yet he never pretended any cordiality, never practised the grimace amiable, and never seemed to care for any human being. After all I do not know that the back-slapping and long-lost-brother style favored by Theodore Roosevelt was so hot. It may be effective in some cases, but after years of observation I am of the opinion that it lacks finish and savors too much of Grand Central Pete.

But if he could not greet you with a handclasp warm and soggy and a smile that wrinkled about his ears, the President of the Fugitive Republic had a way with him about programs, and I found that he had between algebraic formulas worked out a plan for the economic rehabilitation of Ireland that eclipsed anything of the kind I had heard from any others. He not only saw the need to restore the industries and activities crushed (for profits) under the British regime, but he formulated the remedy. Years afterward when he came to speak of world depression at Geneva some American newspapers not before friendly hailed him with applause as a genuine statesman and thinker. So far as I know, he displayed at Geneva no research or brilliancy of coherent statement that might not have been observed in him when he was "on the run" and dodging spies in unusual parts of Ireland.

Some points of information I sought from him to use afterward in America. He suggested that we write out what I wanted to know and his answer. It was at such a task that one could see best how his mind worked, curiously swift, sure, going straight through to the end and as cold as so much granite.

The Free State authorities won out in the civil war and when it was apparent that the Republican cause could make no headway in that conflict, de Valera ordered "arms down," and shifted the contest to other grounds. His capture was still eagerly sought by the government officers, but for months they could not find him. At last there was to be a public meeting at Ennis in County Clare, and de Valera walked upon the platform and made a speech. In the midst of it, a company of Free State soldiers came up, opened fire on the platform, dispersed the meeting, and arrested the speaker.

Everybody now expected that he would be shot. He was locked up in a notorious prison in Dublin, and kept there incommunicado for months. John F. Finerty, Washington attorney and sympathizer, got a court order to see him concerning a law suit. He found the prisoner contentedly studying Einstein and solving algebraic riddles. He never expected to emerge from the prison alive, but after some months the government set him free and the man of so many and strange vicissitudes went forth and began to lead the opposition to the government. He led it to success, incidentally—cold as so much granite.

Chapter XXII

SIR WILL'M MISSES A LUNCHEON PARTY

IN the good old days of Snub-nose and his pals, and for a long time afterward there was dwelling in our town an able lawyer, greatly gifted orator, and learned scholar named Michael Vincent Gannon. He was a neighbor of ours and a most lovable man, and partly on his account I attended meetings of the Land League that were held in the schoolhouse of St. Anthony's Church. It was the time when Parnell was agitating for a betterment of the terrible conditions with which Irish tenant farmers had been cursed for generations. The Leagues in this country were organized by Patrick Ford to support the demand for agrarian relief.

They were good meetings. We had a group of young, bright, intense, ambitious Irishmen gifted after the manner of their race with the command of speech, and they used it to advantage. But one night, about the time I was Saving the Nation by yelling my head off for Free Trade, I heard Mr. Gannon in a full and memorable argument concerning the whole Irish question and thereupon I surrendered.

He spoke for about an hour and a half in the old Burtis Opera House and brought to the occasion all his rich resources of knowledge and eloquence. Here, doubtless, was the ripe fruitage of years of reflection and accumulated lore; he had crammed his address full of historical facts carefully arranged, he had compulsive reasoning and he had a deep and genuine feeling that went beyond doubting. The whole thing swept me from my moorings, and I saw for the first time the Irish cause as it really was; in it lay the epitome, symbol, microcosm, substance, essence of the whole human struggle. So Wendell Phillips had viewed it, but until that night never had it seemed so to me. All stood out in the lightning flashes of one man's eloquence—how, having lasted for seven hundred years, this had become the world's first cause of all causes, why so many men had gone to their deaths for it, why it had persisted from generation to generation, why it could never be eradicated from the Irish heart. That strange persistence had often in my hearing been attributed to the innate stubbornness of the Irish nature, its supposed bellicosity, its fidelity to its form of religion of which this insatiable thirst after independence was alleged to be a part. All such exegesis seemed now but foolishness. It was not because of their supposed love of fighting that the Irish had kept flawlessly all these centuries their loyalty to this cause but because the cause itself was worth all that unequalled devotion; worth it and demanded it.

For if there was in this world any such thing as a right to be free, if freedom meant anything, if all other professions of service for it were not lies, here was one case that admitted of neither doubt nor fleck. Never was so straight an issue. The whole of the Irish resistance was founded squarely upon the doctrine immortalized by Thomas Jefferson. If England might rightfully govern Ireland then the American Revolution was a crime, the duty of oppressed people everywhere was to submit in silence, and again there was in the world no morality but the mediæval bigger fist and harder conscience.

All this was clear, and something else hardly less valuable. The immense power of propaganda, the greatest force in the modern world. Monstrously and almost magically this cause of such solid and noble worth had been twisted, ridiculed, maligned, distorted to the world. The English had not only despoiled the Irishman and dragged him at the chariot wheel of their imperialism but by their control of literature, news, and the world's press had succeeded in making him a figure of fun or of contempt.

It is thus that invariably the wronger contemns the wronged. So long as the weak have anything the strong lust after, the weak must be pictured as despicable creatures. So long as the North American Indians had any lands the white man coveted they were a people merely vile; when they had been perfectly robbed, the white man discovered in them too late that they had admirable traits. It is nothing in the Jewish nature that makes Jews the subject of detraction but only the business ability that the persecutions of a stupid religious fanaticism have developed in them. So long as the Chinese competed in California with white labor they were unfit to live; when they were excluded from that competition, San Francisco welcomed them into the commercial and civic bodies and discovered that they were grand.

In the case of the Irish in America, the process had, in my time, features of barbarous cruelty most wounding to natures with any sensibility. Irish boys we were accustomed to despise as "micks"; this was why. Irish immigrants we despised as "greenhorns"; this was why. At places of employment were signs reading, "No Irish need apply"; this was why. When Home Rule was demanded for Ireland, the English raised ever the clamor that the Irish, being merely veneered savages, were incapable of any degree of self-government; and this was why.

So far as I know there is no Irish blood in my veins, but after that enlightenment, I think I was a fairly good Irishman.

Men talked to me about the violence that had attended the efforts of Ireland to free herself. Violence? What violence? What is violence? The setting of the foot of a single British soldier on Irish soil was an act of violence. The floating of a British flag there was an act of violence. The superposing of British courts and systems was an act of violence. The denial of Ireland's right to be free was an act of violence. The dynamite exploded in the Houses of Parliament and the Tower of London was but a reflex of a million acts of violence on the other side. Wrong begets wrong. What would you have? If you do not wish the harvest do not plant the seed. Remembering Robert Emmet and the men that were hanged after 1798 one can read without wonder of the assassination of Burke and Cavendish. After learning of the horrors of Siberia one can read without shrinking of the assassination of a Czar. To accept the planting and shudder at the tilth is hypocrisy. Wendell Phillips in his Phi Beta Kappa oration flung this doctrine boldly upon the reactionary scholarship of his times. It was sound then; it may be believed to be sound now.

But I started to say something quite different.

Curious are the twistings of the threads that hold things together in this mysterious world. Forty-four years after that night at the old opera house it flowered into a singular episode, which for the sake of its humor I will set down here hoping to be pardoned for the personal references, which are unavoidable. Life is too much lacking in humor. When there is any of it to be had I am in favor of going ahead for it and damn the torpedoes.

While in America on one of his visits de Valera had organized the nation-wide body I have spoken of. It was called the American Association for the Recognition of the Irish Republic. Many Americans that had no Irish ancestry joined it upon what seemed to them an irresistible urge, and I was one of them.

On March 17, 1926, I was a guest of the Cincinnati branch of the Association and made a few cursory remarks about Great Britain and its foreign policy. I had seen much of this policy in the Far East and related what I had seen. For some reason that I could not divine, the newspapers chose to make much of what I said. The next night I made a similar address before the branch at Akron and again was honored with newspaper attention.

About the end of May I sailed for Europe on the good ship *President Roosevelt*. We reached Plymouth, where I was to disembark, early in the morning. My baggage had been placed on the tender and I was lined up with the other passengers for the quaint and curious custom of passport inspection, still a hangover from the war to add needlessly to the traveler's troubles. When I reached the table the passport officer asked me to wait until the others had been passed. Then he informed me that he had been instructed not to allow me to land in England.

Naturally I asked why.

He said he would decline to furnish any information on the subject.

"And if you attempt to land at Southampton," he added, "I shall be there to prevent you."

I thanked him cordially for this delicate attention on his part and remarked that I had no desire to land at Southampton and little to land anywhere in England, and having with difficulty and scant time rescued my baggage from the tender alongside, I proceeded to Cherbourg and thence to Paris, where I was astonished to learn that I had become the centre of an international episode.

I had been excluded from England at the request of the Irish Free State which believed I had hellish designs to slip over from England to Ireland and shake the foundations of the established order, even going so far as to describe me as "a dangerous firebrand" and "notorious plotter," which seemed extravagant eulogy in the circumstances. Reporters met me at the St. Lazare station and informed me of these surprising facts, and wished to know what I had to say for myself.

To be excluded from England struck me as nothing to sit up at night about. So far as I was concerned they could make the banishment perpetual. The world was full of places I had rather be in, and I was satisfied to let it go at that. But just at that time the British Labor Party, being out of power and eager to get in, was keen for anything that looked like a jimmy. With joy its leaders hopped upon my poor little incident as something with which to annoy the hated foe of Conservatism, which was then running the government, and in the House of Commons they gave notice one day of an interpellation on the subject.

Naturally the banished one was not present on this happy occasion, but my son, John Russell, the short-story writer, happened to be in London and went around to see the show. He sat in the gallery of the House of Commons and came near to be expelled for laughing in that solemn adytum, the proceedings were so funny.

It appeared that the chief of the department responsible for the mallet-head performance at Plymouth was one Sir William Joynson Hicks, Minister for Home Affairs, if I have the title correctly. The attack was led by Commander Kenworthy, one of the lights of the Labor Party. With other gifts, the excellent Commander has a sense of humor and he made of my trifling affair a harpoon with which he proceeded to search the innards of the Conservative whale and came hot upon the vaso-motor center.

Ever since the physical demonstration at Belleau Woods, British policy, as I have pointed out, had been concentrated upon one objective, which was to cajole, argue, bunco, or manœuvre the United States into an Anglo-American Alliance. The real purpose of this ardent desire was to preserve the British Empire, already showing sad signs of senile debility and other ailments. But the ostensible aim, as set forth to the gullible and the simple-minded was to bless the world by a union of the noble Anglo-Saxon forces that would shoot peace into these lowly inferior foreigners and make them behave. The whole British nation was obsessed with the belief that this Unholy Alliance was easily possible, Americans being about half-witted anyway, and every British political party had to declare its unswerving and passionate allegiance to the purpose of "closer relations with America." It was this obsession that gave to the worthy Commander his best hold, and before long he had Sir Will'm going.

Naturally enough, the eminent Minister for Home Affairs was unacquainted with certain points in what I am pleased (at times) to call my career, but the Commander must have been looking it up. This man, says he, who had held such and such positions, represented President Wilson on inter-Allied war boards, had been in England as a commissioner for his government and to serve the cause of the Allies in the war, he comes now to visit this country and finds himself stopped at the door and ignominiously slung into the sea. Is that a way to promote Anglo-American concord? Is it thus that we win American friendship? Is this a way to stretch out loving hands across the sea? Shall we thus demonstrate to the world the beautiful harmony and loving brotherhood existing between the great English-speaking nations?

Of course, Sir Will'm did not give a hoot for me or the exclusion stunt, but at the thought that he might have slipped a step, however small, in this supreme chase of the elusive American alliance he was manifestly flustered and worried. He fidgeted, shifted on his feet, jiggled with his eye glass, and finally got in a defense to the effect that the person excluded at Plymouth was notoriously an enemy everywhere of the British Empire and his admission would not be proper. But Kenworthy continued to jab with the harpoon and the Labor leaders rejoiced and were glad.

The next day I was much astonished to receive at my hotel in Paris a letter from Sir Will'm. How he learned my address I have no idea, but it was not the first time I had found reason to wonder at the extent and variety of the knowledge of such things possessed by the British organization. In this letter, which was apologetic and friendly, he suggested that a way might still be found to avoid the blighting of my existence by a continued absence from the British Isles. I replied to the effect that I was not looking for such a way and was content where I was. To this he returned, gently rebuking me for what he called "a belligerent attitude," and inviting me to luncheon at some hour on some day that I have forgotten—to luncheon, providing I would enter into a bond not to blow up Westminster Abbey, not to devise, design, or otherwise originate any devilish complot against the peace and safety of His Majesty the King and not to go to Ireland to incite to riot and insurrection His Majesty's faithful subjects there residing.

Thus with the smile of Anglo-Saxon fraternity mantling his expressive face, held he out the alluring bait. But what is life without spice? Should I for the sake of a luncheon which, being prepared in England, would be sure to be badly cooked and largely inedible, forego my favorite diversions with dynamite, dagger, and midnight conspiracy? Not at all and then moreover certainly not. So I declined the tempting offer and the incident, having thus added innocently to the gayety of nations, lapsed into oblivion.

Not without one more phase. The government of the United States was engaged at that time in playing upon certain unfortunate immigrants a rather shady trick by which it plucked them of ten dollars each. After this manner: It was enforcing, not too considerately, the abominable immigration law that sought to make this an exclusively Anglo-Saxon country and to hell with these dirty dagoes. On various pretexts immigrants arriving from the south of Europe were being denied admission and must be carried back. Each of them had paid to the United States ten dollars for a visa on his passport that was now proved to be worthless. As a rule, it was no fault of his that had vitiated his visa but the United States always refused to refund the money. I had had two or three cases that were peculiarly painful under this species of flim-flam and it occurred to me that I might use my little adventure to call attention to the national scandal. Besides, I think most citizens that try to do business with the State Department come away raging against that prize-winning Circumlocution Office and I had another thought that I might even up one or two old grudges.

The point was that I had paid to the British Embassy in Washington ten dollars for a visa that guaranteed safe conduct in British territory and all the rights and privileges of a citizen thereof. Yet when I had presented this expensive document, and tried to enter under its guarantees, instead of safe conduct and rights and privileges I had been thrust off the door-step. I therefore wrote to the Secretary of State a full account of what had happened, called his attention to the guarantees on my passport, and respectfully requested that he should ask the British Embassy to refund the money I had paid for a piece of junk. In point of fact, the British treasury was welcome to my ten dollars, since by all accounts it needed the money more than I did, but I wanted to find out about these guarantees, rights, and privileges and how about this gypping of immigrants.

I wrote my letter with care and in due form and manner and sent it.

No answer. When I had waited a sufficient length of time I engaged as my counsel Mr. John F. Finerty of Washington, able lawyer and stout champion of all good causes. To him I explained about the plight of the immigrant and sent another letter for use where it would do the most good that recited the failure to extract any response from the State Department and mentioned casually an intention to tell the whole story that winter on the lecture platform.

Mr. Finerty used something efficient on the State Department, a nail-grab maybe, and finally extracted from one of the Secretary's assistants what might be called a reply. I regret to say that it was nothing I could commend to beginners. In evasion as an art, what is needed to excite our admiration is finesse, it is delicacy of touch, it is the swift and agile in side-stepping. This attempt in the useful accomplishment was just journey work. It began, if I remember rightly, with the fall of man and continued to Lee's surrender and in between wandered the green and lushy earth about. But the one thing deducible from its comments was that the State Department had not the least intention to ask anything of the British Embassy and with this deduction, not reached without some deciphering of the cryptic, I kicked the whole subject out of the mental back door and took up something else. But the United States continued to bunco the poor immigrant.

Chapter XXIII

"TWO DOLLARS A HEAD—UNPICKED"

THERE be among the nations of earth those that can go out and do a nice clean turn at piracy and never pretend that it is anything else, but we Anglo-Saxons are not of that order. When it comes to playing pirate we can do it as efficiently as any other people going, but it seems we can never scuttle a ship nor cut a throat without a portable organ, the doxology, and family prayers on deck. Then we proceed with a clear and cheerful spirit to go aboard in the name of the gospel.

How Britain holds India for the uplift of its lowly inferior inhabitants I have already explained, but we of this land of the free lag not far behind when it comes to snivelling while we grind our cutlasses and hoist the black flag. If, without the authority or knowledge of Congress we make war upon Nicaragua and with our marines overrun and annex the country, it is not at the behest of New York bankers eager to extend their investments but because there is unrest in Nicaragua and we are the divinely appointed international policemen to knock the fear of God into alien heads. If we annex Haiti and in the doing kill some hundreds of its inhabitants, we do so not for the sake of a gigantic American sugar exploitation but because the wretched depraved people practise voodoo and we have a mission to reform them—with Krag-Jorgensens. If we interfere in the affairs of Cuba and support a dictatorship there it is not because a New York bank has millions invested in Cuba but because we have an insuperable passion for law and order—as we have proved in Chicago, Herrin, Duquoin, Cicero, and other cultural centres. But taking it by and large I should think the noblest example of our neat union of banditry and piety is to be found in our record in the Philippines.

For some weeks after December 15, 1932, the halls of Congress rang with denunciations of the perfidy of the miserable low French because they had failed to pay us interest on a debt we said they owed us. This was great sport and perfectly safe, no member of either house having so many as five French votes in his entire constituency. The moral obliquity of the miserable Latin was fully illumined in these precious days of the open season for such game, but none of the hunters ever mentioned the fact that we of the superior morality had been guilty of a breach of faith and a broken agreement far worse than anything we charged against the wicked French. Exactly such was the fact, nevertheless. And we next proceeded not only to violate again a national covenant but to accompany it with a piece of legislative trickery and legerdemain beyond anything known among the wretched, dishonest Latins.

Let us see how this matter stands. In August, 1916, the Congress of the United States passed an act that entered into a compact with the people of the Philippine Islands to do certain things on a certain condition. On August 29 the President of the United States signed this act and it became the law of the land.

It was a law providing for the rehabilitation of the Philippine government, being indeed an organic act or constitution. Two paragraphs of it read as follows:

"*Whereas,* it was never the intention of the people of the United States in the incipiency of the war with Spain to make it a war of conquest or for territorial aggrandizement, and

"*Whereas,* it is, as it always has been, the purpose of the people of the United States to withdraw their sovereignty over the Philippine Islands and to recognize their independence as soon as a stable government can be established therein,"——

After which comes another "*whereas,*" setting forth the purpose of the United States to bring about a "speedy accomplishment" of this purpose, to which end the enactments follow, placing in the hands of the people of the Islands 'a larger control of their affairs that they may be able to take it all "as soon as a stable government can be established therein." Single condition, single performance; no covenant could be clearer.

Almost at once a stable government was established. For sixteen years it continued to be one of the most stable governments in the world and for sixteen years the United States on one pretense or another shamelessly evaded the carrying out of the pledge it had made.

The offense was all the more flagrant because this covenant of August 29, 1916, was not by any means the first promise we had made to these people. From the beginning of our occupation of the Islands we had steadily given assurance that we came not to hold them permanently or indefinitely but only to set their house in order and return it. Repeatedly we said this; every President reiterated it. The act of August 29, 1916, was merely the culmination of a long series of such pledges, concreted now with a definite condition and apparently a definite period. If ever the faith of a nation was pledged to anything the faith of the United States was pledged to this.

On what pretext, then, did we dodge this solemn national obligation? The good old pretext of the doxology. We were not in the Philippine Islands for the sake of the profits we drew from them and the investments our financiers had made there; we remained in the Islands in the fulfillment of a high and sacred duty.

We must fit the lowly Islanders for self-government. And we must wait until they were economically independent.

Not a word in the covenant about being fitted for self-government; not a word about being economically independent. Just one condition, just one period. As soon as a stable government can be erected therein.

As for making them fit for self-government, when would

that delectable state have been attained? When the Islanders should have reached the idyllic beatitude reigning in Harlan County, Kentucky, for instance? And who was to decide whether they had really reached this lofty altitude of civilization? And on the way up shall they turn their enraptured gaze upon Mr. Capone's efficient governmental machinery in Chicago for an example and inspiration? Or the high levels of civic rectitude reached in New York when Mr. Walker was mayor? And where was the tribunal that should determine whether they were really of this exalted eminence or only pretending to be?

It is of course true that throughout the sixteen years when with hymn-book in hand we were sprinting away from our engagements, the Filipinos were governing themselves in 1100 barrios or municipalities in the Islands and furnishing an average quality of self-government there rather better than our own; but facts of that order are easily drowned by a good reliable portable organ and a lusty chorus. It was also true that the lowly inferior Filipinos had produced the greatest single mind so far known among human beings, that they had repeatedly shown in every department of endeavor a capacity at least equal to that of any other people; that one of the greatest of political philosophers was a Filipino; that before the bloody assault of the United States, the Filipinos had established a national government perfectly equipped and admirably designed; that the least observation showed them to be of excellent ability and worth; that there must be greatness or the capacity for it in a people that show to the world great individuals.

All this time the people of the Islands never ceased to demand the fulfillment of our national pledge and the freedom we had promised them. And we never ceased to leap so agilely from greasy trick to greasy trick to avoid the pledge that no low, deceitful Latin could have surpassed that bewildering footwork.

Meantime, also to the strains of the dear old hymns, the exploitation thrives apace. Americans own the public utilities of the Islands and squeeze from them such goodly profits that one of their managers says they can afford to spend $20,000,000 to beat the independence of the Islands because if the Filipinos once get control of their affairs they will assuredly root out the plenteous dollar harvest. Americans have investments in sugar centrals, the tobacco business, hemp, timber, banking, copra, all doing well and returning pleasant dividends. They have made an arrangement by which their products come into the United States free of duty. If the Islands win to their independence duties will be exacted upon all such things. Raise the hymns, swell the chorus fortissimo on that organ! A little louder there —turn it all on. So! Let us continue to hold the Islands for the glory of God and the sake of our balance sheets.

The plea about economic independence as a pre-requisite is as disgraceful. Not quite as snivelling but as footless. Where, good side-steppers, will you find warrant for your holy scruples about economic independence? As soon as a stable government can be erected therein, is the reading of the bond. And if you come to that, what is economic independence? If you mean that a nation must raise within its own borders everything it consumes, where is such a nation? But if you mean that under the operation of your tariff arrangement there has been stimulated in the Islands an abnormal production of sugar and that independence would injure the sugar business, you conceal the fact that this injury would fall chiefly upon corporations and investors and that for the commonalty in the Islands, whether the sugar business rises or falls makes not a particle of perceptible difference.

The attitude of the sugar exploiters and their allies was always that the Filipinos were imbeciles and children and must be milk-bottled into adolescency. To one that has been observantly among them in their habitat this notion is the jest of the

"AT THE KEYBOARD"

Puck's idea of the invisible government, March 15, 1905

ages. As a matter of fact they are an older people than we and a subtler. They live in a country with an exceedingly fertile soil and an unusually happy climate. They have successfully met every emergency with which they have been confronted. For more than two years they maintained with inferior weapons and scanty ammunition a war against the best troops of the United States and so doing developed a capacity for military skill that repeatedly compelled the admiration of their opponents. If the whole sugar business were to be annihilated in a day the next year would find them producing something else and plodding along without visible sign of defeat or disaster.

National hypocrisy in dealing with such things was no new trick, of course; but there was another phase of the matter developed in the discussions that had the interest of novelty. It appeared that with jazz, cubism, racketeering, and other delights of the post-war period we had taken on the notion that liberty was the bunk and nothing counted but bread and meat. Give a people these and you gave them all. If the forefathers thought freedom was worth having for its own sake, that merely proved again that the forefathers were sentimental boobs. Nothing counted but the full belly, and among other things thus discovered to be of no value was the nation's good faith. What is a covenant compared with a good brisk sugar trade? Up with the stewpan!

But the trouble about this philosophy of the soupbone is that if you start to disregard treaties and break down covenants in the name of dividends, or the petite marmite, you drift into a position highly embarrassing and full of trouble for the stewpan. For example, when Japan started upon her aggression against Manchuria the United States reminded her of the treaties she was thereby breaking. And Japan with a chilly smile retorted upon our invasions of Nicaragua and Haiti equally in violation of treaties. And if we are to have no validity in international covenants that greed and profiteering need respect, then the only power left in the world is the power of guns, every nation must stand at all times armed to the teeth, and the cost of armament, not to mention the cost of the inevitable wars and their sequels, defeats the whole purpose of the soupbone conception of life.

After sixteen years of adroit evasion of this particular treaty, all the elements in America that favored side-stepping, that is, racial hypocrisy, the dementia precox of imperialism, profit mongering, exploiters and adherents of the bread-and-meat theory, united to put through Congress an act that seemed the attainable summit of duplicity. While pretending to grant independence in ten years (totally ignoring the pledge "as soon as a stable government can be erected therein") it was so cunningly worded and supplied with jokers that in reality it made independence virtually impossible.

And with that the organ pealed again and far and wide floated the entrancing sound of pious hymnody.

Serenely and unchallenged shone forth the true superiority of the Superior Anglo-Saxon. That poor fumbling dago, Machiavelli, had nothing on us.

And we go to the Islands and prove our superiority in other ways, chiefly by refusing to try to understand the people we have assumed to pilot to the heights. Hang them, they're just niggers, aren't they? They have dark skins. Enough. No person with a dark skin was ever anything but a rascal or an idiot. They are a small people, physically. Intelligence and worth are reserved for us that are tall and have white skins. They do not think as we think. But our way of thinking is the only respectable way. People that have another psychology have no business to have it. If they insist upon having it, let them black our shoes and bring our shaving water.

On my second tour of the Islands, I was sitting one night in the lobby of the Manila Hotel, and an American resident approached charged with all the scintillating lumen of one that has discovered a great and novel idea. Without delay he proceeded to share it.

"I've found the best definition of a Filipino," says he. "A Filipino is a creature with the brains of a monkey but without a monkey's intelligence."

Not far away the tropical moonlight poured its silver tide upon the statue of José Rizal. This American had lived for years in the Islands and had never taken the trouble to turn a page of Rizal's record nor to give a thought to what Rizal meant.

Contempt for the Filipino raged throughout the American colony. Sometimes it ran over into hatred. I had seen the same thing in the attitude of the English toward the Hindus, of the English toward the Chinese in Hong Kong.

Blessed Nordic, light of the world!

Manila, a short time before my second arrival, had elected a native mayor. He had closed up the gambling houses and houses of ill-fame. Many Americans were bitterly complaining. How can we do business without plenty of prostitution? What we want is a wide-open town.

It was a sentiment that aroused no enthusiasm among the lowly brown men. For inferior creatures that need our guiding care and all that, they seem singularly unresponsive to the logic of a good lively trade in vice. Perhaps this is one of the respects in which we still owed them that solemn duty so feelingly referred to in high places. The average Filipino has stern views as to personal morality, the poor backward sumph, and I think there is less of the social evil among these than among any other people I have observed except the Irish.

But our task was to instruct them in self-government and God knows we are the premium teachers of that recondite art. I should suppose the orderly government of cities to be as good a test as any of ability in self-government. As I have before pointed out, in most of the Philippine municipalities the whole government is in the hands of the lowly natives—solely in their hands. Well, life and property are safer in these communities than in the average American town or city. In six months in the city of Chicago there were 242 homicides. That is more than ordinarily occur in all the Philippines in six years. There is no part of the modern machinery of government with which the Filipinos are not familiar. They carry on elections, choose public officers, have legislative bodies, enact laws, exercise every function of government. The greatest change the withdrawal of the United States would make is the change between the dun consciousness of an alien domination and the inspiring consciousness of their freedom. If that to other peoples of the world has been worth fighting and dying for, we may be sure it is not less dear to these, maugre the soup bones.

But there is another test of fitness that I want to emphasize now, although I have spoken of it before. It is the quality of the men that have by merit or achievement emerged above the common level of a nation. The English like to be judged by their poets and statecraft men, the Americans by Washington, Jefferson, Franklin, and Lincoln. We do not choose to acknowledge the fact but there have been men of intellects as commanding among the despised little brown men. José Rizal, the most versatile and powerful intellect of whom we have record among all races and in all lands, was one—Apolinario Mabini another.

We are proud, or used to be, of the long array of men in America that beginning with nothing but their two hands and a dauntless determination won their way against the handicaps of poverty to fame or something. None of these has a record in higher relief than this Malay. He was born in the utmost poverty, to win an education he must fight like a man in a desperate battle, he supported himself on his way through college, he studied law when he must live upon scraps, he entered the bar wholly unknown, he rose by nothing but his ability and diligence to be, while still one of the youngest, one of the most respected attorneys of Manila.

He had studied more than law as he went along; he had gone deeply into political philosophy and the relations of man to government, reading all that the best minds of all countries had written on this subject and evolving a compact, reasoned theory of his own. On coldest conviction and without the warm and pliable enthusiasm of youth, he came to the conclusion that government having other foundation than the consent of the governed is in a modern world unworkable. Having reached this formulated conviction, he went deliberately and judiciously to the Katipunan, the secret revolutionary brotherhood of the time, joined it at the imminent risk of his life, and became its chief adviser.

Hard work, no exercise, and bad diet brought illness and a paralytic stroke. He kept on with the revolutionists, was sentenced to a firing squad when the Katipunan was discovered, escaped it, made his way to the revolutionary army, with Palma wrote the remarkable constitution of the Philippine Republic, was at first Secretary of Foreign Affairs and then Chief Justice of the Supreme Court of the Republic, opposed the American aggression, was captured by American troops and exiled to Guam, and all this without a ripple on the surface of his tranquillity. To the end he was the master of his soul; it is agreed that no one ever saw him otherwise.

An exceedingly spare man, rather tall for a Filipino, one is reminded of him when one looks today at the pictures of Mahatma Gandhi, the same suggestion of the student, the same lines of thought, the same expression of a wise and kindly tolerance. He had character as well as a great mental engine, this leader of the little brown men. All the years of his invalidism and through his wanderings and privations he preserved this invariable cheerfulness. No man ever heard complaint from his lips that met everything with the same gentle smile. A great spirit. Let us lay aside for a moment our notions about pigment and admit that he was so. And let us admit, which is also the fact, that the men that stand out of a people are not essentially different from the rest but only their best expression.

We exiled him to Guam, and he died there. He was the Mazzini of the revolutionary movement, Aguinaldo its Garibaldi. Nobody cared. Garibaldi we had lauded to the skies; he was fighting for liberty against an alien oppressor. But he was a white man. Mabini was fighting for liberty against an alien oppressor. But he was a brown man. That made some difference. The fact that we were the alien oppressor made the rest.

But white man or brown, in one remark he once put his finger upon the vital nerve of the whole issue. The United States had not a shadow of right in the Philippine Islands. The plea that it had such a right because it had paid Spain $20,000,- 000 to enable Spain to discharge its debt to British arms manufacturers, was too preposterous to be a pious chanson for deck use, even ours. We had fought the Civil War to prove that people were not to be bought and sold like cattle and smugly we had condemned the piracies of other nations that slipped ashore in the night to burn villages and snatch treasure. The title of Spain to the Islands, if she ever had one, had been extinguished by the revolution. Spain was in possession of next to nothing in the Philippines and the money we pretended to pay for them was the prize of clever lobbying and manipulation.

Taking all these conditions together, the record of their long struggle for independence from Spain, the bargain and sale by which they were taken over, the repeated promises of Presidents and announcements of the American policy to set them free, the explicit covenant of the Jones act, it must be admitted the Filipinos showed a remarkable patience. Superficial observers among the Americans jumped to the conclusion that because they were patient they were content to remain in servitude to American imperialism. They were not so content but they were divided.

The masses of the people and the college-bred men were plump for complete independence no matter what economic hardships might result.

Business men that had much profits at stake, that owned stock in sugar centrals and other ventures, and that had come much in contact with the new American doctrine of the soupbone über alles were in favor of continuing at the cart tail and getting the grub.

The politicians did not give a hang, but being men of exceedingly clever minds, used the popular passion for independence as something useful to them in their business. In the Islands they shouted aloud for it. Beautiful and well worth preserving among the gems of oratory are the specimens of eloquence that fell from those lips on this subject—in the Islands. The Filipino is a natural orator. Like the Russian, he loves speech making and when engaged in it can skate circles all around the average American public man. He certainly can. I have sat one day in the Philippine House of Representatives and the next in the Philippine Senate, and allow an old Washington correspondent to testify that in debate these people leave the Anglo-Saxon beaten and gasping. The politicians had to the full the native gifts of speech and management, and in the Islands they produced a line of fireworks that seemed to be the real thing. Over here, some of them, not all, double-crossed their people and quietly knifed independence in the interest of profit mongers and the soupbone theory.

The bill that the American Congress passed in the session of 1932–33 over President Hoover's veto pretended to provide for independence in ten years. In reality it was hailed and supported by the elements in America that being opposed to independence saw in it one more handy way to side-step the covenant. It did not, in fact, provide for independence in ten years or in any other period, but the jokers were so adroitly conceived and disposed that nearly any one merely looking at

DIVIDE Y VENCERAS
Por Vicente Sotto

DIVIDE AND CONQUER

From *The Manila Union*. A Filipino cartoonist's idea of American imperialism's manœuvre

it would have the impression that it meant what it purported to mean.

It was thus that we redeemed our pledges, justified our exploits with the portable organ and the resounding hymn, and proved our superiority to the deceitful Latin.

There was one consideration involved in the matter that might have dismayed even the most ardent advocate of soup-bones, but was strangely overlooked. He must have been fairly blind that could not at that time discern the menacing situation between the United States and Japan. We need not dwell upon certain features of Japanese tradition, sagas, prophecies, and aspirations well known only to those that have studied at close range these remarkable people. It is enough that week after week fate seemed to shape every event toward trouble. Among the developments were signs that to the experienced were to be recognized as sure premonitions of storm, including even mani-festations of the spy mania, than which nothing is more alarm-ing. The sugar boilers and the rest of the soupbone contingent could not want a war, for it would play far more havoc with profits than Philippine independence could possibly play. When the attention of these powerful thinkers was drawn to the storm clouds in the Far East they invariably laughed them off. If there was to be a war in that quarter the United States would beat Japan to bits.

What? So easily as that? Not if we should be still holding the Philippines. The distance from San Francisco to Manila direct is 6,221 miles, from Nagasaki it is 1,306 miles. Have we forgotten Port Arthur and the events of 1904? Mukden and the fate of the Russian Navy? Instantly upon the declaration of war the Japanese would descend upon Manila. Before we could get a fleet and a force there they would have the place forti-fied and the waters mined. It would be the battle of the Japan Sea over again. We should have to attempt to retake Manila, we should have to fight the war on ground selected by the Japanese and 6,000 miles away from our base, and they would be in the same position of advantage they had in 1904 when they beat the Russian detachments as fast as they could get out of the cars.

However, what are such considerations as these compared with the chances of grabbing off a few more profits? Boil the sugar and take the chances. It may be another generation be-fore Japan strikes.

But while we can have thus no end of fun about sentiment and the queer notions of an antique morality, simply as a matter of most practical wisdom, neither men nor nations can afford to play tricks with their integrity. Tricks do not pay. When we had beaten Spain in the Philippines, every consideration of fundamental good faith, American tradition, the principles of the democracy we had professed, demanded that we should give the country over to its people that had struggled so long and so heroically to possess it. Instead of standing squarely upon our republican creed we went a-whoring after strange gods. We allowed British influences to inveigle us into imperialism that Britain might have a larger chance of our co-operation in the Far East. And we allowed lobbyists with methods leaving only too much suspicion, to lead us into a policy of expansion that was for us merely insane. No one can pretend that if disaster results we did not incur it when we abandoned faith and despite a million warnings plunged into the business of international piracy. It would have been better to allow Spain to pay her own munition bills, particularly in view of the fact that what we were paying for was chiefly shells that had been fired at us.

One statesman of the time seems to have had a prevision of this but his voice was drowned by the exultant organ strains. When he heard that the purchase bill had been passed, this was the comment of Thomas Brackett Reed, canny native of Maine:

"Ten million people—twenty million dollars. We seem to have bought them at $2 a head—unpicked."

Chapter XXIV

LAST NOTES FROM THE REAR RANK

FROM time to time among us arise sad-voiced prophets, or leaders with maybe a biliary derangement, who assure us that all is lost, that mankind is hopelessly wicked, the world grows always worse instead of better, all attempts to reform or improve it are ridiculously futile, and here we all go plunging down the roof together. Occasionally across the blackness of the night of gloom some soul with sorrow laden can descry a gleam from the red, red hope that lies in revolution, riot, and ravin, preluding salvation to be won by wading to the neck in blood. But even this precious deliverance seems at times overshadowed with a doubt. After all, is it really worth while to try to save a race so depraved or so stupid—or both?

As to underlying causes of our dolorous state, it is to be noted that the doctors differ. From one source we learned not long ago that it was all the ductless glands. Either we have them when we should not or do not have them when we should and either way there is no health in us. Before this doctrine had time to soak in and take hold, it was impeached by another that said something might be done with us if we were caught young and subjected to some peculiar style of educational enlightenment, but even in this there seemed to be no real abiding faith. For the next day or so we were back again in the dumps with the assurance that we are only monkeys anyway; so we have always been, so we shall always be, and what chance of redemption can inhere in a monkey?

Far be it from me to controvert eminent authority; and,

besides, who am I that I should seek to deprive any one of the sweet consolation naturally pertaining to the belief that everything is going to hell except that which has already arrived there? Nevertheless, I may be allowed to set down a few humble notations of a mere reporter whose ignorance of ductless glands, being admitted to be abysmal, must place him really outside the boundaries of a serious consideration.

First, then, no one really tempted to take on the wrinkled brow of despair about the world and its state can have been an itinerant newspaper man fifty years ago in America, for in that case instead of lamenting he would now be giving thanks for proof of the unconquerable spirit of goodness in men that despite all untoward material conditions continues to struggle up to the light. For the true wonder is not that we are so bad but that we are not immeasurably worse. If mankind, weighed upon by the present social system, debased by the greed it plants and sedulously fosters, hardened by its insane cruelties, atrophied by its selfishness and brutality, degraded by the wars it causes, can still cling to ideals of honesty, kindness, peace, purity, brotherliness, truly we should exult and not mourn, for the power so revealed is indomitable and unturnable and enough to remake the world.

Next, as a matter of sheerest fact, it is impossible for the old reporter, looking about him now and recalling conditions fifty years ago, to escape the conclusion, reached on purely professional grounds and without doctrinaire accessories, that the world does not grow worse, does not stand still, but slowly grows better. It is not for me to attempt here detailed and picturesque comparisons. Let me rather venture a few illuminative facts that may suggest to those unaware of vanished conditions a way to reconstruct the former American scene and so give over pessimism.

We will first go back to the place whence we started, the great East Side of New York.

And here we are to be understood definitely, if you please, as dealing not with economic conditions of the period in which this is written. Such conditions are bad and always will be bad so long as we cling thus fatuously to the social system that makes them bad. They are bad in this time of general depression; they are bad in the times when Wall Street hornpipes around a bull market. What we are to consider here are the things that reveal the thought, essential spirit, trend, and sympathies of men.

Fifty years ago there were no tenement-house laws and anybody could build any kind of a murderous flat that he might deem likely to return good profits. Fifty years ago nobody on the outside seemed to give a rap about the people that dwelt in those horrible barracks, but the fortunate generally believed that if there were any poor they were poor through their own fault and great laziness. Either that, or God has ordained that some of his children shall be surfeited with too much and many starved with too little, and shall we rebel against a divine decree? Fifty years ago the East Side was uncleaned, wretchedly paved, the streets disfigured with telegraph poles and perilous festoons of wires, was wretchedly policed, got sick or got well as heaven might order, wallowed in political corruption, was the acknowledged kingdom of political thugs and ruffianly bosses, was the gold mine of grafting police officers, had no breathing spaces worth the name and no schools that were not neglected and unsanitary, was infested with dives, boozing kens, and the resorts of criminals, never had an election that was not putrid through and through with frauds everybody knew and nobody cared about. Billy McGlory's dive running full blast as a horrible factory of crime, vice, misery, and suicide was only a type. On some streets every other store front was a saloon, a crooked café, an assignation house, or a house of ill-fame.

You think there is graft in New York today? Right, there

is; much graft. But it is little compared with the organized, brazen, impudent, arrogant overlordship of the plunder-and-vice alliance that prevailed in New York fifty years ago.

Oh, yes; I know! Gangs and gang murders and all that; are not conditions bad in 1933? They certainly are; but gangs, as I have had the honor to point out, are no new thing in New York, and those that dwell much upon the doings of the latter-day thug can never have been in actual contact with the Whyos, the Humpty Jackson gang, the Paul Kelley gang, the terrifying denizens of Hell's Kitchen and of Corcoran's Roost, nor known of that strange band of miscreants that for years kept the region along the North River between Forty-third and Fifty-fourth Streets in one continuous state of alarm.

And, yes, I know the East Side of New York in 1933 is nothing to boast about. I know that 70,000 tenement houses that ought to be pulled down still breed disease and ruin lives. But all this being admitted, it is better than it was fifty years ago, and the great point is that we have now the beginning of a public conscience about these things and the first flush of a determination to end them.

But I speak only of a few scattered examples. All municipal government and conditions are much better in 1933 than they were in 1883. Take Chicago, the maligned and misunderstood, held in 1933 to the world as an awful example of a crime-ridden community. Who that carries in his mind a vivid picture of Chicago of fifty years ago can fail to be exhilarated at the contrast? Yes, straight in the face of the Capones, and all the rest. It is enough to stress this difference, that in 1933 the community cares; it is determined to abolish the evil conditions and is doing so. In 1883 nobody cares; the riot of lawlessness, rampant vice, thuggery, and graft is accepted as inevitable and incurable. Stand now on the lake front at the foot of Van Buren Street, take in that striking panorama of stately designing, and recall, if you can, the prospect from the same spot in

1883. Is it not marvelous? Yes; but that transformation is not greater than all the rest that has taken place. "Old Chicago, you make me shiver," ran the words of a true song of those days. It does not make you shiver now. Old Chicago! How can I make you understand what it was like, the rowdy, dirty, slovenly, slouching, aggressively ugly brute of a place. I give up the attempt. Only one thing I will recite and leave you to imagine the rest. A certain character, whose name must be familiar in the recollections of every old timer, printed at intervals a newspaper called *The Street Gazette,* devoted to the disorderly-house business with correspondence from all important Western cities giving reports about the state of the local trade, with pleasant personal items concerning those engaged in it. And nobody cared.

Or if you wish to pursue the subject farther, look over the files of the old Chicago *Times* from 1876 to 1883.

Every average American city was ruled by a greasy boss who maintained his sway by an alliance with respectable business men on one side and the lowest dregs of the underworld on the other. Elections in these places were farcical. There were virtually no election laws that were enforced. In most places was little or no registration of voters and anything was a ballot that could be stuffed into a ballot box.

I am citing only sample illustrations, kindly remember. Take the state of the worker. There was a ten-hour work-day, apparently fixed forever and regarded as divinely ordered. There was no factory inspection; workers toiled amid any conditions that might be provided for them, sanitary or unsanitary, dangerous or safe. The sweat-shop was unchecked in its fearful ministrations. There was virtually no compensation for a worker injured at his work. Workers were not supposed to have socially defined rights. Women and children in industry were without a shadow of protection. There were no laws regulating hours of labor, no minimum wage restrictions, and no protest

against a general industrial injustice but such as the struggling
and despised Knights of Labor could furnish. Except in a few
larger cities and in a few highly organized trades, labor organizations were mostly impotent. The general status of labor was
rather one of contempt among the more fortunate. John Hay
wrote a book savagely satirizing and ridiculing it. Nobody
cared.

The country had not yet recovered from the mad orgy of
graft, swindling, pillage, and money grubbing that followed
the Civil War, and nobody seemed to care much about that,
either.

There was a distinctly lower tone throughout the public service, less of the sense of responsibility, less of conscience, more
of blind fealty to parties, catch-words, and the private purse.

There was no regulation of railroad companies; they were a
law unto themselves, and maintained unchecked the form of
satrapy we have discussed in foregoing pages; loaded themselves with watered stock and fictitious bonds for the public to
pay and piled high many a buccaneer's fortune. There was no
regulation of public-utility companies; they bribed, corrupted,
rotted, and overcapitalized at their pleasure. There was no
Trade Commission to lay bare the piratical excursions of great
corporations; they exercised upon press and public a power unlimited. There were no effective pure-food laws; exploiters
were free to palm upon the public any impure or deleterious
concoction from which they could make money.

The accepted notions of political and social economy, if any,
belonged to the Stone Age. The purpose of the employer to
grind down to the last cent the wages of his employees was generally applauded as "good business" and salutary. It had occurred to but few that under the existing system of society, the
wage fund was the nation's purchasing power and that when
the wage fund was reduced prosperity was impaired for employer as for employee.

International affairs were conducted upon a basis as primitive as that of Pharaoh. Only a few cranks, Quakers, and silly dreamers had any notion that we could ever get along without war. Every nation looked upon every other nation as a skin-clad troglodyte looked upon a stranger when the supply of cold ichthyosaurus was running low. Russia was crowding down upon India, Britain was butting her way into China, Alexandria had just been bombarded to collect a British debt, and nobody cared.

Well, is it any better today? says Resolute Gloom, pointing to the news from Manchuria. Yes. It is far better. Let us take one comparison, and see.

In 1856 the British were eagerly pushing their advance upon China. Chinese waters were much infested with pirates. The Chinese government was reproached for not more vigorously suppressing piracy. A Chinese gunboat pursued and cornered a pirate craft, which hoisted a British flag. The Chinese commander disregarded this trick and captured the pirate. The British government pretended that this was a deadly insult, demanded apologies, indemnities, and promises. When the Chinese government failed to comply with the last details of the demands, the British instantly bombarded Canton and forced what is called in history the Second Opium War, leading to the capture of Peking and the looting and burning of the imperial Summer Palace, probably the most wonderful thing of its kind in the world.

That was the old way. Now come with me to the Assembly of the League of Nations. It is September, 1926, seventy years later. Sit here in the gallery and look down upon the main floor. There sit together the representatives of fifty-six nations, brown men, black men, white men, yellow men, all kinds, colors, creeds, races, religions, Mohammedan, Christian, Buddhist, Shinto, everything else. Side by side sit such men as fifty years ago would have viewed one another with implacable hatred. Of a sudden, the head of the Chinese delegation takes the rostrum and reveals to the world a fact carefully concealed for many weeks that two British gunboats had attacked and bombarded a town on the Yangtse river. He enters a formal complaint. The head of the British delegation, Lord Robert Cecil, has an opportunity to reply. He makes a lame and impotent defense of the action of the British officers. The world through its representatives there learns all the details of the affair and perceives that the British have been guility of an unwarranted aggression. Note well that there is now no chance to deceive public opinion in Britain or elsewhere about this. The mere force of publicity is enough. The British withdraw their gunboats and will not repeat the bombarding experiment and above all there is no war. Is not this a change?

Yes, I know again. The League of Nations was not able to prevent Japan's housebreaking expedition into Manchuria and Jehol. True; but it could and did express and drive home the world's condemnation, and more than that it could and did propose another way to deal with the emergency than sixteen-inch guns and the bombarding of cities. Even if it failed, was it not something to have such a means internationally offered and urged? Something? It was much; it was an enormous gain! Progress is slow. The peaceful means rejected today will be the world's favorite prescription tomorrow. At last there has been a start. Let us give thanks and be glad.

Mental myopia it is to bound the great world with our own day or think any evil more than transitory.

In 1842 Britain made war on China to compel China to admit opium. Nobody cared. She cannot make war on China today for any such purpose. In 1798 she went about Ireland hanging men that advocated the independence of their country. In 1933 men said with impunity such things as Robert Emmet was hanged for advocating. In 1854 the American ministers to England, France, and Spain met at Ostend and signed a manifesto urging the American government, if Spain refused to sell Cuba for slavery purposes, to make war upon Spain and take Cuba by force—for slavery. How does that document look when held before the modern conscience?

No, never tell me the world grows worse or even stands still. It grows always better. Not swiftly, not with an even motion of progress, not as impatient men desire it to improve. Still it grows better. It is immensely better than it was fifty years ago; immensely better. There is more kindness, more interest in the other man's welfare, more impulse toward justice, more perception of the fundamental truths of human existence and fellowship. Yes, despite all the unspeakable horrors and unimaginable savageries of the World War. Out of that maniac's dream has come the beginning of a conception of a substitute for battlefields, and remembering how slow is all progress, once more we can give thanks for substantial gain.

Again and again, apparent evil proves to be but the outward symptom of wholesome change at work unseen. When banditries increase, kidnapings multiply, and the defensive machinery of society seems to have collapsed, the initial impulse is to throw up both hands and wail aloud that we are slipping backward into chaos. In truth, all these things only signal to the surface a transformation going on within, the ending of one era, the beginning of another. We have increase of crime and of criminals, not because mankind degenerates but because there is breaking down a conception of life no longer able to meet the needs, spiritual and material, of a race that is outgrowing it.

And if with pallid brow and fingered lip comes again some shaken soul to whisper awestruck, "But all these dictators!" he makes for the judicious no more than mirth. In its last throes, capitalism has discovered that it can no longer exist in the same world with democracy. It seeks therefore with these tinseled hot-air specialists that rattle about the old thrones to hamstring an evolutionary force, universal and grown up through ages. Hamstring, quotha! That old giantess will be striding along her great highway when of the last dictatorship will be left not enough trace to make a dust mark on her big thumping feet.

Slowly we go up, weighed upon still by the heavy burden of a murderous system, hobbled by our clinging fondness for old delusions, shackled with our prejudices, groping and stumbling, and still we go slowly up. The notion that men are hopelessly bad and incapable of advancing is merely childish petulance. The notion that we are to sit with folded hands until we shall be washed in the blood of some unnamed revolution is an excuse for personal inertia. The notion that in existing conditions the gift of life is casual, purposeless, and inutile is the delusion of the purblind. The notion that we are to move forward by diving backward, by a recourse to mediæval autocracy, forced labor, and the firing squad, is preposterous. Slowly but surely we go up. When we are rid of the social system that has so long cursed all mankind we shall move more rapidly. But of that system the world can be rid without shedding a drop of blood or sending one more soul to Siberia, real or figurative. Can be and will be.

Of course, the upward progress might be greatly accelerated. Every attack upon every intrenched evil helps the onward motion. And it makes not the slightest difference if in men's eyes the effort is fruitless. There is no such thing in this world as a wasted protest against any existing evil; absolutely no such thing. If the protest is made to no more than a handful of persons and is stifled then, it will some time, if it is true, just, and honest, bear its due measure of fruit. The common error and cherished delusion of reformers is to think that if the particular organization to which they belong goes ashore, all is lost. Reform is not so simple as that, but a vast, complicated, and often mysterious evolution. It is not to be had with the naïveté of a single push. As a matter of fact, nothing in any way good is ever lost. What? All these worthy motions for better conditions that came and went and were forgotten, Anti-poverty, Father McGlynn, James Baird Weaver, Single Tax, Greenback Party, People's Party, Goo-goo, Laroo, Edmond Kelly, William Mailly, were they failures? Not one of them.

Look it up in your histories. The Chartist movement in England—what could seem a greater failure? The societies broken up, the leaders condemned to death and narrowly escaping the gallows, the whole motion suppressed and stamped out. Yet almost everything Chartism stood for has since been adopted into the British constitution and system. Or the successive steps by which the British House of Commons was redeemed from its ancient condition of a landowners' club and made a body representative of the nation's will—the men that advocated these changes were defeated but the changes they advocated went into effect. The successive steps by which the British franchise was broadened and reformed—all these were actually taken by the party that had opposed them, not by the party that urged them.

So it is here. The autopsies we have recorded were held upon outer shell and visible integument. Truly these were dead, but the idea or spirit within was not dead. It could no more be killed than the spirit of man to which it was analogous. When the shell had been buried the spirit went on working, in one way or another working, until some part of the purpose of the movement was attained. Some part; not all. All of any aim is never attained. So far in the world's history, progress has not been made in that way but only step by step and little by little.

From the recorded phenomena of reforming efforts certain general principles may be adduced, which are not the less true because they are not generally recognized by reformers and will not be.

1. Betterment comes if men will to have it.
2. It never comes in the way we think it will come.

3. It never comes at the time when we expect it.

4. It never comes from the source that we expect it to come from.

5. Often when it seems most hopeless it is nearest.

6. Nobody can control these things; nobody can notably affect them. What seems to be required is that there shall be an effort for betterment, a steadfast protest against some evil, a mental loyalty to good. Some other power takes care of the rest of the job and often when they seem strongest the stone walls are shaking.

In the last fifty-two years, this country has seen reform movement after reform movement begin with an auspicious launching, voyage on with swelling sails and humming winds, and pile up on one reef or another leaving only some wreckage and a fading memory. Of such movements that have attracted the stumbling writer of these poor pages, one and one only, the effort to obtain Woman Suffrage, has proved anything but a wreck and a disappointment. Yet betterment has moved steadily on, seen or unseen, and mostly without that leadership that we Anglo-Saxons make so much of. How shall we dispose of that unassailable fact?

Possibly it may be of interest to catalogue here some of the causes that have wrecked these tall ships and brought to an apparent nought so many crusaders and gallant crusaders. Well, then, have at it.

1. The reformers wearied of the voyage before it was half over. The first and indispensable requisites of these adventures are persistence and patience, and most of us have neither. It is hard to believe that the unknown member of a reforming organization that goes to the business meetings and seldom opens his mouth there is serving the cause better than the man in the limelight that makes the speeches and the noise, but this is the literal fact, nevertheless. And as to patience, the real test of reforming purpose is to hold on stedfastly when apparently there

is nothing doing and no interest in the proceedings. No virtue is rarer.

2. Squabbles and jealousies and suspicions. Most reformers seem to prefer to fight one another rather than to front the enemy. Divisions among reformers are the strength of the exploiters. If all the persons in the United States that are opposed to any one form of privilege would unite against it and stay united for six months they could put that privilege out of existence. In 1933 there were in the United States some fifty-two organizations devoted to the ending of war, all multiplicating one another's efforts, all getting in one another's way. If all were in one great organization the government would have to listen to its mighty voice. No government will bother much with the significance of fifty-two almost inaudible whispers scattered over long periods. Intolerance is the reformer's besetting sin. Each usually insists that the way he prefers is the only way and all other roads lead to perdition. Whereas, no human being can tell which way betterment will come and one person that insists only upon betterment is better than ten pulling ten ways and getting nowhere.

3. Personal ambition and personal loyalties, than which nothing is more comical, although the two have wrecked many a good movement. If the cause is not immeasurably greater than any man enlisted in it, then it is a cause not worth enlisting in.

4. Failure of reformers to stand by when attacked. The notion that a Vested Interest will lie down and without a struggle allow itself to be deprived of its advantages is a childish fantasy. For nothing else in this world will men fight as they will fight for profits. Every assailant of privilege will be assailed in return, but as a rule when that happens all reformers of the high-brow, pink, and intellectual order instantly begin to run out. It is not so among the proletarians and wage-workers; they have some understanding of the true nature of the conflict and some sense of the necessity of resistance. But it is true of others.

Troglodyte newspapers can usually break up any reforming movement among the intelligentsia by applying a little judicious ridicule or bitter attack.

Attack, is it? Ridicule? Do but consider the vindications of Time. Wendell Phillips went about with a price on his head, hissed, hooted, hated, threatened with lynching. The thing for which he strove became the rock and the salvation of the Republic. James Baird Weaver was cartooned, ridiculed, denounced, scorned from one end of the country to the other. The world admits today the truth of all he said then about the perils of Concentrated Power and the private control of the money supply. Father McGlynn was silenced for insisting that poverty was unnecessary and a blight upon the nation. The world sees today that he was right. If a Populist were to return to earth and say now what he was excoriated for saying in 1893 he would be condemned for talking old stuff from the back numbers. What do you fear, O Goodman Timidity? Speak it out, say your little piece, and dread not. The furious denunciations of today are the plaudits of tomorrow and the only thing to be afraid of is the closed mind against new ideas.

But however reformers may miss stays and muddle their steering, the cause for which they sail will win in the end if it is based upon any principle and not inspired by the mere steam of the flesh pots.

And now allow the reporter one last suggestion.

Nothing else pays so well as enlistment in some betterment movement. It pays—not in simoleons nor in kudos but in one's right to be on good terms with one's self, which is about all there is in life anyway that amounts to a hoot.

About this there is no sentiment, but only practical fact. I happen to have seen the whole show from overture to curtain drop, seen it in twenty-seven nations all the way from Scotch Cap Lighthouse to Stewart Island, and everywhere one fact has been pounded into my dull head. It is better to be a doorpost on this side of the house than have goose-liver pâte on the other. To make money is nothing; most of the money makers I have known were among the dullest of all God's creatures and led lives flatter than a stove-lid. To get office or position or distinction is nothing; of the men that fifty years ago had all the limelight and the shouting hardly one still clings by so much as a shred to the human memory. To crowd and elbow to the summit of a profession is nothing; who remembers now the leading lawyers, physicians, engineers, of fifty years ago? Even to write literature is nothing; the literary idols of one generation are the jest of the next and the pavement dust of the next. Well, then what is there of a rational object of life as one ricochets from bump to bump through this wild world beneath the sun? Why, looking at the matter judicially and coldly, as a reporter and so only, the one purpose that seems to offer a perdurable profit is to keep some step, however stumbling, however far in the rear, with the vast, silent, often mysterious, sometimes hardly discernible processes that are slowly and surely transforming the world from a wolves' den to a place where man can know some peace, some content, some joy of living, some sense of the inexhaustible beauties of the universe in which he has been placed.

Index

Index